PRAISE FOR THE LIFE AND WORK OF
Edgar Cayce

D0034618

It bothered me a great deal as a child that God spoke to the people in the Bible and did not speak to us. Now I believe that He does speak to us, if we will only listen.

Don't ever think that your life isn't being written in the Book of Life. I found it! It is being written. You are the writer!

God's purpose is that we make ourselves a channel through which His spirit may manifest.

— EDGAR CAYCE

EDGAR CAYCE

MY LIFE AS A SEER:

The Lost Memoirs

COMPILED AND EDITED BY
A. ROBERT SMITH

St. Martin's Paperbacks

MY LIFE AS A SEER

Library of Congress Catalog Card Number: 99–31180

ISBN: 0-312-97144-3
EAN: 978-0-312-97144-1

Printed in the United States of America

St. Martin's Press hardcover edition / October 1999
St. Martin's Paperbacks edition / February 2002

St. Martin's Paperbacks are published by St. Martin's Press, 175 Fifth Avenue, New York, NY 10010.

10 9 8 7 6

CONTENTS

PART III MY PHILOSOPHY

PART IV APPENDIX

ACKNOWLEDGMENTS

This work would never have been undertaken by me had I not been encouraged by Hugh Lynn Cayce to write his biography, *Hugh Lynn Cayce: About My Father's Business*, and enjoyed countless Sunday afternoons talking with him about his life with his father. Nor would this book have materialized had Mr. Cayce's secretary, Gladys Davis, not acquired the habit of throwing nothing away. She was the original compiler of Mr. Cayce's papers who made my research a joy and led me to the priceless documents that inspired this work. I am further indebted and grateful to Charles Thomas Cayce and to his associate, Jeanette Thomas, for facilitating further documentation; to D. D. Cayce, for guiding me all over Christian County, Kentucky, to soak up the scenes of Edgar Cayce's youth; to my colleagues John Van Auken, Joe Dunn, Dan Campbell, Susan Lendvay, and Carol Haenni, who contributed insightful editorial recommendations; to Mark Thurston for his enthusiasm for the concept; and to my devoted wife Jane, whose understanding of my preoccupation with this project during intensive months of development allowed me to complete it with a grateful heart. An editor cannot ask for more.

A. Robert Smith

FOREWORD

My grandfather, Edgar Cayce, once said, "It is a time in the earth when people everywhere seek to know more of the mysteries of the mind, the soul."

His words have a special ring of clarity today as more and more people are turning inward for answers, applying their own powers of intuition, finding that of God in themselves and their fellow human beings. This is not unique to contemporary times, of course, for every culture throughout history has had its own rare individuals who were gifted beyond the five senses to provide insights for life's pressing questions. No one has filled this role in the twentieth century quite like Edgar Cayce.

Not only is his psychic gift the most carefully documented, he has been the subject of more literature than anyone in his field—at last count some 300 books have been published, dealing with various topics covered in his voluminous trance readings. Indeed, the 1996 WorldCat on-line database of 28 million titles of all sorts of publications included 632 titles under the subject "Edgar Cayce"—more than were listed under such well-known intuitives as Mary Baker Eddy, founder of Christian Science (526), or Madame Blavatsky, founder of Theosophy (217). One scholar, K. Paul Johnson, who contributed to this fund of literature with books on both Blavatsky and Cayce, considers the latter "a major figure in the spiritual history of the twentieth century."

Edgar Cayce's wisdom for our age, as one major publisher heralded a series of books pertaining to his ideas a decade ago, is found in the more than 14,000 discourses that are his principal legacy. These psychic readings, dictated while he lay in a hypnotic trance, constituted his work for more than forty years. Transcriptions of this information have been preserved and disseminated ever since his death in 1945, providing inspiration, metaphysical and philosophical insights, and healing help for countless thousands who have applied his alternative remedies and adopted his holistic health recommendations.

While biographers have recounted events of his upbringing on a Kentucky farm and his rise to fame as a psychic healer, this is the first account of Edgar Cayce's life told completely in his own words. He does not dwell on all of the personal aspects of his life, but focuses primarily on those experiences that marked him since childhood as decidedly different from anyone else in his world. In so telling, he reveals how much he yearned to be considered an ordinary boy like everyone else in Hopkinsville, and how he feared for his sanity. Even the Cayce family was divided over Edgar and his strange abilities. But only he can tell this story in all its pathos as he struggles with himself, his family, and with God to discover and come to terms with his destiny.

What saved Edgar Cayce and allowed him to fulfill his soul's purpose as the benevolent spiritual philosopher so widely admired today was his enduring faith and the courage to follow his faith as his guidance directed whatever the cost to him personally. His story, then, is a profile in faith no less than courage, and his humility offers a model for all of us as we face our Maker.

Charles Thomas Cayce
President
Edgar Cayce Foundation
Virginia Beach, Virginia

EDITOR'S PROLOGUE

Like Edgar Cayce himself, his autobiography is most unconventional and merits an explanation. Unlike the life story of many celebrities, it was not ghostwritten or told to a professional writer but is entirely the work of its subject. Mr. Cayce either typed or dictated to his secretary or told lecture audiences all of the stories that appear in this work. And yet it was not written as a cohesive single narrative or as an autobiography. In that sense it is similar to the autobiography of Mohandas K. Gandhi, *The Story of My Experiments with Truth*. Gandhi and Cayce were both encouraged to write their own stories, but both men had higher priorities than self-aggrandizement. "I agreed to write my autobiography," Gandhi confessed, "but I have no spare time." He might have found time, he added, "had I gone through my full term of imprisonment . . . [before] I was discharged." He did find time to write a weekly newspaper article, however, and a publisher later compiled them and called it his autobiography.

This book in Edgar Cayce's own words follows that pattern. He first wrote an essay about his early mystical encounters in 1926 for a booklet explaining his work and how he came by his unique calling. "I have nothing to *sell* and am seeking only to be of help," he wrote. "Not that I expect to write an autobiography of my life, nor do I expect to give in chronological order the various experiences and happenings that have impelled me to arrive at this conclusion, but sufficient that you may have a better understanding, if you are a regular thinker, of *why men arrive at certain conclusions*." In other words, he could imagine writing about himself only if it would be helpful to someone.

Later, in his mid-fifties, Mr. Cayce did begin dictating his life story to his secretary, Gladys Davis, but never completed the task. He also cooperated with a professional writer, Thomas Sugrue, on a biography, *There Is a River*. And he went to his typewriter from time to time and wrote anecdotes from his younger days. But it is obvious that he gave first attention to helping others, which he considered his life's purpose. After his death, at sixty-seven, a few excerpts from his writings were published, but the entire collection was filed away in the archives of the Edgar Cayce Foundation, where I discovered the typescript of what Miss Davis had entitled "Edgar Cayce's Memoirs." I thought that it, like Schubert's Unfinished Symphony, was too moving not to be shared with the world, unfinished though it may have been.

What is the point of publishing an Edgar Cayce memoir half a century after his death, especially when Cayce himself cautioned that the message and not the man is what we are to value—and certainly his message has been widely distributed in hundreds of books, in many languages, on everything from holistic health to reincarnation to planetary influences? My answer, after working with his papers, and getting to know him at a new depth, is that in his case the *messenger embodies the message*, and the better we understand him, the clearer we will hear his message. The overriding value of his writings is not so much the stories never before told, fascinating though they are, but in our taking this very personal journey with him, sensing his inner conflict between fear and faith as he struggles to understand his awesome power and how he should, or should not, use it.

Although he does not write about all of the events of his life, Edgar Cayce reveals himself as never before. Sprinkled freely through his memoir are confessions of doubt, of uncertainty, of yearning to be "normal" rather than blessed with an astonishing talent. His admissions mark him as a truly humble man who never let adulation undermine his motive of service to others. He remained the living fulfillment of that familiar saying of his, "If we ever get to heaven it will be leaning on the arm of someone we have helped."

A word, then, about how this autobiography was compiled. The unfinished memoir served as the foundation. Edgar Cayce had just turned fifty-five when he dictated that document in 1932. Although he did not fancy himself a writer, he was a good storyteller in the great tradition of the South, and he certainly had a good yarn to spin. Another factor that may have inspired his storytelling impulse at that time was that he had just been through the hardest year of his life: the hospital he had spent years trying to build, as well as a university he helped found, had closed for lack of funds; he'd been evicted from his home and was virtually penniless; he had been arrested and humiliated in public. No wonder that he "just wanted to die," as his son Hugh Lynn Cayce put it.

Instead of giving up, he followed his guidance and continued to help anyone who sought him out. Those who benefited by his intuitive counseling never stopped coming. In reviewing his life, he tried to understand what it all meant, and perhaps hoped to bank some satisfaction against all the withdrawals of earlier failings. Given the many people he had helped, obviously there was much achievement in his past on which he could draw a sense of fulfillment. In any event, he continued to live a productive life and went on to give some of his most meaningful discourses in the years that followed.

As for Mr. Cayce's storytelling style, it was earnest and matter-of-fact. As Mr. Cayce dictated his story to Miss Gladys, as he called her, she took it in shorthand, typed it up on leftover letterheads from the Cayce Hospital, and filed away each chapter as the story unfolded. Unfortunately, he stopped dictating his chronicle long before he stopped living it. Fortunately, Miss Davis collected many other documents that are rich in content. One of the most charming had been typed by Mr. Cayce himself a few years before his death. Untitled, and uncorrected, it contained colorful vignettes of memorable episodes from earlier times. Curiously, he wrote these stories in the third person about a young fellow called "Eddy." I had not known that Edgar was ever called by this nickname, but his grandson, Charles Thomas Cayce, confirmed that it was true. Later I discovered correspondence in which he was addressed "Dear Eddie," to which he signed his reply, "As ever, Eddie." Why the third-person subject of his stories was spelled "Eddy" remains a mystery. Perhaps he found it more comfortable to spin out his memories as though he were simply the storyteller and not really the hero. In any event, his stories are rich in feeling—right from his heart, whether his heart was full of joy or aching with pain.

Hugh Lynn Cayce had told me about his father's unique writing style—his disregard for the customary dictates of form, punctuation, and spelling—but I had never encountered it in full flower as in his "Eddy" stories. As an example, here is his version of the famous spelling book incident:

> In school next day eddy missed his lessons as usual-and had to remain to write the word cabin 500 times on black-board. and when he arrived at home that evening his Father was waiting for him- eddy studied his lessons in the evening but seemed not to be able to concentrate, at about 11 that even he had the first experience of hearing the voice with-in-and it recalled the voice of the visitor of the evening before-but it said "Sleep and we may help you" eddy asked his Father to let him sleep five minutes, he slept and at the end of the time eddy knew every word in that particular speller.

The version of this incident that appears in the memoir he dictated to Gladys Davis is more detailed, and explicit in saying he was "slapped for going to sleep" and "received many a buff and rebuff" from his father. This incident occurred, of course, when spankings were still a common form of punishment by parents who believed that to spare the rod is to spoil the child.

The most poignant tale in the book is about what he calls his "puppy love" for a girl named Bess, who had spurned his romantic overtures because her father had told her Edgar was "not right in the head." When Edgar spoke to her father, a physician, about wanting to marry Bess, he was bluntly told that the injury he had sustained when struck by a ball in the head or spine might lead to insanity. We have no idea whether this doctor worked at the local state hospital for the insane and may have recognized what a thin line exists between those on either side of sanity, or whether his cruelty stemmed simply from ignorance. Here is a passage from the original typescript of Mr. Cayce:

> New ideas, new thoughts, new determinations came to eddy from this talk [with the doctor] or were they new, how had he read, but eddy was a warm blooded person at least if this being so different, was going to drive him crazy, why did he have such an accident, was the Dr right, but I had these visions before I got hurt eddy reasoned, that hasnt any thing to do with the visions, but I am different I guess, no I never played marbels, never spun a top, or threw a ball, but never had any of these things, and dont realy care for them he reasoned, but to be like other boys I must like them, must do the things that other boys do, but I dont want to, but will have to, or there is no need talking with the Dr again, and am sure I do love Bess.

The full story appears in chapter 3.

Other documents included in this work were Mr. Cayce's two attempts at keeping a diary. As a diarist, he was no Pepys. Both efforts foundered soon after he began, but what remains offers a glimpse of his daily life and preoccupations.

Another contribution resulted from my cleaning out a closet in my office on the top floor of the old Cayce Hospital, where I chanced upon a file labeled "EC lectures." In it were newspaper clippings from the 1920s, brown and fragile with age, from a weekly, the *Virginia Beach News*. Each article was the text of a lecture Mr. Cayce had given at the hospital. Like Gandhi's newspaper articles, these proved useful in providing elements of his faith and philosophy.

Other documents preserved in the Foundation's vault that proved invaluable included a lengthy treatise by Mr. Cayce's father, Leslie B. "Squire" Cayce, which he evidently typed himself. Squire Cayce's "biography" of his son is effusively flattering—but it contains a number of family anecdotes that reveal the style of life of Edgar's family a century ago. It is clear that, despite serious problems—the Squire's business failures, and his attempts to use Edgar's psychic gift to make

money, which angered Edgar and strained their relationship—
they were devoted to one another. The Squire's fondness for
Edgar is suggested by the salutation on his letters to "My dear
sweet precious boy."

For his part, Edgar says not an unkind or critical word
about his father. Even his account of being slapped was
matter-of-fact instead of self-pitying. There is only one allu-
sion to his father's problems, when Edgar recalls that his
grandmother—Squire's mother—on her deathbed urged
adolescent Edgar to look after his mother—"the best woman
I have ever known," she said—and to "be patient with your
father. He is weak but kindhearted and you can do more with
him than anyone can, for he worships you."

The Squire had squandered his wife's inheritance in farm-
land by borrowing on it to finance business ventures that
failed, Hugh Lynn Cayce explained to me. For the purpose of
illuminating Edgar's childhood and selected episodes in later
life, observations by the elder Cayce have been interspersed
with Mr. Cayce's narrative and set in italics.

Except for his father's comments, all of the material in this
autobiography is vintage Edgar Cayce, compiled from his collected papers and edited into a chronological narrative. In
some instances I have adapted the material to make the narrative flow smoothly, such as modifying the third-person Eddy
stories into a first-person account. A few footnotes expand or
clarify a point. In no case, have I fabricated narrative passages
by imagining what he might have said or thought.

The result is an account of his life that focuses largely on
the phenomenon that made him distinctly different, and his
personal thoughts over the years as he wrestled with his demons. There are obvious gaps, for he wrote nothing about such
troubling incidents as his two arrests—one in New York for
fortunetelling, the other in Detroit for practicing medicine
without a license. And he gave none of his feelings or thoughts
about the fascinating past lives that his trance readings say
were part of his soul's journey.

I was struck by one further similarity between Gandhi and
Cayce—their common purpose was to find God. "What I want

to achieve—what I have been striving and pining to achieve these thirty years—is self-realization, to see God face to face, to attain Moksha (salvation)," wrote Gandhi. Cayce's purpose was set out in the little book which his study group compiled and which similar groups all over the world have used as their text for spiritual enlightenment for some sixty years. It is entitled *A Search for God*. His quest for God, like Gandhi's, serves as a guidepost for all of us.

On the whole, Edgar Cayce's quest—his painful struggle to come to terms with his gift from God and to accept and do honor to that wondrous calling—is at once poignant and powerful, instructive and inspirational, as told here in his own plain-spoken style.

A. Robert Smith

EDGAR CAYCE'S INTRODUCTION

I am often asked, "Are you a spiritualist?" Or "Are you a medium?" I am also called a psychic by many, although I have only tried to be a man of God. Then they ask how I ever became interested in psychic phenomena because psychic phenomena has been taboo for such a long while that when we even speak of it people immediately think of ghosts, weird happenings, spiritual seances, and things of that nature. I have had the privilege of meeting individuals who have made a study of psychic phenomena, and written volumes concerning it, but there are few who attempt to tell what their own personal experiences have been with psychic phenomena.

The dictionary tells us that psychic force deals with the mental, the spiritual, and the soul forces of individuals. There are those who would understand psychic phenomena by studying its manifestations. Such groups as the American or the British Psychical Research Society have studied one phase, principally such cases as those of Mrs. Piper and the Margery case.[1] But there is another phase entirely to psychic phenomena which is worthy of study. Having been a student of psychic phenomena for thirty-odd years, not however from books, lectures, or the like, I have heard a great many people give their opinion on many phases of the phenomena. As I've said many times, I don't know how it works—I just know what has been my experience as a reader for that number of years.

During my first few years, I could not see how the things that were said to be done by me, or through me, while in the psychic state were possible; and after many years of thought

---

[1] Leonore Piper was a celebrated psychic discovered by William James, who presented her to the British Society for Psychical Research for testing. Margery Crandon, a Boston medium, was much publicized during the mid-1920s, denounced as a fraud by Harry Houdini and a group of Harvard investigators, but defended by her surgeon husband and others.

on the subject I do not yet see or know how it is done. How could I, not a doctor, never having studied even physiology, hygiene, or any of the other things known in the cure of human ills, tell when in this condition what would help someone? I did not know, and do not know even now. But can anyone tell me how the phonograph needle takes the music from the record, or how the radio picks the messages out of the air? But it does, under certain conditions. Waver those conditions and you just get scratches, just static force. Nothing definite, nothing certain.

So, with all psychic force, properly attuned, properly adjusted, you receive definite good. Out of tune and the human mind is capable of using it to its own destruction, "for there is a way that seemeth right unto man, but the end thereof is death." Then how are we to judge that which is true from that which is false? For there are many things in life, many things in the Scriptures even, that many wrest with to their own destruction.

My experiences in the work show that the difference is in the intent of those seeking the information. Those looking for material things, sensational things, get them—but the effect is not good for them. The effect upon me is even worse. Only when the desire crept in to make money or to put on the sensational did the work fail. When that was attempted, my health failed, my conscience was rent, and I could no longer even attempt the work.

But when asked to try to assist those in real need, I could not in good conscience say no. And when my wife asked me to give information as she lay ill, I tried giving information with a different spirit within me, for I had to know whether I was on the Lord's side or not. The results were beyond what anyone had ever dreamed, and she recovered fully. Ever since that day I have looked upon all psychical phenomena with a different attitude. People may say hard things about it, but when it gives ease and comfort to our loved ones, then and there it becomes to us something worthwhile, and no matter what others may say, to us it is the *real* thing.

The testimonials from those helped by readings may sound

like a spiel for some patent medicine, yet is there not something of a deeper feeling in what they say? Isn't there something of a note that the individual has received a greater benefit from coming in contact with the Power than mere healing of the body? Let us get this thought. There is not a healing of any form, unless there has come the consciousness of a desire for help, and from a Higher Source than that of our own consciousness. Then that which can add the knowledge of the Higher Spirit must be that which partakes of the *all* good, which is *God*.

I learned about God from my mother and father, and from the Book, long before I learned about the phenomena. In my youth I was told that I was different, but I did not understand what it was all about. As I went along I had many experiences that showed me the way and led me to the work that I do. Many have said they benefited by this work, and they want to give me the credit. But as my mother told me, "Give God the praise."

This is a story of my personal experiences with the phenomena.

Biographical Chronology for Edgar Cayce

YEAR AGE   EVENTS

ran into her room and she sent him back to bed. That day he was in a daze in school and couldn't spell, was kept after class; that night he slept on his spelling book and remembered every word. Until then he had done poorly in school; afterward he did well.

1892 15 Injury to head or spine when struck by baseball on playground may have caused his psychic powers to manifest.

1893 16 Quits school after 8th grade to help support family, works a year for an uncle on a farm.
          Was with grandmother when she died.
          Begins teaching Sunday school, aspires to be a minister.

1894 17 Quits job on farm, moves to town, takes job in Hopper's Bookstore.

1895 18 Meets Gertrude Evans, starts dating her—his first steady girlfriend.
          Meets Dwight L. Moody, other evangelists.

1896 19 Laid off at bookstore, clerks in other stores.

1897 20 Engaged to Gertrude, 16, a few days before turning 20, no wedding date set.

1898 21 Takes job in Louisville for book wholesaler to earn more.
          Gets into Christian Endeavor work there, elected president of Glad Helpers Society that visits jails and hospitals.

1899 22 Comes home for Christmas, decides to stay in Hopkinsville.

1900 23 Takes job with father as traveling insurance agent until voice fails; physicians can't cure his aphonia; takes job in Hopkinsville photo studio.

YEAR	AGE	EVENTS

1901   24   Hypnotized by a magician-hypnotist, who revives his voice temporarily; this connects Edgar with hypnotism and leads to experiments with Al Layne in trance reading for self, which heals his aphonia, and leads to readings for others.

1902   25   Takes job in bookstore in Bowling Green, Ky., 30 miles away.
Returns to Hopkinsville to give reading that cures Aime Dietrich—first "miracle case"—after specialists could do nothing for the child.

1903   26   Marries Gertrude, 22, in June wedding at her family home. Newlyweds start married life in Bowling Green rooming house.

1904   27   Forms partnership to purchase photo studio in Bowling Green.

1905   28   Visits hometown to read for prominent contractor, George Dalton, who broke leg in accident on construction site.

1906   29   Bowling Green medical society observes reading, sticks pins in Edgar.
Cayce Studio destroyed by fire, leaving him heavily in debt.

1907   30   Loses consciousness, pronounced dead, recovers.
First child born, named Hugh Lynn for Gertrude's brothers.

1908   31   Goes to Lexington, Ky., for reading for sick woman, meets David Kahn, who was 15 and destined to become lifetime friend and associate.

1909   32   Takes job as photographer in Gadsden, Alabama.

1910   33   Dr. Ketchum's paper on Cayce is read at Boston medical society, triggers first national publicity in Sunday *New York Times* article followed by wire service

YEAR AGE   EVENTS

stories throughout nation; returns to Hopkinsville, contracts with Ketchum for readings, operates own photo
studio.

1911   34 Publicized in *Chicago Examiner*, visits Chicago; Gertrude gives birth to second son, Milton Porter, who dies
of whooping cough.
Gertrude contracts TB, condition considered hopeless
by her doctor. She asked for a reading and credits her
husband's powers with the miracle of saving her.
This is a turning-point experience, after which he became more confident of psychic ability and more willing to risk trying to help others.

1912   35 Dr. Hugo Munsterburg of Harvard investigates Cayce.
Edgar discovers Ketchum's abuse of readings for financial gain. Breaks contract, moves to Selma, Alabama,
opens Cayce Art Co. photo studio.

1914   37 Son Hugh Lynn, 6, nearly blinded in studio flash powder accident. Boy's sight saved after reading recom-
mends unusual treatment.

1918   41 Third child, Edgar Evans Cayce, born.

1919   42 Called to Washington to read for someone "in high authority," leading to speculation it was for President Wilson after his stroke; asked by Texas newspaper editor
for reading on oil prospects; concludes that wildcatting
for oil may raise money for hospital. Goes to Texas
with Kahn.

1920   43 Forms Cayce Petroleum Co. in Johnson County, Texas.
Returned to Washington for another reading for uni-
dentified authority figure.

1921   44 Drills on oil leases at San Seba, Tex., finds no oil.

YEAR	AGE	EVENTS

1922 45 Gertrude and boys spend the winter with her mother while Edgar, who has been gone nearly 3 years, winters in Birmingham, Ala., lecturing, giving readings, traveling to Denver, Chicago, Dayton, lecturing, seeking funds for hospital.

1923 46 Returns to Selma, hires secretary Gladys Davis; moves to Dayton to work as fulltime psychic, tries to establish Cayce Psychic Research Institute; gives first readings that mention past lives. This launches him into a whole new dimension, the metaphysical. Cayces nearly starve while he builds clientele working as psychic.

1924 47 Edgar meets New York stockbroker Morton Blumenthal, plans a national organization.

1925 48 Cayce family visits New York as Blumenthal's guests; moves to Virginia Beach.

1926 49 Edgar's mother dies.

1927 50 Cayce and Blumenthal organize National Assn. of Investigators, start construction of Cayce Hospital at Virginia Beach.

1928 51 Cayce Hospital dedicated; starting a university is discussed.

1929 52 Cayce Hospital opens, has successful first year. Atlantic University plans developed.

1930 53 University opens, using beachfront hotels for classrooms.

1931 54 Hospital closes in February, university in December; National Association of Investigators disbanded, Edgar despondent.
Meeting of loyal followers organizes Association for Research & Enlightenment, chartered by Commonwealth of Virginia.

YEAR   AGE   EVENTS

First Search for God study group formed in Norfolk, Va.; Edgar, Gertrude, Gladys arrested in New York, charge of fortunetelling dismissed by magistrate.

1932   55   Gives inconclusive readings in Lindbergh kidnapping case. Cayces move to Arctic Crescent house in Va. Beach. First A.R.E. Congress meets there.

1935   58   Edgar, Gertrude, Gladys, Hugh Lynn arrested in Detroit while giving reading for child; Edgar convicted of practicing medicine without a license, freed on probation; ill for some time; has dream of living in Nebraska, as a seacoast area, in 2100.

1939   62   Ailing Tom Sugrue comes to live with Cayces, seeking help. Interviews family for Cayce biography *There Is a River.*

1940   63   Younger son Edgar Evans drafted into army.

1941   64   Hugh Lynn marries Sally Taylor.

1942   65   Edgar's first grandchild, Charles Thomas Cayce, is born; reading says he is the reincarnation of his great grandfather, Thomas Jefferson Cayce.

1943   66   Biography *There Is a River* published.
Hugh Lynn, A.R.E. manager, drafted into army; sent to Europe.
Article in *Coronet* magazine on Cayce brings deluge of mail. People worried about young men in military write and send money for readings; Cayce gives many more than he should.

1944   67   Edgar collapses, has paralyzing stroke, suspends readings.

1945   67   Dies on January 3; Gertrude dies on April 1; both interred in Hopkinsville.

1946   Hugh Lynn returns from the war to begin building the Association for Research & Enlightenment into the international organization it has become.

YEAR	AGE	EVENTS
1948		The Edgar Cayce Foundation chartered.
1967		*The Sleeping Prophet* published, becomes bestseller; A.R.E. membership doubles.
1970		Dave Kahn publishes *My Life with Edgar Cayce*.
1976		Charles Thomas Cayce succeeds Hugh Lynn as president of the A.R.E.; Hugh Lynn becomes chairman of board.
1982		Hugh Lynn Cayce dies.
1984		A.R.E. launches *Venture Inward* magazine.
1985		Atlantic University reactivated as graduate school in transpersonal studies.
1986		Gladys Davis dies.
1987		A.R.E. establishes Reilly School of Massotherapy.
1988		*Hugh Lynn Cayce: About My Father's Business*, a biography, published.
1989		*A Seer Out of Season*, the life of Edgar Cayce, published.
1993		Edgar Cayce readings computerized, made available to public on CD-ROM.

PART I

My Experiences

1

'OLD MAN'

I was born on a farm in south Christian County, Kentucky, Sunday afternoon, March 18, 1877. My father described me in this way:

He was unusually fine looking, large brown eyes, fat rosy cheeks, very bright and cheerful expression showing joy and happiness in his very early life. He was very healthy, strong and active, and with his happy and cheerful disposition, even as a baby, was more interesting to be with than he was a care. He was never a crying baby but reasonably quiet. I recall only two occasions on which he cried unceasingly for any period of time, and nothing his mother or I could think to do seemed to relieve or quiet him. But finally the cause of his crying was discovered by his mother. She had noticed that one of his little hands was swollen. His hands were very fat, and in dressing him a very fine thread had caught between his thumb and index finger and was drawn so tight that it had caused the hand to swell; and the more it would swell the more painful it became and the more the child would cry until both his mother and I were in tears. But when she located the cause and clipped the thread, the child was soon quiet and asleep again. He was about six weeks or two months old at the time.

A few months after that, one night after everyone had retired he began to be restless and soon commenced to cry. He seemed to be in great pain and his mother stripped all his clothing and dressed him several times trying to locate the trouble but could find nothing wrong. She then commenced to doctor him, giving him every thing we could think would give him some relief, but the child continued to cry. The middle of the night came and went and the boy continued to cry. Then there was a knock on the door. It was one of the colored women on the farm. "Miss Carrie," she said, "I think I know what's the matter with your baby."

"Well, Emily, I wish you would tell me because I am almost wild and have done everything for him I can think of and nothing seems to help him."

The child was still crying. Emily had her corncob pipe in her mouth smoking and came and sat by my mother near the child's feet. Puffing away on her strong pipe and drawing her mouth full of smoke, she unfolded the clothes off the baby's feet and puffed the smoke against the bottom of his little feet. Drawing the smoke again and again, she repeated puffing it on the baby's feet three or four more times until the child was easy and closed his little eyes again in quiet sleep. After she went home, he continued to sleep peacefully until morning and I don't think was ever troubled with colic again.

As a baby, as a child, as a small boy, and as a lad, Edgar was always good humored, pleasant, and entertaining. He was quiet but seemed to know always just what he wanted to say. He was a real boy in his likes and dislikes, and very early he became tired of his little dresses, so his mother put pants on him by the time he was eighteen months old. After that he was more ready to travel around and go places and meet people. He would follow me about the house and almost always accompany me when I left home to go about the neighborhood or go to town. He was not a giggler, nor a titterer and not boisterous. Before he could talk, when anyone came in the room with him he would let them know he was present with a coo, a jolly grunt, or a little jump or sudden spring, throwing his little hands and feet and letting known his joy. And after he was talking he almost always had something pleasant to say to everyone he met. Very early he seemed to know everyone, no one was a stranger to him; and as soon as he could, which was reasonably early, he was ready to talk to any and everyone he met.

One day, before he could walk, I came in for lunch and talked to the child and his mother for a few minutes before leaving to go to the store that I operated. It was raining very hard, and pretty soon his mother heard the baby cry. She *found him trying to follow me to the store. He had crawled to the edge of the porch and fell off, landing flat on his back with his little face turned up and the rain falling so fast that he was tossing his head from side to side, kicking and trying to get out of the way of the water, but to no avail. He showed great gratitude when his mother picked him up and dressed him in dry clothes.*

He would never awaken in a bad humor unless there was really something out of the ordinary or cry unless there was something really wrong. And if there was, he would quickly let someone know, and even then almost invariably with some question to ask or some suggestion concerning activities of the day past or the approaching day. Always truly intelligent questions, as though he must understand things. Once he started an investigation, he would usually complete it to his own satisfaction before giving it up. It was not advisable to try to deceive him or even jokingly throw him off by giving him some elusive answer to any question he might ask for such answers never seemed to satisfy him, especially if it was something he could not understand. Usually a plain and truthful answer proved to be best. If the question was evaded, he would investigate further. On one occasion his aunt came into the room where he was, bringing a tall jar of cream to sit by the fire. He asked her what it was, and she looked at him cunningly and said, "It's to catch meddlers and you had better let it alone." He looked at her inquisitively but said nothing more to her then, but twenty-five or thirty minutes later she returned to the room and Edgar had started his investigation and had turned the jar of cream over, spilling it over the floor, seeing what it was. And he had gotten the broom and was spreading the cream thoroughly over the carpet, trying to sweep it up. His aunt realized she was at fault and said but very little to him, but laughingly told his mother, explaining to her how it all happened. So she too realized the child was not to blame and only told him his aunt was joking with him and he had wasted her jar of cream, which meant little to him at the time. Even with his investigative mind and spirit, he was not meddlesome and ordinarily when one put anything down before him and told him not to bother it, saying nothing more, he would not touch whatever it might be. But it was the wrong thing to do, trying to tempt him, pretending there was something curious or not understandable that you were placing in the room. He would find out, or know why he couldn't.

About this time a young bachelor medical doctor began to take his meals with us. He had never allowed a child to eat with him at the table before and modestly protested when he learned that Edgar was going to eat at the table. We gave him to understand that the child would not interfere with him and that Ned, the eleven-year-old boy his mother had hired to look after Edgar, would take care of him. The doctor soon became reconciled and he and Edgar soon became good friends and were very entertaining to one another. The doctor, who as a rule was not fond of children, was so tickled that he laughed profusely at Edgar's mannerisms and said he was "the best and most interesting child he ever saw." It was he who first called him the "old man." That nickname was soon taken up by most of his uncles and many acquaintances who very fondly called him "Old Man."[2]

My earliest remembrance is of accompanying my mother to church. Just how old I was I have no idea. Among my earliest recollections are the conversations I had with my grandfather, Thomas Jefferson Cayce, who, to me, was a most wonderful man.

Edgar was particularly fond of his grandparents and, before he was eighteen months old, would visit them for several days at a time. When they came to visit us, he often went home with them. They were both very fond of him and very glad to have him with them. Naturally, he was a very great pleasure to them. While he was so young his grandfather would take him in his arms when they retired and sleep with him in his arms

---

until Edgar got too restless or too warm. Then his grandfather would place him between the two of them. When Edgar woke up in the night, he would run his little hands over the face of the person he was turned toward. If it was smooth, he would turn completely over and run his hands over the face of the other person, his grandfather, and feel his beard and then nestle down by his side or be taken into his arms again and soon drop off to sleep. He was particularly fond of his grandmother but had gotten into the habit of going to sleep in his grandfather's arms, and I suppose he felt that was where he should be when he woke up. If his grandfather was not there, he would immediately begin an investigation.

I remember riding horseback with my grandfather several times when I sat in front, long before I was big enough to ride behind him. On a number of occasions I saw him do some very unusual things that I have since learned many people attribute to the working of discarnate spirits. I heard people in conversation from time to time ask him to be present at some sort of meeting. I did not know the purposes of these meetings. I also saw him move tables and other articles, apparently without any contact with the objects themselves. On such occasions he would say, "I don't know what the power is, but don't fool with it."

The most impressive incident in connection with my grandfather was his death, on June 8, 1881. He was drowned in a pond at the old home place, and I was possibly the only one who saw him go to his death. I had been riding behind him on the horse when he first entered the pond. He returned to the shore and let me off before entering the pond again. I saw the horse throw him, and as the girth broke he disappeared under the water.

I was only four when my grandfather was drowned, and I often wonder just what effect these associations of thought have had upon my mental being or my activities in this life.

As a child, Edgar was not as fond of playing in water as some children, and really he would avoid water especially when it was cold. And if he could get to the breakfast table without washing his hands and face, he would do so. He was truthful about it and would not tell a falsehood, and if his mother asked him after he had attempted to avoid washing up even if he had taken his seat, he would do it without any grumbling. He just hated water or hated to bathe his face in cold water especially. It may have been his experience of falling off the porch when the water poured so fast into his face and he couldn't get out of the way.

The store I operated was not far from the house and Edgar was a frequent visitor even before he could walk much. He would get Ned to bring him over, not just for the trip but he would know what he wanted. There was a complete stock of goods in almost every line, including choice eatables. He soon learned which merchandise was kept in which rooms, as there were several departments, and when he came into the store if the door to that room was closed he would knock or have the boy knock. He would walk in or be carried in after the door was opened and immediately call for what he wanted almost like the grownups did. Almost everyone who came to the store knew Edgar and always made a great fuss over him. He also knew almost everyone who came to the store, so there was not much time lost before a conversation was started. Occasionally he would address the crowd, not in a boastful way, but in a mild, gentle, pleasant way. In that way he would amuse those present for some time with his sober, matter-of-fact manner. He was the most universally admired and loved child I have ever known. He was very generous and thoughtful of others, even as a child, and very liberal with everyone. It was very rare for him to ever hold anything back.

Many visitors and customers would occasionally take lunch at the store if they happened to be there when they were disposed to eat. Edgar often visited the store several times a day, and often would come in when many others were there. Many times someone would ask him to have lunch with them. If not, he would order and ask one or more people to have lunch with him. Either way there was rarely ever a refusal. Others often invited him more to hear him talk than for any other reason.

In his childhood days it was very rare for him to reply to any remark by anyone, especially if there were several people present. But usually if an unusual remark was made, he would gaze at that person with an assured, pleasant look and express his difference of opinion on his face. The expression on his face would be plain but gentle and kind.

As a small child he would occasionally come in and have Ned set him on the counter out of everyone's way and sit there just listening and watching the crowd for an hour or more, saying nothing to anyone unless someone started a conversation with him. Finally, he would have someone lift him down and he would go back to the house to his mother. Quite often he would hear or see something that he would speak of after returning home.

As a child I loved to be alone a great deal, and quite often had playmates that others, coming upon the scene and hearing the conversation, claimed did not exist.

One day when I was about nine years old my aunt asked me, "Come, Eddie. Don't you wish to help Auntie gather some greens for dinner? I think I saw some lovely wild mustard, as I came through the field from Uncle Jim's the other evening." As we went through the lot by the barn, where many unusual things had happened to me—or so I thought—I began to tell my aunt about them.

"Auntie, I love to play in that barn, I have lots of fun there!"

"Fun?" asked my aunt. "What's fun? You are not old enough to know what fun is, are you? What is so funny about the old barn?"

"Well," I said, "that is where Grandpa used to keep his tobacco that he got so much money for. There is the old beam they used to prize[3] the tobacco with. It is fun to go there and

---

[3] To "prize" tobacco is to pack the cured tobacco leaves tightly into a hogshead, a barrel-like container, for transport to market.

see the pole go up and down, and hear someone cry, 'Up! Down! Up! Down! Up! Down!' And there is a blue jay with a nest there; I saw her building it this morning. And there is one speckled egg in the nest already. I saw a wren also, looking at the horn Grandpa used to call the boys from the field with."

"But," said my aunt, "they haven't prized tobacco there in a long time, and you never saw tobacco prized anyway, I'm sure."

"Yes, I have!" I said. "I see Grandpa there every day when I go there to play, and besides there are a lot of little boys and girls that come there to play with me, and they can climb all over the barn and tell me what is on every pole in the barn!"

"Eddie, you shouldn't let your imagination run away with you like that! You are just imagining things! Don't you know it is wicked to tell stories?"

"What is being wicked, Auntie? I *play* with the children, that I know; and I see Grandpa, and he *talks* to me—as he has talked to the farm hands who prize tobacco. What is wicked? I see it, and it is great fun for me! Why is that wicked? Is it wicked because I see them and say I see them?"

"If you saw them it would be all right," said my aunt, "but they are not there. Your grandfather has been dead for six years now, and dead people do not prize tobacco. So, to say that you do see them is wicked. I will have to speak to your mother about that."

"But Mother sees the children, too!" I said. "She just hasn't been here when Grandpa was prizing tobacco."

"I don't believe it! You are just a bad boy who likes to imagine things! I will speak to your mother. She mustn't humor you in all this tomfoolery!"

We went on to the field and found plenty of wild mustard and gathered a basketful. Coming back toward the barn my aunt asked me again, "Why do you say it is fun to play in the old barn?"

"Because," I said, "I have so many friends to play with there, and Grandpa is great fun. He tells me a lot of funny stories of what happened before the [civil] war, and during the war and afterward."

"Are you sure it is your grandfather?"

"Of course, it is Grandpa! I have felt his chin whiskers, and that is the way I used to tell him from Grandma when it was dark."

"You are certainly a strange child," said my aunt. "I will have a talk with your mother. This thing must not go on, else everyone will know you have gone beside yourself. It gives me the creeps to hear you talk like that!"

"Carrie," she said that evening, "what is this Eddie says about you seeing children playing with him in the barn? There are no children living anywhere near here. You'd better take that child to the doctor—I think he is just out of his mind! He is not normal some way!"

"But, Lou, I have seen the children Eddie speaks of. They can't harm him, I am sure."

"Whose children are they?"

"I do not know. They seem very nice, and I think Eddie is having an experience like we read about but think can never happen to us. I am praying about it, Lou, and I am sure no harm can come of it."

"But what about his saying that he sees and talks with his Grandpa. You know that is out of the question, and what will the neighbors say if they hear about all this foolishness? You need to give that boy a good thrashing, and stop all this fairy business or whatever you choose to call it!"

"Lou, I couldn't whip him for that! Because he is sure he sees all this, and I have seen the children myself. It is not just imagination. I do not know what it is, but I simply can't whip him for such a thing as that. I just wish there was some way he could go to church, study his Bible, and learn what this is all about."

"Tommyrot!" said Aunt Lou. "You don't mean to tell me you think this foolishness is of God! It is more like the Devil, if you don't mind my saying so, and certainly no good can come of such a thing! You had better take the child to the doctor. They will have nothing to do with him in any church, I can assure you!"

My aunt got married that summer and moved to the eastern part of the state to live, so I didn't see her again for several years. But I was reprimanded by different ones of the family as I grew up. This gradually made me ashamed of these experiences, even though to me they were very real. I remember being called "curious" or "different" when I only wanted to be let alone and thought of as any other boy of my age. I did not want to be different, especially in the sense that I was spoken of in most instances.

Quite early in life Edgar began to show a sporting spirit and even as a child was fond of fishing and hunting. On one occasion when he was a child, after heavy rains had filled the ponds and lowlands to overflowing, Edgar decided to go fishing. He got his little fishing pole and started out alone and went over to the pond about a fourth of a mile from the house. He said nothing to anyone about going there. When he got there he found the large flat near the pond full of water because the heavy rains had caused the pond to overflow and a great many fish had overflowed into the flat. As the water drained from the flat, it left the fish floundering in the mud. When Edgar arrived, he soon took in the situation and put his pole down and started picking up the fine fish that were floundering. He got so deeply interested in picking up the many fish that he continued walking and came to the edge of a deep hole that was about twelve feet across. It was slick with mud and very steep and slanting down ten feet or more to an underground stream that carried the water off. As soon as Edgar struck the edge of the banks, he started sliding and went to the bottom under the water. He immediately started crawling up the bank, sticking his hands and feet into the mud to hold and pull by until he got to the top. Just as he was climbing up, one of the hands on the place came along the road nearby with a wagon load of wood and stopped his team when he saw Edgar's hat, thinking he was about to drown. The man got to him in time to catch hold of his hand when he saw

Edgar coming out of the water and pulled him out. After wiping off Edgar's face, he put the child on the wagon with the load of wood and carried him to the house and his mother. When his mother saw him in that condition, and the man told her where and how he found him, it frightened her to think of the predicament he had been in and that she had known nothing of it until he was out of trouble and at home. It seemed almost a miracle that he had crawled out unaided except, when he was practically out, the man reached him and led him out. Slipping into this hole as he did made him slack his hold on the fish he had gathered up in his hands, and when he was out and safe he was glad to get away even without the fish.

In my meditation I often review many of those experiences of years and years ago.

2

An Angel's Promise, 1890

All the schooling I obtained was in the little red school house in south Christian County and the two-room Beverly Academy. Many teachers came and went. I remember some of them with a great deal of pleasure; some I remember with the dread I felt when I appeared before them for class work.

I was considered rather dull, until I began to read, and was not as apt a pupil as many of my schoolmates. It was not from a lack of consideration on the part of my parents, but because of my inability to retain much that was taught me in class.

As a schoolboy, Edgar avoided contentions and disputes. He was not a tattler and I remember one instance when he was going to submit to a whipping from his teacher rather than report another pupil who had violated some rule. One of the older boys who liked Edgar a lot and knew the facts in this case stated very emphatically that Edgar was not the guilty one and did not deserve to be whipped as the teacher had supposed. Edgar was true to his convictions and obedient to his teachers and parents. Yes, he made mistakes and did some things he should not have, but I don't recall an instance in which he willfully disobeyed either of his parents or a teacher.

Soon after learning to read, I heard a discussion from a rather unusual source about individuals in the Bible. A woodcutter told me the first Bible story that made a lasting impression. He said he was "strong as Samson." I wanted to know who Samson was. He told me he was somebody in the Bible and that the preacher had preached about him at church the night before. I went to my mother with the story and asked her to tell me about him. This story of Sampson seemed to attract me more than anything, and I eagerly sought to learn something about this book which taught about the relationship of individuals to individuals, God's relationship to man, and man's relationship to God.

When Edgar was very young his mother and I read the Bible through together, one reading for some time and then the other reading for a while. In this way we read the entire book through, both old and new covenants. Edgar listened almost the entire time. He was quiet all the while, except occasionally asking a question. After we answered the question, the reading would continue and Edgar listened with great patience, which caused us to remark many times about how quiet and interested he seemed to be. Occasionally he would fall asleep, and the reading would cease for that time; but it was rare for him to leave while either of us was reading the Bible.

Quite early in life I became a student of the Scriptures, and love them yet. It seems to me the Scriptures tell us about every phase of psychic power. When anyone begins to make their work or any phase of their work take the place of the Holy Word, then and there they begin to go wrong. It can't be done. Now, we all may be brothers *in Christ*, but to regard ourselves as brothers *with* the Christ and equal to His works, we set selfishness on high and lose the insight into the reason for the sufferings of the Christ. In this, however, we are only bandying words and are losing the thought I want you to get, though in the end it must lead back to this phase of it, or there would be no virtue in anything done.

My grandmother's old home in south Christian County burned when we were living there, so I was separated from my three sisters and parents, as I stayed in the homes of relatives for a time. In the home of one of my aunts there was a large, profusely illustrated Bible which excited my imagination. I decided that I was going to know more about this book. When I questioned people about it, I was told that it was God's message to His children. Understanding little as I read, I seemed to become more and more anxious about the proper interpretation of the stories, promises, and the actions of people recorded in the Bible; some of them seemed to me good, and some very bad.

When I was about ten years old my mother asked if I would like to go to Sunday school. So I began to go. The lesson was the first chapter of Genesis, the creation, and I found it very interesting, in fact, all absorbing. I asked my father to procure a book for me that had the whole story in it. A few weeks later a Bible was given to me, the gift of a book dealer to whom my father told the story. I began to read, and the more I read the more certain I became that these happenings in the barn were real and not foolish. Yet, the more others questioned me, the more of a recluse I became.

I taught a Sunday school class of boys and young men for many years, and while Edgar was quite small he sat in that class while they recited the lesson each Sunday. It was in that class that he commenced to answer Bible questions before an audience or in a class. He surprised the other boys as well as other members of the church. He kept that up, rarely ever missing one when asked by the teacher, until it was not long before he was considered one of the class. A little later when the men's Bible class would come to questions they could not answer, invariably someone would say, "Ask Edgar," and he was usually so prompt and accurate in his answers that most members of the Bible class would delight in asking him. The Bible was a favorite study with him and he spent much time reading it. He never boasted about it. It was very remarkable even at that tender age, with so much attention from others, both young and even the very elderly people, it never seemed to make any difference to him or to interfere with his courteous manner or to make him seem uppish or boastful. No success seemed to make him egotistical or unjustly proud. He never seemed to think what he knew was anything more than should be expected, so it did not make him vain or puffed up. Modesty and lack of pomp continues with him.

The year I turned ten our family moved to a little house on the edge of a wood, one with a great variety of vegetation.

There were large oaks, hickory, white oak, poplar and beech in timber wood; hazelnuts, paw-paw, and many other fruit and nut trees. I became acquainted with all the beautiful dells and glades in that wood, and built myself a retreat in a very pretty spot a quarter of a mile from the house. I kept my Bible there and read it every day, reading and re-reading many portions of it.

Edgar took membership with the Christian Church [Disciples of Christ] in 1889 when he was twelve years of age, and continued a faithful member, not one whose activities are just to "hang on," but a real active member, recognizing his privileges and his duties and fulfilling them in a very capable and satisfactory way. Many times the older members and officers of the church would call upon him to perform duties. The ministers were particularly fond of him and would talk with him a great deal. They often kept him pretty busy about the church service and especially during a series of meetings of several weeks. They admired his willingness to take hold, never refusing a request or making excuses. Therefore everyone felt free to call upon him or make any reasonable request for the performance of almost any task. His church membership and his Christian life as a young man was very beautiful, and it has continued to the present time.

By the time I was fourteen, I had read the Bible through several times, understanding little; yet to my developing mind, this book seemed to contain that something that my inner self craved. As I read of its promises and the prayers of those who sought to commune with the one God on high, I felt that this must be true, and to me there came a peace, and then a *promise*.

More and more I sought the companionship of teachers and ministers that chance brought my way, ministers of all creeds and denominations. I remember very well some discussions I had in my earlier years with a very devout Mormon woman, who was forced to leave the colony after the passage of the law that no one could have more than one wife. She had been one of the wives of a leader. She knew her tenets well, and a great deal about the Scriptures. Also I remember very well the conversations I had with an elder in the Methodist Church, and ministers in the Baptist, the Presbyterian, the Christian, the Unitarian, and the Congregationalist churches. For some time I was with a priest of the Catholic church, seeking I knew not what. Is it any wonder that I was called peculiar by my schoolmates? Few of them, I found, liked the association or companionship of teachers or ministers. They were rather looked upon as above ordinary, with some special mission in life that cut them off from all of life's material pleasures. But I found them much as other men—some were thinking mostly of others, some were carrying the burdens of many as well as their own.

It was during such a period that one evening I had my first vision. I had read through the Book several times by then. I had been reading of the vision of Manoah, for I loved the story of Samson. I do not know whether I can put into words this experience, this vision, this promise, in order that you may understand what it has meant to me, and what it means in my life today.

I prayed very earnestly that afternoon as I sat in the woods by my favorite tree that had so often seemed to speak to me, answering many of my childish questions, as the birds and little animals of the section would gather about me. Even, in time, I seemed to hear the answer that God was just as near and personal as we would allow Him to be, speaking to us through His creatures. It appeared to me even then, if God had made the little birds, the trees, the flowers, the beautiful sky, and set the stars in their places, given to the sun and moon those laws governing them, so they might shed their glory for the benefit of all He had made, He must be in every one of these little creatures in some manner or form. As I gradually saw their fear subside, because of something I was able to say or do for them, was not this affection, this companionship, something akin to what would, if properly understood, show His presence in relations between individuals?

That day I studied hard on my lessons, but seemed far, far

away. Many of the things I had heard from the little birds, squirrels, and rabbits in the woods seemed to crowd into my mind. Their very actions seemed to say to one another, "Hurry, hurry, he is here and will give us something to eat, and stroke us—we need not be afraid."

As I was rudely called back home by my father, who was giving the lessons, it seemed that everything was all awry, that we were studying about things which didn't mean very much.

Kneeling by my bed that night, I prayed again that God would show me that He loved me, that He would give me the ability to do something for my fellow man which would show to them His love, even as the actions of His little creatures in the woods showed me their trust in one who loved them.

I was not yet asleep when the vision first began, but I felt as if I were being lifted up. A glorious light as of the rising morning sun seemed to fill the whole room, and a figure appeared at the foot of my bed. I was sure it was my mother, and I called to her, but she didn't answer. For the moment I was frightened, climbed out of bed and went to my mother's room. No, she hadn't called. Almost immediately after I returned to my couch, the figure came again. Then it seemed all gloriously bright—an angel, or what, I knew not; but gently, patiently, it said: "Thy prayers are heard. You will have your wish. Remain faithful. Be true to yourself. Help the sick, the afflicted."

There was little sleep for me after the vision gradually faded away. I could only rush out in the moonlight; and I will never forget that it seemed to me I had never seen it shine so gloriously as it did that May night. I went to my favorite retreat, or tree, and kneeling there, I thanked God for letting me know He cared. I will never forget how, in the early morning after day began to dawn, two little squirrels came down that tree and hunted in my pockets for nuts I did not have. I couldn't even tell my mother what had happened, though she said, "My boy, why are you so happy, yet look so very strange this morning?" I could only say, "Mother, I will have to tell you later."

In school that day I seemed to be still in a daze and, of

course, missed every word that I was given to spell. We were in school at eight and didn't leave until four. That day I wrote "cabin" five hundred times on the board, so it was quite late when I had walked the three-and-a-half or four miles home. My father was waiting for me, and in no too good a humor for my being the dunce in school.

"You will certainly know that lesson before you go to bed this night," he remarked.

I studied, or thought I did, and was very sure I knew the lesson well, but when I handed him the book my mind became a perfect blank—I had forgotten everything. During those two or three hours I received many a buff and rebuff for my stupidity, as I labored heavily over that spelling lesson. As you remember, I hadn't slept much the night before, and the fatigue of a growing boy had begun to tell, so around eleven o'clock I began to fall asleep. Several times I picked myself up off of the floor where I had been slapped for going to sleep. Finally, I suggested, "If you will let me sleep five minutes, I can learn this lesson," for something had spoken within, "Rely on the promise." My father told me to go to sleep. When the five minutes were up I handed him the book, for I knew that I knew the lesson. Not only was I able to spell all the words in the lesson, but any word in that particular book; not only spell them, but tell on what page and what line each word could be found and how it was marked. As many of the pupils said later, "Cayce knows every mark in that book, unless somebody has made one since it was printed."

From that day on I had little trouble in school, for I would read my lesson, sleep on it a few seconds, and then be able to repeat every word of it.

To be sure, the next day I was as much a curiosity to my teachers and schoolmates as I had been in the days before, and the peculiar thing about it was that I knew all my lessons as well. I only had to lose consciousness, even in school, to retain whatever I had read in the book. I often felt that Miss Cox, my teacher at the time, must have had a greater insight into what was taking place than anyone ever credited her with having. From then to the end of school I advanced rapidly. I was accused of memorizing all my lessons; but I only read them, slept on them, and they appeared before my eyes as I recited.

What this was I did not know. It was a wonder to my parents, my classmates, and my teachers; yet I did not attempt to reason *why* this had happened, and to this day I do not know *how* to reason it, for my present position is a combination of many experiences, varying in their way and manner of presentation, seemingly necessary for the evolution of my mind.

As a child he was the leader among his young associates, and usually looked upon as the spokesman in many crowds. One of his favorite ways of entertaining his little acquaintances was to have them be seated and relate to them miraculous or very unusual happenings, usually of things he had seen, heard, or experienced in some way, and in this way would occasionally entertain the little ones for possibly an hour or more, occasionally relating conversations and incidents that took place before he was born, not often giving dates but relating in detail conversations or occurrences, and among his acquaintances his word was final, no one doubting any statement he made. Occasionally his mother would speak of his activities, his unusual statements and narration of occurrences, sometimes under very peculiar circumstances and at others very simple and everyday like, much of which was never understood. At the present time, it seems plain to me that such conversation, statements, and activities were psychic, possibly received and spoken psychically, if that is what it should be called. Not a great while after such activities it seemed that he was able to prepare his lessons in that way and did, or in some like manner, that also was far from being understood by his parents or teacher. I feel confident he did not understand what it was or how it was accomplished at the time.

A year later I was talking with the principal of the school about the subjects I desired to take when he asked me, "Eddie, how is it that you need to lose yourself in sleep even here in school to recite your lessons? I heard something about this a year or so ago, but how do you retain the lesson—do you memorize it, or does it appear before you as you recite the lesson? My father was a captain on the Merrimack, when it fought the Monitor in Hampton Roads, and it is said that he visioned or dreamed the manner of armoring the Merrimack and as a consequence had its sides covered with armor plate. He saw it all as pictures in his vision. Is that the way you see the lesson?"

This, of course, was news to me, and it gave me for the first time the sense of being different. Was it something to be proud of? I didn't know. And my study of the Scriptures gave me a sense of humbleness—and fear of being a prevaricator. Yet to my developing mind it seemed to contain something my inner self craved.

Edgar was just a real boy with his likes and dislikes, not peevish or contentious but what some might call a good sport, not given to any frivolous or childish habits. He was very fond of games, particularly pitching quoits, and was very good at the game even when quite small. Often at the store men were playing quoits, for it's a man's game, and if Edgar was in sight, one of the men would call out that he and Edgar would play some other twosome. Edgar was hard to beat at that game even though so young.

I didn't enjoy playing many games with the other children at school—baseball, football, marbles, etc.—for I never could shoot a marble, spin a top, throw or bat a ball, as well as other children. I preferred to sit and argue with the teachers, when they would listen, concerning the mysteries of life. Often Professor Thomb and others insisted that I run out and play, but I could not keep up with the bigger boys and I was often in disgrace for wanting to play with the little boys or girls—if they would let me.

One day I tried to follow their admonition to play normally with other boys. We were playing a ball game called "Old Sower." To be sure, I was the one who had to stand with my

back to the others and have them throw the ball at me for
having been unable to keep up with the others in the game.
Someone must have struck me in the middle of my spine or
the back of my head, for I remembered nothing that happened
the rest of the day even though it was said that I rather me-
chanically went through all the classroom activities. It was
nothing unusual for me to be peculiar to the rest of them, but
in the evening my sister had to lead me home. I gradually
seemed to grow worse, later throwing things at the table, and
when I went into the kitchen, finding a pan of coffee that had
recently been roasted I told them it needed sowing and proceeded to scatter it over the yard. I was reprimanded and put
to bed.[1]

There was a celebration of Cleveland's election the next
evening in the county seat, and I asked my father if I might
accompany him to this celebration.

*In his annual message before the United States Congress,
President Cleveland vigorously advocated a revision of the
tariff in the direction of free trade. I was a great admirer of
Grover Cleveland, both as a man and as a public official, and
was very strong for "tariff for revenue only." Naturally, that
speech attracted my attention and hearty endorsement. I felt
that it would be good for every citizen to hear it. Edgar was
in school at the time, and at the close of the term there was
to be an exhibition of speeches, essays, recitals, and such for
the entertainment of the patrons and the improvement of the*

---

[1] The authorized biography of Cayce, *There Is a River*, makes more of this
incident, saying that once in bed Edgar "gave instructions for a poultice to
be put on the back of his head, near the base of the brain. He was suffering
from shock, he said, and would be all right in the morning if the poultice
were applied." There is no mention of a doctor attending him. After going to
sleep, "several times during the night he shouted 'Hurray for Cleveland!' and
pounded the wall with his fist, but did not wake up. To keep him from harm-
ing himself the squire pulled the bed away from the wall. When he opened
his eyes the next morning, neighbors and relatives were sitting around keeping
vigil." He remembered nothing when he awoke from the time he had gone
out to recess at school, but he professed to feel fine.

students. Edgar was to prepare something for the occasion. As you may suppose, the president's speech was very long; but I felt confident that Edgar was equal to the task, and I was very anxious for it to be repeated at the close of the school and anywhere else possible, and knew that it would be wonderful for Edgar and show something of his ability along these lines. I showed him a printed copy of the speech and asked him if he thought he could deliver it at the close of the school term. He looked at it and read a few lines to get an idea of the words Cleveland used and said to me, "If you will read it to me a few times, I can. Will you do that?" I assured him I would. After making a few changes in the introduction to make it suit the occasion, I read it to him, I think three times, and he said, "I have it. I know it." I was very much surprised to have him say so quickly that he knew it, but he did. And when the time came, he delivered that speech perfectly. I thought it was a marvel, and so did everyone present, and it was. He was perfectly cool and calm, with no excitement whatever, and spoke as deliberately and with as much understanding as one would or could who was much older and more experienced. I did not think of such a thing at the time, but I believe now that the speech was prepared psychically, whatever that means. I believe it would be impossible for anyone to prepare an article of that length with words and subject so unfamiliar, as that necessarily was to Edgar, in so short a time and with so much ease and effort in the old way, as one might call it. However, he was not asleep on that occasion when I was reading to him. But other incidents in his childhood give me the feeling that he has always been endowed with the power or gift, and these experiences are evidence of it.

3

'WILL IT DRIVE ME CRAZY?'

One of the young ladies of the school, Bess, gave a party one summer evening, and for the first time I went to an old-time country moonlight party. My association with this young lady grew into friendship and ripened into young love. This was a new experience for me, the arousing of a desire I had known nothing of before. We experienced all the little glances and antics that bespeak of "puppy love." But, to be sure, other boys also wanted the company of Bess, and this brought me a new realization. Jealousy, a new emotion, filled my heart and mind and made me neglect my studies of Holy Writ. I was often sad and lonely. I became defiant and stubborn, which was unusual, but I didn't know who to turn to. Once my mother questioned me. Then I had a dream—a dream that has repeated itself again and again through the years, but which I did not fully understand then. In the dream I am walking through a beautiful, sparsely wooded place. All trees are small but cone shaped, the ground covered with a mat of vine on which there are small, white star flowers. The lady on my arm is veiled and says nothing, but I have a feeling of contentment, happiness, complete love. The ground seems to slope downward. As we walk, we come to a lovely little stream of crystal clear water, beautiful white sand and white pebbles with tiny fish in the stream. We step over the stream and start up the slope on the other side, and are then met by a "messenger," a lovely bronze-colored figure, nude save for a loin cloth, with wings on his feet and shoulders. In his hand he has a lovely gold cloth. He stops us from speaking and says, "Will you join your right hands." When we have done that, he lays the cloth of gold over our hands, saying, "United, you may accomplish anything; alone, very little. Do not lose the cloth." Then he disappears. We continue walking and soon come to a very muddy road. As we stand undecided as to how to cross, the messenger appears again, saying, "Use the cloth." We wave it over the road and the mud disappears. We pass over on a very lovely path and soon come to a high cliff which we must scale. There is a large knife there with which niches may be cut into the wall of the cliff. I begin to cut and climb, pulling the lady up one step to the next.

In all of the fifty-seven times that dream has been repeated identically, except as to heights I climbed up the wall, the veil has never been lifted or the wall scaled.[1]

When I told Mother of the dream and of my feelings for Bess, as well as the feeling of resentment toward other boys on whom she might smile, her advice was to read the Book again and see just how one should act under such circumstances. I searched the Bible for such stories and read what was recorded there, and I knew that the day must come when Bess and I must discuss our feelings for one another.

One day Bess and I and some friends went on a picnic in the woods on my grandmother's farm. Bess and I wandered away from the others and came to the cove that was my retreat and sat down among the scenes that had once meant so much to me. I felt welling up within me a feeling—I didn't know what to make of it—that I wanted to have this girl apart from others, to have her alone for my own—her body, her thoughts—but I did not know how to put this into words. But when there is sympathy between a boy and a girl in their teens, usually such feelings find a way of being expressed. We may be very stumbling, very halting, but we convey how we feel to one another.

The place and the girl were so sacred to me that I couldn't help tell her of some of the things that had happened there: how the place came to be made, how the little folks had dug a spring here that was, after several years, still running clear and beautiful; the flowers they had planted that were now

—

[1] Many years later when Mr. Cayce submitted this dream for interpretation through a reading, the message was that "together all may be accomplished, alone nothing will be accomplished."

blooming and seemed yet to be cared for by a loving hand; how I had come here to read the first note Bess had written me in school, and had sat here to reply to her.

But all my words seemed to fall on deaf ears, for Bess laughed at me and my mysterious tale of the little people. She said she liked me but didn't care for all these things that I talked about, which to her were unnatural. Bess said she liked to play and romp and go to parties, go buggy riding, sit and talk, dance, go places for entertainment. I tried to tell her I loved her and that I wanted her for my wife and that we would build for ourselves a place in the world.

"I know we are just children," I said, "But I can study hard and be something—maybe the best preacher in the country, and we will have a church like Old Liberty, and a lovely garden and fields of pretty crops and the like."

But Bess laughed all the more and said she would never be a preacher's wife.

"And besides, this foolishness of seeing things isn't right, only crazy people talk about such things. Besides, Dad says you are not right in the head and can never come to any good end. Even if you grow up to be a man, I want a real man, a man of the world who will go out and be something, not a dreamer of dreams, not one that likes the Bible better than a good love story. I want a man who would make me love him by force and take me in his arms and make love to me, kiss me and make me love him. You think all that is foolish, but that is what every girl hopes for."

About that time, our friends found us in the woods and teased us about being in love. And soon we all went home, but it was a sad, sad day for me.

A few days later I went to see Bess's father, who was a doctor, and asked him about what Bess had said about me being touched in the head. I also told him what I felt for Bess. His reply was a real eye-opener for me.

"Eddie," he said, "you are a good boy, but you are just a kid, not sixteen yet, are you?"

"I was sixteen last March," I told him.

"Well, anyway, you are too young to think of getting married. While it is every father's wish that his daughter marry a fine upstanding man, one well thought of in every sense of the word, he must be a man, Eddie, and you can never be a man. That accident[2] that happened to you a few years ago has robbed you of that possibility. You may have all the desires of a man toward a woman, but you would never be able to have children, and that would eventually bring discord. All this unusual vision you have I am sure comes from that injury, and it will grow on you and sap the very never fiber of your body. After awhile I am afraid it will cause insanity. You should be like other boys, be with other boys, but you never played marbles, spun a top, or threw a ball or did any of the things other boys do. Don't you feel the difference when you are with other boys? But you don't go with other boys, do you? Do that and after four or five years, come talk with me again."

This talk with Bess's father made me more determined but gave me new questions to think about, or were they really new? I was at least a warm-blooded boy, but is that so different? Was the doctor right that it was going to drive me crazy? Why did I have such an accident? But I had these visions *before* I got hurt, I reasoned, so it had nothing to do with the visions. I *am* different, I guess. It's true, I never played marbles, never spun a top, or threw a ball, but I never had any of these toys and didn't really care for them. But to be like other boys, I must like them and do the things that other boys do. I don't want to, but I'll have to or there is no need talking with the doctor again, I thought. One thing I was sure of, I did love Bess. And so my thoughts ran. I began to think how and whom to make friends with.

About that time a young man named Tom asked Mother to let him a room at our home because he was going to work

---

[2] Evidently he referred to Edgar's being struck by a ball which caused his silly behavior for a day. This blow to his head or spine may also have helped bring his psychic ability to the surface, judging by the experience of Peter Hurkos and other known psychics who trace their gift to a blow or injury in a fall.

with his uncle who lived in the neighborhood, so she took him in. Tom had been a cowboy, a ranch hand or general roustabout out West, going from ranch to ranch during roundups— branding and marketing cattle and all such—and the tales I heard from him day after day were like a new world to me. "He is the answer to my prayer to be like others," I thought. "This boy knows the world and what is expected of a man." So I wanted and begged for Tom's friendship more and more. Of course we didn't always go to nice places nor be with the best of company. I saw many a man drunk and was thrown with many regular and occasional drinkers, but I scarcely tasted hard liquor myself. Before meeting Tom I had concluded that drinking was the way to steel oneself for the escapades boys get themselves into. Tom, however, discouraged me from drinking. He never took a drink himself and would not stay long in the company of those who did drink. All this did keep me from attending Sunday school for a few months or showing any interest in the teachings of the church.

Tom was not one to mix with the girls of the community. Instead, he played all sorts of games for boys—baseball, boxing, riding unbroken horses—and teased the boys and girls who were supposed to be sweet on one another. He led me into such things until I was equal in some ways to the best of them. A group of us were into all sorts of pranks about the countryside; none very mean, many quite questionable. One night Tom and I passed a Negro dance and stopped to watch a crap game when shooting started.[3] I was hit by a stray bullet in the collar bone. It was a spent bullet, painful but not serious. Tom took me to a doctor many miles away, for he didn't want my parents to know about it. We rode a stallion that had not been broken to take double riding, but we got there. The doctor removed the bullet and Tom brought me home and put me

---

[3] Social events were racially segregated in Kentucky a century ago. These two white adolescents undoubltedly were attracted by the sound of music in the summer night, stopped to watch the fun out of curiosity, and were amused until the shooting started.

to bed. It was months later before the family found out about it.

One evening Tom asked my cousin, L. W., if he wanted anything from the neighborhood store. At the time L. W. was very much taken with a young lady from California named Winnie who was visiting her married sister in town. So L. W. said to Tom, "Tell Miss Winnie I will be over to see her at eight o'clock."

Tom said, "If you let me talk to her once, you won't ever see her again."

L. W. thought Tom was a roughneck and a woman-hater generally, and he said, "How some people do talk. How well some people think of themselves."

Later Tom saw Winnie and talked with her, and L. W. never saw her again, for she went with Tom to California that night. They were married on the way.

After Tom left, I felt lost for awhile but continued to keep the company of the boys who had hung around Tom and his boxing group. But I sought other means of entertainment and would slip out of the house of an evening and ride here and there, seeking whatever companionship I might find. There seemed to be some peculiar twist to my desire to be out with other boys. We rigged up a mode of communication with the boys on adjoining farms, for I wanted to run around with them at night.

One afternoon word reached us that John Robinson's Circus was in town. I had not been to a circus since I was a small boy—I had gotten lost at one—so I was determined to go. None of the other boys could go, but I decided to go alone. I saddled my pony and started out, not even asking my mother's permission. My father was away on business. As I rode past the little country store on the way to town, an elderly gentleman, Mr. Carter, was seated on the porch. He was quite well-to-do and said to be the stingiest man in the county. Quite often I had questioned him as to why he was a member of such-and-such a church. He spoke to me, and was immediately ready for an argument, but asked me where I was going. When I informed him that I was going to the circus, he began to tell me about the evils that one encountered at the circus, the danger of the associations with individuals who were attracted by such entertainment, and pled with me not to go, saying that I was too good a boy to undertake such a trip alone at night. "It will cost you twenty-five cents to put up your pony for something to eat when you get there, and fifty cents to get into the circus. If you will turn 'round and go home I will give you a dollar, Eddie. I have been thinking of you a great deal of late and have missed you from church now and then. The path you are choosing isn't the best path. Won't you reconsider, come back and take your place in church and be the boy we have known for several years? You are out of the company of that ne'er-do-well, Tom, so don't go to the circus, that is the weapon of the devil. I have never let one of my boys go to the circus."

But I was determined to go. When I had gone a little way, my pony suddenly became very lame and refused to go. Something inside me seemed to say, "You had better turn back." I dismounted and found that a rock had stuck in my pony's shoe; however, I turned back to the store. Mr. Carter was still there on the porch and called to me; he gave me the dollar, and I will never forget the little prayer he said with his hand on my head. Immediately after this I left off the associations I had recently cultivated, and seemed to swing as far in the other direction of wanting to be alone as I had in my younger days. My life was all changed again. Circumstance, you may say. Or was it? What is the figment that shapes circumstance? How was it that Mr. Carter was there that day? Chance? Why did the pony balk? He never had before nor did he afterward, even though I rode him for a year or more after that to many places, but never doing any of the things I had done with Tom. Do we not with each decision set in motion laws that must carry through on their course? Is there not a destiny shaped for us by the deeper desires of the recesses of our hearts?

Soon afterward, evil days seemed to fall on me and my family. Not only sickness, but a place to live became a real question. It became necessary for me to quit school in order to add something to the family income.

4

FARMING, 1893–1894:

'ANOTHER CELESTIAL VISITOR'

I went to work farming with my uncle, living in familiar surroundings at my grandmother's place, where I could often go
sit in the barn when my duties permitted and again have many
conversations with my grandfather. This was a real treat, but
I never said a word to anyone about such happenings. During
the evenings I read everything. I could procure and talked a
great deal with my grandmother. In the spring she was taken
very ill and my mother came to nurse her. On the anniversary
of my grandfather's death, my grandmother said she wished
to talk to my grandfather. She said, "Eddie, would you go out
and see if you can't find me a peach on the last tree your
grandfather planted—for I would like to eat one more peach
from that tree. Fix it and bring it here."

After I did that, she talked with me. "You are a good boy,
Eddie. You are like your grandfather and I know you were
very fond of him. I heard you tell your mother several years
ago that you had seen and talked with him at the barn. Have
you seen him since you have been here this time?"

"Yes, ma'am," I said, "but I was afraid to say anything
about it, for so many people seem to think it is foolishness."

"No, it isn't foolish. Your grandfather did many wonderful
things. He could move tables and chairs, and hear raps, even
make broomsticks dance, never touching the broom. While he
did not make a show of it, he believed that there was something good about it all. Don't be afraid of it, Eddie, just don't
abuse it. I don't think your grandmother is ever going to be
well again and I want to tell you what I wish you would do
for your grandma: Be good to your mother, she is the best
woman I have ever known in all my life. She is kind and true,
a good mother and wife, and the best friend anyone can ever
have. Be patient with your father. He is weak but kindhearted,

and you can do more with him than anyone can, for he worships you. When I die there will be a little money for you, Eddie, to help you take care of your mother and help at least to educate your sisters. Will you do that for me, Eddie, for you know Grandpa and I will be listening for you to tell us what you have been doing real often."

I told my grandmother what Bess's father, the doctor, had said and asked her what she thought. "No, Eddie," she said, "you will never be bothered from that injury. For remember, it was I who helped you that night, not the doctor. You will get all that straight sometime soon. But keep reading your Bible, and Jesus will tell you what and how to do everything. You can trust Him, Eddie, and don't let these voices and speeches from anyone confuse you, for although some come back from the dead and tell you something other than as Jesus told it or tells you, don't have anything to do with it. They that speak to you rest in Jesus, I'm sure, but some may try and fool you, or so your grandpa thought. And I'm sure he knew, Eddie. But love your mother. She is the best friend and counselor you have, and she will never tell you anything that is wrong. You were with your grandpa when he drowned, weren't you, Eddie? Well, I am going pretty soon and will be with your grandpa, I am sure. Stay with me to the end, Eddie, won't you. The others will understand, I'm sure."

A month later she died. I was alone with her and held her hand when she passed over. Although she was sick for many months and suffered a great deal at the end, she said, "It is all right, Eddie, I see your grandpa coming for me."

Days of sorrow and confusion followed my grandmother's death. I didn't know which way to turn. I often went to the barn, but no answer came. Then I sat in the little graveyard by the graves of my grandparents, but no word or thought came to me. Then I remembered what my grandmother had said, "Your mother is your best friend and counselor." So I talked with her, again and again. I felt that my sisters, who were younger than I, must have the advantage of school, and I was very argumentative in the suggestion that my parents move to town where the girls could have the advantages and not have to walk so far to school. We reasoned together and it was finally decided the best thing was to move into the country seat, Hopkinsville. There my sisters might go to school at least, for no place out in the country was near enough for them to go to school alone since I had to go to work.

So, on a cold January day our few belongings were stowed in a wagon and we started toward the little town. I drove a cow, the gift from an aunt. We moved into a house on West Seventh Street, next door to John S. Young, the hardware man. There was a nice little garden in the back, a stable, and a barn where we kept the cow, through whose wanderings I later met Dr. Dwight L. Moody. The girls entered public school.

Getting settled in the new surroundings was a problem for each member of the family with their likes and dislikes to be accounted for in the companionships the new environs created. I soon grew restless. There was too much hustle and bustle for my strange soul, so I went back to the country to work with my uncle, C. H. Cayce, on what was known as the old Anderson farm, coming to see Mother, Father, and my sisters every Saturday night and to Sunday school on Sunday mornings. Each Saturday I heard tales from everyone at home— new problems, new faces, new surroundings. And I realized that a gradual change was taking place in each of our lives. I had many worries and anxieties for my mother, to say nothing of my new environs. There was a great deal of Negro help on the farm and I was not old enough nor experienced enough to be considered for overseer or boss. So it was not an easy task for me to fit into these surroundings.

One of the first jobs I was given was to plough a field of corn. With a mule to pull the plow, I was sent out alone to a one-hundred-acre field. That evening when it was getting dark, I unhitched the mule from the plow and rode it back to the house. The owner and the other men were in the lot as I rode up. I noticed all the men looking at me strangely, when the owner rushed out and yelled, "Get down, get down, that mule will kill you. She's never been ridden before." But she hadn't shown any sign of disagreement to my mounting her. A few days later when one of the men attempted to ride her, she immediately threw him and was never ridden again, so far as I know, by anyone but me that one time. She was not given to me to plow again. Everyone is still wondering how or why she allowed me to ride her that evening.

I spent a full year working on the farm. On Friday afternoon, the 8th day of August, the anniversary of my grandmother's death, I was sent to fallow a field for planting the next season's crop when I had another celestial visitor. I had just returned from dinner to the field with four mules and dismounted to repair something on the plow when I heard a voice behind me. Thinking it was someone from the farm, I answered before looking around. But I had a strange feeling of pleasantness, a lightness not of an earthly nature, and when I looked, I beheld what appeared to me to be the same vision I had seen in the cove in the wood. This time I was told: "Leave your plow, go to your mother, she needs you near her. A way will be provided. Go now."

I drove my mules around to the nearest place toward the house, took them out, went in, and told my uncle that I was through. I didn't know where I was going, nor what I was going to do, except that I was leaving the farm. This didn't please him very much, so he refused to carry me or to supply a way for me to get into town, which was about thirteen-and-a-half miles away. I bundled up my few belongings, hung them on a stick, and struck out boldly around two-thirty or three o'clock in the afternoon. Late in the evening I arrived home, where my parents and sisters were. My uncle was sitting at the supper table when I came in. He had followed the highway, while I had cut across the field. He had relented and come to see about me and to know what had been the reason for my decision. Most of the night was spent talking with Mother about what I had experienced in the field that afternoon.

5

HOPKINSVILLE, 1894: HOPPER'S BOOKSTORE

The day after coming into town from the farm I went about the various stores trying to decide where I wanted to work. The first place I went in was Hopper's Bookstore on South Main Street. I liked the looks of the place and the appearance of Mr. Will Hopper when I met him. He was a tall man, six feet or more, slender, dark hair and eyes, and had a most pleasant voice, but was inclined to be rather quiet, as I soon learned. Before deciding, I went across the street to speak with Mr. Charles M. Latham about a job. He had a dry goods store, a very beautiful one. A few years before, Mr. Latham had shown a great deal of interest in me when I had come to town on some business for my father. It being a very cold day, I was almost frozen when I got to town, riding a white Mexican pony. Mr. Latham had noticed that my clothing was thin and very kindly had given me a pair of mittens and shown me how to put newspaper under my clothing to protect me from the cold. Now, speaking with me about a job, he told me that when I decided where I wanted to work to come back and see him.

Then I went next door to R. C. Hardwick's Drug Store to see about a job. Then I went up the street to Burnett's Shoe Store, then into Wall's Clothing Store at the corner of Main and Seventh Street. Then across the street to the Hopkinsville Bank, where I spoke to Mr. McPherson. Then next door below that to Hoosier's Tailor Shop, which was next door to Hopper's Bookstore. Then to Thompson's Hardware, where I talked to Mr. J. A. Meadows, who was manager.

Considering all the things I had seen, I decided that the only bookstore in town would be the best. There seemed something appealing to me in the place. So I went back to Hopper's. This time I met Mr. Harry Hopper, the elder of the two brothers who owned the store. He told me that the Bible my father had given me had come from his store. He was a man about five-feet-ten-inches, fair hair, and a blond handlebar mustache, but not too large a one. Mr. Will Hopper told him I had been in to ask for a job. They both told me that they didn't particularly need anyone, but I insisted that was where I wanted to work. They finally told me I might come to work on the next Monday morning, which I did.

On arriving at the store Monday morning, I met the handy-man who swept up the store. He told me that Mr. Will Hopper had a bedroom upstairs in the store. Pretty soon Mr. Will came down. He told me that I could acquaint myself with the stock, and that I would find most everything marked. He also showed me the combination to the cash drawer, as he was going home to breakfast. He rode a bicycle which he kept in the back of the store. The Hopper brothers, as I learned, lived in a large home out a little distance from town. They had quite a number of sisters who lived at home. Mr. Harry looked after the place, and other properties, and came to the store only a few hours each day, unless it was in the busy season.

I began to inspect and to dust the stock in the store. In front was quite a space with showcases in which there was a display of framed pictures and a bookcase for current literature on the opposite side. On the bookcase were schoolbooks, not only the public school texts but those for the two colleges, as well as the boys' school in the town. Then came inks and office supplies. On the opposite side, next to the picture frames, was stationery of all descriptions. Then samples of picture molding and a large rack in which unframed pictures were kept. In the rear on both sides was a storage rack and display rack for wallpaper. All across the back was Mr. Will Hopper's desk and a very large safe. The entrance to the staircase was here. Upstairs was the work room for making the picture frames, as well as the storeroom for uncut frames, and Mr. Will Hopper's bedroom.

From the labors of a farm hand to clerk in an up-to-date bookstore was some transition, and adjusting to the new environs was not an easy task nor did I always make decisions wisely. But try I did, first acquainting myself with all the stock the store carried and their purposes for our customers. Many items, to be sure, were entirely new to this clodhopper—books of all kinds and sizes; stationery of all descriptions; pictures, art studies, picture frames, and mouldings to prepare frames of all kinds; wallpaper in many variations and patterns; window shades; as well as many art objects, such as vases, urns, statuary, and the like. What a far cry these were from the things I had known all my life on a farm, where tending chickens, work mules and horses, spreading manure, plowing, seeding, and harvesting crops were what I thought about morning, noon, and night. One was the expression of material things for sustaining the physical man, the other was for sustaining the mental man. But was not there beauty in both? Were they for the same person, or is there one thought for the city or town man and another for the tiller of the soil? No, the basic truth is the same. They are different phases of man's experience and must be treated as one, or so I reasoned.

The first thing I did after acquainting myself with the source of the store's stock was learn how to prepare the goods for proper display. Keeping things clean and fresh was necessary like keeping one's barn or stable or fence corner clean. A few days later I had an experience in which each brother said something different about my work. I was quite anxious to be well acquainted with every bit of the store and to have it one of the cleanest, nicest places in town. I was dusting off the top of the bookcases where statuary was kept when Mr. Harry came through and said, "Be careful, don't break anything up there." When Mr. Will came in, he said, "That's been needing attention a long time. Be careful, don't fall and hurt yourself." Just a bit of difference, but what a difference! You can possibly know which of the two brothers I felt more drawn to. That endeared Mr. Will to me as few people I had ever known. I loved him as a brother; I loved his company, his association, and his counsel. I do not believe he would have been counted as a success financially, but spiritually, morally, I know he was a wonderful success. When we find a person interested in us, we are usually interested in him.

I soon found that people don't respond to the same treatment like nature. People have free will. They can disagree whenever they choose, no matter how well an article may be presented, how clean it is kept or beautifully displayed. A clerk has to show some personality and often sell himself along with the merchant's goods. A clerk also has to learn to meet people, which I had never done.

I was soon given a bunch of bills to collect. Asking others to settle their bills was all a new experience to me. Here again, I needed to compare it with a familiar experience: if you give honest labor, the soil produced, and you harvested your crop; and if you sold honest goods, the buyer must pay with interest for the handling. But how was I to convey this in presenting a bill? Here again, it seemed that personality must be used, but I soon felt that something else was needed—individuality. Bill collecting also was an opportunity to become a laggard, idling time away visiting with customers. So self-analysis is necessary.

One afternoon I was alone in the store when a very fine, dignified-looking man came in. He asked me what was among the bestsellers. I named several titles, but told him that one was particularly interesting to me and we were selling a great many. It was *Jucklins*. I pulled down a copy to show him. He asked me to tell him the plot, which I attempted to do. He listened attentively, smiled broadly, and said, "Very interesting, as I happen to be the author of the book." I can't think of his name now. He was lecturing at the tabernacle that evening and gave me a pass. I felt rather conspicuous that night when, in his opening statement about the wonders of the town, he remarked on what a wonderful bookstore clerk they had in their town who could give in detail the plot of his book.

At the time I desired to be a minister, and I often talked with Mr. Will about my love of the Scriptures. The years I remained there seemed to be the stepping-stones, yea, even the door, to life itself, for I was just sixteen when I went to work at Hopper's. I often talked with and sought the acquaintance of evangelists who came to town, and I count as the high points in my association with men the few hours spent with the Rev. Sam P. Jones, George B. Pentacost, George Stewart, and most important, the Rev. Dwight L. Moody.

6

REVEREND MOODY, 1895: CALLED TO THE LORD

I will never forget the morning I was hunting for the cow that had strayed from the lot along the river bank, and came upon the famous evangelist, the Rev. Dwight L. Moody, alone, kneeling by a log, praying.

Each morning before breakfast I milked and fed the cow—the same cow I had driven into town when we first moved from the farm. But one morning the cow was missing. There was a creek a few hundred yards behind the barn, and cow tracks led in that direction. I followed the tracks, crossing the creek, and a little way up the other bank I came upon a man seated on a log reading the Bible. As I approached, he said, "Good morning, young man. I'll venture you are looking for the cow just beyond me, behind that bush. She just came up this way from the path you came over."

"How did you know?" I asked. "Do I look that much like a farmer?"

"Not that so much," said the man, "but the anxiety in your face told me you were seeking something. And the cow having just passed, I was sure that was it."

"What are you reading, may I ask?"

"Certainly, my son. I am reading the word of God, the Holy Bible."

"There is a story there," I said, "about a man looking for his father's asses who came to the man of God, Samuel."

"Yes," said the man, "I see you know something of the word. Do you go to Sunday school and have you read the Bible?"

"Yes to both questions," I said. "I haven't read it as much as I would like as yet, for I don't understand it as I would like to. I've only read it through about fifteen times so far."

"What is your name, my boy?"

I told him my name and that I had been working in the bookstore for a few months. "I lived on a farm all my life, as you have guessed. What is your name?"

"My name is Moody and I just came here to your city to hold a meeting. I came down to look the town over and pray and read a bit and ask God's guidance while I am here."

"May I ask you a question, Mr. Moody, and you won't think I'm crazy, as so many seem to that I have asked this same question? You say you ask God's guidance, but did God ever speak to you?"

"Do people tell you it is crazy to ask that question, Eddie?"

"Yes, sir."

"Well, it isn't. I know you are in a hurry to get your cow and mind her, but meet me here tomorrow morning and we will watch the sunrise together, and I'll answer your question. I'd like to talk with you at some length, if I may."

I drove the cow home in wonder and amazement at what was going to happen, and that night I went to hear Mr. Moody preach. There were possibly five thousand people or more at the meeting. His text was Luke 10:25–37, in which Jesus tells the parable of the Good Samaritan who fulfilled the law to love thy neighbor. As I sat there listening, I could not help but think of the possible meeting with this man on the morrow. I thought, Is he my neighbor?

The next morning bright and early I was up and told Mother not to wait breakfast for me if I were not back in time. I set off for the river and the hill where I had met Mr. Moody. Arriving a few minutes before him, I wondered what he would say when he arrived—and if he would really come. But I did not have long to wait. I soon saw Mr. Moody making his way along the bank. It was not sunup as yet. "Good morning, Eddie, I see you are here and waiting. I hope you had a pleasant night and are feeling refreshed for the day's tasks."

"Yes, thank you. And I want to thank you for a very lovely sermon last evening. I have of course often heard the text used but never treated in just the same way as you did."

"Very good, my boy. But you said some things yesterday that I have thought very much about since meeting you. I wish to answer your question, of course, but tell me more about yourself. Have you really read the Bible through fifteen times?"

"Yes, sir."

"How did you come to do that? You must have a very devout mother and father."

"It was not their doing that caused me to begin reading the Bible," I explained to Mr. Moody. "They have helped me a great deal since I began to read, but it was like this. As I told you, I used to live in the country, and about five or six years ago I was cutting wood one day with a Negro who was thought to be not quite right in the head—Crazy Bill, they called him. He never did anyone any harm, and he was very strong. He was rolling a log over and he said to me, "I am as strong as Samson." I asked him, "Who is Samson?" He said, "He is someone in the Bible, the strongest man that ever lived. He pulled a whole house down and killed a thousand men with the jawbone of an ass. The preacher was preaching about him last night.

"Naturally, I asked my mother about what the man had said. She told me a bit more of the story, as did my father. We did not have a Bible at the time, as our home had burned a year or so before, and a new Bible just hadn't been purchased. A few days later I saw my grandmother and asked her about Samson, and she got the big family Bible and showed me the picture of Samson pulling down the pillars of the temple. She read me the entire story of Sampson. I liked it very much, so I asked my father if he would get me a Bible of my own. He did, and funny thing, the man I am working for now, well, it was his father who gave my father a Bible for me when he heard how I had asked for the Book. Well, of course, I couldn't pronounce all the names, but I began to read it and liked it so much that I kept on and on until I had read the whole book. After beginning to read it, I asked Mother and Father if they wouldn't like to hear me read it of evenings, and for a long, long time we did, and we had prayers morning and evening. Oh, that was fine. Ever since I have wished to read it every year. One of the ministers that we used to have come to Liberty—that was our church in the country—said that if you read three chapters every day and five on a Sunday, you could read the entire book in a year. So I have kept that up."

"Very unusual," said Mr. Moody. "But what made you ask, 'Did God ever speak to you?' "

"Well," I said, "ever since I can remember, I have had playmates that others did not see. Many people told me they did not exist. But Mother has seen and talked with them, too. So it wasn't so bad.

"But I believe the Bible is true, Mr. Moody, and that God did appear and speak to people of old. And I don't think He has changed a bit, and if we ask Him, He will make Himself known to us today. For once, while I had a little hideaway place where I went to read the Bible and dream and study, not only did the little playmates come there but once a beautiful angel came to me there—or it looked like what I think an angel should look like. He talked just like the figure did to Cornelius, or to Manoah. He told me I could have what I wished for."

"What did you ask for, Eddie? Were you frightened?"

"No, sir, for I was to have God speak to me. I had read where it said, 'If ye call I will hear,' and I believed it, and still do. Yet, many people have said that I am beside myself, and it isn't easy to get along with people who don't believe you. So I have to keep quiet about such things and it hurts at times. But after the figure appeared to me, it didn't help me in school at first. But when they spoke from within in the "still small voice" and told me to sleep and they could help, I didn't have any more trouble in school after that. I could read my lessons, just fall asleep for a few minutes, and would know them. As I came to be fairly good in the facts, or some of them, of the Bible, the minister asked me if I wouldn't like to have a column in his paper of Bible questions. And I did that for a while."

"What kind of questions did you ask, Eddie?"

"As I remember they were like this: Who waxed fat and kicked? What was Moses's mother's name? What was

Joshua's name before Moses called him Joshua? And like that."

"Very good," said Mr. Moody. "Normal questions of a mind seeking knowledge from such reading, I would say. But what about this business of people saying you were foolish to ask if God ever spoke to them?"

"You see, Mr. Moody, I'm like most boys, I guess, who've imagined they were in love with some particular girl. When she made fun of the experiences I have told you about, I went to see her father who is a doctor. He thought it was all foolish. I have tried to justify myself through the study of the Scriptures, feeling that I had really had an experience similar at least to those of old. Next I questioned the elders of the church I attended. They told me I shouldn't speak of such things, but a few referred me to the ministers. So I began going to one and then another meeting, and each minister I asked the same question. All of them except you told me I was foolish and was very liable to get off into spiritualism or seek after things as did Saul when he went to the witch of Endor. But I don't feel like that, Mr. Moody. That isn't what I seek at all. True, I have seen and spoken with my grandfather, but I did not ask God for that, nor was it what I expected. But I was expecting the vision when it came to me in the woods."

"Why were you expecting something to happen then, Eddie?"

"I believe the Bible, and somewhere it says He will answer if we call. And I mean we shall hear Him."

"Well, Eddie, I have had a bit of experience here and there of people telling me of their experiences. Some say they receive messages in all sorts of ways. Many, I am sure, are very sincere in what they think or believe, but the Book tells us all, 'There is a way that seemeth right unto man, but the end thereof is death.' It also tells us if the blind lead the blind, they both will fall into the ditch.

"But to answer the question you asked me yesterday, I am sure you will want to hear the whole story. You know, Eddie, there are very definite laws given by God to Moses regarding those that have familiar spirits and are wizards. See here in

Leviticus 20:27 it says, 'A man also or woman that hath a familiar spirit, or that is a wizard, shall surely be put to death: they shall stone them with stones: their blood shall be upon them.' So I do not hold to such as that, but we may suppose from that that some people are endowed with the power to have such communication with the departed, or the powers of darkness, whatever may be the state from which such proceeds—but from the command—such must not be well pleasing to God.

"But in Numbers 12:6 we are told, and it is God speaking to Aaron and Miriam regarding Moses, 'Hear now my words: If there be a prophet among you, I the Lord will make myself known unto him in a vision, and will speak unto him in a dream.' These words seem to me to be quite different, of and from a very different source, and are worthy of accepting. The question is: Does the life of the individual claiming to have such a vision bespeak that of God?"

Mr. Moody then told me of an experience of his. "Some years ago I went to Cleveland to hold a meeting that was to last some weeks. We had fine attendance and a very fine response, but one night after only a few days I was told in a dream, 'Close the meeting at once and go to London, England.' I had never been there, nor had I ever seen any interest shown in my work by anyone there. This dream was out of the ordinary, but I was faithful to the vision, for I believed it expressed the will of God toward my work. The next evening I announced that the meeting was closing. Many of my associates thought me very foolish, for I was much younger then and hadn't yet gained popularity in any part of the country. I couldn't explain to any of them why I was impelled to close the meeting, and many told me, 'You are being very foolish. You have an open field here and are going off to some place where they never heard of you.' But I went to London as a definite reply to the vision. In London I was a stranger and wandered about the streets asking myself, 'Are you sure that you know what you are here for? Are you sure it wasn't someone fooling you and not a real vision or real instruction?'

"So you see, Eddie, what you have to combat, for you are

still young. But hold fast, my boy, to the faith you have in God directing you, and not in voices or messages of any sort that do not conform to His written word, as revealed in Jesus Christ."

I wondered what Mr. Moody did in London, and he told me: "One day I was walking along in a more humble section of that great city when I noticed ahead of me on a ledge a window box in which a geranium was blooming. I was attracted by its unusual color. As I approached it I heard a sweet, lovely voice singing, 'Sweet Hour of Prayer.' I stopped to listen, and after a bit felt impelled to climb the stairs to find the singer. At the head of the stairs there was an open door from which the song came. I peeped in, asking if I might join whoever was there. And I saw a poor, little lame girl, who said, 'Oh, Mr. Moody, it's you! I knew God would answer my prayer and send you here. I read of you in one of our newspapers and have been praying for you to come to London for several weeks now.'

"My meeting in London started right there in that little girl's room. I knew it was God who spoke to me. What channel He used, I don't know, but I heard a message from Him to go to that child praying there for Light and for a message from me.

"So, Eddie, you may be assured that I do not think you foolish. But what are you planning for your life's work?"

I told him about the vision I had in the field and about moving into town. Mr. Moody told me to meet him again the following morning, then we read some scripture and prayed together before I went home for breakfast and then to work.

That evening I attended his meeting and heard a wonderful sermon. The text was, "I beseech you therefore, brethren, by the mercies of God that ye present your bodies a living sacrifice, holy, acceptable unto God, which is your reasonable service." There were many references to what we had talked about that morning, without any names or places being mentioned. Chills ran up and down my spine as I listened, and I often felt like speaking out on what Mr. Moody was saying.

So the next morning I was up early with great anticipation and told Mother where I was going.

Mr. Moody was there, sitting on the log, when I arrived. It was not light enough to read well, but he was making marks on the ground when I came up and greeted him. Immediately, he asked me more about my childhood from the time I started to read the Bible. I told him about attending Sunday school and how it began with me asking if I might take care of the church. After being given permission, I swept the church on Saturdays. I told Mr. Moody that when I began I couldn't reach the door fastener, but when I left I could reach the top of the door. I told him about the people I had met at church, the older men, the officers and the ministers, and how I had attended several Sunday schools or groups that met during the week. I said I couldn't make up my mind which church to join, as none of them conformed to my idea of what was required. I told him how much I had learned to recite from memory, and how it was all changed by reading the various translations and hearing it translated from the Greek, especially by a man named Cook, who spoke when there wasn't a regular minister. Mr. Cook, who was in the neighborhood for a few months, had been a missionary in Africa and taught me to say the Lord's Prayer in the language of the natives, like this: "Baba wati mbe li orum; Owo li oruko re Ijoba re de; Ife ti re ni ki a se, bi ti orum beni li aiye. Fun wa li onje wa loni. Dari gbese wa ji wa, bi awa ti ndariji awon onigbese wa. Ki o ma si fa wa sinu idewo, sugbon gba wa ninu tulasin. Nitorin ijoba ni ti re, agbara, atiogo, lailai. Amin."

"Very good," said Mr. Moody. "But what would you like to do?"

"Well, I wanted to be a minister, or a missionary, and that's why I went back to the farm. But after that last experience, I believe there are other fields of service. And I must remain close to my mother."

"You are quite right," he said. "Be true to the vision. But can't you do some special work in Sunday school or study missions and possibly persuade others to go who are free to leave home."

"But I haven't the training, the education," I told him.

"Haven't you said that you believe His is a more perfect way? Who is better qualified to give instruction than one well versed in the Book of Books? Were you not commended for your study of the Bible while in the wood? And your lessons came easy after that, so that other students had a hard time keeping up with you. Might not some such be your help now? Isn't it shifting the responsibility were you to fail to take up some special work?"

"But here everyone is a college graduate, or at least most of them I've met in Sunday school have finished high school. And I haven't been through grammar school."

"Eddie, aren't you putting God on an intellectual basis? Does He have need of you, then you were sent here. To fail would be to become fearful of that promise you profess to believe in. Do you recall what the Disciples said to the Fisherman when they were sent out with a message? Do you think they were better equipped to give that message than you are? And don't you have the advantage of their experience, as well as having received the assurance directly? This isn't something to get puffed up about, to be sure, but it is something you must use in your daily life. Oh, to be sure, all manner of things may be said about you, but in whom have you put your trust?"

Mr. Moody gave me much to think about.

"It has been a real privilege to have known you, Eddie. Remain faithful and I will expect to hear great things of you one of these days. And may the blessing of the Father be with you all along the way."

Mr. Moody and I met there many mornings. We sat on the log and talked of many things given in the Holy Book. Many mornings we watched the sun rise and prayed together. We planned to talk some more by the river before he left town, but rain prevented any more meetings. It was many years before we met again.

Good intentions are one thing, fulfilling them is another. No one realized this better than I as I set out, filled with longings to do things in a spectacular way, to make myself heard and recognized. But who would listen to me, a poor boy with the air and mien of a country lad? Certainly none of the other young people who were in school or college, few of whom wanted to arouse the world to study the Bible and enlighten others in out-of-the-way places. Then there was my lack of ability to appeal to a crowd, to talk before groups. I realized that this ability comes from practice, but I had known so little social life that I was awkward in everything I attempted. I even had misgivings about speaking up in Sunday school classes. Yet I felt a burning desire to carry on in some way, as I had told Mr. Moody.

It is very peculiar how little things so often grow to be something near turning points in our lives. It was during one of Sam Jones's meetings that I came home one evening with a friend, an old schoolmate from the country, expecting him to share my room with me that night, when I found the house completely full of visitors and no place for my friend. I was asked to sleep on a couch in my mother's room. It upset me to have to tell my friend he would have to drive five or six miles home, or go to the hotel. I was so upset that I refused to even undress. At first I was determined to go out, even though snow was on the ground, and spend the night somewhere else—anywhere; but a harsh word from my father and a gentle word from my mother caused me to throw myself upon the couch without undressing, except removing my shoes and coat. Somehow, the house caught fire that night, or I did, for the couch was almost entirely destroyed, and the cover and most of my clothing. I succeeded in carrying the couch outdoors, along with the bed clothing and clothes that had caught fire. Of course, it was soon smothered in the snow that was on the ground. Little material damage was done, though a great deal of excitement reigned for some time in a large house so full of people.

My experiences at these religious meetings changed me. I sought more and more to be associated now with the people of the church. A Sunday school class was given to me. And an opportunity I had never had before was offered when some of the young people of the town united in Christian Endeavor work. There were periods when the things I had been told by both Mr. Moody and other ministers were approached, haltingly, to be sure. Something seemed to call for special study of missionary work. Of the group I started during my search for a means of expressing my urge to do something, more than half became foreign missionaries—in China, India, Mexico, Africa, Tibet, and other fields.

I also sought to aid some of the Methodist circuit riders, accompanying them on some of their trips, several times filling appointments for them when they were unable to go. In one of the classes I had there were thirty-eight students; I was nineteen years old.

7

ENGAGED, 1897: 'THE ONLY GIRL FOR ME'

Hopper's Bookstore was a natural center for students from both the co-ed schools or colleges and the girls' school and boys' academy. I became acquainted with many of the students. Many of the friendships among the students ripened into love, and I became the "post office" for many a love note passed between girls and boys from either school. I was also invited to their social gatherings. And many changes occurred in my life during this period when for two or three years I socialized with boys of all kinds, good, bad, and indifferent. There were many temptations for this country lad and all his good intentions! Shall I say it was from this, or was it just built in me, that in a few months I again sought other men associates, some that were of questionable character? I was not always wise in my choice of companions.

One evening in the company of one of these boys we passed a saloon. Harry suggested we go in and have a drink. I told him I didn't drink but I'd go in with him. We went into the saloon and sat down at a table in the back. The bartender (whom I did not know personally, as I had never been in this place before) came up to the table. I will never forget his remark: "Hello, Harry. Cayce, what are you doing here? I would as soon expect to see Jesus Christ walk in here as you. Harry, you can get anything you can pay for in here, but Cayce certainly cannot get a drink of any kind—not while I am here." Turning to me he said, "Cayce, you don't know me, but I know you. I know all your family, and many of them, most of them drink here. Many boys drink a great deal too much, but you are too good a boy to commence such associations, and I certainly would not want it on my conscience that I served you your first drink in a saloon. Keep away from such boys as this and go home to your mother."

I left that saloon thinking many, many things and very much perturbed and upset at myself. The next day I talked it over with Mr. Hopper and that evening had a long talk with my mother. From that time on, I made quite a change in my choice of friends—and soon sought the company of young ladies rather than boys.

During the time I worked in the bookstore I had a great experience. A teacher I had met while still living in the country came into town one afternoon in a very smart buggy. She taught in another school district, but had been a judge in a debating contest in which I had won the medal. I was standing in the doorway of Hopper's Bookstore when she drove by with a young lady, and she stopped and beckoned to me and said, "I want you to meet my cousin Gertrude. We are having a social at our home this evening and would like you to come."

I thanked them and said I would come. When I left work that evening, Mr. Will said to me, "Are you going to see that pretty girl I saw you meet this afternoon?" "I hope so," I told him, and went home and told my mother about being invited to the moonlight social. She agreed, but my father said, "No." So I didn't go to that social.

A few days later I had a talk with my father about his habits and activities of one kind and another, and also about his dictating what I could do and who I could associate with. We had differences of opinion, but after that talk several changes took place in both our lives.

The following month I was invited to a moonlight party at Gertrude's grandfather's home, which was a much prettier place for a party than her family's own house. I attended this party, and during that evening had an opportunity to talk with this young lady. What is it—Fate? Destiny?—that brings two young people together? For as we stood there in the moonlight, she with a lovely rose in her hair, I thought she was the most beautiful creature I had ever seen—black hair and eyes, eyes that flashed fire and determination, and the most kissable-looking mouth ever. I went home that night with the feeling in my heart that I had met the one and only girl for me.

Now and then that summer, Gertrude and I were together

again, and each time I felt more sure that I was really falling in love. I talked with Mother about her and said I didn't care to be with any other girl; yet I realized that Gertrude had not said or done one thing that would lead me to believe she had more than a passing interest in me.

That fall a young man who worked next door to Hopper's roomed with me at our house. His name was Ed. He met a cousin of Gertrude's and when they began to keep company, the four of us began to do things together—Sunday afternoon drives and visits, walks to Wednesday evening prayer meeting, and all forms of entertainment. Our visits began to be rather regular.

The following spring we planned a Sunday all-day outing to Pilot Rock. The day was bright and beautiful, but my sister was ill and Father had had an accident in the country. What was I to do? I knew my father would object if he had been at home. But I couldn't go to him, or could I? After a talk with Mother, I decided to go to the outing, feeling full well that this was possibly a turning point in my life.

It was quite a nice group of about five couples. All of them knew one another better than they knew me, but we spent a most pleasant day climbing over the rocks, visiting the spring, taking pictures, and the like. Their conversation during the ride out to Pilot Rock and back was something new to me, for I had never in my life been in such close company with a group for so long a period. Gertrude's beauty, her manner, and the closeness I felt just about turned my head, and from that day on I was sure this was the only girl for me, the only one I could love. My problem was how to adjust my life, my thoughts and activities in harmony with hers.

Some say that familiarity breeds contempt. Why it didn't happen with us I do not know, for wherever Gertrude went you were sure to find me. Rarely would you see one at any gathering without the other. Other boys might come and go with the other girls, but I was always on hand with Gertrude.

After a year or more, I finally summoned up enough courage to tell her I was in love with her. But she certainly didn't fall all over herself to tell me that my love was returned.

One cold evening when we were alone at her house, I asked her to marry me. Her answer was, "You will have to let me think this over. I like you better than any other boy I have ever known, but since getting to know you I have been with few or no other boys. You will have to let me think."

I asked her for an answer the next week. Finally, she promised to give me an answer the next time I came to see her.

The night I was to see her was a cold, rainy night—one too bad for anyone to be out—but I felt that I must know her answer, so I went to see her. This time she said "Yes."

I soon gave Gertrude a ring to seal our pledge to one another. The diamond ring was the first investment I had made in my life, and my guess is it was the best. So we became engaged. As for when we would be married, nothing was decided about a date: to Gertrude, it meant when she knew she really loved me enough to marry me; and to me it was all anxiety and plans for ways and means to carry out my wish and support a wife.

About this time a change I had not expected came about. Mr. Harry told me he was getting married and moving to Tennessee and it was necessary to make a change in their business, as he was selling his half in the store to Mr. D. W. Kitchen, and I was out. I was so astonished I hardly knew what to do, so I went next door to Thompson's Hardware Store and took a job to look after the wallpaper and picture-framing department. These had interested me most while I worked in the bookstore, though of course I read many books. I was there for only two or three months because business was slack, and I was out again. Then a struggle began. At first I didn't know what to do with myself. Then one day I went down the street and followed a crowd into Richards Dry Goods Store. I went into the shoe department and someone asked if I worked in there. I said, "Yes," and started selling shoes. Mr. Cooper, the manager of that department, said, "Cayce, is that your name?" I said, "Yes." "Run up to the bank and get me some change," he said, which I did. I worked through the rest of the day. That night he asked me why I had gone to work. I said, "Somebody asked me for something and I just gave it to them." I worked in that store for eighteen months or more.

During this period, Gertrude's grandfather, of whom I was very fond, and a bit later her grandmother, both passed away. These circumstances seemed to draw me closer to her whole family, as if they accepted me as one of the family—but not for a wedding. I felt consumed by one idea, marriage, and had many thoughts about devising ways to achieve this. Then Gertrude became ill, and the time, or prospects, for our wedding seemed to fade.

Things at home, however, seemed much better. My older sister, Annie, had gone to work; my next sister had graduated from high school and had a very nice position as bookkeeper and cashier; and my father's health had improved. I felt that I must get out and try something else and see something of the world. But what to try now? Considering my experience, I decided to try the wholesale book and stationery business. So I wrote to John P. Morton & Co. in Louisville, Kentucky. Louisville was a metropolis to me, and a thousand miles from all I held dear. But I asked that they send me their catalog, as I wanted a place with them. I learned their catalog by the same method I had used in school, reading a little, sleeping on it, and knowing it. A good bit of the old catalog of 1898 is still fresh in my memory.

I wrote the firm and asked for a job. I received their stereotyped letter informing me they needed no one, but would place my application on file and if they needed me they would acquaint me with the fact. Then I asked all the people in Hopkinsville who bought materials from John P. Morton to give me a letter of recommendation. I inquired concerning the mail and arranged it so that the company must receive at least two recommendations in each mail they opened. In a few days I received a wire, "Quit sending recommendations and report for work Saturday morning, the first of August." That was only two days away and it came somewhat as a shock. I had to borrow money for my train ticket to get to the job, but the hardest thing was telling Gertrude goodbye.

8

LOUISVILLE, 1898–1900: 'A MAD WHIRL'

What a change Louisville was for this poor farmer boy who had scarcely even been on a train before. I had never been to the city or seen streetcars or busses, and people, people, people everywhere. It was all a mad whirl to me.

Fortunately, a friend had given me a letter of introduction to a lady who had a rooming house where he thought I might find a room and board. I looked her up and found a very lovely lady in a fine home with a very select crowd of roomers. Paying money for room and board was new to me. And it was only two meals a day, which was unheard of to me, and it would cost all of five dollars per week in advance. I had no idea how much I would be paid; but upon being shown a room on the third floor, I grudgingly paid five dollars, set down my little trunk and bag, and set out to find the place I was supposed to work. It was Saturday and the business closed at noon on Saturday during the summer. I finally found the place and presented the telegram offering the job. I was told to report back on Monday at 7:30 in the morning.

I wondered what to do with myself the rest of the afternoon and night and Sunday. So I went back to my little room, unpacked my few belongings and, being tired from loss of sleep, slept until called for dinner.

Dinner at night was new to this country lad, but I was introduced to many people around the table. After the meal, the man of the house took me in hand. I was glad to learn that he had lived in Hopkinsville and been in business there for several years and knew practically everyone in the county, including all my family. He asked about each one and made me feel that I had at least one friend. He told me how to get to and from the store and something of how I should conduct myself and made it as easy as possible for this already lonesome, lonesome boy.

Sunday morning I went to Sunday school at the First Christian Church. Everything was different. There were hundreds of people, whereas in the little church back home I knew everyone. I met the minister and had a talk with him in his study. I found him to be a most lovable man. When I told him where I was from, he said he had been a pastor there. He asked about many people that I knew very well and invited me to join the minister's Sunday school class, which consisted of two young men and ten young ladies—and what a class. I also reorganized the Christian Endeavor work in this city church and became president of the Glad Helpers Society. Our work consisted of visits once a week to the city prison and to the city hospital.

The boarding house where I lived had a different type of people from any I had ever known—a medical student, a government worker or two, artists, musicians, a writer—with a new type of conversation and such varied interests. To them I was an enigma.

When I reported for work on Monday, the head of the company sent for me. I will never forget my first conversation with Mr. Griswold, the manager of the place. He asked, "Why did you come here? Was there trouble at home?" Very frankly I told him what my purposes were—to see the world, to meet more of my fellow men, and to be of greater service if possible.

I had not asked what I might expect to receive as remuneration for my work there. "No one has ever come to work here with such recommendations as you have," Mr. Griswold said. "But you will have to prove yourself here, and we can only pay you five dollars a week."

"But I have to pay that much for my board," I told him. "What will I pay carfare with or laundry?"

"Get a cheaper place," said Mr. Griswold.

"I couldn't do that," I said, "for even living with acquaintances who know some of my family is hard enough. I'm sure a cheaper place would not be the right environment for me or offer the right associations."

"Well, we will see what can be done, but five dollars is all we can start you with."

So I began work. On the weekend when I received my pay and offered to pay the landlady, she said, "It is only three-fifty this week. The store where you work will take care of the rest."

Of course, I wrote Gertrude every day, spending most of my evenings that way. For the first few weeks I was seldom coaxed out of my room. But ways and means of increasing my income troubled me. And while I wanted to stay with the book company, I looked for other means of adding to my income. One afternoon I went into a picture frame shop where they were quite busy matting pictures. I showed them some of the ways I had developed where I worked back home, and a few days later they gave me piece work to do in the evenings. Many evenings I was able to make as much as a whole week's pay at the bookstore. Also, there was a young man among the roomers who was chief clerk at one of the railroad terminals who told me he could put me on extra in the evening if I liked. This was not a regular thing, but it helped for several months. It was sufficient, however, to get me a railway pass to go home for the Christmas holidays, which helped a great deal.

My knowledge of the catalog at the book firm was considered uncanny to many of the people who worked in various departments of the store, and soon everyone was asking me about lists of this and that of everything supposed to be carried by the company, as well as for special customers. That week my pay envelope had seven-fifty in it, and I hadn't even asked for a raise.

One day a lady came in and I was sent to the sample room to wait on her. She was very pleasant and ordered what seemed to me, without regard to price, the most beautiful things carried by the company—urns and all kinds of toilet articles. The order amounted to several hundred dollars. She said, "Send them and charge it," and handed me a card—her name was Margaret—and asked me for mine. When I took the order to the credit man, he said, "You have very much impressed the wealthiest girl in this city. You had better watch out, young man."

The next afternoon I was called to the office by the boss.

"Eddie," he said, "you are a very unusual man here. You have interested someone, or the family of someone, whom we have been trying for years to interest in the business. The young lady whom you were evidently so nice to wants to meet you, and you and I are invited to her father's home to dinner this evening. Her carriage will call for us. It will pick me up first and I will call for you. What is your address?"

"929 Second," I said. "That is very nice, but I can't go, I have nothing to wear to such a home as hers must be. How could a seven-fifty-per-week man and a country boy, a farmer, dress for such a place? I have on the only shoes I own, and my Sunday suit isn't any better than the one I'm wearing."

"Well, Eddie," said Mr. Griswold, "I'll take you out and buy you what you will need for the occasion, for neither I nor you can afford to turn down this invitation. It is plain that I am not wanted without you, and I have tried for years to talk with this man and have not been able to. And here you, a country boy as you call yourself, in less than three months make it possible for me. Now this will not come out of your pay, and your salary from this week on is ten dollars."

So I was fitted out in new clothes and we went to this home that evening. It was a magnificent home, with servants, which was all very, very new to me, and furnishings so luxurious that they made my head swim. Entering the home, we were conducted through the long drawing room to a small sitting room in which the host and hostess were in view. It was not an easy journey for me as thoughts raced through my mind that I must be dreaming, for this couldn't be real.

After the introductions, I knew little about how to make small talk. But soon dinner was announced. Here again I was at a loss how to conduct myself but was made to feel easier by Margaret's very gracious manner during dinner. I was asked from what part of Kentucky I came. When I told them, her father remarked that that was where certain types of tobacco were raised. This was common ground for me, as I had spent most of my early days in a tobacco patch, and some time in the prizing and handling of tobacco for market. I was told that tobacco was what the man of the house was engaged in and from which he had made his fortune.

After dinner Margaret and I had some time alone while her father and Mr. Griswold talked business. She asked about my interests and social life when I was not at work. I told her of my interest in Sunday school and that my social doings were solely with members of the class. Margaret was acquainted with several members of the class, and a few weeks later she joined the class. That is how a very unusual friendship grew between Margaret and me. And I advanced rather rapidly in my connection with the stationery firm.

About this time the Sunday school class began to hold services at the jail and the hospital. Quite an interesting happening came of our visit to the jail. Among the prisoners was a young man who had been arrested with his father for making moonshine liquor. He was seventeen years old and sincerely unaware that he had done anything wrong. He became very much interested in what our Sunday school class members had to say, but he couldn't read—and didn't even know his letters. He asked if some of us would teach him to read. Margaret and I and a young lady who later became a famous author undertook this task while telling him the story of Jesus. One day our minister went along with us to visit the boy. As we approached the cell, we heard him saying over and over, A—B—C—D, and so on through the alphabet several times. When we got to the door we saw him on his knees by his cot. The minister asked him, "What are you doing, Jim?" He replied, "If this Jesus is what you say He is, He will put the letters together to say just what I want to pray for because I don't know what to ask for yet." After he got out, this boy was given an education by members of that Sunday school class and he became a real minister in the mountains of Kentucky. I am sure he has done some wonderful work in eastern

Kentucky. Many people have heard of this man and the work he has done.

Other boarders at the house where I lived took an interest in me in many ways. The railroad clerk was especially nice, taking me on weekend trips now and then. At least I got acquainted with trains and their advantages. The medical student invited me to go with him to special meetings when surgical operations were conducted before the whole student body or were of some special nature. I witnessed quite a number of them. The artist also invited me to her exhibits, and on one occasion I went forward to receive the prize ribbon for the young lady. To celebrate her prize, she took me to my first stage play, "When Knighthood Was in Flower," with Julia Marlowe and E. H. Sothern. Another time the man of the house took me to a political meeting, a prize fight—young Corbett was fighting—and a Salvation Army meeting, all on the same evening.

The first time I was ever hypnotized was at the store, under very unusual circumstances. Herman the Great, a hypnotist, came in one afternoon to buy some playing cards. I happened to wait on him, not knowing who he was. When he went to pay for the cards, he appeared to take the money from my pocket. Then he said the cards were so cheap he'd take another dozen packs. This time he appeared to take the money from the mouth of the cashier. Then he asked my name and said, "I think you are a good hypnotic subject. With the manager's permission, I'd like to try it." As it was just about closing time, permission was given. He turned me around with my back to him and said, "Sleep—sleep—sleep." Next thing I was lying on one of the tables.

Afterward, I told him of an experience I had had with Hart the Laugh King at a theater in Hopkinsville a year or so before. I had volunteered during his show, but he asked me to leave the stage because I was not easy to put under. Before he left, Mr. Herman gave passes to his show for two performances to a member of the firm and me. I went to see him and talked with him in his dressing room.

Some changes at the store resulted in some animosity toward me, for I was accused of being the boss's pet. But my knowledge of the catalog stood me in good hand here, for I was able to help the catalog group prepare the new catalog, which was revised each year, and to keep our traveling salesmen acquainted with changes in price and style and abreast of the times in every way. This somewhat quieted the other boys. But each time Margaret and her father came to the store now, I was teased by several of the office force. But, through the meeting of Margaret's father and the boss, funds were realized for expansion of the main business. After that, little more was ever said.

At Christmas time I went home for a few days, using a pass obtained by working at the railroad office as an extra. Margaret sent some lovely, appropriate gifts for members of my family. To see Gertrude again was heavenly for me. But I didn't know how to arrange a wedding, for none of her family wanted Gertrude to go to Louisville to live. My chief worry was how to make sufficient income. At the beginning of the new year, I knew that I would be given an office and another raise, yet it was not enough to support two people. Also, I had to have spending money, because I was spending more time with the young people I had met, and I thought, "Isn't that going to increase as my circle of friends grows?" Some people at the store concluded that one day Margaret and I would get married, for the investing of considerable monies in the firm by her family seemed then to hinge on that happening. But that didn't fit my idea of being true to my promise to Gertrude at all. The question was this: Were circumstances to so shape my life that there was little I could do but drift along?

When I returned to Louisville after the holidays, my father came with me to arrange to become district representative of the Fraternal Insurance Company. I was offered a job with the company, too; and after some consideration, I felt I must leave Louisville to become associated with my father in the insurance business.

My last week at the store, which was in January 1900, my

pay envelope contained forty dollars. There were many people, I know, who had worked there a quarter of a century who were not making that much. I took the train home to Hopkinsville that evening.

9

HEALED, 1901: 'GIVE GOD THE PRAISE'

My father was already in the field organizing lodges[1] when I joined him in January 1900. I soon received word from my former employer, John P. Morton & Co., that I would be sent samples of a specialty line and would be kept on the payroll as specialty salesman in blank books—checkbooks, ledgers, and such.

During our travels, Father and I were quarantined once in the hotel in Madisonville, Kentucky, because someone had smallpox. While there I saw a man hypnotized and told to play the piano, which he did even though he could not normally play. It was tried on me, and I also played the piano and was very good at that.

After the quarantine was lifted, the lodge completed organization, and I went to Greenville, Kentucky. The first Sunday I was there I met a girl I had passed many notes to in school for one of the boys in the boys' school. Her name was Anna Belle. We renewed our friendship and spent some very pleasant evenings together.

My combined effort in selling for John P. Morton & Co. and organizing lodges paid very well, and I felt that at last I was accomplishing something. When I finished in Greenville, I went to another small town, and the day I arrived I was taken with a very violent headache. I had been subject to headaches for some time, so I consulted a doctor. He seemed unable to locate the cause and gave me a sedative. I took one dose and went to sleep and the next time I was conscious, I was at home in Hopkinsville with two doctors with me. I had been brought

---

[1] Insurance was offered to members of fraternal lodges at a group rate, so in order to stimulate insurance business the Cayces went from town to town organizing new lodges.

home by a friend who found me wandering around the railroad yards several miles from the town where I took the dose of medicine. At home I finally went off into a natural sleep.

When I woke up the next day I could speak only in a whisper. I didn't have a cold. The doctor called it aphonia, but nothing he tried helped me. I consulted many other physicians, far and near, all to no avail. Margaret even had a specialist from abroad see me, but nothing seemed to help. I began to lose weight. I had no control whatever of my voice and for twelve months or more I could scarcely speak save in a whisper. Everything was tried but I continued to fail in health during the whole year that I was unable to talk.

This condition, of course, disqualified Edgar for the insurance business, which he well knew, and as time went on and his condition did not improve, he seemed to feel that he was disqualified for almost every occupation or business. After he was able to be up and about, he consulted other doctors, but with the same results. They all told him his throat looked perfectly normal and they could see nothing they could do to relieve the condition. This was very discouraging, and after consulting every doctor available and trying everything, he decided to take up some other work, something he could learn readily and that he could do without very much talking.

I tried to accept it as best I could, feeling there was something amiss in my spiritual life. It gave me the opportunity to review in my mind all the events of my youth and boyhood. I had just turned twenty-three a few days before this happened to me. Many people prayed for me. It was real torture to hear people pity me as I walked down the street. Feeling neither well nor sick, I realized that I must find a job, something among people to occupy my mind. I tried canvassing, but this was too much. Finally, I began working around a photo studio and learned to take photographs. While I was working there, a hypnotist guaranteed he could cure me if I would allow him to hypnotize me. He hypnotized me in the presence of several local men, including the psychology teacher at one of the colleges.

While under hypnosis, it was said that I was able to speak, yet when brought from under it I could not speak. Successive attempts to hypnotize me seemed to "get on my nerves." I was unable to sleep, so this was discontinued for the time. But, as the experience was witnessed by many people, I received a good deal of publicity in the local newspaper. A noted physician of New York City, Dr. Quackenbush, visited me. He was quite an exponent of hypnotism, which he tried, with no results. He then took down the history of many of my experiences as a boy and was especially interested in my studying lessons while asleep. After he returned to New York he wrote to the local psychology professor and an associate that he felt that I was an auto-hypnotist. He suggested that if I would put myself to sleep, as I did when studying my lessons, letting someone suggest to me, "You see yourself, tell us what is the trouble and what to do about it," I might obtain help.

My parents, having little or no faith in hypnotism, were afraid to try this physician's suggestion because of my exceedingly nervous condition. I now weighed less than a hundred pounds, whereas I had weighed one hundred sixty-five before the trouble began over a year before. After several months I was unable to even whisper, and many declared I had galloping consumption. I pled with my mother and father to at least let this man who had hypnotized me try the experiment this specialist had suggested. Finally, I persuaded my parents to let me or the professor try the famous Dr. Quackenbush's suggestion. There was no one present that Sunday afternoon at our home but my mother, father, the hypnotist Al Layne, and me.

Mr. Layne was a very delicate-looking individual, quite thin, weighing not more than one hundred fifteen to one hundred twenty pounds. He had dark gray eyes, a little gray mustache, quite gray hair that was rather thin on top, although he was probably not more than thirty-eight or forty years of age. I first knew him as the bookkeeper for his wife's millinery store where my sister Annie first went to work. Mr. Layne's wife was quite heavy and a most pleasant person. It was over her store that Mr. Layne later on had his first office and where all of my early readings were given, and where he treated people through suggestive therapeutics and massage that he had learned through his osteopathic correspondence course.

I told Mr. Layne of my experiences as a child sleeping on my school texts and that I felt sure that I could make myself unconscious, for I felt within me the same condition taking place when being hypnotized as I felt when putting myself to sleep. He suggested that this was why the hypnotist was unable to give me post-suggestion, but that if I would put myself in the unconscious condition and one talked with me, I would be able to tell them the trouble and how to get rid of it. Can you imagine what that meant to my mind?

I lay on the couch and gave the first of what is now called a reading. In a few minutes I had lost consciousness.

Edgar's mother and I knew nothing about this investigation up to this time, but Edgar suggested that he and Mr. Layne were coming out to the house that afternoon and that Mr. Layne said Edgar would talk, and he believed that he would. They came and Edgar stretched out on the couch and in a very short while seemed to be asleep and Mr. Layne started talking to him about his throat, and Edgar answered in an audible voice. He described the condition of his throat, giving the cause and suggesting the remedy to bring it back to normal, which was to increase the circulation to the throat and carry away the congested condition so the throat would be normal and the vocal box would work. He was asked if that could be done, and he answered in the affirmative and said watch the increase and see that condition pass off. Mr. Layne told him he would awaken in a given time, which he did, and he talked in a very audible voice and continued to do so, the happiest and proudest boy one ever heard talk. This, of course, was not understood but was very gratifying to all who knew Edgar.

*   *   *

They told me after I woke up that, in response to Mr. Layne's suggestion that I would see myself, I said: "Yes, we can see the body. In the normal physical state this body is unable to speak, due to a partial paralysis of the inferior muscles of the vocal cords, produced by nerve strain. This is a psychological condition producing a physical effect. This may be removed by increasing the circulation to the affected parts by suggestion while in this unconscious condition." In five or ten minutes I am told that I said, "It is all right." Then he told me to wake up at a certain time, and on awakening, with little or no effort, I was able to speak clearly and plainly.

My mother and father and I were overjoyed and expressed our thanks and praise to Mr. Layne for what he had done. Mother wept and left the room, but later she told me, "Mr. Layne had nothing to do with it. Give God the praise."

Later on Mr. Layne told me, "I have had stomach trouble for years. Let's see what you say may be done for it." This was very confusing to me. I felt that I owed Mr. Layne real consideration for what had happened, but I didn't care to become a guinea pig for a lot of experiments with hypnotism. But he said, "If you can do that for yourself, there is no reason you can't do it for others. Let's see what you will say about me." I agreed to try to help him. The suggestion to him was to take certain compounds, use certain diets, and to exercise. In a week he said he felt better. All this was new to me. I had never studied physiology and knew nothing about anatomy or suggesting compounds of things I knew nothing about. I thought it must be all wrong. Where did such information come from? What did it all mean? Did it have anything to do with the promise made to me by the figure that appeared to me in the little retreat? This troubled me and, if anything, I was ashamed of it all.

But the aphonia returned, and for several days I was unable to talk. When Mr. Layne tried the experiment again, I talked in a normal voice. I couldn't do it without losing myself into unconsciousness.

During the following year I had several more attacks. Each time I was treated by Mr. Layne in the same manner and my voice was restored. These attacks gradually became further and further apart, and my general health began to improve and I even put on more weight.

Over the next year, every few days Mr. Layne would ask me to do this stunt of telling someone what was the matter or what to do for some special condition. I didn't tell anyone about it, for I really didn't believe in it—it seemed too fantastical, too unreal. Or was it? Such thoughts kept me all astir inside. I realized that either I was different from other people or it was all a fantastic stunt being pulled by Mr. Layne or something.

Mr. Layne, however, opened an office over his wife's shop and began to treat people. Every few days he asked me to try to read for someone. I felt I couldn't refuse because I seemed to have to go to Mr. Layne to get my voice back. So each time I lost my voice, someone would say, "Layne has you under his power and won't let you loose."

This went on for possibly six months or more. A number of readings were conducted by Mr. Layne for many individuals whom I did not know then or afterwards. Sometimes I would be asked to come to his office five or six times each week, and each time it meant going to sleep and talking about someone I rarely, if ever, knew. No stenographic reports were kept of these readings during the first few years. Many were benefited, I was told. I could not believe it, for I had never seen anything done by a hypnotist other than make some man or woman do something to make other people laugh, and I felt that I was only making laughter for someone else. However, after a while, others began to tell me of the many things I had given in the readings and of the benefits others were receiving.

One of the cases was a little girl, daughter of a local physician. I was told the reading stated she had swallowed the back from a celluloid collar button, and it had lodged in the throat before entering the stomach. X-rays showed nothing. Eventually the button was located and dislodged in a hospital. The parents denied any knowledge that such information had been given through a reading, but several people testified they were present when Mr. Layne sought the information concerning the child.

During this same period a Mr. Stowe requested a reading for his wife, giving her name as Mrs. H. Stowe. It was said by those present that the reply came, "There are several here—which one?" for he had been married several times. Then her address was given, and the reply came that she had only a few days to live—complications of some kind.

I also gave information through a reading for I. H. Cayce, a cousin of my father. Cousin Ike's conversation with me some weeks later was possibly the first convincing argument to me that the unconscious spells, or readings, might be of practical value to others, though to me they were only unusual experiences.

Nonetheless, I felt decidedly embarrassed by what other people said to me and often I felt ashamed at being considered peculiar or different from others. So that spring I asked the picture man about my trying to make pictures in the little towns thereabouts. He agreed, and I opened a studio in Pembroke that did fairly well. But I was questioned several times regarding my association with Mr. Layne, which didn't set very well with me, for I felt I was the laughingstock of many. So I went to LaFayette, and there I met many young people who were exceedingly nice to me. Business was especially good there. While working in LaFayette I received a telephone call from Mr. Potter in Bowling Green, Kentucky. He wished to employ someone in his bookstore. I went to see him and arrangements were made for me to go to work there. In May of 1902 I moved to Bowling Green. I was twenty-five years of age.

10

BOWLING GREEN, 1902–1909: HERETIC OR HEALER?

I found Bowling Green a beautiful little town on the Barren River on the main line of the L&N Railroad from Louisville to Nashville. Main Street, running east and west, runs from Reservoir Park past Fountain Square, around which the main part of the town is built, past the railroad and on out toward the lower part of the river. The other two principal streets run north and south—State Street, which runs on the east side of Fountain Square; and College Street, on the west side of Fountain Square, runs from what was then Potter College, on out to the road that leads to Louisville.

I went there to work for L. D. Potter Company bookstore, which was on the ground floor of the Mitchell Building on State Street, four or five doors from Fountain Square. The Morehead Hotel was on the corner of Fountain Square and Main and State streets. Next to the hotel was Mrs. Taylor's Coat and Suit Company, one of the largest made-to-order suit companies in the country.

When I arrived by train, Mr. Potter carried me to Mrs. Hollins's boarding house, a large frame building painted cream with white shutters on lower State Street five or six doors below Fountain Square, just out of the business district. The house had a reception room and, to the left, a large dining room. A stairway went up from the reception room to the second floor where all the men boarders stayed, while all the ladies were on the main floor. Mrs. Hollins, a widow, was a stout, little, lovely person with laughing, twinkling eyes that made everyone feel at home. Her two daughters lived at home, one married to a man who worked at the post office, the other, Miss Lizzie, worked in one of the banks.

At Mrs. Hollins's boarding house I met many people with whom I was later closely associated, among them Dr. John H.

Blackburn, a young physician who had just a year or so before come to Bowling Green to establish his practice. Dr. Blackburn was about five feet, eleven inches tall, weighed about one hundred fifty pounds, had dark brown hair and eyes, wore a full Van Dyke beard cut rather close, and was a very lovable and genteel Christian gentleman.

Others included his brother, Dr. James Blackburn, a dentist; Joe Darter, secretary of the Y.M.C.A.; Bob Holland, a young man associated with one of the department stores; Mr. Mottley, a barkeeper at one of the saloons; and Dr. Hugh C. Beazley, a young eye-ear-nose-and-throat specialist who was from my hometown of Hopkinsville, although I had not been personally acquainted with him. Dr. Beazley was my roommate the greater part of the time I stayed at Mrs. Hollins's boarding house. He was a little man, possibly five-feet, six-inches tall, weighed possibly one hundred thirty-five to one hundred forty, was very quick, alert, and a thorough Christian gentleman.

Mr. Layne began coming to Bowling Green to seek information for those who came to him for treatment. From the experience with my father's cousin Ike, I felt inwardly that it was imperative for me to attempt to serve when people sought me as a channel, though I was mentally rather ashamed of the whole performance.

One of those I was asked to give information for was the daughter of C. H. Dietrich. I had first known Professor Dietrich as the principal of the high school in Hopkinsville. To me, he and his wife represented all there was in culture and learning. He was of medium stature, a bit stern in appearance with a short-cropped mustache. Mrs. Dietrich was medium height, very lovely in appearance. When I gave the reading for Aime, their little girl, Professor Dietrich was the representative of the American Book Company of Cincinnati, Ohio, a publisher of school textbooks.

Mr. Layne conducted all the readings. I'll never forget my experience on that occasion, nor my inmost feelings. I journeyed to Hopkinsville, where the professor met me at the train with his carriage, drove me to his very lovely home on South Walnut Street, introduced me to his wife, then asked if I would

like to see the little girl and examine her. How foolish I felt!
I didn't know whether I wanted to or not. I knew, of myself,
I could tell nothing by examining her. I had never studied
anything of the kind and didn't know what it was all about.
They led me into a room where the little girl was sitting on
the floor on a very beautiful rug with a nurse attending her.
They were playing with blocks on the floor. She appeared to
be one of the loveliest children I had ever seen—very curly,
light brown hair—and to all intents there appeared nothing in
the world wrong with her. She looked as well as any child I
had ever seen, and I couldn't imagine what in the world would
be said regarding such a perfect-looking specimen of childhood.[1]

From there we entered another room, which apparently was
Mrs. Dietrich's bedroom. She told me of having met in Cincinnati Mr. William A. Wilgus, who had first told them of
what I could possibly do and had advised that they get in touch
with Mr. Layne. I had known Mr. Wilgus a good many years.
He had often been to the farm when I lived at my grandmother's, or near there, to go hunting. I had often been with
him, and I still carry in my face, to this day, a shot that glanced
from a bird he killed during one of those hunting trips. He
showed considerable interest in me the whole time I knew him.
When I lost my voice, he asked the president of South Kentucky College to offer me a scholarship, and he would take
care of all expenses. I did not accept it, feeling timid about
being in classes and unable to speak, so that I would have
needed individual instruction. Possibly that is where I missed
a real opportunity. Mr. Wilgus left his fortune to the children
of Hopkinsville for playgrounds and their upkeep.

---

[1] An affidavit dated October 8, 1910, signed by C. H. Dietrich states that
Aime, born January 7, 1897, had an attack of "LaGrippe" in February 1899,
causing convulsions, loss of balance, and "spells." She was having twenty
convulsions a day by the time she was six, her mind a blank, all reasoning
powers gone. A Cincinnati doctor said there were only nine such cases in
medical history, all fatal, and as nothing could be done she would die in one
of her convulsions.

Mrs. Dietrich asked if I would try to help their little girl. I removed my coat, collar and tie, lay on a couch in her room, went through the proceedings as I had done for myself and went to sleep. When I was conscious again I saw the father and mother in tears. The mother put her arm around my shoulder and said, "You have given us the first hope we have had in years for our little girl."

She had been playing with a doll when the first spasm came on. For the first time she called for that doll and recognized her parents one from the other as well as the rest of the household.[2]

How did I feel when told about what had happened? Who can say or know what to think, for I knew that I did not know what had been said, and it was all hearsay. I knew I did not know anything about physiology or anatomy or hygiene, to say nothing of the intricacies of the mind. Then what was it? Was the promise made so long before in the little place in the wood being fulfilled? If so, by whom—Mr. Layne or me? I didn't feel worthy of such a trust, if it were a gift. But what must be done about it?

Years later when Aime came to see me, I don't think I have met many prettier girls. She was then possibly sixteen or seventeen years of age.

I joined the First Christian Church in Bowling Green and was made a Sunday school teacher. I joined in the social life more than I had in the past, for there were advantages there that were new to me, such as the Y.M.C.A. There were several colleges, among them a school for young ladies. Many of the teachers as well as the pupils became my friends. It was here that one of the art teachers and I made up the game of "Pit" or Board of Trade for a Y.M.C.A. entertainment. The director was a very close friend of mine and put me on the entertain-

---

[2] The Dietrich affidavit states that: A reading by Mr. Cayce diagnosed Aime's condition as "congestion at base of the brain" and outlined the treatment. Layne treated her daily for three weeks, using occasional readings to follow up. "Her mind began to clear up about the eighth day . . . within three months she was in perfect health, and is so to this day."

ment committee. I also helped organize the young people's societies of the churches into a union, holding meetings regularly. More social life brought more young lady companions, and among several groups I was considered a favorite. That summer Anna Belle, the young lady from Greenville, visited Bowling Green. I was among the last to call on her. Considerable effort had been made to make our introduction quite an affair, but to the astonishment of the whole crowd Anna Belle embraced and kissed me. And were they all taken aback.

I, like every man, I suppose, wondered if I was still in love with the little girl back home. But a visit from her to Bowling Green settled that. And the next June—1903—Gertrude and I were married. Dr. Beazley and Bob Holland, with Gertrude's two brothers, stood up with us.[3]

After our wedding in Hopkinsville, some friends of mine who had married just a week before us arranged to meet us on our way to Bowling Green, and they accompanied us to our new home next door to them. We lived in a room at Mr. J. A. McCluskey's large white home directly across the street from Mrs. Hollins, and we took our meals at Mrs. Hollins' for several months. Mr. McCluskey was a mail clerk on the railroad. Several other couples had rooms there, most of them taking meals at Mrs. Hollins'. Our room was on the second floor overlooking State Street. Dr. Beazley also lived there after he married. Everyone was very nice to Gertrude and me and entertained us quite a number of times.

We were married on a Wednesday, and the following Sunday was a blue day for Gertrude because Mr. Layne came for a visit. He had been coming to Bowling Green for some time to have readings. This Sunday there was a newspaper reporter at the dinner table where we boarded. He asked Mr. Layne how it was that Bowling Green was favored with a regular Sunday visit from him. Layne said he came to see me.

"He isn't sick, is he?" said the reporter. "He has several very fine doctors here with him."

---

[3] They were married by the Rev. Harry Smith, minister of the Hopkinsville Disciples of Christ Church in which both Gertrude and Edgar were members.

"I come to ask Eddie about my patients," Mr. Lane replied.

This was astonishing to Gertrude, as well as to everyone at the table.

"Well," asked the reporter. "Is Eddie a doctor? He must be keeping something from us."

"If Eddie has no objections," said Mr. Layne, "you may witness the most unusual experience of your life."

So I spent the entire afternoon with the doctors and the reporter who boarded there. They asked Layne about his results with such information. He gave them case after case of how this and that condition had been helped. Then one of the doctors asked how he went about applying such varied types of suggestions and what school he had graduated from.

"None," he said. "All I have learned I have gotten from just such information during the last two years."

This experience caused a great deal of comment after one of the first newspaper articles appeared in the Bowling Green *Times-Journal* the next day and was copied in the Nashville papers.

This happening also brought me trouble with my bride, who was in tears when I got back to our room. And who could blame her, having her first Sunday in this new town all torn up? And later, talk, talk—everyone asking her questions, and she and I both acting as if we were ashamed of it all.

It also brought Mr. Layne trouble. The medical fraternity stopped his practice. As a consequence, he enrolled in osteopath school at Franklin, Kentucky. During his stay there I went to see him twice to have him bring my voice back again. During one of these visits, I was asked to give a reading for someone at the school. The head of the school was in another room within hearing of what took place. When the reading was over, I was introduced to the president, Dr. Borland, and found that he was blind. He asked me where I had studied anatomy, for he knew the patient well and thought that was one of the most perfect diagnoses he had ever heard even though I never saw the patient. All this was rather exasperating to me. I went home all in a muddle. Was there something taking place while I was unconscious that I knew not of? And was it a worthwhile experience for the seeker? Could anyone but Mr. Layne do this? Did I, as well as others, have to depend on Mr. Layne to conduct the performance, if a performance it was? Such questions troubled me, and I prayed long and often about it.

Then I had the dream again of walking with the lady through the woods. But this was no answer to me. So what must I do?

A few weeks later the aphonia, or loss of speech, returned again, so I went to Dr. Blackburn, in whom I had all confidence and trust. I had tried to get Dr. Blackburn to experiment, as had Mr. Layne, and to tell me what he thought of it. In the whisper which I was forced to use, I asked if he wouldn't conduct a reading, as I didn't want to have to go to Mr. Layne the rest of my life. Dr. Blackburn had seen Mr. Layne that Sunday afternoon nearly a year before. He finally consented. I'll never forget the experience.

I went to his office and lay on his examination table, lost consciousness, and when I became conscious again I realized I was all right and could speak—but Dr. Blackburn was as badly confused a man as I ever saw. He was standing at the door, with it partially open, and seemed very much upset, continuing to ask me if I was all right. He had conducted his experiment, he said, very much as he had seen Mr. Layne do before.

So one question was answered in my mind: Others could do it, not just Mr. Layne. But what about getting help for others? I invited Dr. Blackburn to try. He made several experiments; that is, while I was unconscious he asked questions regarding several of his patients, the names of many I never knew, with just as good a results as when Mr. Layne tried.

But what was it? No one seemed to know just what to call it. With these experiments came many unusual experiences. People from all walks of life came to look on.

There was quite a bit of unpleasant notoriety which came with the medical board stopping Mr. Layne, and about my connection with him. Some of the meetings were reported in the local paper and copied in some of the state papers. I was questioned before the board of the church of which I was a member. Being an officer in the church, I was accused of heresy. A professor at the Bowling Green business college, Mr. Dickey, came to my defense, as he had obtained readings for his wife, daughter, and himself, through Dr. Blackburn's experiments. In his reading he was told he needed to take a leave from teaching for at least two years and do something that took him into the outdoors most of the time. His doctor told him that was good advice, and the professor heeded it and was out of school for two years. Later he became president of the school.

During the time he was out of school, I was tried for heresy. And because of the attitude that some in my church had taken, I did not show as much interest in my church work as before— or was that just an excuse for me? But some of these church people said those close to things psychic are inclined to free love. Yes or no, they demanded, what is your experience or observation?

Professor Dickey defended me before the church board. The result was that I was only relieved from any office with that church, but I was exonerated of heresy.[4]

About that time I received a request from a Mr. Andrews in New York City for a reading on himself. This was my first experience in trying to give information for someone at a distance. Mr. Layne conducted the experiment in the presence of several physicians, for I made a trip to Hopkinsville for that purpose. In this reading "Clarawater" was prescribed for his relief. We did not know whether this was a preparatory or patent medicine or whether there was any such thing or not. But the information was written up by a stenographer that it

—

[4] The Rev. Joseph B. Fitch, a Disciples of Christ minister, wrote an article about Mr. Cayce for *Disciplianea*, a periodical published by the Disciples of Christ Historical Society, in which he explained this incident: "The reason for examining him ostensibly was that he taught a Sunday school class, and the Church officers were uncertain whether such a man should be permitted to continue." The Disciples Historical Society had no further information on the case. Fitch adds: "Cayce was retained as a church member, but he was uncomfortable."

might be sent to the man, and for the first time I read a report of what I had said during a reading. This was a mystery to me, for I had never seen many, many of the words before and I had little or no idea of their meaning. Yet two or three physicians who were present said they made sense and were used in the right place and in the proper connection.

The reading was sent to Mr. Andrews. Some weeks later, as he had been unable to obtain the preparation, he asked that we try to give the formula for making Clarawater. This reading was conducted by Dr. Blackburn in Bowling Green, with quite a number of prominent people present—businessmen, professors, and doctors. A formula was given. Something like a month later I received word from Mr. Andrews that he had received a letter from a man in Paris, France, who informed him that his father had made and marketed a preparation under the name of Clarawater, and the formula was identical with that which had been given in the reading. Mr. Andrews reported receiving a great deal of benefit from taking the Clarawater.

What was this, I wondered—spiritualism? If so, not so good. Or was it? For I remembered my conversation with Mr. Moody and Leviticus 20:27—"A man also or woman that hath a familiar spirit, or that is a wizard, shall surely be put to death: they shall stone them with stones: their blood shall be upon them."

Dr. Blackburn invited several other doctors to witness these experiments. Some very unusual results were obtained at practically every experiment. Just a few are noted here:

A lady from Tennessee described her condition as laceration of the stomach. Dr. Blackburn and others were present, and the reading told her to forget the doctors and each morning to take a lemon, cut it in half, eat one half and then walk just as far as she could and still get back to her house. Upon returning, she was to sprinkle salt on the other half of the lemon, eat it, and drink at least two glasses of water. Her nephew who was with her fainted when he heard the description given of his aunt. A few weeks later she reported that she never felt better and could walk several miles and that everything now seemed to agree with her.

Several months later a doctor from Minnesota came into the store where I worked and said to me, "I understand there is a man who works in this store who goes to sleep and tells what is the trouble with other people. Do you know him?"

"Yes," I said, "I guess I should because I am the man."

"But what do you think of this phenomenon?" he asked

"I don't know, for I don't know what is said. Yet many people say that what is said makes sense, and people do get help who use or apply the suggestions."

"Well, I would like very much to witness one of these experiments," said the doctor. "I wish you would tell me what you find with me."

"All right," I said, "it's only a little while before the dinner hour. If we can get hold of Dr. Blackburn, we'll see what may be said."

So I telephoned and made an appointment to meet Dr. Blackburn at his office. We went over at noon and he introduced himself as Dr. Z to Dr. Blackburn and told him he had had the unusual experience of calling on one of his patients who had been with him for several months and finding very little improvement. "Then a few weeks ago I received a letter from her telling me about seeing Eddie here and his telling her to drink water and eat lemons and walk each morning, and she said, 'I am well.' "

"Yes," said Dr. Blackburn, "I was present and took the reading, heard his description, and have seen her letters. It is quite interesting, isn't it?"

"Certainly is," said the doctor. "And he has promised to give me one of those readings."

I lay down on the examination table and went to sleep or at least was unconscious. After a bit I described conditions regarding the doctor's body and suggested that certain things be taken. Then I was awakened.

"That is the most amazing thing I ever heard," said Dr. Z. "How many experiments have you tried, Dr. Blackburn?"

"Oh, I have seen some ten or twenty, I would think. And

each is just as amazing as that one. And practically all say that he describes what they are feeling. But he doesn't always give drugs, and doesn't always use the same school of treatments."

"Well, can't you change that by suggestion?" asked Dr. Z.

"I don't know," said Dr. Blackburn. "And would it be the right thing to do if you could? But I don't think you could."

"I have a friend who must see him," said Dr. Z. "He is the author of *Spiritual Law of Psychic Phenomena.* Do you know him, doctor?"

Blackburn said, no, but he'd like to meet him. Dr. Z said he would wire him to meet us if I were willing to conduct other experiments.

On the day that the author came to Bowling Green, several psychology professors were present for the demonstrations. Some were good, some not so good. During one experiment, post-suggestion was attempted. It worked almost exactly. The suggestion was made that when I awakened I would be given a drink of plain water but that it would act upon my system as if I had been given a dose of salts. And the reaction when I drank the water was as if salts had been taken. Later something similar was tried with no results at all. I was asked to read books, letters, and give the contents of wrapped packages. Those present knew what was in some of them, but no one knew the contents of the letter or packages. A great number of these experiments were successful.

Then physical readings were attempted, some where the person was present, some at a distance. In each case the analysis was pronounced correct, even where the sex of children was asked from the day before its birth to three months before. In nine such cases, each was correct as to sex.

Many other physicians in Bowling Green then began experiments of various kinds. Many individuals of science and note were invited to be present. During the next year I met Dr. Thomson J. Hudson, the electric wizard Thomas A. Edison, Byron W. King, Elbert Hubbard, as well as many others, for considerable interest was expressed by various faculty members of the different schools in Bowling Green. Quite a number of notable visitors to these schools from time to time came to see me during their stay there.

Gertrude and I moved in 1905 to Mrs. Ernest Vick's lovely cottage on Twelfth Street. As her husband traveled for a paper bag and cord company, Mrs. Vick had us in the house more to be with her than taking lodgers. We took our meals down the street some six or seven doors on the opposite side with Mrs. Ed Lawson, who was an officer in the First Christian Church that I attended. The Vicks' home had a beautiful front yard. It had sugar maples, which we enjoyed sitting under in the summer, talking with Mr. and Mrs. Vick, as he came home on weekends. We lived here a year or so, and moved just before Hugh Lynn was born, when we went to housekeeping in a little five-room, cream-colored cottage with a tiny front porch. It was on Park Street, the second door from the head of Main Street, opposite Reservoir Park. Hugh Lynn was born in this house on March 16, 1907, Dr. Blackburn attending. Miss Daisy Dean was the nurse. Gertrude's mother, Lizzie E. Evans, was also with us. It was a lovely sunshiny Saturday afternoon.

While working at Potter's bookstore, I became very good friends with a distant relative of the owners, Frank J. Potter, a tall, blond man with a very pleasing personality who was the assistant county clerk. In 1904, in partnership with him, I purchased the Harry L. Cook Studio on College Street. Frank insisted that I spend a little time at a photography school, which I did, attending the Southern School of Photography at McMinnville, Tennessee. The instructor, Mr. J. W. Lively, later became well known, especially during World War I days when he was instructor to army photographers. I attended this school for eight weeks, during which time Gertrude stayed with her family in Hopkinsville.

While I was there, a good deal of talk came up about the readings, which had been reported in one newspaper or another. The brother of the head of the school was connected with the Southern Railroad. There had been an unusual wreck in one of the rail yards of this railroad, and he asked me to try to tell him something of what had happened. While I was

averse to doing this, I finally agreed to try it. They claim that
I gave an accurate report of the men and conditions in the
yard. I also said a certain individual who had been discharged
was responsible for the wreck. The officials of the railroad
disregarded this explanation. However, a few months later one
of the vice presidents asked if he might have one more reading
on the matter. He wanted to know how he could prove the
information being given was correct, and the answer came
back, "If the one we have named that caused this trouble is
allowed to remain in the service he will, before the first of
December, be the direct cause of an accident which will mean
the death of the one who refused this information. It will happen in Virginia and West Virginia." And, it is said, I named
the one directly responsible for the wreck. This was in February. On the 29th of November of the same year this man,
who was still working for the railroad, let through a train. The
high official was in his private car near the scene. The car was
struck in one state and ran over the line; he died in the other
state.

In August 1904, after I finished photography school, we
returned to Bowling Green and opened the Cayce Studio in
the one-story Girard Building on College Street, four or five
doors from Fountain Square. The Girard Building also contained Girard's Undertaking Parlor at Tenth and College, then
Dr. Stone's office, and then the studio, which occupied space
for two stores. There was a display case in the center of the
store and a large floor showcase for pictures as you entered.
It had a large operating room in back and the printing and
negative room next to that, the finishing room between the
two front rooms and the operating room. There was a dressing
room also between office and operating room. Back of the
office on the left was the darkroom. Back of the office on the
right was the room in which we handled Kodaks, Kodak supplies, pictures, and picture frames. The studio was heated with
a coal stove in each room.

The next offices on College Street were Cook's Insurance,
Stone's Grocery, and Pushing's Dry Goods Store on the edge
of the square.

Business was very good. That fall I made a very nice picture of a very prominent matron and her son, which we put on display in a showcase in front of the studio. Mr. Elbert Hubbard, who was in the city for a lecture, passed the studio and stopped to look at the picture, then came in and told me to enter that picture in the *Ladies Home Journal* contest of mother and son pictures and it would win a prize. I entered it and won first prize. Mr. Hubbard, it seems, was one of the judges.

I went to St. Louis later that fall to attend the national photographers meeting. Some of my pictures were put on display and three won honorable mention. In 1906 Frank Potter and I purchased the Clark Studio on State Street and took in as partners my brother-in-law, Lynn Evans, and Joe Adcock, who had been working for us. The Clark Studio was quite large, as it extended over Potter's bookstore, where I had worked, as well as most of the saddle and harness shop next door. The Clark Studio had a front room which at first I used as a frame room.

In January 1907, Lynn, Joe, and I bought out Potter's interest in the studios. But in December the College Street studio burned, and afterward Gertrude and I lived in the State Street studio, using the large front room as a combination living room and bedroom. There was sufficient space in the back for a kitchen and dining room. The reception room and the operating room here were quite large. In September 1908 we had quite a fire in this studio.

One day Dr. Stone, whose office was next to my studio, asked me in for an experiment before one of his visitors. As I said before, no records were made of these experiments, but this is what I was told happened during this experience: While I was unconscious, Father Haynes came in with a bundle under his arm that he had received through the post office. Not knowing the contents of the package himself, he asked Dr. Stone to question me as to its contents. The reply came, "Altar candles," which proved to be correct.

During the same experiment Dr. Stone also made the suggestion that my system would react as if I had been given a large dose of salts. My own experience bore it out, as the reaction a few hours later was very much as if I had been given the salts.

Dr. Ford conducted an experiment about the same time, with many others present, and it was told to me as follows: He asked about the condition of his mother, his brother-in-law being the physician in charge of her case. Some questioned whether the information came simply from reading people's minds; so a question was asked concerning conditions in the woman's sickroom. There was a minute description given of every individual in the room, also the location of various articles of furniture, where they were manufactured, and when. The bed was described in such detail as to include where the metal was mined, the factory where it was made, where the cotton was grown for the mattress, by whom sold, etc. Just why such detail was given, or just how true these all were, I have no idea, though many of these statements were verified as far as possible. The mother improved under the suggestions made and applied.

Dr. Cartwright, with Dr. Blackburn, asked about a man whom neither of them had seen, but who had, through Dr. Stone, asked that information be given for him. They later examined the man in person and reported that the diagnosis was very thorough, the suggestions for improvement logical, and the applications very helpful.

Dr. Blackburn also conducted an experiment before the Psychology Club at Potter College. I cannot remember a complete description of this experiment, but it was for one of the young ladies from Louisiana, in reference to misappropriation of funds by someone in her father's employ. The psychology class declared it a most interesting evening and later presented me with a watch, engraved with my name and the name of the class, in appreciation of my efforts.

Dr. Blackburn also conducted an experiment before the County Medical Society. Gertrude asked the doctor not to do anything that would hurt me in any way, and he promised that he would not. I had to do without my dinner, as the session was given in the evening. When the time came for the exper-

iment I lay on a couch in the presence of the group and seemingly went into a deep sleep. I was presented with a name for
a person who was supposed to be just outside the door. While
I was unconscious, I am told that I replied, "It is a Negro, we
can't help," and there was the refusal to give any further information about the case. Many questions were raised as to
why I refused.[5] Many of those present had never witnessed
such an experiment and wished to see something, so, I was
questioned about a patient of Blackburn's at Potter Bible College three miles out of Bowling Green. The reading stated that
the young man was recuperating from typhoid fever; that his
temperature was 101 degrees, his pulse 96, respiration was so
and so; and that it would be necessary to take precautions
regarding his diet. Someone asked Blackburn if this was true.

"Yes, that is my patient and he is recovering from typhoid.
As to his temperature and pulse, I don't know."

Then a committee of three was sent to ascertain whether or
not these things were correct. On their return they reported
that they were absolutely correct.

While they were gone, much unfavorable comment was
made to Dr. Blackburn because of his experiments, and questions were raised as to just what state I was in. Some of the

---

[5] Given his rural Kentucky upbringing, Mr. Cayce was quite progressive in
his personal attitude on race and gave readings over the years for people of
all races, including African Americans. Hugh Lynn Cayce, his eldest son,
noted in his biography, *About My Father's Business*, that his father showed
no racial bias despite the racial prejudice of his father, L. B. Cayce. The Cayce
readings were clear about race. When he was asked: What should be our
attitude toward the Negro, and how may we best work out the karma created
in relations with him? Mr. Cayce responded: "He is thy brother! They that
produced, they that brought servitude without thought or purpose have created
that which they must meet within their own principles, their own selves. These
should be taken in the attitude of their own individual fitness, as in every
other form of associations. For He hath made of one blood the nations of the
earth." Reading 1260–1 states: "For they are all one; there's no races, they
are all one—they either have enjoined or have separated themselves, and as
has been indicated from times back the environmental influences have made
for changes in the color, or the food or the activity has produced those various
things . . ."

doctors said it was hypnosis, some didn't agree. Mr. Hudson said there was evidence from the experiments that he witnessed in the last few days that there is something similar to hypnosis, yet something of the trance state also. "I have never seen anything just like it." Others insisted on testing to prove I was really unconscious. Needles were stuck through the back of my hand, my arm, and feet; and a long needle or hatpin was stuck entirely through my jaw. No response whatever was indicated, not even more than a drop of blood. Then someone suggested that I had been hardened to such things, and to stick a knife under my fingernail. The nail on the forefinger of my left hand was lifted. They said there was no perceptible pain and no blood until I awoke.

Well, I was not in a very good humor. I berated the doctor who had promised my wife that I would not be submitted to tests that might hurt and told them all they would not witness any more experiments with me if they had no more regard for their word than that. I said I would only try when help was needed and sincerely asked for, and that I did not care whether a doctor was present or not. I had been subjected to their experiments for nearly two years, and this was the way I was treated by them. Mr. Hudson said, "You are quite right. This should never be used except for beneficial hopes for the ailing."

That evening several of the psychologists present said to me, "After you have given these readings for several years, if there is anyone who comes to you again and again, say for a period of five years or more, then you may know what you are doing is worthwhile." Among those who had readings in February 1903 there was someone who came for another reading in February 1940, so there must be something worthwhile in this.

There was a young lady in Potter College from Mississippi, whose mother had been quite ill; in fact, the local doctors had despaired of doing anything for her. She asked my wife if we would give a reading for her mother, and she was brought to Bowling Green on a cot from Mississippi. The diagnosis outlined a treatment that was administered by Dr. South. She began to improve almost immediately and in a few months was perfectly normal and well. Dr. South then experimented with quite a number of patients and declared the information was very helpful, often assisting him in locating trouble that he had not before suspected.

In one of the readings for myself, while Dr. Blackburn was experimenting, it was suggested that my severe headaches were produced from a condition in the appendix area, and that it would be well for me to have an operation. Several physicians tried to verify this, but all were of the opinion that my trouble was from some other cause.

One day I received a telephone call from Dr. House, who had married my wife's aunt Carrie and lived in Hopkinsville. He said his wife was very ill and would not be satisfied until I gave her a reading. When I arrived I found that she had been in bed for several weeks, under the care of two other physicians besides her husband. A specialist who had also been called decided she had a tumor and that an immediate operation was necessary. She could not sit up, but she insisted that she hear what was said; so I lay near her, and Dr. House for the first time heard a reading, conducting it himself. The information insisted that she did not have a tumor, but rather an impaction. A treatment was outlined to remove this. Each day for several days a reading was given to check up on the following of previous suggestions. The condition was removed. She did not have an operation. This was some thirty years ago, and she has never yet had an operation.

Several months later I was again called by Dr. House. Their son, who had been born prematurely, was very ill. Two other physicians were present. One said, "Well, if you're going to fool with that fake, I'm through." The other stayed to listen. The suggestion was that an overdose of belladonna be given, followed with other applications when this had created the desired effect. The remaining physician was very insistent this proposed remedy not be tried. Carrie reminded him that he had despaired of her condition sometime before, but the reading had prescribed a treatment which prevented the operation he had deemed necessary. I saw the father measure out the dose and the mother administer it, with the physician standing by saying the child would not live through the night. The young man today is as strong and healthy as anyone you would care to see.

Then a very unusual thing occurred that was not a test, but just a happening. I went to Hopkinsville for the Christmas holidays and returned on the late train, as I had an appointment to make photographs at the furniture factory the first day of January 1907. Most of the next day I worked in the factory without any heat making photographs. It was rather cold and there was a little snow on the ground. I returned to the studio late in the afternoon and went to the darkroom to develop my plates. When I came out two of the boys were sitting around the stove. I made a remark on the possibility of what I had gotten that day and soon lost consciousness and fell to the floor. This is what happened, as it was told to me by Tom Barnes and Frank Potter: They picked me up from the floor, carried me into the next room and laid me on the bed, and called Dr. McCraken, who came. Several other physicians had been called before they tried Dr. McCraken; among them Blackburn, who was in the country. McCraken said I had a chill and gave me some medicine and told one of the boys to get some whiskey and give me a stiff drink. They got the whiskey at once, but when they attempted to pour it down, my jaws seemed to lock. Another doctor had arrived in the meantime. In trying to pry my mouth open to force a drink of whiskey down my throat, several of my upper and lower front teeth were broken out. I was still very rigid but shaking like a leaf. One of them gave me a hypodermic of morphine. Others came in, and in the course of the next two hours I was given two or three more hypodermics, one of strychnine and another of nitro. As I continued to have convulsions and got very cold, they put hot water bottles, hot stove lids, and bricks to my feet, wrapping me in hot packs. Finally I was pronounced dead.

A few minutes later Dr. Blackburn came in, and Dr. McCraken said to him, "You and Cayce have been pulling these stunts for a long time. Tonight you will have to be

Cayce's Jesus, for he is dead." Blackburn asked what they had done. When they told him, his answer was, "You shouldn't have done anything. I believe he has gone into one of his trances for the protection against an overworked physical body."

Blackburn worked with me by giving suggestions, and in about thirty minutes I showed some return of life. I came to consciousness with the realization that the room was full of people, practically all of them doctors. I heard McCraken say, "John, now what in the hell are you going to do? The stuff that is in Cayce would kill him if he was a well man. How will you get it out?"

I was in great misery. My feet were blistered, and there were long streaks of blisters on my limbs. My arms showed the effects of the hypodermics, my mouth was bleeding where they had pried it open to prevent me from chewing my tongue. Several of my teeth were missing. Blackburn asked me, "Cayce, what shall we do?" My reply was, "Let me put myself to sleep, if possible. Talk it out of me if you can." I was able to concentrate sufficiently to lose consciousness in a few minutes, but I didn't expect to wake again. I slept for two or more hours, then he woke me. The blisters were entirely gone. He had been able to press the solution from the hypodermics as my system did not assimilate it, the whiskey had come up, and I walked out of the room, got in the buggy with Dr. Blackburn, and he carried me home and stayed with me the rest of the night. We were aroused in the morning by flowers being delivered—they all thought I had died. There were no ill effects whatever from the experience, except my teeth were still missing. This experience caused me many confusing thoughts, not all good either.

Another confusing experience happened one afternoon when Dr. South came by the studio to tell me that a Mrs. Goodman had just been brought into the hospital, and he was very anxious that I get information for her that evening. Her son, son-in-law, and grandson were doctors, and I asked him if they were not attending her; he said yes, but they had despaired of doing anything for her. I wondered if he thought it would be well for them to request the information; later in the afternoon they did. Going home, I told my wife I wouldn't want any supper until I came back from giving the reading about eight o'clock. For a little while I played with the baby, then lay down across the bed—and wondered what it was all about. Did these good people really feel something might be given through these channels to aid their loved one? Was Dr. South willing to risk his reputation by saying he believed in such information? I lost consciousness.

When I woke up the room was dark, and I was puzzled to find myself in bed with most of my clothes on. I went to look for my wife and told her I must hurry over to give the reading.

"If you look at the clock you will see that you have scared us most to death," she said. "Dr. South called for you but we couldn't arouse you. I got uneasy and phoned Dr. Blackburn. He worked with you nearly an hour and assured me you were all right and put you in bed."

The next morning I went by to make my apologies. Dr. South assured me that he felt he knew what had happened. They had told Mrs. Goodman of their intention to get the information, and she was very anxious for it. "You must have gone to sleep about seven-thirty as she did, and must have awakened about two-thirty as she did. She awoke feeling a great deal better, and this morning she is anxious to be up." Soon afterwards she was entirely well again.

For some reason, people whose character might be questioned appeared to be attracted to me. This was a new experience for me. Yet to meet those who were light of love, well, I listened possibly too often. But one evening I had a telephone call from a minister in another city, who said, "My sister is in your city, so I understand, at a house of ill fame. I am worried and can't give her up to such a life. Will you try and help me? Won't you find her and see if you can't persuade her to come home before it is too late?"

I went to look for the girl, which was not easy for me. Most of the inmates saw, heard, or talked with me and were loud in protesting my trying to persuade this girl to go home.

Such associations and surroundings didn't improve my confusion. But I finally got her to agree to go meet her brother. In fact, I went with her to meet her brother. Today she has a lovely home and family out West.

11

TEMPTATION: 'WHO CAN GUIDE ME ARIGHT?'

There were people who said to me, "Old Man, you ought to make all the money there is in the world. You ought to read the races, the stock market, find lost people, lost articles. People will pay you anything for that sort of information." Half-heartedly, I submitted to some of these experiments, some with a great show of success. Almost immediately, however, the results were fearful, dreadful.

One day, for example, a young man named Joe came to see me.

"I know you owe three hundred dollars over at the bank," he said. "If you will tell me what wheat will do for the next three days, I will pay that note."

This was a new phase of the phenomena to me altogether, one that in some ways appealed because I was in debt. And yet something about it wasn't good. But I finally agreed, the reading was given, and the note was paid. Joe made some twenty thousand dollars during the three days' deal. This, however, only made him anxious. So he came to me again with another proposition.

"I have a friend in New York City that I've written to about you, and I told him my experience with you. But he doesn't believe me. He says one can find many people there in the city who will tell you anything you wish to know for a dollar or so, but it would take real money to bring you and Eddie to New York. 'Give me proof that you can do this and I'll talk to you,' he said. Now what can we do to convince him? We could make real money in New York."

"Well," I said, "let's knock him down."

"What do you mean?" asked Joe.

"Let's tell him what he is doing right now."

"That would be fine, but can you do it? I don't even know where he is."

"All right," I said, "let's tell him where he is and what he is doing."

We undertook it, and this was the report:

"It is now two minutes to 10 A.M. in New York. Paul is walking along Williams Street in New York. We will make him do things so that he will remember. He goes in a cigar store, he smokes cigarettes but we will have him buy a cigar so that he will know. He does, then goes out of the store and walks up the street to a building in which his office is located. Instead of riding up, we will have him walk up three flights whistling 'Annie Laurie' so he will remember it. At his office he finds a man waiting for him with some business about a piece of property at the end of Williams Street bridge. It will be tried in Surrogate Court at three today. The man leaves. He turns to his desk and finds three letters. One is a bill, one a letter from his sweetheart which begins, 'Darling Paul.' The telephone rings, he answers and talks with a man named Donagan."

This report was wired to New York. In an hour the answer came back to Joe—"Report absolutely correct. Leaving for Bowling Green today to bring you and Eddie to New York." Paul came to Bowling Green and spent several days attempting to get me to go to New York City, but I refused. The man gave me the creeps when I was around him.

My father then came to see me and said he had been having rather a hard time making ends meet, but that a couple of businessmen in Hopkinsville felt we could all make plenty of money if I could be persuaded to give information on the market, especially on wheat. They were willing to advance sufficient money to justify my staying there at the hotel for a few days in order to get the information and phone it to them every morning. Reluctantly, I agreed to do it. They were to report each week as to what their earnings had been. The first week they made several hundred dollars, although I got no part of it. The second week was very satisfactory. Still desiring to have the information day by day, they felt justified in leaving their business to go to Chicago where they might be closer to operations at the Board of Trade. It was insisted that a certain man named Leiter would corner the market, and that wheat would go to $1.19 and then break very suddenly down several points. They were persuaded this couldn't be, and failed to follow Leiter's transactions and lost a lot of money. This whole transaction brought troublesome conditions mentally and physically for me, as well as to my father. I was forced to discontinue giving the information, and operations were necessarily suspended. Most unsatisfactory conditions arose, and some animosity that has never been wholly overcome.

Dr. Blackburn also wanted to locate a buried treasure on his old home place. The reading described two houses practically in the same location, which made it rather confusing to him and his brother who were present. When they consulted the family, however, they were told that no doubt the information was correct, as the former house had burned and the present one had been built almost on the same place. The treasure was supposed to have been buried before the present house was built. A very small portion of the treasure was located.

One day a young medical student, son of a physician, came to me requesting information for his sister. Her condition was described as appendicitis, with symptoms of a growth. Dr. Blackburn assisted in performing the operation in Nashville; it was a true case of appendicitis, though there were only signs of a growth which were removed at the same time. She had no return of the trouble.

Right here I might digress to say that out of the sixty-two cases diagnosed as appendicitis, only four operations have been advised—one of them being my own.

On another occasion, the founder of the osteopathic school asked questions about a patient who was suffering from infantile paralysis. The information came so fast that the stenographer was unable to get it. Dr. Lundy, a dentist who was interested in the phenomena, placed his hand about the central portion of my body and said, "Up, up—not so fast." Later they told me that my body rose from the couch to the level of his hand, then fell. For several days following this experience I was almost in a state of nervous collapse.

Dr. House visited us for several weeks. His wife's family had a legend of there having been money buried on their place. Through the information he attempted to locate it. The reading began with a description of soldiers coming to occupy the town and the state institution nearby. Their activities were followed around the place where the treasure was supposed to have been put, and many minor happenings were described that were later checked. There was a description of the changing of a road, how the deeds were drawn, the pages on which the record would be found, purchase of land adjoining the property, when fences were run, and such details. A skirmish between Federals and Confederates was described, and the hiding of the treasure by someone, and a letter he wrote to his people about it, their receiving the letter, and years later the search by two men who recovered the gold, then had a subsequent fight, and the death of one man.

All of this happened many years before I was born, of course, and much of this information, if it had ever been known, had long been forgotten. But so far as possible, all the stories were checked and tallied.

A professor in the high school, who was a Canadian, told me of a mystery in his hometown and asked if I would undertake to ferret it out through my psychic abilities. I hesitated, but consented as an experiment. While Blackburn was conducting this reading, he was called out on an emergency case; so he gave the suggestion for me to wake and left me with the professor, thinking I would be all right. When he returned four hours later, I was still lying there unconscious. Prof. Lambert wired the information to the chief of police. It said, "Dig at the intersection at such and such a number, where the tragedy occurred, and you will find the gun, number such and such, bought at Roanoke, Virginia." A few days later Chief of Police White wired the sheriff of Warren County to locate Lambert and Cayce and hold them in connection with the tragedy. We knew the sheriff very well, and he jokingly told us we were in for some questioning. Police Chief White came, and we did have some tall explaining to prove that neither of us had been out of the state. In a subsequent reading for White, a description was given of the incidents leading up to the tragedy, which was verified.

Another case of the same character followed. On a visit to my home, my father—who had an acquaintance who had acted in the capacity of plainclothesman in two or three cities—spoke to me about a mystery which had occurred in western Pennsylvania. A large reward was offered for information leading to the whereabouts of the people who were supposed to have gotten away with several thousand dollars' worth of bonds. I still disliked anything of the kind, but very reluctantly agreed if they would leave me out of it entirely. The man said he would get a description of the lady in the case. I remarked to him that if the reading could tell where she was, it could certainly describe her. A description was given of the principals in the case. The woman who had left her husband with her lover was said to have a birthmark on her body which was not visible ordinarily; and it described her left foot from a burn which caused two toes to grow together.

My father gave the description to the husband, but didn't tell him how it was received—and the husband told him over the phone that it certainly was his wife. A reward was posted, and the police attempted to locate the people. They seemingly got on the move at once, and it required quite a number of subsequent readings to follow them from hotel to hotel across the country, finally locating them in Columbus, Ohio.

Some weeks later Joe came to me and said, "Why can't we read the races and make a lot of money?"

"I don't know if I can," I said. "I never tried. Let's try it this evening for tomorrow's race and see if it is correct. Then if you want to try it, we'll do so, provided you have a certain man go with us." We tried it and the information gave six out of seven races, saying the other race had been fixed and it wouldn't do to bet on it at its present status. So these two men and I went to Cincinnati.

The next morning a reading was taken that indicated that

only four of the seven races to be run at Latonia that day were not already fixed. Joe bet on these races and won in each one. The next day we tried again, but after the reading I was taken with a violent headache and couldn't go with the others to the track. I was absolutely a wreck, as was Joe.

A few weeks later he was put in the state institution for the mentally unbalanced. And for nearly a year I was unable to give information. My health seemed to fail. I was supposed to have TB or something worse. So I decided to leave it all, quit messing with it, quit experimenting, and try to determine in my own mind whether there was anything in it or not. I closed out my business in Bowling Green and went back to my old home and rested for several months. I took up the study of the Scriptures and prayed very sincerely about the whole business, for I realized that the attempt to use such information for speculative interests had brought a sudden, definite change in my whole being. I realized that my likes and dislikes had changed. My associations that I sought were different. What produced it? I wondered.

Several attempts were made to get information. More often I was not even able to put myself into the unconscious state, no matter how I tried. I began to find that even when I desired to enter this state I could not. For a time I determined I would never attempt a reading again.

This was the test. Edgar didn't say a great deal, but he would make up his mind based on all the facts concerning the work, including his church connection and the criticism of some church members and the feeling there might be a possibility that he was doing wrong. He had several very hard battles trying to decide the right and the just thing to do. But when someone would come and say to him they were in a serious condition and the doctor had told them the chances were not very good, and ask him to help them, he would say, "I will gladly do what I can." And he would. And possibly in a very short while the patient might be well or fast improving. But still much of the criticism would continue, along with great praise from many others.

As far as writing down the readings, he had no one who could do it. Consequently, no records were kept of each case. And he never knew what became of many of them. Since he had no record of what he said about any case, many people who knew nothing about it ridiculed the idea, poked fun, and made funny remarks, or so they thought, and looked at him as though he was to be shunned. Others would praise him to the very top, for they really felt that he was the greatest boy living. Of course many of those were his very close and dear loved ones who believed in everything he was doing; but many of those, too, were almost shunning him and would not even talk about what he was doing even when they were asked about it. So it went back and forth, and he knew nothing except what different people said to him about the work.

This controversy continued from month to month for several years. Because of these conditions and such division of the people and so much criticism, Mr. Layne did not ordinarily say very much about Edgar and his work and what was being accomplished unless someone asked him a direct question. Again, possibly Edgar felt the pressure of the unreasonableness of so many acquaintances, many of whom he felt so very near to. But many others continued to come and ask for help for themselves or someone in their family. Occasionally there was no one to listen to the reading except possibly the one who was conducting it and placing the case before Edgar, while at other times there were as many as could get into the room. Such crowds, of course, were divided in their opinions of the work—many very favorable, and others severely critical, some saying how marvelous it was, and others saying how ridiculous it was to give credence to such impossibilities. The critics would say that such things were impossible, and everyone knew it, and that Edgar should not try to deceive the people as he was doing. And yet there were others who had really investigated the work and were very strong believers even that early before there were any records kept, based on the testimony of those who had received help from the readings and others who were close to them and knew the facts. Usually those denouncing the work knew nothing about it, and

would not try to find out anything about it or listen with much
patience to those who had received benefits themselves. They
would just say it was impossible.

With so much adverse talk by many people, Edgar began
to wonder in his own mind whether or not he should continue.
He censured no one for their opinion or for the stand they
took concerning his work and only seemed to think about the
possibility that he was in the wrong since there was such a
preponderance of opposition, and much of it among his own
dear friends and loved ones. To those who looked to discover
some secret or fake about it, he would say, "If it's a fake, it
is not my fake."

As for me, I needed no further proof of the reality and
wonderful help that could be received after seeing the imme-
diate restoring of Edgar's voice by some unknown, supreme
power or whatever one might be pleased to call it. To me, it
was the power of the Great Creator working through Edgar
and for him.

There was a relative of mine who had been ill a number of
years. He was a middle-aged man. He asked me to see what
I'd say of him. I did. Seemingly, then, on the improve, he sent
for me. I will never forget! When I entered the room, he was
lying there on his bed, and looking up, calling me the old
familiar name, he said, "Old Man, I'm glad to see you! I want
to talk with you." Motioning to the others in the room, he
said, "I would like to talk to Old Man alone." When they had
gone, he asked me to take a seat by his bed. Taking my hand
in his, he said:

"Now, I want you to tell me something. Do you or do you
not know how you do this thing you do? How do you tell
people what's the matter with them? Where did you learn all
of this? Here I have been sick a long time. I've been to the
best people in the country, to the most expensive hospitals.
They keep me there a week, ten days, two weeks—two to
three doctors made examinations every day, ask me every
question imaginable and then say, 'We don't know what's the
matter.' Here you, a boy I've known all my life, knew your

mother and father when they were children, have seen you practically every day of your life until the last two or three years, you walk in the room, don't ask me a question, lay off your coat, collar tie, and lie down there on the bed, seemingly go to sleep or something, then begin to talk about me, tell me how I feel, what hurts me, when it hurts me in what place, what causes it and what, if they will do it, will help me, and this you tell to a man that I know doesn't know any more about such things than you. How do you do it? It isn't that you've gained the knowledge from him, I know. It isn't that you've gained the knowledge from me. Now, what is it?"

And all the answer I could give was, "I do not know!"

"Old Man, God has given you something He has given to few people. You must consider well to what use you put this gift He has given you. Do not abuse it, but *use* it. Do not be ashamed of it as you have been, but help poor suffering humanity, such as I."

Again and again I found myself bewildered. If only I had had some living friend who knew something of what was going on, who could have guided me aright! Would it have been different? Would it have been better? Someone has said, "Experience is a dear school, but fools will learn in no other." Is this true? Or, is it not true that we never learn anything in the physical sense except by experience? For the mental mind can only reason by comparison. The subconscious mind reasons from the experiences of the physical and soul minds. Hence, it covers a broader and greater scope. So, I studied, I thought, I tried to reason.

During this time I met many people from different walks of life. Some questioned, some sneered, some felt sorry, some sympathized. I tried to keep away from the work, and it was only by insistence that I would consent to give these readings; yet time and again there were individuals who said over and over, "It has given my child back to me." "It has given me new hope." "I see life entirely different." But could I make it compatible in my mind with the tenets of the church of which I was a member? What was I to say when my Sunday school pupils asked me concerning it? Was it in keeping with good judgment; was it consistent with ordinary reason? I wonder if anyone will ever know what trials and what torments I went through! Finally, I said, "I'll get rid of it all! I'll forget it! I'll go away somewhere else. I'll never mention it. I won't let people know anything about it."

So, I moved to another state, still studying, trying to see if there was a grain of truth, or "could any good thing come out of Nazareth?"

12

DR. KETCHUM, 1910: AN UNLIKELY PARTNER

After my experiences in Bowling Green, I went to Gadsden, Alabama, where I became associated with a young man in the photography business. My wife and boy remained in Hopkinsville, so I stayed in the home of this man's parents, who were the most devout Christian people it has ever been my pleasure to know. I often talked with them about some of my experiences, but did not attempt any readings during my stay there.

My work as a photographer took me into the country a great deal, traveling about to schools, conventions, and various meetings in several counties. I chose to work outside the studio deliberately on account of wanting to be alone in the open, close to nature, as much as possible. I walked many a mile through the forests from one school district to another in Calhoun and Talladega counties.

In May of that year, 1910, the president of the state normal school at Jacksonville, Alabama, had some correspondence with some of the more prominent investigators of the phenomena who had visited me in Bowling Green. He and one or two physicians undertook some experiments, several with very remarkable results—one an operation, one a deformity in the lower limbs, another a child with some very unusual condition, all responding under the treatments suggested. These were the first readings I had been able to do since my attempt to read the races in Latonia.

These cases caused considerable comment, and several other readings were then attempted in Anniston and other towns close by. Most of them were conducted by one of the young men students at Jacksonville, A. J. Hyde, who later became the postmaster at Nauvoo, Alabama. The Anniston paper had quite an article regarding some of the experiences.

While working in Anniston, I returned home to Hopkinsville to visit my family for a few days. My father told me there was a physician in town, Wesley H. Ketchum, who was very anxious to meet me. We went around to his office and found Dr. Ketchum a very amiable, pleasant young man.[1]

"I have heard many stories about the things you have done through this country," he said to me. "In fact, I live in the home of a lady whose hair was turned white overnight through one of your readings."

"What do you mean?" I said.

"Well," he replied with a smile, "You told her the dye she was using was injurious to her health."

Father and I smiled at that one. Dr. Ketchum also had seen Professor Dietrich's little girl, Aime.

"Dietrich and his wife are very enthusiastic, and I think they really believe in you," said Ketchum. "I would like to see a demonstration."

I told him of my sad experiences during the latter part of my stay in Bowling Green, and about the young man who had been sent to the feeble-minded institution and was still there, and that I had tried to do something for him but had failed. My inability to give readings, I told him, led to my decision to leave it all alone. Only in the last few months had I been able to again experiment in physical diagnosis with several physicians in Alabama, I added.

"Well, I want to see it," Ketchum said. "What do I have to do to get a reading for somebody?"

If he could get a written or verbal report from somebody who really needed it, I told him, I would try it. He asked me to wait a few minutes. He was gone from his office some fifteen or twenty minutes, returning with a piece of paper in his hand.

"I have this written request here. When can I get the reading?"

---

[1] Dr. Ketchum had a different version of their first meeting. He said he had gone to Bowling Green once with Dr. House to consult Edgar about a difficult case—an incident evidently less memorable to Cayce.

"We can try it now."

So I lay down on his examination table, and my father conducted the reading. I did not know Ketchum had a stenographer taking down what was said, as she came in after I was unconscious. When I awoke, Ketchum was standing over me, his thumbs in the armholes of his vest, rocking back and forth on his feet. He said, "Well, that is the most remarkable thing I ever saw in my life, but it is a *fake*, pure and simple, and I doubt if anyone except someone like myself would catch it. You are a mind reader. Do you know whom you were talking about?"

I said, "No."

"Well, I think you do, for you talked about me, and I know what is the matter with me. I have appendicitis. I am going to be operated on next week, but you go along with a lot of bunk and tell me that so many moons ago I had an accident in which I wrenched my spine, which formed something of a lesion, which produced an unpleasantness in my right side, causing me to feel like I have appendicitis. Your reading suggested that I, a regular doctor, go to an osteopath for an adjustment, and that in a few days I will be all right. It is a lot of bunk. I know I have appendicitis, for I have been to six of the best doctors in the state and they all say so."

"I have never seen you before," I told Ketchum, "and I had no idea on whom the information was to be given. I don't even know what was said. I have not claimed anything; I was not trying to show you anything, but merely trying to be of service through a channel by which many have told me they have gotten relief."

Ketchum wasn't the first doctor who didn't believe in the phenomenon. But he surprised me by offering a proposition.

"Cayce, if you tie up with me we can make a whole barrel of money," he said. "I can take you to various centers, exhibit you, and collect real money for such experiments as you have done here, but in reality there isn't a thing to it."

"Doctor," I said to him, "it may be a fake and everything you say about it may be true, but it isn't *my* fake. If you will prove to me that this is a fake, and that the information is incorrect, I will certainly thank you and will never do another reading. As for trying to make money by fooling someone, far be it from me." And I walked out of his office.

About nine o'clock that evening the telephone rang in my mother's home. My father answered and it was Ketchum, asking that we come to his office. Ketchum met us at the door, holding his side with his right hand. Reaching his left hand to me, he said:

"Come in here. You are not a fake. I was just a plain fool. When you left here I got to thinking about what you said and I thought if that had happened, could it have produced the condition with which I am suffering, and the more I studied it the more plausible it seemed. Did you know that I have a copy of what you said?"

"No."

"Well, I have, right here. So I said to myself, 'Ketchum, don't be foolish. He has dared you to prove it—now prove it.' So I went up to see Dr. Oldham, the osteopath, and had an examination. As I sat in his room before he examined me, I asked if he knew you. He said, 'Yes.' I asked what he thought of you. He said, 'Well, he does some very remarkable things. I treated the boy for several months. It is quite remarkable as to how well he outlines a case, but I believe the most he knows he learned from me. He gets an idea as to what is the trouble and has a general smattering of physiology and anatomy by his association with me for several months.' Then I told him I had never seen you before this afternoon, and that you made no examination of me. I told Oldham, 'He didn't know whom he was going to give information on, and he has dared me to prove he is wrong. I want you to help me.'

"Oldham ran his hand along my spine and came to a certain area and named the specific vertebra, saying, 'Here is your trouble.' Then I asked him to look at the report you gave and it was the same! I asked him, 'Oldham, what would that produce?'

"He said, 'I suspect, Doctor, you think you have appendicitis.' Then I asked him what he would do about it? 'I will place my hand here, I will have my wife hold your feet, and

I will turn your body until we reduce this pressure,' he replied. I said, 'Read the next line on what Cayce said I should do, for that is precisely what he said!'

"Cayce, I am convinced there is something very, very unusual about this. You have no right to hide this as you are doing."

I told him I had had many unpleasant experiences and, although several people had obtained real help, I didn't know what to do with it.

About a month after I returned to Alabama I received a wire from Dr. Ketchum asking me to come at once to give information for a very prominent citizen there. As he sent my railroad fare, I took leave of absence from my job, and I went back to Hopkinsville.

When I got home my father had in his hand a written request from the man's family. When the reading was given, the man's family was in an adjoining room, so I did not see any of them. Two stenographers took this report. There was very little comment after we had finished the reading. Ketchum simply said, "Well, this is a case where I will have to make further investigations to prove whether this is correct or not." I then returned to my work and heard no more about the case.[2]

The middle of the summer I moved to Montgomery, Alabama, to work for another photographer, Mr. Tressler. Several local cases were attempted during the latter part of the summer, with my cousin, Thomas E. Cayce, conducting the readings.

In October, without any warning or idea of it happening, I learned from the newspapers that the case on which I had been called to Hopkinsville to give a reading had been presented to the American Society of Clinical Research in Boston by Dr. Ketchum, and it had been reported by the Associated Press.

---

[2] In an interview many years later, Dr. Ketchum said he followed the reading's suggestion, his patient recovered, but he never told the family about Cayce "because in that day and time it wasn't healthy to mention such a weird proposition as that!"

The New York Times newspaper published an article, too. The headline said:

ILLITERATE MAN BECOMES A DOCTOR WHEN HYPNOTIZED
Strange Power Shown by Edgar Cayce Puzzles Physicians[3]

Other newspapers smelled a story and were trying everywhere to locate me. Since it had been reported that I was born and reared in Hopkinsville, my family was besieged by reporters. For some time I withstood all efforts by the press in making a report. Finally Dr. Ketchum, with Albert Noe, a Hopkinsville hotel owner, insisted on my coming for an interview. I found on arrival that over two thousand dollars in cash, checks, and money orders and more than twenty thousand letters had been received at my home. A great deal was carried in the newspapers throughout the country for several months in the fall of 1910. I did not know what to do about it all. Many friends and acquaintances advised this way and that. When Dr. Ketchum and Mr. Noe proposed to conduct a research society on a scientific and businesslike basis, that appealed to me, for I didn't want to fool myself nor, most of all, anyone else. If I could be of help through these channels, was it a duty I owed my fellow man? Or was I seeking an easy way to induce my fellow man to invest money in something that was the bunk?

I asked several prominent men in political circles—judges

—

[3] The article ran in the Sunday edition of the *Times*, on October 9, 1910, complete with large photographs of Edgar Cayce, L. B. Cayce, and Dr. Ketchum. Edgar had not been identified by name in Ketchum's paper at the Boston meeting, only that he lived in Hopkinsville. Evidently, his father was interviewed by inquiring reporters and was the source for some of the exaggerated claims made in the *Times* and the AP article. The text of the story from the *Times* appears in the Appendix. Ketchum attended the following year's meeting of the society in Boston and read another paper, extolling Cayce's miraculous results with several of his patients. "But it was all foreign to them, even then," he wrote years later. "Nobody accepted it; and they looked at me as though I was something out of the woods!"

of the city, county, circuit, and state courts—to be present at
one of the experiences and to give me their honest opinion as
representatives of the people and the law as to whether I would
be considered a charlatan and a fake, or whether there was
some real information that could be of interest and help to my
fellow man. They reduced their opinions to writing, all agree-
ing that good would be accomplished with the record.

A contract was drawn between Mr. Noe, Dr. Ketchum, and
myself. The contract specified that they were to do certain
things and I was to do certain things, and whatever profit was
made out of it was to be divided equally. In other words, they
were to establish an office, furnish the necessary means, etc.,
for the work to be conducted, and charge certain fees for the
work, and so on.[4] Before I would enter into the contract, I
asked several attorneys and doctors, who were supposed to be
honorable, upright, good businessmen, to listen to one of the
readings, question it themselves, and tell me whether I had a
right to make such a contract or not. They approved. The contract was drawn. The judges of the court told me it was legal
and everything. Offices were opened in Hopkinsville. Stenographers were employed, and every bit of the money that had
been received was returned, with the request that the individuals become better acquainted with the channels through

---

[4] Ketchum's memoir explained that he and Noe agreed to back Cayce in
establishing his own photo studio: "Cayce did his own buying and we paid
for it. Prettiest stuff you ever saw! Dandy new camera and all. Must have
spent the biggest part of five thousand dollars, just to outfit the office. I figured
that *that* was his vocation, and this other was a side issue . . . All his readings
were given at the studio. Cayce was a good photographer. He was a fine chap
all the way. Couldn't beat him. Sometimes he would say, 'I don't know how
to do this,' and we would answer, 'Well, just keep on doing it! Never mind
how!' He was embarrassed because the medical profession wouldn't endorse
him—and wouldn't endorse me either. There were others that 'sneaked' to
him for advice. Some day it will all come out about some of those other
doctors! But once you come from a reputable medical school, endorsed by
the medical society, and you don't stick to the book, well, you're just
'branded'—right away! It's the biggest wonder in the world that I didn't get
a 'black mark'; but instead of its hurting me, I built up the town. The whole
thing was just too big to be true!"

which they expected to receive information before sending their money.

The office was on the second floor in the building adjoining the bookstore where I had worked. On the door was painted ED-GAR CAYCE—PSYCHIC DIAGNOSTICIAN. Just across the little hall was a door painted CAYCE'S STUDIO, for I had made it part of the agreement—when I agreed to associate myself with Dr. Ketchum and Mr. Noe—that they would supply the space and equipment for a studio and furnish the office with as nice office furniture as could be had. This they had done.

Upon entering the psychic diagnostician's office, there was a little hallway about six by nine feet, with a nice rug, table, and a couple of chairs. A door led into the main office, which was about eighteen by twenty feet and had quite elaborate furniture—two very large overstuffed rocking chairs; two easy chairs, not rockers; a center table; a large desk at which my father officiated; and a typewriter desk and typewriter. Off the main room was the reading room. It had a high table, specially built, overstuffed, sufficiently long for me to lie upon to give the readings. There was a table and chair for the stenographer, but no chair for the conductor. He had to stand, as the table was too high for him to sit on it.

I've never been able to give more than two—and sometimes three—readings in a day; consequently not a great amount of work could be done, so we were kept busy for the next few months. We attempted many cases locally and some at a distance.[5]

One case got written up in the newspapers as taken down by Miss Poole:

This psychic reading given by Edgar Cayce in Hopkinsville, Ky., this 1st day of December, 1910. Present: Edgar Cayce; L. B. Cayce, Conductor; L. P. Poole, Steno.

---

[5] Ketchum recalled that the local medical society threatened to ostracize him for "messing with a freak called Cayce who was nothing but a faker." But when he challenged them to let Edgar diagnose their toughest cases, they backed off.

EC: Mr. Boehme, yes, we have him here. Pretty near wore out.

Begin this at the head. Very poor capillary circulation through the whole body, especially near the head and facial muscles and brain and head proper and all the whole head. Capillary circulation is very weak, you see, for the whole system shows it just as it is shown in the head. Down the spine, refractory, dorsal, lumbar, cervical and shows abnormal condition throughout the eighth dorsal, second lumbar. Stomach all swiveled up and the liver too large, much impurity of blood. Circulation is weak through the trunk, through the extremities. Nerves very good for the circulation, you know. Pretty good nerve, pretty good willpower. This condition of the whole body is brought about by the whole system being run down, wore out, from lack of nutriment. Supply to the rest of the system from the stomach itself. Lack of the stomach in itself to supply the quantity needed by the system; the building material for the bone, muscle, nerve, for the blood, brain, for each different organism in itself. Supply from what is taken in by the digestion carried on in the stomach itself. Here we lack the amount of nutriment to carry all this. Calcium, iron, dirt—need more.

The impoverished condition of the rest of the system depends on this, you see, from the condition we have here in the stomach now. We destroy this and we see it is gradually impoverished. Thus, we find the whole system here depended on what is taken in here. If you don't get enough into the stomach to supply life we don't have it. He has been able to take it. It hurts, it don't hurt his head, his stomach hurt, wore out, needs a new one to rebuild this one and you cannot put a new one in it. To rebuild first cleanse with water. Wash it clean, thoroughly fill the system with water—pure water—and we take a light diet (not flesh, but cereals and vegetables), until the system is thoroughly cleaned and take iron and calcium. A reaction from the blood to the lungs and get a fuller capillary circulation. Digitalis and strychnine begin to supply the need. It is wore out, and get enough into the stomach to cleanse it thoroughly.

Boehme obtained another reading a few months later. Before we gave this reading, a gentleman from the press came in. He informed me that his name was Roswell Field of the *Chicago Examiner* and he wanted an interview. It was the first time I ever was interviewed by one of the big Chicago papers.

13

CHICAGO, 1911: EXAMINED BY THE *EXAMINER*

Roswell Field was the brother of Marshall Field, a big businessman of Chicago. Roswell worked for the *Chicago Examiner*, a paper owned by Mr. Randolph Hearst. He did some interviews while he was in town and reported two or three articles for his newspaper. The first article ran on the front page with a picture of me with my baby, Hugh Lynn, and another picture of me giving a reading for Mr. Boehme, with my father standing beside me asking the questions, and the stenographer taking it down.[1] This is what the Chicago newspaper said:

PSYCHIST DIAGNOSES AND CURES PATIENTS IGNORANT OF MEDICINE, TURNS HEALER IN TRANCE
Kentuckian New
Puzzle for Physicians
Admits He Can Remember
Nothing That Occurs in
Hypnotic Sleep

———

Solves Murder Mystery

———

Remarkable and Successful
Treatments Are Sworn To in Affidavits

———

By Roswell Field

———

[1] Hugh Lynn was five years old when the photo of him as an infant appeared in the *Examiner*. By this time Gertrude was six weeks away from delivering another child. Tom Sugrue reported in *There Is a River* that Field's stories about Cayce ran in all the Hearst newspapers, from New York to Los Angeles.

HOPKINSVILLE, Ky., Feb. 18—"You have before you Mr. August Boehme of 632 Overton Street, Newport, Ky. Go over him carefully, examine him thoroughly and tell us what his condition is now."

So spoke the "suggester," the father of Edgar Cayce, Jr., the auto-hypnotist, or psychic diagnostician, to the man lying in a trance before him. Very slowly came the reply from the sleeping body.

"Mr. August Boehme of 632 Overton Street, Newport, Ky. Yes, we have him here. We have had him before. His condition here is much improved along the circulation, through the digestion, etc., etc."

But I am beginning at the wrong end of the story. Who is Edgar Cayce, Jr., and why should he, in a hypnotic condition, be interrogated as to the unseen Mr. Boehme of Newport? That is the question that is exciting the people of his town, perturbing the doctors and delighting the spiritualists, the psychologists and all other seekers after the truth if truth there is in the occult.

Tobacco War at Hopkinsville

Far back in the mental recesses there is a lurking memory of Hopkinsville as once a center of sensations in which the famous Joe Mulhatton figured. There is a haunting recollection that in this pretty town first appeared the only original seven-legged calf, together with other prizes, the delight of Mr. Barnum's professional life.

There was a genuine sensation two years ago when the Night Riders swooped down on the town and suburbs, for Hopkinsville is the heart of a great tobacco raising country, and the tobacco war is a distinct part of martial history. But all these manifestations, great or trivial, have not the flavor of mystery and amazement caused by Edgar Cayce, Jr., farmer's son, photographer and psychic diagnostician.

And I am going to tell you his story as nearly as possible as he told it to me.

Near the end of Main Street in Hopkinsville, at the side of

a narrow flight of stairs, is the sign, "Cayce Studio." At the head of the stairs are two doors, one of them leading directly into a photography establishment, the other indicating a suite of rooms on the glass entrance of which is painted "Edgar Cayce, Jr., Psychic Diagnostician." Know then at the outset that the photographer and the psychic diagnostician are identical.

Possessed Psychic Powers

Locally for six or seven years, more or less nationally for perhaps four or five months, the fame of Edgar Cayce has been extending. It was rumored that although a simple, easygoing modest young man, with very little education, he possessed marvelous psychic powers. He was enabled to demonstrate that while in a trance, a cataleptic state, or whatever you may choose to call it, he departed from himself, became seemingly another person, could bring before his mental vision people a hundred, a thousand, three thousand miles away, and without the slightest previous knowledge of their physical condition, diagnose their cases and prescribe treatment for their ailments as his extraordinary mental sight directed.

More than this, he would talk in the parlance of the medical profession, discourse with a marvelous knowledge of anatomy and physiology, and make his diagnoses with extraordinary quickness and accuracy.

When the doctors at the homes of the patients made their own diagnoses, they were compelled to admit that Cayce had not merely corroborated their own conclusions, but had given suggestions which had escaped them.

Called Fake by Doctors

Doctors are a very ethical lot of gentlemen, and do not approve of such dabbling with the black art. So many of them, while openly wondering, declared that Cayce was a fake—but how and where? To conclude this imperfect introduction, it is necessary to say that when Cayce came out of his trance he was

neither doctor nor diagnostician; he was merely a simple
farmer's boy, a photographer, if you please, who wouldn't
know a solar plexus nerve from a capillary circulation. He says
so himself, and I take his word for it cheerfully

As I was only mildly interested in the photographer, but
much so in the psychical gentleman, I turned from the studio
and sought the diagnostician. I found him with his father sitting in a reception room, apparently "killing time" in the most
approved Kentucky fashion. His appearance was neither con-
spicuously encouraging nor disappointing. His photograph,
which is an admirable one, bears out the impression of a tall,
slender young man, with good, honest eyes, sufficiently wide
apart, a high forehead and just the ordinary features.

He admitted that he is thirty-three years of age, although
he does not look over twenty-five, and he told me how the
Cayces came from France many years ago, and how one of
his grandfathers married an Irish girl, thus showing the possible confusion of Cayce for Casey, pronounced exactly alike.
He was born in Christian County, where his father was born
also, and the Cayces have been Kentuckians for a hundred
years.

Mr. Field then reported how the phenomenon was discovered when I had aphonia and used it to recover my voice. He
asked me: "Didn't it occur to you to use this power for your
own advantage?"

I replied: "No, sir, I was ashamed of it. It seemed to me
that I ought not to be exhibiting myself in such a way."

Field asked how I happened to take up the psychic diagnosis seriously. I told him about my father's cousin who was
an invalid whom I had diagnosed. "He used to tell me that
God had given me a gift, which I should use for the benefit
of my fellow creatures. I was always ready to do what I could
for sick people, but I couldn't quite bring myself to take up
the work as a business. I suppose I was still ashamed. Yes, I
went into frequent trances for the benefit of local physicians,
and I found that the 'sleeps' did not hurt me."

"Do you mean to say that the trances do not affect you nervously?" he asked.

"On the contrary, they seem to do me good. I always feel refreshed and better when I get up. But I have an idea this is because I am really doing good for somebody else, or think I am. And the only times I ever felt languid or depressed were when I was gratifying idle curiosity or doing something I felt I shouldn't have done. In those days the doctor would ask me to consider three or four cases during one sleep, but now I take only one at a time or three a day."

When the reporter asked me how I accounted for my power, I told him: "I don't account for it. I don't know anything about it. I simply know that they show me the copy when I get up, and it's all Greek to me."

He asked if I'd done any other kind of psychic work.

"Yes, but I don't like it. I really think that if I were to trifle with this gift, God would take it away from me."

Somebody in the room mentioned the Canada murder case, which happened when I was in Bowling Green. Field asked me to tell him about it.

"A friend of mine there was from Canada, and his father sent him a newspaper containing a murder mystery. A girl had been found dead in a house, and her sister was shrieking hysterically, but unable then, or later, to say anything about it. My friend asked me if I could solve the mystery.

"I went to sleep and described the murder as I saw it. The two girls had quarreled about a man, and one of the girls shot her sister and threw the pistol down the bathroom drain. I was able to repeat the conversation of the two girls, to describe the pistol, and to tell the police where to look for it. The plumbing was of the old-fashioned kind, and the pistol had gone way down into the sewer, where it had lodged. They found it at the spot I indicated. They also told the girl the conversation as I had repeated it, and she owned up to the murder. The Canadian people sent me the reward advertised, but my wife wouldn't let me keep it. She said it was blood money. And I never needed money so much in my life."

Field wrote:

This impressed me as a pretty good story for a February morning, and I was in the humor for more. So I got out of him the story of his prediction of the death of President Spencer of the Southern Railroad, which was afterward corroborated by citizens.

Cayce, in all his talk with me, betrayed nothing more than a passing interest in his accomplishment . . . He betrayed no feeling of animosity toward any of the doctors who do not subscribe to his feats, and, in short, manifested, so far as I could see, the greatest indifference to opinion which merely reflected on his power.

It was about the time when he was to diagnose the condition of a gentleman from Newport with which this story opens, and I was glad of the opportunity to witness the modus operandi. The sleeping room, if we may call it such, is just off the reception room. It is a small but well-lit room, and Cayce smiled when I asked him if I shouldn't put out the electric light which shone in his eyes and would drive the average human being to the verge of frenzy.

A long, high couch is placed in the middle of the room with a chair and a table for the stenographer at its side. Cayce takes off his coat, waistcoat, necktie, and collar and lies flat on his back on the couch. The stenographer seats herself at the left, and Cayce's father stands at his right. It was 4:15 when Cayce stretched himself on the couch, lying flat on his back with his hands folded on his stomach. He was wide awake but entirely free from restlessness.

In four minutes his eyelids began to droop and his father repeated a formula, somewhat after this fashion: "Edgar, you are going to sleep. You are in perfect health. Your pulse is normal. Your respiration is as it should be and you are in every respect a well man."

Two minutes later his eyes closed and his father said: "Edgar, you are now asleep." Then the following inquiries and answers are found in the appended stenographic report. The psychic voice at first was low and feeble, but it grew stronger, until toward the end it was the normal voice of a man awake.

The questioning lasted about seven minutes, when, with the

final "No," the father said, repeating the former assurance of excellent physical condition, "Edgar, you will wake up in one minute and twenty seconds." I took out my watch, and at the time specified he opened his eyes and rose from the couch, evidently not the worse for his experience. It seemed to me nothing more than a short, healthful nap, and I could discern nothing unusual in his manner at any time.

They say that occasionally he comes out of the sleep exhausted and nervous, but that is only when his visions have been peculiarly trying and unpleasant. So far as I could observe there was no manifestation of the rigor and coldness often associated with the cataleptic state. It would be a joy indeed to snatch forty winks with such ease and seemingly beneficial results.

The stenographer transcribed her notes immediately after the diagnosis. I give them just as they come from her, following copy, spelling, and terms. As I remember the words, the transcription is faithful. It has been urged, and doubtless properly, that many mistakes are made either by Cayce's manner of talking or by the stenographer, but physicians who are unhampered by prejudice say that this is natural and excusable.

This is the report of Miss Faxon, the stenographer, omitting the father's formula:

This psychic reading given by Edgar Cayce in Hopkinsville, Kentucky, this 16th day of February, 1911. Present: Edgar Cayce; L. B. Cayce, Conductor; Katherine Faxon, Steno.

LBC: You have before you Mr. August Boehme, of Newport, Kentucky. Go over him carefully, examine him thoroughly, and tell us what his condition is now.

EC: Yes, we have him here; we have had him before. His condition here is much improved along the circulation, through the digestion, that is, the trouble we have had here in the digestion tract in the stomach itself, through the duodenum, through the effect of the pancrean juices on to the digestion, has been much improved by the treatment, both from the exterior and from the internal treatment, interior. What has been taken into the stomach has assimilated well, has assimilated with the juices made by the stomach itself, or by the body itself.

We find the capillary circulation, or that given out by the lymphatics, the action of the sympathetic nerve force in the system, is very much in the same condition as we have had before. We have the closeness of the skin; we have the pains here to the head at times; a filling up of the stomach, or that is, from the sympathetics of these actions impairing this, between the sympathetic, and cerebrospinal nerve force of the system, as it were a disconnection here along the regions of the solar plexus nerve at the stomach; they coming in conjunction then with these forces of the cerebrospinal and sympathetic nerve system, have produced on the system, this lackness of capillary circulation or lymphatic circulation. This, being carried to the extent it has, has produced then a condition in itself of closeness of the system, or lack of fat in the body.

The condition in itself has been improved here, in the stomach, but the lack of the connection between these, has made some nervous effect on the body . . .

Q. What treatment would you prescribe for this now, to relieve these conditions?

A. Keep what he has, in the system, that is, more of it, as we have taken it along into the intestinal tract of the stomach, but create a unison between the sympathetic and cerebrospinal nervous system, either by electrical force to these nerves, as along the spine and over the body, or by manipulation and resting of the muscular force of the body, by the hands. Perhaps in either way.

Q. Any other treatment?

A. No.

(signed) Katherine Faxon,
stenographer

This reporter from Chicago wrote another article about the case of Mr. Lucien Davis, a prominent man in town who was a patient of Dr. Ketchum. This is what his article said:

One of the most remarkable cures the young man has effected was that of Lucien H. Davis, a prominent politician and wealthy contractor. Mr. Davis had been ill for some time and a number of physicians had told him he was a victim of appendicitis. Davis was about to undergo an operation when Cayce was called in and diagnosed the case as one of spinal trouble.

The diagnosis and treatment from a stenographer's report, incorporated into a sworn affidavit, follow:

At the first cervical vertebrae, the second to the eighth dorsal, second and third lumbar, we find lesions which influence this case through the ganglia on either side, or through the sympathetic nervous system; in the region of the tenth and eleventh dorsal, there is a lesion that affects directly the solar plexus, which lies immediately behind the stomach—in other words we have spinal congestion.

We have in this case poor excretion of all waste products due to the overtaxed condition of the whole nervous system; all reactive forces are now affecting directly kidneys, liver and spleen. The whole system is easily irritated, pains shift from one part of the body to another, caused by lack of nerve force.

This condition has been brought about by long-continued overwork, overtaxed condition of all the animal forces—in other words, everything has been running at too high a tension. We find the slowing of the circulation subnormal pulse and sub-normal temperature. We find a lack of leukocytes; the spleen, also is not performing its functions properly; its functioning ability has been overtaxed, consequently inaction.

Treatment is outlined which included electrical treatments and adjustments for the lesions. Definite reference is made to the appendix as follows:

Trouble in the region of the appendix, is due to a lesion in the spine. Subcostal nerve being irritated at its root or origin produces pain and irritation at its distribution, which is in the caecum and vicinity of appendix; no organic trouble, purely functional.

It is necessary only to add that Mr. Davis did not die 'within six weeks' as previously announced from time to time, but got well under the treatment and is now extremely alive and existing satisfactorily to himself.

After Mr. Field returned to Chicago, I received a request from his managing editor that I be the guest of the newspaper in Chicago, and they would make arrangements for a demonstration. So Mr. Noe, my father, and I went to Chicago and were quartered at the LaSalle Hotel with one or two people to act as escorts, or guards, I do not know which. We were told arrangements were being made for the deans of some of the schools to see a demonstration.

After three or four days, about 10:30 or 11:00 o'clock one evening, we were told they had been unable to make connections but they had three physicians there, and if I would agree, one of them would present the case of one of his patients. They asked the physicians present if they would allow their names to be used if it was a success. They said no, and they also refused to let a physician we might select examine the patient. There was much discussion back and forth.

They insisted that I try to locate a missing woman named Dorothy Arnold and unravel several other mysteries that were troubling them locally at the time. My father was very insistent that we not attempt anything of that kind, but several of the reporters argued that I owed it to them, after all the newspaper notoriety they had given me. About two o'clock the next morning I finally agreed to take the case for the doctor.

When we had finished the reading and I was conscious, one physician asked the other if that was a description of his case and what was the matter with his patient.

"From what you have heard, what would you say was the matter?" he replied.

"I would say there wasn't very much in the beginning, but you have allowed the case to gradually develop into locomotary ataxia."

"That's what he has now," he replied.

The third physician insisted that I attempt information for a very close relative of his. This man was a specialist, I learned later. Very little or nothing, I am told, was gotten on the case.

The reporters listened at the doctor's description, wrote it up, and asked him to sign it. He absolutely refused. The next morning the headlines on the second section were, "He Came, We Saw, But He Did Not Conquer." This article said I claimed many things and refused to do this, that, or the other; the doctors had said there was nothing whatever in what was given; the stenographers had failed to write anything at all, saying it was such gibberish that was not understandable and was a lot of bunk.

That afternoon's *Chicago Examiner*, however, had an article from Hopkinsville containing some fifteen or sixteen affidavits from individuals who claim to have been helped by my readings. That so many thought it was not bunk made me think there must be something to it.

14

FAMILY CRISES: LIFE AND DEATH

About this time my wife, who had been ill for several months, began to get very much worse.[1] Several physicians were attending her. The one in charge called me to his office after she had had a very bad night and said:

"Cayce, I'm sorry to tell you, old man, but your wife can't live another week. There's absolutely nothing we know in medical science that can do her any good, in her present condition. You know she has tuberculosis. One lung is choked. No air has been going through it for months. The other is now affected and you must know from the hemorrhages that it is bleeding. With her high temperature and with her little resistance, she cannot hold out. She is very weak, and the hemorrhages are very bad. She cannot stand another one of them. If there's anything in this monkey business you've been doing with these fellows around here, you'd better try it on your wife."

Up to that time I had not given a reading for a member of my immediate family, except myself. I asked my wife's mother and her aunt, Dr. House's wife, to talk to Dr. Jackson. He told them the same thing. They suggested, "Let's try a reading." Of course, I knew the conditions were rather desperate.

At some point we all have to face our own deeds, our own conduct before our fellow man; for we must surely meet our

—

[1] Gertrude had given birth to a son, Milton Porter, on March 28, 1911. But the child developed whooping cough and died about six weeks later. Mr. Cayce wrote nothing about this family tragedy but is said to have felt considerable guilt for not having given a reading in time to diagnosis the child's condition. Gertrude was ill for months after the baby's death, and by late summer her condition had become perilous.

own selves often in the lives of individuals whom we have influenced by our activity. But will anyone ever understand what it meant to me to know that I was taking the life of one near and dear to me in my own hands and that the very force and power that I had been wishy-washy with for years must now be put to a crucial test?[2]

I asked physicians and druggists, and sent for one specialist, to listen to the information and to tell me if there was any hope. When I awoke from this experience, the specialist told me, "Most remarkable! Most wonderful lecture I've ever heard on tuberculosis, and I've lectured at home and abroad, but I don't see how she may be helped. May I see the case?"

The druggist said, "Well, you offered a remedy—but I don't believe it will compound." But he said he would try it and see. It did compound, and with the first dose she took there were no more hemorrhages. Perhaps she wasn't ever going to have any more anyway. In a few days there was no fever. Possibly the fever had already broken, I don't know. Within two weeks she was decidedly on the mend, though it was several months before she was able to go about her household duties.

The results were all one could ask, far beyond what anyone had ever dreamed. Then I began to think in real earnestness, for I had been told by some that I was all right when I was asleep but was too big a fool when awake to ever be worth anything to anyone to make money. Perhaps I am so even now.

I laid it all aside again and went back to picture making. But it would not rest. Ever since that day, when the one so close to me was given back to me, I have looked upon all psychic phenomena with a different attitude. For after all, we come to this: no matter what the object in question, until it strikes home, it is a thing far off. For the Savior must become our personal Savior before He, to us as individuals, is *the* Savior. Just so, we may bicker and haggle and say all manner

[2] Mr. Cayce evidently felt like surgeons who refuse to operate on members of their own family, preferring that a more detached colleague take the case.

of hard things about anything we observe, but when it reaches in and gives ease and comfort to our physical bodies, and to our loved ones, then it becomes something worthwhile; and no matter what others may say, to us it is the *real* thing.

A few days after the reading for my wife, in January or February 1911, I was at home with her. We were living at Gertrude's mother's cottage on East Seventh Street. The house had been redecorated a few months before. It was beautifully finished on the inside. All the woodwork had been grained like the floors. The outside was painted white and trimmed in green. A bookcase was in the hallway, the living room to the right as you entered the hall, the bedroom to the left, where Gertrude was ill.

One afternoon our doorbell rang. I went to the door and there stood a rather large, very imposing but brusque-looking gentleman.

"Is this Cayce?" he asked.

"Yes, sir."

"Well, I'm Munsterberg from Harvard. I'm here to expose you. There's been entirely too much written about you in the newspapers lately for this not to be a fake. I've exposed more fake mediums than any man in the country. Is this where you do your work?"

I told him no, that I had an office in town.

"Well, what sort of a cabinet do you use?"

All this time he was advancing into the house and I turned toward the living room. When I said, "I have no cabinet," he said:

"Then what is your modus operandi?"

I had no idea what he was talking about.

"Well, how do you do it?" he asked.

I told him I would just as soon lie on the floor, or outside in the street, or in the yard, as anywhere else. I did not know what it was, and I could only judge it by its results. "I am becoming convinced that the preparations have to be as much in the individual seeking the information as in myself. I do not claim anything for myself. The more I have seen of the readings the less I know. I would *like* you to investigate it, and if I am fooling myself or my fellow man, please tell me. Suppose, Doctor, that you see Mr. and Mrs. Dietrich. Suppose you see many of the individuals for whom this information has been given. Here is my wife who is very ill now. Would you like to see what was said? Would you like to examine her? Would you like to see what the physicians say about the compound suggested for her improvement? Would you like to see what has been prepared for her from the suggestions? The results are the only proofs I have. From my experiences with some people, however, I know there is something wrong, else there would not be such a confusion in my own mind. What it is, I do not know. Possibly it is in myself."

I produced a copy of the reading for Gertrude from the bookcase, asked him to read it, and if he was a doctor to examine her and see what he thought. But he informed me he was not an M.D.

Then he asked me about my education, what I had read, and went to the bookcase. There was a very good set of E. P. Roe, a few magazines, and quite a number of books of current literature, as I had made it a rule to give Gertrude a book each month of the bestsellers during the time I worked in the bookstore. He pulled out many of these, leaving some of them where they fell on the floor. He left in about thirty or forty minutes, telling me, "I will look in on you again."

The next morning when I arrived at the office, my father and the stenographer were there. I asked my father if there was an appointment that morning. He said there was a man coming from Cincinnati on the ten o'clock train. While I was telling my father of my experience the day before, Dr. Munsterberg arrived, wearing a great heavy coat, for this morning there was a little snow on the ground. He took a seat in one of the large rockers, had little to say, merely observing my father, the stenographer, and someone who had come in—I don't remember whether it was Dr. Ketchum or Mr. Noe. He looked at many of the reports which were then being made by the stenographers.

I went into the studio, as I had some plates to look after. I was printing proofs from these plates when my father called to me that Mr. Bomie had arrived for his reading.

Mr. Bomie talked with my father, who was conducting the readings at that time. Dr. Munsterberg, still sitting in the rocker, had not removed his overcoat, though the room was sufficiently heated. I asked if he cared to witness the reading. He said:

"You're going to lie on that table?"

"Yes, sir," I said.

"Well, I can see it from here, and hear all I want to hear," he said.

He preferred to sit at the door where he could see all the proceedings—yet not be in the room. I lay down on the elevated couch and gave the reading. When we had finished and I came out, Munsterberg called to Mr. Bomie—he didn't rise from his chair—and asked:

"Where did you hear of Cayce?"

Mr. Bomie replied, "I read of him in the newspaper, the *Cincinnati Star*, I think it was."

"How much of your condition have you told Cayce?"

"Nothing whatever. I never saw him before my first visit in my whole life. I only read something about him in the paper—I'd been a sufferer for a long time with no results, so I came to see him."

"Well, what do you think of what he just told you?"

"I think it is a better description of myself than I could possibly make."

"Are you convinced?"

"I certainly am!"

"So am I! You do whatever he suggested. It may help where everything else has failed."

Turning to me, he said, "Cayce, I would like to know more about this. I've never encountered anything like it. If you never do another case other than the little Dietrich child, your life has not been in vain. My opinion is that you are tied up with the wrong bunch. Keep your feet on the ground. Do not try to force anything. Keep just as sincere as you are at present. Be a constant listener to the voice within. I believe you will go far. You will hear from me again."

But I never did.

I continued to read for Dr. Ketchum's patients.[3] But one day I awoke from a reading with the realization that something was wrong. Unknown to me, my associates felt we should turn to making money.[4] Something was being misrepresented to me, for the old trouble that I had experienced during the latter part of my stay in Bowling Green seemed to be coming back. Immediately, I tried to get in touch with some of the people for whom we supposedly had been giving readings. Some of them informed me that they had not requested or received readings. When I faced my partners with this information, they said we had to make money faster. They had been getting information on the horse races. I told them I was through, that I could not go on.

Several months after I felt Mr. Noe had abused the privileges that had been given him, my father, being a party to the contract, brought suit to try to make *both* of us carry out our contract. The case was tried before a judge who had given me a written opinion that the contract was legal, and who had later offered to buy the contract for several thousand dollars from Mr. Noe. But now this judge ruled from his bench that the contract was illegal and dismissed the case.[5] Something within me at the time made me rise and ask the judge if I might speak without being ruled in contempt of court. He said I might speak. That same something within me compelled me to say, "For the lie you have this day enacted, the worms of your body will eat you up while you are yet alive!"

In less than two years this was proved true, and he lived two years in this agony. Possibly it was only a coincidence—

---

[3] Notes by Miss Addie Pool, one of his stenographers during this period, indicate that she took approximately 150 readings under contract with Ketchum, Noe, and Cayce.

[4] Ketchum said "people would come to him and want him to locate a gold mine or an oil well or play the horses—we tried to keep this type of person away from him, and in this we were fairly successful, because he was utterly uninterested in such things."

[5] Hopkinsville historian William Turner reports that the breach of contract suit was settled out of court in March 1913.

possibly it was because he was playing with fire.

After that, I took a job working as a photographer in Selma, Alabama. My wife's health had not improved sufficiently for her to accompany me. During the next several months, two or three readings were given on my wife's condition. A physician was present, and some new friends I had made, but I did not talk about it very much, as I was trying my best to determine in my own mind whether I should forget about everything of the kind, or whether I should devote more time and thought to the readings.

15

SELMA, 1912–1919: CAYCE ART COMPANY

I had much time to myself after moving to Alabama, as there was little business in my studio, my family was still at home, and I had not yet become acquainted with many people in Selma. I often reviewed my life's experiences to that time in a very prayerful, meditative mood.

One afternoon when I had been praying practically all day, and it had been raining steadily—it was very necessary for some finances to come from somewhere in order to meet my daily needs—I heard someone coming up the steps to the studio, which was on the second floor. I wondered, "Could this be an answer to my prayer? Am I going to be shown a very conclusive demonstration that God can and does use unseen channels to show us the way?" An elderly, little lady, all wet and bedraggled, her poor little bonnet sticking to her face, appeared. As she pulled it off and brushed her hair back, she said, "Mister, do you make large pictures here?" and I said, "Yes, ma'am."

She fumbled in her dress and brought out a little tintype. "I have a picture of my boy who is in Alaska. I would like to have the very best picture you can possibly make of this."

I looked at the little faded print and told her what I thought could be done. She said, "Well, I will be very glad for you to do that, and I will pay you now if you will get this check cashed for me. This is from my boy. I have been to everyone in town, but nobody will cash it. I don't know what to do."

I took the check and asked her to wait a moment while I went down to the bank. Mr. Armstrong, the banker, told me, "Cayce, that check has been here three times today already. I am sure it is good, and I suspect this poor mother needs it. If you will endorse the check I will give you the money." She had already endorsed it.

I told him, "Well, you know I haven't any money here."

"No, but you and I together will do this little mother a good turn," he said.

The delight expressed in her face as I gave her the money would be hard for anyone to forget. She paid me for her picture, which enabled me to take care of my obligations for the moment. Then she told me of her little girl, who was afflicted with infantile paralysis, and I in turn told her of some experiences I had had in the years before I came to Selma. She asked me to give her little girl a reading.

A few days later she brought her daughter in. I got Mr. Alfred D. Butler, one of the boys in my Sunday school class, to conduct the reading. The child had a very crooked foot and limb. One physician in town agreed to give his services to see whether what was suggested in the information would help. In less than a year the little girl's limb was almost perfectly normal. And as long as I lived in Alabama there was scarcely a week that some member of this family did not come in to see me; and they never came without bringing something as a love offering and saying "Thank you."

The father of the physician who took care of this little girl had been quite ill for some time. The trouble on the side of his head had been diagnosed as cancer. He asked if I would see what a reading would suggest for him. The suggestion was given for a compound, which has proven most helpful in hundreds of cases since then, though its preparation and combination in many instances has been changed for individual use. In this particular case the sore healed and never gave him any more trouble. He died several years later from another condition entirely, or was so diagnosed by his son and others.

In the latter part of that year I had a request from a lady in Lexington, Kentucky, whose husband had met Professor Dietrich. She was very anxious that I visit her home to give her a reading. After two or three letters were exchanged, I finally agreed to go. I arrived at her home without being able to induce anyone to accompany me, as I had no money to pay anyone else's train fare. The lady who had called me was in the most pitiful condition of anyone I had ever seen. She could not move hand or foot, and appeared to be very badly swollen. It all seemed so hopeless to me, but I told her and her husband, as well as the physician present, some of my experiences throughout the years, especially of my wife's condition. Gertrude's healing, it seemed, was of special interest to them, as they had heard considerable from Professor Dietrich and others from the western part of the state, and insisted that I try to give the reading. I described to them as best I could what had been told me of how Mr. Layne, my father, and others had conducted the readings, and agreed to let the husband conduct this one. Afterward, they seemed well pleased with the information.

After returning to Selma, I had a letter from the husband, asking that I make a check reading. This information insisted that she was somewhat improved, but there had been a substitution for one of the ingredients in a compound by the doctor who prepared it, and that it had produced a bad rash over the body, but if they would change this she would improve steadily. About a month later I received a wire asking that I come once again to Lexington.

When I arrived in the home I was never more astonished in my life than to see this lady, who had looked so hopeless. She was sitting in a chair and looking very comfortable. Her feet and lower limbs seemed very much better, not swollen so badly. She asked the nurse to loosen her hair and give her the comb and brush. After she had done her hair, she told me, "A few days ago I was able to feed myself for the first time in three years, and it has been five years since I even attempted to raise my hands high enough to do up my own hair, and I wanted you to see the improvement."

About eight or nine months later she invited me to her home to a reception which was given for her birthday, and to walk across the floor with her. During this party I met David E. Kahn, who lived next door to her. The Kahn family invited me over for a visit, and my first evening in the Kahns' home will always be remembered. We discussed and recounted many of my experiences far into the night. I discussed with

Mother Kahn my slant on life and the many changes in my outlook produced by my various experiences in relation to others who sought information through the readings.

She asked for a reading for Dave's little brother Leon, who had been injured in an accident. Some help was promised, provided they could get the wholehearted cooperation of one who could give the suggested treatment. This was never accomplished. Very little help was obtained for the young man, and none permanently, with the result that he died.

I spent several days at that time in their home. The sincerity manifested by Dave, and especially the consideration and friendly advice given by Mother Kahn, have continued ever since to endear them to my heart and mind.

The first mental and spiritual reading, as they are called now, was given on one of these visits to Mother Kahn's home. It was conducted by Dave himself, and it was for him. He acted in the capacity of questioner and also stenographer, for he took down the information in longhand. Many of our experiences together since that day in many parts of the country are a matter of record with him, and how we were guided by the readings, though I have no copies in my possession of information obtained at that time.

In other readings received it was suggested that in a few years there would be a mighty change in the country, and that as conditions developed Dave would leave home; his work would be in a line in which he had not been trained but which would affect his life throughout; it would be well for him to make preparations; that his family would be very much averse to this change, yet it would be better for him, as it would better equip him for experiences to come later.

Later that year Gertrude was well enough to bring our boy, Hugh Lynn, and join me in Selma. In February of 1913 Hugh Lynn had a very bad accident. He had seen me make flash pictures in the studio. Some people came in one evening with several pet squirrels. I had made a picture of them, using flash powder. Through negligence I left a quantity of flash powder in a box on the camera stand. The next morning, as the maid was cleaning up, she knocked this box off on the floor. The boy found it. He said later he intended to scare the maid. He struck a match as she came down the stairs, and the head of the match fell in the box of powder. He was bending over it, and the flash and burn got him just above the nostril. There was very little hair left on the front of his head. It was literally blown and burned out.

I rushed downstairs when I heard the explosion and his scream and took him to the doctor. On examination, he informed me that it was quite hopeless with both eyes. My son was blind.

Hugh Lynn suffered great pain and agony. By the fifth or sixth day several doctors and a specialist had seen him. I was advised that if they were to save his left eye it would be necessary to remove the right one. Hugh Lynn's Sunday school teacher was sitting by the bed trying to quiet him, and the doctor told her to acquaint him with what it was necessary for the doctors to do. To the surprise of everyone, the little fellow raised on his elbow and said to the doctor, "Don't take out my eyes. When my Daddy's asleep, he is the best doctor in the world. He'll tell you what to do, and you'll do it, won't you, Doctor?" Neither my wife nor I had considered it practical or reasonable to attempt a reading. But after his request, a reading was taken—and the suggestion was made to change the treatment somewhat, to add certain things. With the first application of tannic acid packs on his eyes, the child asked the nurse, "Is this Daddy's medicine? I'm easy now."

A few days later I saw all of the eyelid slough off, and the doctor who was present said, "Cayce, it does look so hopeless." But the child insisted he was feeling better and didn't have any more pain.

In twelve days from the beginning of the treatment, a scale, as it were, dropped from his eyes as he got up one morning and he screamed out, "I can see!"

Of course, much care was taken in protecting his eyes for a year or more, but his eyes healed completely, and by the time he was twenty-five years old there was not even a scar—

unless he got very mad, and then it was livid across his face and forehead.[1]

A year later, while making some photographs in a nearby town, I had quite an attack of cramps and nausea, which was diagnosed by our family physician, Dr. Gay, as appendicitis. He gave me some treatment for a few days. I improved somewhat and was able to keep going. Then I decided, if I really believed in the readings, I had better get one for myself. The information still insisted that an operation was necessary and should be performed immediately. That evening I called the doctor again and showed him the information. He examined me and carried me to the hospital that night. The next morning they performed the operation. It was said that I had a very bad case, which evidently had existed for several years. So, this was a verification of information given in Bowling Green many years before.

The latter part of that year the president of the Sunday school class of which I was a teacher came in one evening and requested a reading for his sister, as the doctors insisted she was mentally ill and there was no hope. Her family and physicians were present, though she was not even in the city at the time. The reading suggested that there was an imbedded wisdom tooth causing the greater trouble, and that the removal of this tooth would clear up conditions in a short while. A hurried trip was made to verify this condition, the tooth was located and removed. A few months later the young lady was herself again and in training for special work.

Another member of my Sunday school class, Mr. Jones, had a good deal of trouble with loss of weight, and complained of headaches; seemingly nothing had done him any good. He asked that I give a reading for him. The treatment outlined for

---

[1] Hugh Lynn Cayce, in *About My Father's Business* by A. Robert Smith, remembered eating "lots of grapes," as prescribed by his reading. "I thought Dad was a miracle man, the most important person in the world. If you can imagine being blind for weeks, and having doctors tell you that you aren't going to see with but one eye and the other one must be removed, perhaps you can understand why I had no trouble believing in my father."

him proved most beneficial. A month or so later he got a reading for his oldest boy which straightened out the lad. Later he had information for his wife and younger son. All of these proved to be very satisfactory in every way. As he said to me, "A reading a year keeps the whole family in good shape, with no need of worrying about their health."

In the spring of 1915 I had a return of my trouble, aphonia. The specialist there declared it to be purely psychopathic, and he solicited the aid of a hypnotist who was one of the county officials. This man, on experimenting, declared that I was very susceptible to suggestion, but he had never seen a case exactly like mine. While he could control me to the first stage of hypnotic influence, I seemed to take control of myself after that and he was not able to do anything other than suggest that I wake up.

My condition lasted for several months, and I remember one incident during the time that was a wonder to many people. The building in which I had my studio and apartment caught fire. They were all very sure the excitement would make me speak out, but it seemed to work just the opposite. I could say and do nothing except stand and look, wave my arms, run in and out, assisting the firemen to get things out.

One evening we were trying to get information for myself, as I had been feeling badly, besides the return of the aphonia. The conductor made a mistake in stating just where my body was located; giving the address of an office across the street. When the body was not located there, he asked that the office be described, and there came the statement that a man in the office had been short in his accounts with the government and was trying to get it straight. We had no intimation otherwise that such a thing had even been suspected, but in a few months it was discovered. Of course, the reading had nothing whatever to do with bringing about his questioning. When the correct address was given, my body was located. Apparently, when information is given for me, there has to be just as specific an address given as for anyone else seeking information, and my body isn't known from anyone else except by the suggestion.

One day a gentleman who was connected with the gas company came in and told me he had been a student of suggestive therapeutics and the like for some time. He had been in with some of the others watching the experiment. He said he would like to try a reading.

I am told that his suggestion was, "Now we are going rabbit hunting, and I want to you to call the dogs." Those who were present said I seemed to take on the air of one who was watching a chase and very soon began to whistle for the dogs and after a bit quieted down, and the suggestion was given that I would wake up feeling all right and be able to talk normally, which I did! This man also had a reading a little later for his boy, as the physician had declared he was tubercular. Under the suggested treatment, he got along nicely and was able to throw it off entirely.

This same man came to the studio one day almost out of breath. He had been running. "Cayce, do you want to save a woman's life? Down where I am boarding is a lady whom the doctors say is dying, and they have already left her with the nurse."

The reading suggested something which might be done immediately for relief, and pronounced the condition as the effects from pneumonia. When I was conscious again the man seemed quite excited. He said, "I have to go right now, but I must come back and tell you some of the things you gave that we weren't looking for."

That evening he came in and said, "Well, the patient is resting easy. A new doctor who has been called says she is out of danger and there is no reason why she shouldn't get along all right." She did and is still living.

Then he said, "What I wanted to tell you was, this morning in the reading you said, 'Do this (meaning what you had outlined, I suppose) and she will be all right, but the physician who has gone off and left her has only six months and six days to live.'"

Six months and six days after that time this physician dropped dead in front of his home. This was verified, for many knew of the prediction, if it might be called such.

In the early part of 1916 I was again called to Lexington

by Dave Kahn to give a reading for some of the people who had been present at the experiments during my previous visit. This proved to be a very satisfactory reading for a patient who had been pronounced a hopeless mental condition. He improved very fast, soon becoming well and strong,

During the same visit Dave asked questions as to what his life work would be. It was said that he would be away from the fold for some time; he would go across many waters; he would go in honor, come in honor, and there would be a change entirely in his surroundings and line of work when he settled again; but it was not intimated what would be the cause of his leaving or as to how long he would be away.

Just before war was declared between the United States and Germany in 1917, I received a wire from Dave in New York, asking that I tell him what he was doing and how he must proceed with his undertaking. The reading said that war would be declared, there would be a call for volunteers, establishment of training camps and the like; that he was already trying to use political influence, which would get him nowhere, but he should apply through the regular channels and he would be commissioned in a department where he might be of the most service and have a more agreeable situation for himself; and that in the training camp to which he would go, he should arrange entertainment for the troops.

It was some months before all this came about, but it did, and almost identically with what his reading outlined. In camp he spoke to some of his superior officers about the readings, and we had considerable correspondence and some very satisfactory exchange of ideas, eventually a reading for a professor of Howe School in Indiana, which proved to be very satisfactory. He reported aid coming to his family, where seemingly everything else had failed.

Some months later Dave was sent to Fort Worth, Texas. From there we received the request for information concerning his association with his superior officer. His reading said that he would not embark for many months, though they had already had orders to move, but when he did they would move to the East Coast and there he would have the opportunity either to remain in this country or go abroad with his division. It was recommended that by all means he should go. This offer would be made by his superior officer, who—though he expected to go—would *not* go abroad. This also came to pass and it was almost identical to the information in the reading.

Dave and I exchanged many letters while he was in France, and many people in various parts of the country wrote to me following the interest aroused by Dave's telling his experiences with the readings, as well as some of mine. One which seemed to be of particular interest was from a consul in Italy. A reading was given for him and his wife about his return to his post in Italy. A request came through this consul for a reading from one in the house of royalty. The letter was written in Italian, and of course I couldn't read it, as I didn't know any other language save American (I couldn't even say that I knew English).

I succeeded in getting a fruit vendor in Selma to translate it for me. He seemed very excited to find that someone of so high a position in his own country was writing to a little photographer in Alabama for information concerning his wife's physical condition. He was present when the information was given. To the astonishment of everyone, much of it was not understandable except to the fruit vendor, who declared it was given in Italian. The request was made that it be repeated in an understandable manner so that the stenographer could make a report to send to the individual, and this seemed to be most satisfactory.

Quite a number of requests locally and throughout the country came about this time. I was called to Washington to give information for one high in authority. This, I am sure, must have been at least interesting, as I was called a year or so later for the same purpose.[2]

My last experience with a return of aphonia was possibly

---

[2] Dave Kahn, in an oral history interview nearly fifty years later, said Mr. Cayce made trips to Washington because he had been "asked to give a reading on President Wilson." More details are found in the Appendix.

the most noteworthy. I do not know that I yet understand its whole import. This was the experience:

For about ten days I had been unable to speak above a whisper. I felt that if I were able to get myself into the sub-conscious state, possibly I could again find relief. It was Sunday afternoon. My wife sent the older boy for a walk with his younger brother,[3] who was then a very small baby. We retired to the bedroom, where I proceeded to put myself into the un-conscious state. The experience lasted possibly thirty minutes, and it is the only one where I have been able to recall anything that transpired. There have been quite a number of times when I have had dreams in such a state. Was this a dream?

Apparently, there was spread before me all the graveyards in the world. I saw nothing save the abode of what we call the dead, in all portions of the world. Then, as the scene shifted, the graves seemed to be centered around India, and I was told by a voice from somewhere, "Here you will know a man's religion by the manner in which his body has been disposed of."

The scene then changed to France, and I saw the soldiers' graves. Among them were the graves of three boys who had been in my Sunday school class. Then I saw the boys, not dead but alive. Each of them told me how they met their death—one in machine-gun fire, another in the bursting of a shell, the other in heavy artillery fire. Two gave me messages to tell their loved ones at home. They appeared much in the same way and manner as they did the day each came to bid me good-bye when they left for the army during World War I.

As the scene changed again, I apparently reasoned with myself "This is what is called spiritualism. Can it be true? Are all these we call dead yet alive in some other plane of expe-rience or existence? Could I see my own baby boy?" As if a canopy was raised, tier on tier of babies appeared. In the third or fourth row from the top, to the side, I recognized my own

---

[3] Gertrude gave birth to their third child, Edgar Evans, February 9, 1918.

child, Milton Porter, who had died as a baby some years before that. He knew me, even as I knew him. He smiled his recognition, but no word of any kind passed.

The scene changed and there appeared a lady friend who was being buried in the local cemetery during that same hour, someone I had known very well and from whom I had purchased many flowers that were distributed by the children in my Sunday school classes. She talked with me about the changes that we call death, saying that it was really a birth. She spoke especially about the effect that a gift of flowers has upon people and that they should be given in life rather than at funerals or in death. As for what they mean, she said flowers speak to the invalid, the shut-ins, and mean so little to those who have passed from the material to the spiritual plane. Then she said, "But to be material for the moment, some months ago someone left $2.50 with you for me. You are not aware of this having been done, and will find it in a drawer of your desk marked with the date it was paid, August 8th, and there are two paper dollars and a fifty-cent piece. See that my daughter receives this, for she will need it. Be patient with the children, they are gaining much."

Again the scene changed, and a man appeared who had been a fellow officer for years in the church of which I was a member. He spoke of his son, Malcolm, saying that he would no doubt return to his position in the local bank. But he said that Malcolm would rather accept an offer that would be made from a moving-picture house. Then he spoke about the affairs of the church, and I was physically conscious again.

When I awoke my voice was all right, I could talk normally, though my wife told me I had not said a word during the whole thirty minutes. After I told her about the dream, I went to look in the desk, and sure enough there was the envelope that the lady described. It had been received in August by one of the young ladies who had since left the studio (and this was in December).

The next day I had occasion to go to the bank, and the young man, Malcolm, took my deposit. When I asked when he had returned, he said last night. I asked if he expected to remain in the bank and he said he thought so. Then I told him I had something I would like to tell him, but that he could act as he felt right. He came to the studio within the hour, and I related to him the whole experience with his deceased father. Malcolm told me that on his way home from Washington he had stopped in Atlanta, where he had been approached by a friend who asked him to take over the management of a moving-picture theater, but that morning he had mailed a letter rejecting the offer. After hearing what his father said, however, he said he would immediately wire him accepting the job, which he did.

Whatever this experience meant, I do not know whether I have the whole interpretation. One thing I do know is that I have traveled in many portions of the country, north, south, east, and west. There are few, if any, cemeteries that do not appear familiar, so much so that when I see even a corner of one I can, with a few minutes' reflection, tell many intimate things about that particular cemetery. What was it all about? I do not know.

Some of the boys in my Sunday school class asked if I would undertake information as to just what might be expected in the affairs of the world. This was recorded on several dictaphone records. These were later destroyed by someone not knowing their meaning, after the young men who had hoped to preserve them had gone to war. This reading told about the breaking up of the western front in Europe, the fall of the Russian government, the rejection of religion that would come in Russia—but it stated that out of Russia would come a religion that would have a worldwide influence. This remains to be seen.

In December 1918 I received a request from a Mr. J. D. Thrash, who was a newspaper editor in Texas, asking for a physical reading, as well as some questions regarding business. Some letters passed before any information was given. Among these letters was one in which he asked for my birth date, saying he desired to have my horoscope cast. Soon after this I received several communications from astrologers telling me that on March 19, 1919, between 8:30 and 11:00 o'clock in the evening, I would be able to give a reading that would be of more interest to mankind as a whole than any I would be able to give during that year. This phase was so new to me that I think it bewildered rather than encouraged me. I was curious, however, and asked my wife to conduct this reading and present questions which we had prepared on the subject of astrology. I was asked to make this reading public. I did not care for notoriety, which I felt this would give, yet being curious and desiring to know what the reading would give at this time, I attempted it—and the following information (254–2) is the result:

You will have before you the body and enquiring mind of Edgar Cayce, and you will tell us how the psychic work is accomplished through this body, and will answer any other questions that I will ask you respecting this work.

EC: We have the body here—we have had it before. In this state the conscious mind is under subjugation of the subconscious or soul mind. The information obtained and given by this body is obtained through the power of mind over mind, or power of mind over physical matter, or obtained by the suggestion as given to the active part of the subconscious mind. It obtains its information from that which it has gathered, either from other subconscious minds—put in touch with the power of the suggestion of the mind controlling the speaking faculties of this body, or from minds that have passed into the Beyond, which leave their impressions and are brought in touch by the power of the suggestion. What is known to one subconscious mind or soul is known to another, whether conscious of the fact or not. The subjugation of the conscious mind putting the subconscious in action in this manner or in one of the other of the manners as described, this body obtains its information when in the subconscious state.

Q. Is this information always correct?

A. Correct insofar as the suggestion is in the proper channel or in accord with the action of subconscious or soul matter.

Q. Do the planets have anything to do with the ruling of the destiny of men? If so, what? and what do they have to do with this body?

A. They do. In the beginning, as our own planet, Earth, was set in motion, the placing of other planets began the ruling of the destiny of all matter as created, just as the division of waters was and is ruled by the moon in its path about the Earth; just so as in the higher creation, as it began, is ruled by the action of the planets about the earth. The strongest power in the destiny of man is the Sun, first; then the closer planets, or those that are coming in ascendancy at the time of the birth of the individual; but let it be understood here, no action of any planet or any of the phases of the Sun, Moon, or any of the heavenly bodies surpass the rule of man's individual willpower—the power given by the Creator of man in the beginning, when he became a living soul, with the power of choosing for himself. The inclination of man is ruled by the planets under which he is born. In this far the destiny of man lies within the sphere or scope of the planets. With the given position of the solar system at the time of the birth of an individual, it can be worked out—that is, the inclinations and actions without the willpower taken into consideration. As in this body here [Edgar Cayce] born March 18, 1877, three minutes past three o'clock, with the Sun descending, on the wane, the Moon in the opposite side of the Earth (old moon), Uranus at its zenith, hence the body is ultra in its actions. Neptune closest in conjunction or Neptune as it is termed in astrological survey, in the ninth house; Jupiter, the higher force of all the planets, save the Sun, in descendency, Venus just coming to horizon, Mars just set, Saturn—to whom all insufficient matter is cast at its decay—opposite the face of the Moon. Hence the inclination as the body is controlled by the astrological survey at the time of the birth of this body, either (no middle ground for this body) very good or very bad, very religious or very wicked, very rich or always losing, very much in love or hate, very much given to good works or always doing wrong, governed entirely by the will of the body. Will is the educational factor of the body; thence the patience, the persistence, the ever faithful attention that should be given to the child when it is young.

As to the forces of this body, the psychical is obtained through action of Uranus and of Neptune, always it has been to this body and always will, just outside the action of firearms, yet ever within them, just saved financially and spiritually by the action of great amount of water—the body should live close to the sea, should always have done so. The body is strange to other bodies in all of its actions, in the psychical life, in all of its ideas as expressed in the spiritual life as to its position on all matter pertaining to political, religious or economical positions. This body will either be very rich or very poor.

Q. Will this work hurt the body?

A. Only through the action or power of suggestion over the body. This body is controlled in its work through the psychical or the mystic or the spiritual. It is governed by the life that is led by the person who is guiding the subconscious when in this state, or by the line of thought that is given to create ideas of expression to the subconscious.

As the ideas given the subconscious to obtain its information are good, the body becomes better; if bad or wicked it becomes under the same control. Then the body should not be held responsible save through the body controlling the body at such times.

Q. Can this power be used to be of assistance to humanity and also to obtain financial gain?

A. There are many channels through which information obtained from this body in this state would be of assistance to humanity. To obtain financial gain from these is to obtain that which is just and right to those dependent upon this body for the things of life. Not those that would be destructive to the bodies themselves, physically or mentally, but that which is theirs by right should be obtained for such information.

As to which is the best channel, it depends as to whether the information desired is in accord with the ideas of the body from which they are attempting to obtain them. When credence is given to the work in a material way, anyone is willing to pay in a financial way for such information; but without credence there can be nothing obtained.

Q. Is there any other information that this body should have now?

A. The body should keep close in touch with the spiritual side of life; with sincerity to the spiritual side of life, if he is to be successful, mentally, physically, psychically and financially. The safest brace is in the spiritual nature of the body; sincerity of the work done or obtained through any channel with which this body is connected is governed by the masses through the action of the body towards the spiritual.

This record has been described by many students of psychic phenomena to be the most phenomenal they have ever seen. The life readings (as they are called today) are an outgrowth, no doubt, of this experience, though they were not begun until several years later, in 1924 to be exact.

I had a telephone call one day from a man who wanted to make an appointment for a friend. He came to the studio that evening and we attempted to get the information. My father conducted the reading and said I apparently went to sleep as usual, but was unable to locate the patient. The next evening this was tried again with no results, and the next. On the fourth attempt very satisfactory information came. The friend, however, at that time was not present. There had been no information given that would suggest the trouble, nor have we ever been able to determine in our own minds why at times we are unable to get information. This had occurred before, though there had not been as concerted an effort to insist that information be given. There have been many times since that the same thing has occurred. We do not know why.

Then there was the case of a relative. Her family had no confidence whatever in the readings, but they had despaired of her life. She asked her younger sister one day to please wire me, as she felt I could help, for she had been told so in a dream the night before. Upon receipt of the wire I made the attempt at once. It was said there was little hope for her recovery, but there could be something given to keep up the strength and vitality until her baby was born, which would be perfectly normal and all right, and a girl—but the mother would die soon after. This was sent to the sister who had sent the wire. She had a physician prepare the compound; and when it was given, the patient asked, "Isn't this what Edgar sent? I feel better already." She lived forty days, but died a few hours after her little girl was born.

Two years later I was in the town where this child lived. I had never seen the child nor the father. As I sat down in a barber shop, a child playing around the room looked at me very straight and came over to climb in my lap; she put her little arms around my neck. The barber who was shaving her father told him somebody was talking to his little girl. He raised up—he didn't know me—and asked the barber if he knew who I was. When the barber told him, the father got up and came over to speak to me.

"The child is not affectionate with others," he said. "Do you suppose there is anything in intuition, and the child knows who you are from what you did for her mother?"

I am still wondering.

16

Texas, 1919–1923: 'The Proposition'

I received a request from a man in Texas for information concerning oil developments there. As I had never undertaken anything of the kind from a distance, having only had an experience of locating a place to drill for oil in Kentucky one time, I didn't answer his letter. About a week later I received a wire from him asking me to please let him know within a week if I would give the information, that he was sure from reports on me he had received from astrologers that I could if I would.

In talking to my wife about this, I said, "I don't know but one person in my acquaintance that I would like to handle this, and yet I don't know whether he would consider it or not, even if he were back from France."

At that moment the doorbell rang and I received a cable from Dave Kahn, to whom I was referring, saying he would arrive in Lexington on Wednesday of that week and asking that I meet him there.

On my way to Lexington I reviewed my experiences up to that time, trying my best to consider every phase of the phenomena. I thought over what had been given in 1910, in Hopkinsville: that the phenomena was worthy of being studied in an institution; and that Virginia Beach, Virginia, would be the best place for such an institution to be established. Then, as the proposition from Texas presented itself, I thought that if it were possible to make money, would it be a plausible thing to do that in the oil business and invest it in an institution? I felt this could be presented to Dave, and he could act as he saw fit. I would not persuade him to become interested; he must interest himself.

*   *   *

Edgar's attitude was always the same—he was ready to do what he could to help anyone in need. He decided that if he had a hospital that could be used for the benefit of those who came to him for help, the money to build it would have to be gotten from his efforts. So he yielded to many propositions, including the oil business.

I reached Lexington shortly after Dave arrived home from the war, and we spent the rest of that day and the next morning recounting his experiences in France and my experiences with the people who had written me at his suggestion and the varied things which had come of these; how I had been called to Washington and the many other places from which people had written or come to see me. He said he was not out of the army yet, but expected to be stationed somewhere until demobilization was completed. Then I showed him the letter and telegram from Texas. He said, "This is interesting, but what does the reading say about it?" I repeated what I had told my wife, and explained that we hadn't attempted to get anything concerning it. He said, "Well, let's take a reading." The reading stated that the man had written a long letter giving much information as to the particular undertaking in Texas. Dave questioned the contents of the letter and it was repeated to him word for word. We wired to Selma for the letter, and when it came a few days later it was very interesting to make the comparison. It was identical with that obtained in the reading.

Many unusual things happened about this venture. Dave purchased an interest. Later, while he was in Washington, a reading told him about a development in Kentucky. We looked over the proposition there, and if he had not already invested in Texas, no doubt he would have undertaken a development around Scottsville and Bowling Green; however, we had no capital nor the experience to know what to do with information we had (which I realized fully a year or so later).

Dave was advised through a reading to send one of his associates to Texas, a man who had been with him in France and who was just then being let out of the hospital in Washington but whose home was in Louisville, that he would no doubt make his home in Texas. He was sent as Dave's representative and in less than six months married a girl in Texas.

Soon afterward Dave was sent to Atlanta by the army. I visited him there several times, and through him I made the acquaintance of some most prominent people—bankers, businessmen, lawyers, journalists, people in almost every walk of life. We had many experiences during these visits. I met a relative of President Wilson's, a Major Wilson Dave met in the army and who later became associated with Dave in the oil business in Texas.[1] I also made a trip to Texas in company with Dave and Major Wilson. On this trip we attempted to prove to ourselves whether or not the information would be correct in locating drilling sites. We met an operator in Fort Worth who had several wells drilling in the Desdemona territory.

There was the insistence through a reading that one well was in the heart of the pool, that while it would not begin with the largest flush production, it would be one of the longest lasting wells in the whole district. This has absolutely proven to be true. It was given that another would prove very unsatisfactory, for it was already a crooked hole and so much time would be lost in trying to straighten it that it would be better to move over and drill another hole. This they didn't do, but eventually lost the hole entirely. It was also advised that another would come in with a very large flush production, but would not be long lasting.

When these proved out, considerable comment was made by those who became acquainted with the facts. Not everyone who heard believed these things, but those who knew the facts

---

[1] "For Cayce and me, the gushing promise of the Texas oil appeared to hold the answers to all needs," wrote Kahn in *My Life with Edgar Cayce*. "I've got friends all over the East, North, South. I can get backers for us." In Johnson County, Texas, in 1920 Cayce, Kahn, and a driller-investor, M. C. Sanders, organized the Cayce Petroleum Company of Texas. On the strength of Mr. Cayce's psychic ability, investors put some $50,000 into the venture. But efforts to sell stock in New York failed for lack of proof of an oil discovery, for as the securities dealer explained, "outside of Cayce's personality we had nothing else to sell."

became very much interested. Eventually a banker in Cleburne, along with Dave, induced me to give some information on a particular location, also in the Desdemona territory. They were advised that if they went over three thousand feet where they were drilling it would be called a dry hole, but if they would come back to a certain distance and shoot with a hundred and fifty quarts of nitro, there would be a production of six hundred barrels flush production—and be a commercially paying well; however, if they would drill another well on a specific location in a given direction from that location, they would find even a better production. While not so great in its flush, it would be longer lasting. The people in charge drilled below the three thousand feet and pronounced it hopeless. Mr. Long requested that they try out the information which had been given. They shot with fifty quarts. I was in Selma at the time. He wired me, "Shot well with fifty quarts. Just a slight trace. What would you advise?" The reading advised that they clean out the hole to the same depth and shoot with a hundred quarts, that it would produce six hundred barrels on flush production. This they did, and Mr. Long wired me as follows: "Lucky Boy Number One turned in pipeline today. Registers six hundred and two barrels on flush production."

With such experiences, is it any wonder that a number of men in Dallas, Fort Worth, Cleburne, and the adjoining county allied themselves to explore for the elusive liquid gold?

In the meantime, Wilson and Kahn had become interested in their first proposition, the Sam Davis well, which had gone ahead. A number of people in Atlanta invested in the proposition to continue work on this well, which had been abandoned. It never worked out, however. They were never able to clear it. Why? I still wonder. Neither did the operations of the Cayce Petroleum Company prove to be worthwhile. They never got production. I am still wondering why.

I met numbers of people all over Texas during this time, and many readings were given for physical ills with wonderful benefits; but never again while I was there was any information obtained which assisted in bringing in a producing well. I don't know why. It would be very hard to give all the details, yet I saw an instance where men were carrying guns for one another because they had fallen out over a proposition—and both sides agreed to abide by a reading, and it settled difficulties which seemingly could not have been settled without bloodshed. The wife of one man was very ill. Information through a reading saved her life. The incident was sufficient that a son of this couple wrote me many years later requesting information for his wife, referring to what had been done for his mother years before in Comyn when he was only a small boy.

Friendships were made during the operations in Texas that I am sure are as beautiful as any that ever existed. And no doubt there were crosses made for some, and unless they have changed a great deal there will always be resentment in their lives.

In one place in Central Texas where operations were being started for the Cayce Petroleum, much had been said about me to the natives. When I first arrived, one of these long, rawboned natives, dressed in high boots with high heels, long spurs and chaps, and a large hat, a typical cowboy, said to me, "I understand you can tell anything. It hasn't rained here in four months. Tell me when it's going to rain." Why I answered this way I don't know, but I looked up and said, "Next Friday afternoon at four o'clock."

The next Friday afternoon at four o'clock, for half an hour I don't think I ever saw it rain harder. Now, I know I didn't have anything to do with it—but tell me how I happened to say just that? You can well imagine what this meant to all those who knew of it. I was also asked to locate water for many farms or ranches. I don't believe there was ever a failure; and some drilled less than fifty feet, and a few less than twenty, and found an abundant supply of water. Many had been driving their livestock miles for water for years before that.

During the organization of the Cayce Petroleum Company, Dave and I made several trips over the country seeking investors. I met people in New Orleans, Jackson, Memphis, Denver, all over Texas, St. Louis, Chicago, Indianapolis,

Cincinnati, Washington, New York, Philadelphia, Florida, many of whom I now number among my best friends. Many of the people I met in other places wired, wrote, or came to see me, even at that distance, for further aid, and many whom I had never attempted to help before. In Memphis, there was an offer to build a hospital such as we had planned during the first discussion of the oil proposition, but we were hoping to continue our own undertaking in Virginia Beach. During this time I was offered a million dollars if I would turn over all the holdings of Cayce Petroleum to this concern, and not give readings except for them. The directors of Cayce Petroleum decided against this; yet nothing came of our efforts to produce oil except a financial loss to many people. Not any large sums of money, particularly, for I never drew a salary for myself as president of this company, nothing save traveling expenses.

There were also conflicts within the group. Some of the principals went so far as to separate Dave from the proposition, as they felt he was at fault. This didn't change matters one iota, except it made it very much harder for me personally.

One man became involved with another man's wife, and it looked as if there would be bloodshed. Some of the family appealed to me to intervene. I talked to these people, gave a reading for them, and prayed very hard for evidence to convince me I had done right. At least I felt sure I had done right in preventing bloodshed. If I never had any other material manifestation of the rightness of the readings, I certainly experienced one that night. These families are good friends still.

The many experiences I had during these two or three years of traveling and work during the operations in Texas may not be given in chronological order, but I will give a few of them so that we may be able to draw comparisons from time to time. Many traveling companions heard verifications of stories that had been told and experiences I had through the years, as in Memphis one day coming out of the hotel I met Professor Lambert and introduced him to Mr. Kahn. Lambert asked if I had seen Dr. Lundy, as he was living there also. As we walked up the street to Lundy's office, Lambert asked Dave if he had heard of my experiences in Bowling Green, then made several references to the case of the girl who had killed her sister and what the readings said about it. In Lundy's office, as we reviewed the experiences, Lundy asked Dave if he had heard of the time I was talking so fast that when he attempted to stop me there had been levitation of the body.

In Memphis we met a very prominent businessman who said he had made some experiments with other psychics, but he would like to see a reading from me on his mother-in-law. Arrangements were made, the reading was given, and then we were invited to the home of the mother-in-law. It was astonishing to us to see her do just the things described in the reading. The reading suggested that she could be carried to another city to a hospital and get relief. She did receive much relief, temporarily.

In Birmingham we had many experiments with the superintendent of a hospital there. Several patients requested readings and in each case the suggestions were most helpful in bringing relief or permanent cures.

As we left Birmingham, we received a phone call from Nashville asking for an immediate reading for a young lady we had met there. The reading insisted that because of a personal disappointment, she had decided to end it all and had taken poison. It suggested something to help, but we were unable to convince the doctor in charge even to try it in time. When he did agree, twelve hours later, the information said he had waited too long.

The next day, while in the office of a specialist, I was asked to give information for an orphan. The doctor said he had been examined at the clinic at Vanderbilt University and appeared to be hopeless. I assured him I would be very glad to help if possible, that I would like the boy, as well as the matron, to request the information. They did so that evening, and the next day arrangements were made for the reading to be given at the Maxwell House Hotel. A number of prominent physicians were present, as well as businessmen. The young man was not in the room. Afterward someone brought him in, so the doctors could examine him, as someone present had asked the question (since they thought it was mind reading, as all the doctors present knew what was the trouble). The answer came back, "There is something the doctors haven't seen. Poisons in the system have produced a rash, which has only today broken out on the toes of the left foot, since the examination. Look and you will find it." The reading suggested an immediate operation for a growth in the head that was causing pressure, producing partial blindness. Surgery was to be performed through the nose. A few days later this operation was performed and proved to be most successful, to the astonishment of everyone that had known of the case.

In Atlanta we met some people who had experimented in Bowling Green, and we had several cases where physical readings were given that proved very helpful. We were called to do some special work in Washington again. There we met a lady who was very anxious that we give information for her niece who lived in Cleveland, so we went to Cleveland over the weekend. It was a case of pernicious anemia, and the suggestion given proved to be quite helpful. A very interesting thing came of this meeting, and is how I happen to have the nickname Judge. This lady insisted that if we ever came to New York we must let her know, as she wanted her husband and brothers to meet us. A few weeks later we were in New York. The first evening I was invited to a stag party on Long Island. At dinner I was seated at the head of the table and the man on my right said, "Are you from the South?"

"From Alabama," I replied.

"You don't happen to be from Selma?"

"Yes."

"You don't happen to know Alec Cawthon?"

"Yes, he is a very good friend of mine."

Then he said, "Well, he killed my brother some years ago. I have never been satisfied with the verdict given, and I want you to judge the case from our point of view; they judged it in Alabama from their point of view."

For several hours I had to listen to what all these people had to say about that murder case. I did not give a reading on the situation because of the condition of many at the party.

There were possibly not quite as many hard feelings toward
Cawthon afterwards, as there had been previously. Ever since
that night I have been called Judge by Dave and many others.

We met many people in New York who were interested in
psychic phenomena. A question was raised as to whether I
would be allowed under the city's laws to give any readings
while I was there. Some of them went to the city attorney for
an answer. He told them if they had three affidavits saying the
work had been helpful, we might go ahead. We sent five
wires—to Hopkinsville, Bowling Green, Birmingham, Selma,
and Texas. As soon as the mail could return we had possibly
fifty affidavits, about twice as many letters, many of which
are still on file. After this we met some very interesting people,
many of whom were very desirous of establishing the institution as we were seeking to do through the oil business, yet
we still held to the idea that we would carry out the program.
This never worked out, however. I am still wondering why.

I went from New York back to Texas. Dave, in the meantime, had begun another proposition somewhere else. At this
time a very influential and wonderful man from Chicago, Mr.
M. B. Wyrick, who was associated with the Western Union
Telegraph Company and had some experience with psychic
phenomena during his college days, became very much interested in seeing the work carried on. He had his own oil proposition in Texas and asked for readings about that. His
proposition did not prove successful, but many individuals for
whom he had physical readings received benefits. Many were
restored to normal health who had given up all hope. He received wonderful help through the readings for his health.
Later an accident brought back much of his trouble, but the
counsel and advice of this man has meant a great deal to me.

It seems strange at times how or why we are influenced so
much in our lives by people who have heretofore been strang-
ers. What is it that draws us together? What is it that makes
the associations of one individual mean so much more to us
than another? It isn't the mere abilities; it isn't just the position
in life. I wonder.

While in Texas this time I received a wire from Mr. Frank

Mohr in Columbus, Ohio, saying, "I have been trying to locate you for some time. What you said years ago would happen to me did, and I was blind for two years. Eventually I persuaded the physician to carry out the suggestion in your reading, for what must be done if I should go blind, and now I see. I must come and see you at once, that I may thank you personally."

Mr. Mohr came, and it was real good to see how enthusiastic and well he felt. Although he had lost everything financially, he had regained his health wholly, overcoming both his blindness and his rheumatism, though the treatment for his blindness didn't assist his rheumatism. As soon as he was able to have prepared the machine suggested in the reading, the third treatment cured him entirely. He spent two weeks with me. During that time he requested information for several people who had asked him to do so while he was in Texas. I decided to go back with him, and several people had readings. While there I received a wire from Dave in Denver, saying he felt he could arrange to refinance my oil proposition in Texas. Mr. Mohr went with me to Denver. The editor of a paper in town, the *Denver Post*, heard I was there, and sent a reporter to see me. He later asked for a personal interview and arranged for a demonstration—one of the few tests that has proven absolutely satisfactory to the patient, to the doctors, to the reporters. The editor then offered me a proposition, to build an institution in Denver, provided I would dress very queerly in very oriental style, never see anyone without a chaperone, and never drive about unless chauffeured. Money would have been no object, for he seemed to be willing to supply any amount I might name. He also proposed that if I would accept this proposition he would have some of his associates finance our oil operations in Texas. I may have done a lot of worse things, I don't know, but my conscience didn't allow me to accept the editor's proposition.

Stranded in Denver without funds, I received a wire from Birmingham, Alabama, asking me to address the women's clubs of that city on psychic phenomena. Never having undertaken anything of the kind, I still wonder how or why I was asked to do that, especially as they offered to pay very well, including rail fare, for the two addresses they asked me to make. I accepted the invitation and left by train with Mr. Mohr.

We arrived in Birmingham on October 6th expecting to be there only a few days. On the 6th of the following February I was still in Birmingham. To tell about each case or experience would be impossible. All the readings made there, however, are a matter of record, and more than an average of two readings a day were given.

A reading for one man suggested that he should use radium water under the direction of a physician. We had never heard of radium water. Several physicians from different hospitals, who came in now and then, were unable to locate it for this man. Later another man came in with his physician, who was superintendent of a hospital. Already I had lost consciousness when the physician came into the room. When I was again conscious, I was introduced to him and I thanked him for his courtesy in trying to help me find out whether I was fooling myself and other people. He told me:

"I know you don't know me, Cayce, but I have known of your work for some years. My head nurse had a niece down at Tuscaloosa for whom she obtained a reading from you. I went with her to Tuscaloosa, made the examination, and to my utter astonishment found you had been absolutely correct. The operation was performed that day, and I carried the child home. Also you did not know it, but a few weeks ago you gave a reading for a cousin of mine who has been my patient for the last sixteen years. You indicated the case was hopeless, as she has cancer, but there was certainly nothing to indicate it. Also you advised what might be given to ease her pain. It took me some time to decide that I could write that prescription, but again—to my astonishment—it brought the first relief the poor creature had received for weeks. The post-mortem examination certainly proved that you were correct. But I think I've got you now. You told a man sometime ago he should have radium water under the direction of a physician, and to-day you have suggested the same thing for this patient. I wrote on a piece of paper asking Mr. Mohr to ask you where we could find radium water, but before he could put the question you answered it by saying that radium water could be obtained from this place in Pittsburgh. I've already wired for it, and I'm going to wait here and see if you were right or wrong." He did, and in about forty-five minutes he received an answer, "Your shipment of radium water goes forward today."

In another instance a reading suggested that a culture be made, and described how it should be done. One of the experimental laboratories had a representative who heard the description and made this culture for the patient, which proved most helpful in the condition.

During my stay in Birmingham, I addressed the Women's Club, Writers' Club, Theosophical Society, Unity, Psychology, Applied Psychology, College Club, Business Men's Club, and many other organizations there.

Quite an amusing incident happened one evening while Mr. Mohr, Alf Butler, and I had seats up front attending a mystery show. A stranger sitting next to me turned and said, "Do you know how that man does all those tricks?" I said, "No, I don't!" He said, "Well, there's a lot of things we don't understand—but I think I know how this fellow up here at the Tutwiler Hotel does his tricks." Alf, hearing him, said, "Well, tell us how." He answered, "Well, he has his appointments a long time ahead, and he has somebody who finds out everything about the patients. He's a pretty smart fellow, from what I hear, and then he just tells it back to them."

Mr. Mohr spoke up then and said, "Are you sure of that?"

He said, "Well, I'm pretty sure, because I've had some friends who have been up there."

Mr. Mohr said, "You are sitting next to the man now. We don't know how he does it, and he doesn't know. If you do, come up and show us and expose the whole thing!"

The man came, but if he found out just how it was done, he never told us. Quite recently he had a reading for himself and is studying to be a leader of study groups concerning this work. So, at least his confidence and faith has lasted a good many years.

A man made an appointment, and after the reading was

finished, Mr. Mohr said, "Well, there isn't anything much the matter with you physically." He answered, "I know it, but I just wanted to see whether Cayce knew it or not."

Another time, when I became conscious after the reading, Mr. Mohr seemed quite out of sorts. I asked what was the trouble. He said we didn't get anything, as the man had given his name wrong. The man eventually acknowledged this, and later had a reading under his real name.

An attorney had a reading and one for his wife. He told us later that he had been sent by the authorities to investigate, but he was certainly satisfied there was no hokus-pokus about it.

There was considerable in the local press about what took place in Birmingham. Many local people proposed to establish a hospital in Birmingham, but the readings still insisted that a more satisfactory location would be Virginia Beach.

A man in New York who was interested in the oil property wanted to make arrangements with me for the oil leases that Cayce Petroleum had held in Texas, and that is how I met Tex Rice, possibly the most notorious character of my experience, though I did not know it at the time. I must say now that in all of his dealings with me he was absolutely straight, and if he ever used the information itself in any of his crooked dealings, I was never aware of it.

From Birmingham I went with him to Texas to see about the leases. They were renewed and money paid for them. From there I went with him to Chicago. He attempted to conduct a reading, having seen it done in Birmingham and also in Texas, but he never did so again. Several readings were given in Chicago, all physicals. Later we were in Pittsburgh, and several physicals were given there. Later in Altoona, then New York. I introduced him unsuspectingly to my friends. I learned later that he used them. No doubt some have felt that I aided and abetted him; but I did not consciously.

We went to Dayton where I remained for several months, giving many readings, and met some people whom I still count among my friends. I met for the first time the mother of the little boy whom I had two years before tried to aid while in Birmingham. All the nodules had disappeared except one under the left eye. One day this child, while playing around a pool, tripped and fell on the concrete, striking the place that was then no larger than an English walnut and bursting it. In a few days it had grown to the proportions of an orange. Each day a reading was given, until this gradually decreased in size, and physicians of three schools who were attending him declared it to be the most marvelous thing they had ever seen.

Then I was called to St. Louis by one of the stockholders in Cayce Petroleum and had been there a week when I received a wire that the child had fallen again, and that the place had opened. He died before I arrived back in Dayton.

I remained in Dayton for several months at this time. While there I received a letter saying my mother was very ill. A reading was taken at midnight. Though they had despaired of her being any better, the suggestions followed brought her almost immediate relief, and in a few weeks she was up again—though possibly she was never entirely free from the weakness produced by this spell. She lived several years after that.

From Dayton I returned to Texas, waiting for Rice to complete his negotiations for beginning operations on Cayce Petroleum again. I was in Meridian nearly a month, staying in the home of the secretary-treasurer of the company. I gave an address and a demonstration under the auspices of the local chamber of commerce, half of the proceeds going to the work of the chamber. A number of readings were given, one most astonishing for a little lady whose son was a physician, who had complained of having spells of getting very cold. She had for many years been a practical nurse herself. The reading suggested that she use a little appliance (telling her how to make it) when having these spells. She could drop it in a pail of water and attach it to the body, and it would warm her up. To be sure, her son called this imagination—but, as Mother Campbell said, "If that's imagination, then give me some more imagination, for it certainly relieves me." The last I heard from her, she was still carrying her little appliance[2] around with her wherever she went.

About this time I received word that Tex Rice had been apprehended for defrauding. I was very loath to give up on the oil proposition, but I gave up any idea of further work. I considered that my two or three years should be accounted as experience that might or might not be useful and returned to my picture making in Selma.

When it came to the final test, it seemed plain that the readings were not to be used in that way under the existing conditions. That was a very hard lesson for Edgar to learn because the information proved correct but the final results were not satisfactory, never turning just the way he desired. Possibly Edgar prayed over that as much as any one material undertaking, so great was his anxiety to have a hospital for the benefit of those who were interested.

---

[2] Apparently this was what came to be called the radio-active appliance, which the readings recommended for improvement in circulation, reduction in stress, normalization of blood pressure, pulse rate, kidney functions, and other benefits. Sometimes called the impedance device, it looks much like a battery because it has two terminals, which are connected to electrodes that attach to the body; but it contains no electrical energy of its own. Instead, it utilizes the body's electrical currents. Stanford University physicist William Tiller has theorized that it balances the body's energy flow through the acupuncture meridians. Research at the A. R. E. Clinic in Phoenix, Arizona, showed that it causes a possible significant increase in the level of serum dopamine, which helps control the motor function and circulation in the body (see *Venture Inward*, May/June, 1989). Many who have used it claim beneficial results, including several people suffering from degeneration of the nervous system caused by Lou Gehrig's disease.

PART II

My Work

17

DEFINING THE WORK: 'SERVE MY FELLOW MAN'

It took great effort on my part to come back to what might be termed normalcy, for, as I studied over the happenings of the years I had been away, I realized there must indeed be a change in my outlook on life. I wondered if my purposes and aims were just as sincere as they had been and if I had an ideal, or if I had just been through all the rounds, ups and downs, with just an idea. Why had it, so far as the world's outlook is concerned, all come to naught? Did it mean that I should never have an institution as the information had suggested, or had I gone about it in the wrong manner? Would it have been better to have accepted some of the offers? Was that the way it was meant for the work to serve my fellow man?

All these and many more thoughts were considered during the weeks I was making a decision concerning my work. When I thought of the individuals who claimed to have been helped so miraculously, over and over it was repeated to me what the readings had said, "First to individuals, then to classes, then to masses."

I talked with many friends in Selma, some of them physicians, and a very mysterious thing happened. I had been assisting a physician with his X-ray work, and he seemed very enthusiastic about my ability to read the plates for him. I was often called in when he had work for out-of-town physicians, as well as local doctors, to discuss with him what the shadowgraphs indicated, not by giving readings, but from visual observation. He insisted that I knew physiology and anatomy, whether I had ever studied it or not; that my being interested and making the X-ray exposures, then being in the darkroom with them as they were developed, had done something to my intuitive powers. He and some others suggested that I take a course in electrotherapy and become associated with them in that capacity in the hospital. They arranged for me to take the course as well as to cover my personal obligations during my absence. We had made some wonderful plates the day before the contract was signed, but something happened from the day it was signed. I was not able to make a plate, not one. They showed double exposure, full figures on the plates when the plate itself did not cover more than a very small portion of the body, and such things as that. What this was, or what produced it, I can't even guess. The opinion of the physicians was that it was not meant for me to use my abilities in that direction. But then I had to ask myself, had I been using my abilities in the wrong direction all over the country? Can you imagine what I went through, trying to determine what I should do, or what course I should pursue?

The number of requests for readings that continued to come in from all sections of the country may be imagined when I tell you that in one day's mail there were five requests from Texas, one from Arkansas, two from Oklahoma, two from Missouri, one from Chicago, three from Ohio, one from Kentucky, three from New York, one from New Jersey, one from Maryland, one from Virginia, one from North Carolina, and six from Georgia—all in one day!

Was I trying to capitalize on the credulity of my fellow man? As I thought back over the experiences in every place, however, I realized that I had not claimed anything for myself (and don't yet), yet all had reported getting results when it was for their personal ills or for their own mental development or understanding. Were they not better judges of what was helpful to them than I? Would I be doing right to withhold from them what they sought? Just how should I go about it? Should I ask some people in Birmingham, Chicago, or Memphis to establish the institution, as they had suggested, or should I accept the offer from the man in Denver who wanted to make of it something mysterious and possibly offered—as far as money was concerned—the greatest possibilities of all?

"Well," I said, "I will leave it to the reading. I will be guided by that."

"Use that in hand," it said. "Start where you are. You will go the rounds again, as it was given years ago, before you are awakened to the whole truth. The institution should be in Virginia Beach."

So we made preparations for the opening of an office in Selma in the same building as my photography studio. I told my friends we would call it The Office or the Spook Room. And I asked them to furnish it for me, to send me anything from chairs to penholders, something so personal that when I went into that room my best friends would speak to me. I wanted old things rather than new.

I also wanted a stenographer. I had experienced a great deal of trouble in having an efficient stenographer, except when we used court reporters; so the first thing we had to do was to try and locate one.

For several years it was only occasionally that a copy of the reading would be made with any accuracy. Many stenographers were tried without success. I recall on one occasion when we were in Louisville, where Edgar had been requested to come and give readings, he used a Dictaphone, which at that time was a very poor substitute for a stenographer. But that was what we were using in the office, so he carried it along to Louisville, hoping he could get a competent steno. After some effort, a court reporter with ten years' experience was retained, and with the help of the Dictaphone he recorded the readings for several days. But afterward he said the job of writing and transcribing them was the hardest task he had undertaken in a very long while and that he would not do it as permanent work for a large sum of money because it was too nerve-racking. The difficulty for him was not the speed necessarily but the unfamiliar words. And if he didn't understand a word, there was no way to stop Edgar and ask what he meant or what he was talking about.

*   *   *

We interviewed fifteen or twenty women who attempted to write the information as given in a reading. Most of them were miserable failures. Finally, I located Miss Gladys Davis, a local girl who was working in the office at the hardware store. She had learned shorthand in high school and business school and then got her first job as a temporary steno in the drug store that was downstairs in the same building as my studio. Miss Davis reported for work and took a reading in shorthand for the first time on September 10, 1923. She was but eighteen years of age, and from the first Miss Davis wrote the readings better than anyone we had tried before that time. We then began by making appointments for a number of individuals, many of them coming to hear their own readings. Miss Davis took the information down each time, then typed them up. We never had cause to look for another stenographer after that, as she liked the work and stayed with it.[1]

One day I had a phone call from a Mr. Arthur Lammers in Dayton, Ohio, wanting to know if he would find me at home, as he wanted to talk with me. Lammers came to Selma and told me something about a man who was trying to interest him in oil lands in Texas and he proposed that I go with him to look over the proposition.[2] We went to Texas. On our way we discussed the readings. He wanted to hear in detail many of my experiences. In Dallas we discussed the experiences leading up to and during the activities of Cayce Petroleum. From there we went to Cleburne to talk with one of the officers of the company. We sat in front of the hotel that night and I related my experiences until three o'clock in the morning. We

---

[1] Gladys Davis worked for Mr. Cayce not only for the remaining twenty-two years of his life but for the Cayce organizations until her own death in 1986, a total of fifty-three years.

[2] Mr. Cayce evidently thought Lammers, a businessman, was interested in investing in oil and might revive the prospects of Cayce Petroleum Co. and the hopes of its principals.

went on to Meridian and had several meetings with the officers of my company there, including the treasurer, Mr. McConnell. Mr. Lammers then told McConnell, "I am very much interested in Cayce and his work, but I am candid to say I believe you have all been working at the wrong end of the proposition."

He thought we should organize a psychic research society and suggested that I go with him to meet some people in St. Louis and Chicago who might also be interested. I agreed to look into the matter with him, at least. He had outlined questions for a reading on how an organization might be perfected for research work. After seeing a few more people in Texas, we went to St. Louis, meeting with a young engineer there from Western Pennsylvania, George Klingensmith, and another officer of the Cayce Petroleum. We decided to get some people from Chicago and Dayton to meet with us in a week in Dayton to get a reading. I left for Chicago and met Mr. Wyrick again, and he, with a man from Cleveland, promised to be in Dayton for the meeting.

I went on to Dayton, where I met Linden Shroyer, Lammers's secretary, whom I had come to think a great deal of, and I asked him to conduct a reading so that he might be more familiar with the procedure and be able to conduct the one we were to have in a few days with the other men. On the appointed day, all those who had promised were present, and Shroyer conducted the reading. The information signified that a research institute could be very helpful. There was a note of doubt, however, as to the advisability of it being organized with just that group. This was construed to mean that possibly we should interest others in the East and South. There were also many questions about what type of readings might be given, and it was intimated that any question of vital interest that did not give one person the advantage over another, or that was not of too speculative a nature, might be answered.

When the outline for the organization was drawn, it was decided to have an office in Dayton where Mr. Lammers had

his business. I told my family my decision.[3] After some consideration, my family, along with Miss Davis, moved from
Selma, Alabama, to Dayton, Ohio.

---

[3] Edgar wrote to his wife about the move: "9/30/23 Ask Miss Davis—(and-
now, talk with her yourself)—if she wants to be connected with the work all
the time, and if *you* have to leave soon to join me will she come with you?
Can you arrange for Hugh Lynn to stay there until Christmas? Would he want
to change then to finish term? Talk this over just between you and Hugh
Lynn. Will get you some money this week sometime. Love me. Love me
whole heap, for I do love you, Gertrude. Will write you again real soon. Kiss
boys for me. Always, Your Edgar." Hugh Lynn did remain behind, living
with the family of his best friend in high school, in order to complete the first
semester of his junior year before transferring to a private school in Dayton,
his tuition paid by a businessman friend of his father. The Cayce Art Co.
photo studio remained open, run by Squire Cayce, but soon, as Hugh Lynn
recalled, "a man came along and offered to run it for him because my grandfather wasn't really good at running the business. So Dad said to this man,
'Fine, do that,' but he never made a contract and never got paid."

18

DAYTON, 1923–1924:

THE CAYCE RESEARCH INSTITUTE

We secured an office for the Cayce Research Institute in the Phillips Hotel in Dayton and began by giving readings for Arthur Lammers in October of 1923. He arranged for a steno to take the information until Miss Gladys arrived with my family, and Linden Shroyer conducted the readings. Mr. Lammers had drawn up a list of metaphysical questions that we had never considered before.[1] He wanted to know from what source came the information. The reading said my conscious mind becomes subjugated to the subconscious, superconscious or soul mind and communicates with like minds. Information may be obtained from any subconscious mind, either from this plane or from the impressions left by the individuals that have gone on before as we see a mirror reflecting that which is before it. It is not the object itself, but what is reflected. The suggestion that reaches through to the subconscious or soul, in this state, gathers information reflected from what is real or material, whether of the material body or of the physical forces. And just as the mirror may be waved or bended to reflect in an obtuse manner, so that suggestion to the soul forces may bend the reflection; yet, the image itself is what is reflected.

These are some of the other questions Mr. Lammers posed and the information that came through:

• What is the soul of a body?

That which the Maker gave to every entity or individual in the beginning, and which is seeking the home or place of the Maker.

---

[1] Lammers appeared to be a solidly fixed, middle-aged family man who operated a printing company and had a strong interest in astrology and metaphysics.

• Where does the soul come from, and how does it enter the physical body?

It is already there, "and He breathed into him the breath of life, and he became a living soul," as the breath, the ether from the forces as come into the body of the human when born breathes the breath of life, as it becomes a living soul, provided it has reached that developing in the creation where the soul may enter and find the lodging place. All souls were created in the beginning, and are finding their way back to whence they came.

• Does the soul ever die?

May be banished from the Maker, not death.

• What is meant by banishment of a soul from its Maker?

To work out his own salvation, the entity or individual banishes itself, or its soul, which is its entity [to Saturn].

• Where does the soul go when fully developed?

To its Maker.

• What is the subconscious mind of the body?

An attribute of the soul or mind of the soul.

• To what place or state does the subconscious pass to receive this information it gives?

Just here in the same sphere as when the spirit or soul or spirit and soul are driven or removed from the body or person.

• Is it possible for Edgar Cayce, in this state, to communicate with anyone who has passed into the spirit world?

The spirit of all that have passed from the physical plane remains about the plane until their development carries them onward or they are returned for their development here; when they are in the plane of communication or remain within this sphere, any may be communicated with. There are thousands about us here at present.

• Is memory thought, or thought memory?

With the evolving of the individual, the thought becomes a part of the memory. Physically, memory and thought are not synonymous, neither are they of the same beginning in physical forces. In that of the soul and spirit force, they become one and the same in evolution.

• In the physical plane, do the thoughts of another person affect a person either mentally or physically?

Depending upon the development of the individual to whom the thought may be directed. The possibilities of the developing of thought transference is first being shown, evolution, you see. The individuals of this plane are developing this [possibility just] as the senses were and are developed.

• Define the word evolution with reference to the human family?

Evolution with reference to the human family means resuscitation of those forces that have gradually brought man to understand the law of self from within, and by understanding such law has brought the better force in man to bring about the gradual change that has come to man, known through all the ages.

Man was made as man. There [were] only three of the creations—matter, force and mind. All flesh is not of one flesh, but the developing of one has always remained in the same, and has only been to meet the needs of man, for which there was made all that was made, and man's evolving, or evolution, has only been that of the gradual growth upward to the mind of the Maker.

• Is the Darwinian theory of evolution of man right or wrong?

Man was made in the beginning, as the ruler over those elements as [were] prepared in the earth plane for his needs. When the plane became that such as man was capable of being sustained by the forces, and conditions, as were upon the face of the earth plane, man appeared not from that already created, but as the Lord over all that was created, and in man there is found all of [what] may be found without in the whole, whole world or earth plane; and *other* than that, the *soul of man* is that making him above all animal, vegetable, mineral kingdom of the earth plane. Man *did not* descend from the monkey, but man has evolved, resuscitation, you see, from time to time, here a little, there a little, line upon line and line upon line.

The needs of those in the North Country [are] not the same as those in the Torrid region. Hence development comes to meet the needs in the various conditions under which man is placed. The theory is, man evolved from first cause in creation, and the preparation for the needs of man has gone down millions of years for the needs of man in the hundreds and thousands of years to come. Man is man, and God's order of creation, which he represents even as His son, who is the representative of the Father, took on the form of man, the highest of the creation in the plane, and became to man that element that shows the way.

• What is the law of love?

Giving. As is given in this injunction, "Love thy neighbor as thyself . . . Love the Lord thy God with all thine heart, thine soul and thine body." We see again upon the physical or earth plane the manifestation of that law, without the law itself. We find the manifestation of the opposite from law of love—giving, with hope of reward or pay is direct opposition of the law of love. Remember there is no greater than the injunction, "God so loved His Creation, or the World, as to give His only begotten Son, for their redemption." Through that love, as man makes it manifest in his own heart and life, the law becomes a part of the individual. *That is the law of love*. Giving in action, without reward for that given. So we have *love is law, law is love. God is love. Love is God*. We see the law manifested, not the law itself.

Now, if we, as individuals have all of the other elementary forces that make for the bettering of life, and have not love we are as nothing—nothing. "Though one may have the gift of prophesy, so as to give great understanding, even of the graces in hope, in charity, in faith, and has not the law of love in their heart, soul, mind and though they [manifest] even these graces, and [have] not love they are nothing."

Mr. Lammers also asked about astrology and experimented with what he called a horoscope reading, which gave more about the planetary influences upon the individual, the personality, and what could be made out of this life. It also told about *why* such a personality existed, or his individuality, for we know that the individuality is what the individual really is, that which has been builded within the individual. The personality, then, is a reflection of the person's individuality, and what we are today—our personality that is seen by other people—is a reflection of all that we have builded within our own selves, whether it has been done through one life or a thousand lives.

After we gave the first horoscope reading, we decided to go to one of the best astrologers and get a reading so as to compare the two. Klingensmith and Lammers and I went to New York and made an appointment with Miss Evangeline Adams for an astrological reading. I told Miss Adams I was born on March 18, 1877, in Hopkinsville, Christian County, Kentucky, at 1:30 o'clock on a Sunday afternoon. However, I have had several astrologers tell me it was impossible for me to have been born at that time, else I would have been a girl. But this is the actual record from my parents, the physician, and the birth certificate.

The horoscope given by Miss Adams was certainly very interesting and I tried to make a digest of the information as given. I must say, however, that I wasn't able to get very far. However, apparently to me, just what is said here is almost positive proof of what was in a reading that we got later when a question was asked regarding the worth of horoscope readings, and it gave this: Horoscopes give the inclination by the relative position of planetary effects upon the earth and human beings; however, the *will* being the greater factor in the human being, and *mind the builder*, all planetary influence may be made null and void. Consequently, a reading that will give the inclinations, the urges, with *how* the will is being applied to same is of a great deal more worth to individuals than plain horoscope readings, other than to warn them of impending conditions that may be avoided at specific times, though this would necessitate having horoscope readings given quite often.

Astrology, we were told, is helpful in that the positions of the planets give the tendencies in a given life, without reference to the human will. So, while astrology may be called an exact science in a manner of speaking, still the human mind and the human will can override the astrological influences, just as the human will may cause man to deliberately break a law of the Creator's, for man, as we know, is a free-will being. While subject to all of the laws, he may *break* the laws.

This was a great deal of help in understanding readings that we had gotten, even though they were physical, just as the physical readings assisted in understanding the information given by Miss Adams. This, as we see, is a great big subject and a very interesting one, but one that certainly cannot be covered in one statement; in fact, it is very much like religion, a thing to be lived and can scarcely be explained by theory or theorem.

The horoscope reading for Mr. Lammers gave the first information we had about former appearances in the earth plane.[2] At first it was hard for me to separate the idea of reincarnation and past lives from transmigration, but I later realized that they are entirely different. Reincarnation had been considered a part of the Eastern religions for so long that we had cause to consider it foreign to Christianity. For many years I thought and taught that it was foreign. To the Christian way of thinking, a man has only one life; and as a man doeth, so is he. Or as the tree falls, so will it lie.

However, I doubt if anyone who has really studied the Bible could say that reincarnation was not contained in the Book. Throughout the ages the question has been asked, "If a man die, will he live again?" One of the poets said, "Dust thou art to dust returneth," but he was not speaking of the soul. Consequently, it has been generally considered that if a man live again, it is his soul that lives.

After giving the horoscope reading for Lammers, as I read my Bible I saw new meaning in some passages, such as when the disciples asked the Master, "Who did sin, this man or his

---

[2] It said that Lammers had had a previous incarnation as a monk. That winter Mr. Cayce gave such readings for each member of his family and on February 9, 1924, he gave the first of several for himself, 294–8. These readings portrayed many previous lives in which Edgar, Gertrude, Gladys, and Hugh Lynn had been associated, notably in ancient Egypt. Please turn to Appendix A for the text of several of these life readings.

parents, that he was born blind?" Jesus answered, "Neither hath this man sinned, nor his parents, but that the works of God should be made manifest in him." Now it wouldn't have been possible for the man to have sinned in *this* life that would cause him to be born blind. They must have believed that the man lived *before*, else they wouldn't have asked such a question.

Again, the Master said to His disciples that some of them would not taste death until they had seen the Son of Man come in His glory. After six days He took with Him Peter, James, and John and went up to the Mount of Transfiguration, and there they saw Moses and Elias.[3] The disciples, or at least Peter, recognized them and wanted to make it a permanent thing, wanted them to remain with them forever. But this wasn't to be at that particular time. But as they came down from the Mount, Peter and John asked the Master, "Why then say the scribes that Elias must come first?" And Jesus answered and said unto them, "Elias is come already, and they knew him not, but have done unto him whatsoever they listed. Likewise shall also the Son of Man suffer of them. Then the disciples understood that He spake unto them of John the Baptist."

In another place, He said, "Verily, I say unto you, among them that are born of women there hath not risen a greater than John the Baptist: notwithstanding he that is least in the kingdom of heaven is greater than he. And from the days of John the Baptist until now the kingdom of heaven suffereth violence, and the violent take by force. For all the prophets and the law prophesied until John. And if ye will receive it, this is Elias, which was for to come."

Later Paul said, "The first Adam brought sin into the world, but the last Adam brought life." Whether that's figuratively speaking or not is for us to determine within our own experience.

I also considered the idea of reincarnation as an answer to

---

[3] Elias is the name used in the King James version (Matthew 17:3), which was Mr. Cayce's favorite Bible. Later revisions used the name Elijah.

the question of how it is that when we meet some people, we immediately feel as if we had known them all our lives, and others we have known for years in this life and still do not feel close to or understand. I don't believe anyone can answer that question unless there is more than just this life. I'm sure none of us feel within ourselves that this span of life is all there is to life; for we remember that many writers in the Book say, "You do not live again unless you die." Nothing lives again unless it dies. Even the grain of wheat—if it dies, it lives again. But it doesn't live again unless it dies in bringing forth that which will propagate its own self. That in itself seems to be an answer, or a reason, for believing that each individual will have that opportunity to choose to come into the earth's plane, even as the Son of Man chose to become our Savior. He chose that. It wasn't forced upon Him. It isn't forced upon the individual to enter the earth's plane, that he may make manifest God's love, because we are each a portion of Him. It isn't a forced issue with us. We may work out our own salvation through whatever sphere in which we find ourselves. We have an opportunity to come into the earth to make manifest what we may have gained through whatever experience we may have passed. God gives us that opportunity. It is our job to do the working out. He is willing to aid us in doing the job right, but it's our job—and we have to do it! Too often we want to do the work our way and take the credit to ourselves.

In another horoscope reading, we were told that four of us—Lammers, Shroyer, and Klingensmith and myself—had been associated in a previous life during the Trojan wars in Greece. Having worked together for destructive purposes, it was said we had to learn to work together for good. We did all work together for a short time, but circumstances brought it to an unexpected end. Mr. Lammers became tied up in a lawsuit in Cincinnati and we heard little from him after that. We did not have many contacts of our own in Ohio, so Mr. Wyrick insisted that what we needed more than anything else was publicity. Until some prospectus is circulated among the people, he said we cannot expect many applications for readings. My associates agreed that we must get out a little booklet to publicize the institute. I gave Miss Gladys the information and she typed it up but it was many months before we could get this booklet out. Mr. Lammers had said that it would be taken care of; yet it didn't get done because he was tied up in court, so seemingly there was nothing whatever to be expected from him in any way. Whether it would have been done had he been in Dayton, I cannot say. I soon gave up hope of the promises he had made. I was not pleased with the way things were allowed to run along, with the promises he had made, but I was helpless to do otherwise than to sit still and do the best I could. I had hoped to have some returns from some other prospects that we had had on readings, and I felt sure there eventually would be some, but the returns were put off from day to day. Naturally, that made it rather hard, trying my patience, for I believed that which is right and just will come when we do our level best and are striving to do right ourselves.[4]

Mr. Wyrick believed that he could successfully raise the money to develop the oil lands he had in Texas, which would enable us to put over the Cayce Research Institute proposition whereby we could carry the good work to the people in a scope that would justify the effort. Finally, he had the booklet printed up in Chicago.

We also got up a manuscript for a book, hoping that we would realize something on the sale of the books once it was published, and that we had every right to believe that several thousand copies of the book would be distributed. But we were under financial strain at that time and, of course, needed to find someone to pay for the printing. We were put to considerable expense by having been forced to move but we were still eating, *sometimes*.

---

[4] When Hugh Lynn arrived in Dayton at Christmas, he recalled: "My father was distraught and looking gaunt and tired. It was snowing but he wasn't wearing an overcoat. When I hugged him as I got off the train I heard crackling sounds. It came from newspapers he had stuffed under his clothes for warmth . . . Dad said Lammers had gone bankrupt and they hadn't seen him for a month or more . . . So suddenly there was no money."

I did not know what was happening with my other associates, who were trying to raise money for their oil propositions. Klingensmith told me point-blank that they had twenty thousand dollars in the bank, but I understood from Mr. Shroyer and Mr. Lammers that he told them he had about thirty thousand in the bank that he had raised in Cleveland. I did not understand such statements. I understood from Mr. Shroyer that Mr. Lammers gave him some money.[5] How much I do not know. I saw Mr. Lammers one Saturday for the first time in over a month. Mr. Shroyer, Miss Davis, and I had been going along with the work as best we could and tried to forget as far as it was possible that Mr. Lammers ever had anything to do with it, for that was the way that we had been treated after he had made so many promises, and of course it was on his promise first that I moved to Dayton. I presume where one tries to do good, such things come along with the rest. Time seems to be the one thing that changes conditions, and the undesirables are gradually eliminated, or eliminate themselves, and when conditions are correct things will happen so that we get along with what is the right thing.

After we began sending out some of the little booklets, we were soon a week or more ahead on engagements, but the thing we had to do was get them to turn a little bit more of the "wherewithal" so we could get along on our own resources. I thought that if I wrote the right kind of letter to these people whom we had done work for in the past that they should be willing to help us out. I did not want to become a beggar, but I believed the work should be carried on, and that the people who had received benefits were the ones to contribute to the work, that it might be carried on. That I was giving my entire time, I thought, should have made a difference in how they felt. There was no great return financially

---

[5] Shroyer had worked for Lammers as a bookkeeper before Mr. Cayce came to Dayton, but Edgar thought Shroyer might make a suitable conductor for the readings so Lammers evidently offered Shroyer's services to the proposed Cayce Institute. Apparently it wasn't clear who was to pay him for his services.

from the letters sent out with booklets, but quite a number of requests for the larger book entitled *Psychic Phenomena Through the Subliminal.*

George Klingensmith was also trying to raise money to start the institute. He was to talk to people while on a business trip to Birmingham. It was my hope for our institute to secure a physician who was at the time one of the officials at Western State Hospital at Hopkinsville, Kentucky. That was Dr. T. B. House, a graduate osteopath, also a practicing M.D. who knew the work very thoroughly. He was willing to act either as the attending physician in the institute or take charge of the drug department and head the research work.

George also had the promise from a group of men in Nashville, Tennessee, among them two physicians, who proposed, if I understood correctly, that if the institute were organized and we were able to have such an investigator as McDougal of Harvard, or one of equal reputation in the study of psychic phenomena, associated with same, they would donate sufficient funds to carry on the work for at least five years.

As to George's mission, it seemed to me that George should have been able, with the number of people that had been interested in Birmingham, to obtain sufficient financing for us to get located somewhere. Naturally, the prospectus set forth Virginia Beach as the place. I was very much in hopes that he would get sufficient help to at least get started in a way which would make expenses very small for the work and then by the continual doing of this case here and there, and getting the results, we would gradually be able to build up to sufficient knowledge of the work attempted to make it self-sustaining. Most of the people seemed to think that work should be paid for, but that the other fellow should do it.

As for Mr. Lammers, I rarely saw him, and about all the information I got was either from the newspaper or from Shroyer, who was helping him out with the books.

About this time, Mr. Wyrick let us know that a reward had been offered by the *Chicago Tribune* for information in a murder investigation in Chicago. He suggested we might give information and collect the reward. I had thought of undertaking that after seeing the first account in the newspapers. But soon a confession was made, and curious as it may seem, I had met both of the young men who confessed to the crime. One of them was engaged to a young lady in whose home I visited a couple of times and gave a reading for her father and grandmother. The case was certainly sensational, and though I was only in the company of these two young boys one afternoon, it is hard to conceive of them being so depraved in mind as to commit the crime that they both acknowledged.[6] It seemed peculiar to me that such things come in once in a while, and I have no doubt had I given a reading beforehand, that this would have been given in the reading, and perhaps it would not have been bad in this case, but I was glad it had been ferreted out without my taking a hand. However, it would have certainly been very nice to have had the reward that was offered.

Things continued in a bad way financially for me, but I trusted that something would turn up, or it would have been very embarrassing for me for I would have been put out of house and home if I couldn't make some money or raise it somewhere. I remained hopeful for I had quite a number of requests on hand—but the returns were not sufficient to meet the daily needs. We stayed fairly busy, but there was hardly a sufficient amount to keep up all of our expenses. We managed to squeeze by with the help that comes in now and then. Many were the days that we wondered when we left the house after breakfast to go to the office at the hotel whether there would be anything to eat when we returned in the evening. But from day to day our needs never failed to be supplied. One day I recall very well, Mr. Shroyer, Miss Gladys, and I were in the office when lunch time came. We counted our

---

[6] This was one of the most celebrated murder trials of that time in which Nathan Leopold and Richard Loeb had as their defense attorney, Clarence Darrow, who obtained life sentences instead of a death penalty. Wyrick commented in a letter: "If we had the money that will be spent on this defense, we could equip a well-appointed institute and endow it for many years to come."

holdings and wondered who should be the one that day to have a bowl of soup, as we had only thirteen cents among us. As we were preparing to draw straws, a stranger came to the door and said, "I want a reading for my sister. I'll pay for it now—here's twenty-five dollars. I'll be back to see you this afternoon, as I'll have to acquaint my sister with the fact that I'm going to get it for her, as she is in New Jersey." That same day we had a letter from a man in Chicago enclosing a check for twenty-five dollars for a reading; and so it was for our first year.

A dispute arose between Klingensmith and Lammers about finances, which caused the Cayce Research Institute to come to naught before it was really begun. Others insisted, however, they would like for me to continue with the work, giving my whole time to it, as they felt a laborer was worthy of his hire—though we did not make charges and accepted only such free-will offerings that might be contributed by those seeking such information.

As Mr. Lammers gradually withdrew from the picture, leaving us entirely on our own initiative, my wife suggested we might move the office to our house, discontinuing the office at the hotel and having all the work at my residence. She told me she could conduct the readings and it wouldn't necessitate our having to have someone else at the office and that would make the expense a great deal less. I didn't know just what the effect would be on the business, for we still had groups that came in once in awhile from out of town, but I supposed they would find us at the residence. I thought I could arrange it very well so that it would not seem too crowded in the place. But we had to delay moving to my home until we could get even with the people at the hotel.[7] We were about forty-five dollars in arrears until Mr. Wyrick sent us a check for fifty dollars. My residence, at 322 Grafton Avenue, was just a good walk out from the hotel. The work continued there until we moved to Virginia Beach the following year.

---

[7] Hugh Lynn recalled: "He was afraid if he moved out he'd be arrested for non-payment of rent. He stayed on and promised the manager it was coming."

That summer Frank Mohr suggested that if we would come to Columbus, Ohio, he felt sure he could interest some people there in obtaining readings. I had met Mr. Mohr through Dr. Ketchum many years before in Kentucky where he owned a coal mine. He had figured with Dr. Ketchum to build a hospital at Nortonsville, Kentucky; in fact, he had gone so far as to break ground, the foundation had been laid for a small hospital, the grounds had been cleared for a hotel, and such like, when an accident happened to him in the mine. Dr. Ketchum conducted a reading for Mr. Mohr. The information insisted that a curvature had been caused in his spine that would gradually produce such poisons in his system as to cause blindness in a few years unless corrected. The physicians made fun of this, saying it was unreasonable. Mr. Mohr's condition gradually grew worse, however, and he had to be removed to his home in Ohio. His business failed and he was unable to proceed with building the hospital. He did go blind later, but remembering the information as given, he was able to regain his sight. After that he was a great supporter of the work.

So, at his suggestion, Miss Gladys and I went to Columbus. We were there four days and no appointments materialized. We were counting our money even for breakfast, to say nothing of our hotel bill, wondering what we should do, when I received a wire from a man in Chicago whom I'd never heard of, asking that I call him on the phone. He told me he was eager that I come to Chicago at once and wired me five hundred dollars. That night we left for Chicago. The reading was given for this man, who brought in his own family physician, as well as the physician from the Board of Health. This gentleman was very desirous of establishing an institution in Chicago and went so far as to select the building, which was already equipped as a general hospital. We called in some of our friends in Chicago who had been interested in forming the other organization, and they decided to take a reading. The reading insisted it would not succeed in Chicago because it wasn't the place to establish the institution—it should be in Virginia Beach. Later they decided we would go to a town about a hundred miles out of Chicago and look over the situation there, as we had a reading for some doctors in that vicinity. This also seemed an ideal place, but a reading on this site also insisted it should not be.

We had a wire from a friend, asking that we return at once to Dayton and give a reading for her. She had been diagnosed with a case of gallstone obstruction. Her reading suggested that while an operation had been advised, and under ordinary circumstances might be necessary, it was possible and plausible for her condition to be reduced osteopathically without an operation. The leading osteopath of Dayton, Dr. William A. Gravett, who was very well acquainted with the work by this time, disagreed with the information and said she should have an operation at once—but a younger man who had come as his assistant, Dr. L. A. Lydic, said that he would give the treatments as outlined in the reading. So Dr. Lydic treated her and she never had the operation.

We returned to Columbus, and this time had quite a number of people who came in to see us, some who are still very much interested in the work, many who have received a great deal of help through the readings. It was while we were there at this time that I first had a phone call from Mr. Morton Blumenthal of New York City.

19

NEW YORK, 1924:
THE BLUMENTHALS OF WALL STREET

Morton Blumenthal had heard about me from my good friend David Kahn, who had gone into the furniture business in New York City. Dave asked that I come there and give information for this man. It was impossible for me to go to New York under the unsettled conditions at that time. I was working out a proposition with two gentlemen concerning an attachment to a radio. And I did not want to take a chance when I might have had the very thing here that was going to work out *big*.

But Dave wrote to me about how much he thought of this young man, who was his own age [29], and that he was thinking of going into business with him. He said Mr. Blumenthal was well connected and that his brother Edwin had married into wealth. The Blumenthal brothers were in a stock brokerage firm, and they wanted to see me. So I wrote to Mr. Blumenthal and explained that it was one of my rules, that I feel I should in no way ever break, not to give a reading on anyone unless they desire it themselves, assuming of course, the person is in their right mind and capable of making that judgment for themselves. I was sorry indeed that it was impossible for me to go to New York at the time Dave wired for me. My financial condition at the time was such that I could not spare the time away nor meet the necessities of the family with the existing circumstances.

Mr. Blumenthal expressed disappointment in my inability to come to New York, but later sent three hundred dollars for my fare and to take care of things at home while I was away.[1] It was the beginning of a very close relationship. His readings

---

[1] Hugh Lynn recalled a family visit to Manhattan as Blumenthal's guest in which he stayed at the bachelor Blumenthal's apartment while his parents and Gladys stayed at a hotel, and they all were Morton's guests for dinner at a nightclub and at a Broadway show.

began with concern for his health—he had ear trouble—but his interest in the phenomenon extended to metaphysics, his business affairs, and a certain young lady from New Orleans, Miss Adeline Levy. Dave later said I was so good at selling Morton on the idea of marrying the young lady that he would like to see me selling furniture for his company.

Mr. Blumenthal also wanted information about his dreams. The subject of dreams had come up in one of the metaphysical readings for Arthur Lammers, in which it was said that not enough credence is given to our dreams. When asked how dreams should be interpreted, the reading said, "Correlate those truths that are enacted in each and every dream that becomes a part of this, or the entity or individual, and use such to the better development, ever remembering [that] develop means going toward the Higher Forces, or the Creator."

Mr. Blumenthal, however, was the first person to ask for information about the meaning of one of his own dreams. In fact, Morton asked for an interpretation of three of his dreams, and seemed satisfied with the information (in reading 900–8).

These early dream readings prompted me to seek an interpretation of my own dreams, including one about the veiled lady which I had had many times. In the dream I am walking down a glade with a lady holding my arm. The lady has on a veil, so I never do see her face. There is a carpet of vines on the ground, all with star-shaped white flowers on them. We find all the trees and evergreens are trimmed to represent a pyramid. We come to a brook with very clear water, beautiful white sand, and pebbles. We step over the brook and start up a little hill and are met by a messenger dressed as Mercury, wings on feet and shoulders. He asks us to join hands, which we do. Then he lays across our united hands a cloth of gold. The piece is about six inches wide and a little more than a yard long. Then we walk on, up the hill, the messenger having vanished. We come to a road that is all muddy. As we stand looking at it, the messenger suddenly appears. He tells us to hold hands with the cloth on them over the road. We do this and the muddy road dries up. We walk across the road and come to a very high cliff. It seems made of chalk. We are to climb it. I have a heavy knife with which I cut niches in the rock and begin to climb, pulling the lady up as I cut niches and climb.

This dream has rarely varied with the years. Sometimes I get a little higher on the cliff than others, but I have never seen over the top. Usually I fall.

The interpretation given to me was that this vision came when there were changes coming into my life. And if studied properly, it might be seen as a warning of certain conditions which were arising. The messenger was seen as the bearer of new thoughts, ideas, or ideals. Then, as the gold cloth was presented to us, there was the injunction that *together* all can be accomplished, *alone* nothing may be accomplished. The scaling of the wall depends upon the ability to stick together. As seen in this present dream, the wall is scaled, and a vision or vista of that to be gained is seen. Yet, in the ecstasy of approaching the ideal, there is the cry and the fall. The lesson is that as these changes come into one's life and ways are presented in which the furtherance of those ideals may be carried out, beware that the thought, the intent, the purpose of the entity is not shadowed by success, fame, glory, or gold.

Since then, in giving information for many individuals to help them understand their dreams, we learned that dreams are of different types. Many are about relationships with other individuals, some are warnings about conditions to be met, some suggest how to solve a problem. Dreams often contain advice or lessons, and some are as a prophesy of future events. Mine often had to do with the work. We wondered whether all my dreams should be interpreted through the psychic forces. The answer given was that those that make such an impression on the conscious forces as to become a portion of the mental activities of the mind should be interpreted. Those that are caused by foods we have eaten are of a physical nature and need not be interpreted. The difference between the two is that one is well remembered and the other may be a worry or a nightmare without any specific point.

There was another dream that I had a number of times. I see myself as a tiny dot out of my physical body, which lies inert before me. I find myself oppressed by darkness and there is a feeling of terrific loneliness. Suddenly, I am conscious of a white beam of light. As this tiny dot, I move upward following the light, knowing that I must follow it or be lost. As I move along this path of light I gradually become conscious of various levels upon which there is movement. Upon the first levels there are vague, horrible shapes, grotesque forms such as one sees in nightmares. Passing on, there begin to appear on either side misshapen forms of human beings with some part of the body magnified. Again there is change and I become conscious of gray-hooded forms moving downward. Gradually, these become lighter in color. Then the direction changes and these forms move upward and the color of the robes grows rapidly lighter. Next, there begin to appear on either side vague outlines of houses, walls, trees, etc., but everything is motionless. As I pass on, there is more light and movement in what appear to be normal cities and towns. With the growth of movement I become conscious of sounds, at first indistinct rumblings, then music, laughter, and singing of birds. There is more and more light, the colors become very beautiful, and there is the sound of wonderful music. The houses are left behind, ahead there is only a blending of sound and color. Quite suddenly I come upon a hall of records. It is a hall without walls, without ceiling, but I am conscious of seeing an old man who hands me a large book, a record of the individual for whom I seek information.

Another time when I again had the experience of going to the hall of records, to the old man with the books, I felt myself to be a bubble traveling through water to arrive at the place where I always got the information. When we asked the significance of the bubble, it was explained like this:

> To bring from one realm to another those experiences through which a soul may pass in obtaining those reflections that are necessary for transmission of the information, it becomes necessary for the understanding of those in that realm, seeking to put it into the language of that being as near as possible to do justice to the subject. So, the body,

in a symbolized form as the bubble, arrives at a place where the records of all are kept. This is signified as the Book of Life to symbolize that each entity, each soul in its growth, may find its way back to the Creative Influences that are promised in and through Him that gives—and is—life. The keeper of the records is as the lord of the storm, of the sea, of the lightning, of the light, of the day, of love, of hope, of faith, of charity, of long-suffering, of brotherly love, of kindness, of meekness, of humbleness, of self.

So, in the materializations of the concept for those that seek to know and to be enlightened, the question naturally arises: Are there literally books? To a mind that thinks books, literally *books*, it must find the materialized form of that portion of the Maker that the soul would enjoy. What is more real, the book with its printed pages, its gilt edges, or the essence of what is told in the book? Which is the more real, the love manifested in the Savior for His brethren, or the essence of love that may be seen even in the vilest of passion? They are one. Each portion of that one whole in what we call life, as it uses the attributes of the physical forces of a created form manifested in a material world, makes a record, as truly as is seen in the cylinder of the plate of the phonograph, or as is given to the radio transmitter on the ethers of a material world. Only those become conscious of same that have attuned themselves to that which is in accord, or seeking to know His will; for each soul should seek to attune its mind, its soul, its body-vibrations to what He, the Son of man, the Mother-God in Jesus the Christ, lived in the earth. Tune into that light, and it becomes *beautiful* in what you think, what you are, what you live!

Many of Mr. Blumenthal's dreams had to do with his work as a stockbroker, and information about buying and selling stocks began to appear in some of my dreams as well. For example, one dream had me on a train trip and getting left. The interpretation was that stock of the L&N Railroad was declining but changes would come, causing the value to rise again. The reading said, "Sell, then buy, see?" I had no money to buy stocks but the Blumenthals did.[2]

Dreams arising from individual experiences are experiences of the soul or cosmic body in periods when the consciousness of material things is more or less subjugated to the mental or spiritual forces of an entity. And these come either as lessons, forewarnings, or symbolic experiences that may be applicable to the experience of the one having them—or those with whom he is associated.

Sometimes dreams tell what you have done right. One of mine said that if Gertrude and I had not married, she would have died in 1906 of TB, and I would have died in 1914 from stomach trouble. That was right to the point. But in most dreams we learned that symbolism is used to deliver a message, such as one in which I was passing through a gate and trying to keep the pigs from coming through after me. One got past and I chased it, not knowing how to keep them all back. Then a peacock flew up on the fence and was strutting about and hallooing. The reading explained that I could have no confidence in those who would hog the show when it came to the work or who made a great cry about such but accomplished nothing.

Dreams often contain lessons. In one of mine I met a pretty little white pig, which seemed to be a woman, and we went into a hotel room, where some people saw us, and I turned the pig into a wasp and myself into a horse fly. One of the men shot the wasp and it flew into pieces. Then I was wondering how to change the wasp into something so it wouldn't be hurt, when the man started to slap me with a big board. There I woke up.

This was only a portion of the dream. The reading (294–67) said that while this portion is the emblematic lesson to be gained, the whole of the dream gives a better connection, as follows: There is a school building, which symbolizes the seat

—

[2] Morton Blumenthal obtained 468 readings from Mr. Cayce between 1924 and 1930, probably half of them to interpret his dreams, and many others seeking tips on investments.

of the higher learning, and entrance is gained by the intuitive knowledge rather than by pay. The school represents lessons gained through projection of self into the subconscious forces, through which and from which the greater lessons and experiences of the universal forces are obtained. As these are gained, then comes the warning: Let not fleshly desires present themselves in the way which would prevent the fullness of development to that perfect condition. Present self in the way and manner that brings no reproach; or, as it has been given, "Let not thy good be evil-spoken of."

Members of my family, friends, and acquaintances appeared in other dreams many times, playing a symbolic role. One morning I dreamed I was wading in water with Miss Gladys and Mildred.[3] I stepped in a place over my head, and I yelled for Miss Gladys and Mildred. Miss Gladys ran for help and Mildred came after me. I got hold of her feet but couldn't get up to save my life. Mildred said, "Can't you climb up?" I said, "No!" She said, "Well, pull me down." I woke up.

This was explained as a vision of forces that may manifest in individuals. Water is a source of life and understanding. In one's activities, let each action be such as brings the proper understanding without wading into depths that may be hard to overcome without calling for aid. Yet, as visioned in this dream, each may aid the other in the proper understanding of the experiences of life and light, that they bring better understanding to all.

In one dream I talked with my mother after she passed on about concerning the return of individual lives, born or reincarnated. The reading said this was proof for me that there is the fact of the rebirth, physically, of a soul; and that my mother would be reborn in the earth—and among those near and dear to me.

In another dream I was with Mr. and Mrs. Lot and their two daughters running out of Sodom when it was raining fire

—

[3] Mildred Davis was Gladys's cousin from Oklahoma.

Edgar Cayce, 1877–1945

Edgar's father, Leslie B. Cayce, was "weak but well meaning," and his mother, Carrie, was "the best woman I know," Edgar's grandmother told him.

Edgar at age 15 was troubled by taunts from other children, and some adults, for being "not right in the head" because he was different. His formal education began in this country schoolhouse and ended when he dropped out to go to work at age 16.

While working as a bookstore clerk, Edgar met "the only girl for me," Gertrude Evans. They were engaged when she was 17, he 20.

Although he left his hometown to find work, Edgar remained close to his family in Hopkinsville: (seated) his parents, Leslie B. and Carrie Cayce; (standing, l. to r.) son Hugh Lynn (held by Edgar), Gertrude, and his sister Annie.

The Cayces had three sons, two of whom survived. Edgar Evans (left) and Hugh Lynn (right). Milton Porter died in infancy

Dr. Wesley Ketchum used Cayce's diagnostic abilities with patients and publicized the successful results.

Dave Kahn joined Cayce in wildcatting for oil and later helping build an organization.

When Edgar abandoned photography to become a psychic diagnostician, he hired 19-year-old Gladys Davis (right), whose stenographic transcripts over the next twenty-two years would make him the world's most documented seer.

New York stockbroker Morton Blumenthal (left) financed moving the Cayces to Virginia Beach. They rented a summer cottage within walking distance of the ocean. (top right)

Edgar realized his dream when construction of the Cayce Hospital began in 1928 (above).

Opened in 1929, the hospital resembled a Southern mansion with a wide front porch overlooking the ocean.

The Cayces in the early 1930s bought a house on a Virginia Beach lake and added a library wing that held offices of the newly formed Association for Research and Enlightenment.

Edgar seated on the couch he used as "the sleeping prophet." Photo shows table where Gladys Davis took shorthand notes of his every reading while he lay before her in a trance.

Although challenged financially, socially, and emotionally, Edgar and Gertrude stuck together and never lost their sense of humor.

The Cayces' youngest son, Edgar Evans (between his parents), chose an engineering career outside the family, while his older brother, Hugh Lynn (far left), worked as manager of the Association.

Edgar remained close to his four sisters: (seated l. to r.) Ola and Annie; (standing) Mary and Sarah.

Gladys Davis not only served as secretary but lived with the Cayces like a dutiful daughter until they died in 1945, after which she married but continued working for the Assocation until her own death in 1986.

Thomas Sugrue, a college friend of Hugh Lynn's and a writer, came to live with the Cayces, suffering a debilitating disease, and stayed to write the biography of Mr. Cayce, *There is a River.*

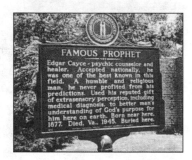

Wartime demands for readings from anxious families overtaxed Mr. Cayce, who sufferend a stroke shortly after this 1944 photo with Gertrude. Within a year, both were buried in Hopkinsville, where this historical marker stands.

This image of the thoughtful seer has appeared on numerous books containing the philosophy and message that are the Edgar Cayce legacy.

and brimstone. When "she turned to a pillar of salt" [Gen. 19: 26] because she looked back, they really passed through the heat that came from the fire from heaven. I got through the fire. The interpretation was that I would pass through an episode, in terms of mental attitudes, much as Lot did. Whether I would escape, as then, would depend upon my attitude and activities through these trials.

Another dream was about an old horse that died many years ago. It was climbing up a hill. We turned it loose so it could pull itself up, and we walked behind in the tracks the horse made. I said it was a good thing the horse had just been shod so that the feet would make tracks for us to climb up by. The message of the dream was that we should follow in the footsteps of the Messenger, or the Prince of Peace, and take it step by step as necessary for advancement and meet those conditions as they arise, either in the physical, mental, or spiritual plane.

I also had dreams of spiritual reassurance, such as one in which I visioned God, and He promised that He wouldn't turn His face away. This was called a vision, not a dream—and the promise was, as of old, that while the body itself was going through a period of transition, in the material sense, this was given: "If ye will be my people, I will be your God."

On another occasion, while giving a group reading [262–12], I saw Jesus giving the message, and His face changed in appearance as He gave it to each one. This was a vision of the source from which the information as received came to each individual.

Morton took his dreams seriously, as well as the readings which recommended Virginia Beach, Virginia, as the best location for an institute to sponsor the work. We did readings on this work, and within a few months he made it possible for my family and me to move from Ohio to begin the work in Virginia.

20

VIRGINIA BEACH, 1925:

Association of National Investigators

We arrived in Virginia Beach in September 1925 after all the summer visitors had gone home. As the house Mr. Blumenthal had rented for us was a short walk from the seashore, it seemed like the fulfillment of the readings that had said I needed to be near the water. While pleasant in the warm season, the house had no heat other than the fireplace, hence our first winter there was trying. Our youngest boy, Ecken,[1] had an accident in which his night clothes caught fire while he was sitting close to the fire to keep warm. It was very painful for the little fellow.

Our financial situation was also very close. Morton requested many readings, sometimes every day by telephone, so we were not idle. Morton by then had become a married man, and his young wife was expecting a baby. I often feel no one knows how to appreciate a body's position until they have experienced such a thing themselves. Having experienced such conditions some twenty years before when our first child was expected, I could still remember that awakening of something from within that is indefinable and incapable of being put into words, the expectancy of seeing a miracle enacted before your very eyes—and I knew they would both be bigger, better, and drawn closer and closer to the Giver of good and perfect gifts,

---

[1] Ecken, nickname for Edgar Evans Cayce, was eight years old when this occurred. As he explained: "A spark popped out on some flannel pajamas I had on and they went up like celluloid film. My mother was coming down the steps with a shirt in her hand and grabbed me and wrapped the shirt around it and put out the fire." One leg was so badly burned that "for weeks pieces of burned shirt would come out of my leg when they dressed it." Ecken missed school for three or four months. "But I never had a doctor. Dad told me what to do for that. He even told me what to rub on it to remove the scar." He later excelled in athletics and felt no ill effects of his injury.

and realize, too, the wonderful trust and responsibility that had been placed in their hands.

Morton came down from New York to discuss plans for the organization. We considered the feasibility of opening an institute at once. Our plan was to organize it in a benevolent corporation, put a physician in charge, start in a small way, perhaps rent a house that could be fitted up with six or eight rooms to take care of anyone who would come in—start, of course, first with the regular physician, nurse, and orderly— then the physician could call in any specialist he saw fit to use under the circumstances. This, we figured, ought to be almost self-sustaining from the start. It would require a whole lot of work on the part of the physician, and perhaps without a great deal of pay for the first year, except board and keep and a good lot of prospects. We believed we had the right sort of fellow interested with us—Dr. Thomas B. House, who had a good deal of experience in institutional work. We could also have prepared, under his supervision, all of the prescriptions that were given for people that were not in the institution. We felt like, with the number of readings we were getting, that we ought to have at least one or two every month who would come to the institution. That ought to have kept us going fairly well—in a small way, of course.

I let Dr. House know that the men who were principally interested were members of the New York Stock Exchange. They felt like it was possible to increase their capital by the use of the information in speculating on the stock exchange. The capital was very much tied up in stocks and bonds, the income of which at the time amounted to about fifteen hundred dollars a quarter. Should, however, any of that been liquidated in such a manner as to create a large fund, then there would of course have been no trouble financially.

I told Dr. House there were others interested in the institute work. One of them was Mr. Wyrick, who had a prospective oil well that we thought would provide sufficient capital, irrespective of any other, to carry out the work in almost any manner we might desire. Then, we had another man in Dayton, Ohio, Tim Brown, who was manufacturing the applicator. He

hoped to have sufficient capital to start the manufacture of
these on a large scale. It would have been necessary, in that
case, that he be associated with someone of the medical fraternity to test the work. From this source there would also
have been a small amount turned into the treasury of the institute. I thought that if the work had continued to multiply,
as it did in the first year or six months, there should have have
been sufficient in this fund to do practically most anything we
would want to with the institute work.

I also advised Dr. House that Virginia Beach had possibilities for a practitioner, irrespective of all this development in
the work. Of course, I hadn't been here long enough to know
what the various seasons meant for a resident of the place—
winter with all its outgo of people, summer with all of its
summer people returning, with the thousands of visitors that
come here annually. While the place is old, it had only recently
attracted prominence as a summer resort. For until a few years
ago it was merely a fishing village; but when the war came
on, Cape Henry being a strategic point, the government built
many good roads, and we know what good roads and auto-
mobiles mean to any place that already has wonderful possibilities. So, in a few years it grew to be a considerable place.
There were perhaps only about three thousand year-round inhabitants of Virginia Beach proper, it being about sixteen to
eighteen miles almost due east from Norfolk, a city of about
a hundred and seventy-five thousand inhabitants, and one of
the greatest seaports on the Atlantic seaboard. The exports
through the port amount to three to five million dollars weekly.

Now there has been a great deal of outside capital, and
more all the time, is being invested in Virginia Beach, and I
have seen few places where there was as much building going
on as here, for each real estate man is hoping to make his plot
of land the center of the city.

There has been a great deal in the magazines and papers
concerning the healing properties to be found in the sands of
Virginia Beach. As you know perhaps, it lies at the point on
the Atlantic Ocean where the Gulf Stream turns across toward
England and France. Therefore, there is brought in the tropical

sands to its shore, and where the northern shore, or the Chesapeake Bay, with its James and Potomac and other large rivers, bring from the mountains of Virginia, West Virginia, and Pennsylvania, its properties to the same shore, and downstream from the Delaware and New Jersey shores. This combination of properties makes this a nature resort and a natural place for an institution, such as we hoped to build, for with nature's assistance, and with the building up of a place where thousands of people come in, we naturally could see the possibilities of the city.

We had only one medical man in the town, Dr. Robert W. Woodhouse, a man about forty years old who took over the practice of his father. He was a good man and a regular medical practitioner. There was also a lady specialist for her sex and the ills of same, who, as I understand, stayed only in the summer season.

I did not know what the local business for my work would be in Virginia Beach. Consequently, I couldn't say whether this would mean anything to a local doctor or not. However, *I did know* that it would mean something, if nothing more than to verify the data that we obtained and give medical advice to those whom we give the work to through correspondence. I suggested to Dr. House and Miss Carrie they should make a trip here, provided they would deem what I said worthy of being considered, to look over the situation and then decide for themselves.

Another question was what would be my official connection with such an institution. The institute would be under the supervision of trustees or managers, and I wanted as many of them as possible to be my own close personal friends.

We were keeping several weeks ahead with appointments. We were not getting as many contributions as we would have liked, or as we could have *used*. I believed that having the institution would change this somewhat.

We also had a group of supporters that included Frank Mohr. When I heard again from Mr. Mohr, he was in Florida working with his brother-in-law, who was connected with two businessmen, Thomas J. Peters and A. C. Preston. Mr. Peters was quite a wealthy man, having made the money himself in truck farming and in real estate. A year or more before, he took Mr. Preston in as an associate for his business abilities. They had millions of dollars worth of real estate in their names that had never been paid for. Mr. Mohr, being of the turn that talks about those things that are of interest, recalled some of the experiences of the Dietrich family with the phenomena as it worked out for their little girl Aime. As a result, both of these gentlemen obtained readings for themselves. They were interested in an oil proposition and sought information concerning that. So, they wanted to get us together, especially when the information had been given about the treasure that was supposed to be buried on an island near the Florida coast where they had acquired property.

Until Ecken was healed enough to travel, I declined to leave home, but we did give a reading, and the information was that on this island of Bimini a cache of buried gold and silver might be located on a high point there. Before Mr. Mohr and his associates could explore for this location, however, a hurricane struck the area. In Miami they tell me the wind was traveling at the rate of one hundred fifty miles an hour. Barges, dredges weighing four hundred to five hundred tons were left high and dry on land. Many dwellings of light construction were completely destroyed, while roofs were torn from at least fifty percent of the homes in the path of the storm.

When they looked for the cache of treasure on the island, they found the storm had altered the landmarks. The hurricane had also severely damaged their holdings and put them in a very embarrassing condition financially.

While trying to decide what to do, I had a dream that was inspired by these conditions. In this dream the ruler of some oriental country died, and I couldn't save his people unless I married his daughter. But, as I was already married, this country was to pay a whole lot of money to my wife to free me so I could marry, which she agreed to. The boys didn't like it, but she insisted that it would be all right, as they could have plenty of money and could get whatever they wanted. Preparations were being made for the wedding with a great many dignitaries from the oriental country being on hand, but I kept putting it off, as I couldn't bring myself to go through with the performance. It finally came down to the time I was to bid my family goodbye at one o'clock, have my divorce at two o'clock, and before three was to marry and leave on an aeroplane. Again, I saw this almond-eyed girl. She was pretty as such beauties go and very elaborately dressed, especially in a very high hat. Then it seemed we had to have a baby to carry back to this country, and I went to Mrs. House who had just had a tiny baby; so she and her husband agreed that I could have the baby if I'd pay them so much money. I looked at the child, but in handling it, it slipped out of my hands and went between the bedstead and the bedding, and I couldn't find it. She finally located it, though, and fixed it up into a little bundle so it could be easily carried on the plane. It lacked twenty minutes of one when all these dignitaries filed in again, and I felt very much impressed with their silk robes and pajama-like vestures. But I sent them away again, and told them I had thirty minutes yet before I had to decide. That's when I woke up.

This dream was said to be emblematical of conditions which arise in my life from time to time. It represented the specific condition regarding a trip to a warm country, in this case Florida, and the dignitaries represented men of means, as did the daughter and the people to be saved. The monies represent the returns that may be gained through such efforts.

The next day I had another dream about some beautiful girl—I didn't know what her name was, though she told me when I went to her home and to her room. We felt very much in love with each other. I then met her mother and grandmother, and told them I was very much in love with the girl and wanted to marry her. Although I was fifty-two years old and she was only eighteen, we were very much in love with each other, and I was sure it could be arranged with my wife in some way. We then seemed to be preparing to go to church, and I was to have lunch with them. If possible, I was to arrange so they would think I was gone, but I wouldn't leave and would go to the girl's home again. We went out to get in a carriage when I saw two of my sisters coming up the street in a little phaeton, driving a bay horse, and I told the girl that I wanted her to meet my sisters, so we let the carriage with the mother and grandmother go ahead, and we crossed the road to the righthand side and stopped the carriage as it drove up. My sister's little girl was sitting on the lap of one of the girls. I asked them if we couldn't ride with them, and they said yes. I went to introduce them but I realized I didn't know what the girl's name was—but I told her what their names were. She got in the buggy and sat in Mary's lap. I sat in the foot of the buggy.

Again, the reading said these were symbolic conditions respecting the same forces and elements which enter into one's life, and it showed that only by the most openhanded, most concrete manner, may the conditions or elements be handled, that the best may come from same. For any underhanded manner would bring reproach and prove detrimental to me and to the families connected with same. The message was that I was to act in an openhanded manner.

With these messages in mind and in hope of being able to locate the treasure through the information obtained in readings, I accepted their offer to assume the expense of our coming to Florida in person to try and locate it. My wife, Miss Gladys, and the boy and I took the train to Miami. Mr. Peters met us at the train with two big Packard cars and carried us to the Halycon Hotel, which he owned. The next morning I went to Bimini with the menfolk and stayed three days and gave four readings on the ground. But they were not able to locate any treasure. Why this did not follow to a successful end, I did not know.

It made me wonder a whole lot after I came back. Everybody took special pains to make things pleasant for us, everybody went to a whole lot of expense—and yet possibly we were all worse off in the end than if it hadn't been. I know we all were from the financial way, if we look at it from that end. But whether we are to judge things like that in that way or not I don't know. And I've tried mighty hard to find out what's the trouble—and the nearest thing I got was what was given us in this last reading: We were not in accord one with another!

Edgar's great desire was to help his fellow man, not especially to make money. He realized that it was necessary for him to provide the necessities of life for his family, but his object was not to accumulate or horde money. He had the opportunity to do that many times, but that has not been his object in life. So you may rest assured that he has not piled it up and he does not seem to worry over that fact either. He is of the flesh, of course, and has need of the material things of this life just as other people, and he appreciates those things when he has them, but not to grasp after them as the object of life.

I told Morton that while it was disappointing from a financial standpoint, one of the best things that was accomplished in Florida was the better cooperative influences that developed from this trip among our own selves—meaning my wife, Miss Gladys, and me—for, being thrown constantly with individuals, as a group, who were seeking to gain some knowledge concerning the good that might be accomplished through the work we were trying to do. We found ourselves expressing our own ideas concerning the work in such a way and manner that we were drawn closer and closer together, and it made us all appreciate the part played by each individual and their relation to those seeking advice, help, and aid. I am sure that this is almost like creating new blood in the work. This I think is the biggest thing that was accomplished.

This was possibly the first *group* of individuals that we tried to interest as a group. Naturally, each individual was already more or less interested, each with his own development, with the idea of what might possibly be accomplished through the work; yet we can see, from *our* understanding, just why they never located the treasure; for there are cosmic or psychic laws just as we have a penal law, and these people, I think, realized this. Perhaps in our first week's visit they realized it. Then, they went about, even with all their other worries, to try to get their individual selves straightened out. The readings had told me—

and these people heard them given—that when we had given each individual of the group the opportunity to see themselves, see what was wrong from within, then it would be time for us to go home, and let them digest what they had in hand. I don't mean to imply that they had given up the idea of locating the treasure or that the information that was given would not assist them in locating it, but they gave up the idea of finding it until each one came to the consciousness of making himself right with the Creative Forces.

So I believe, all in all, it had not been in vain—though, of course, it placed us in a very embarrassing financial position for the moment, but each of us felt better and felt more like meeting the conditions from day to day and working harder toward the goal that is set before us; and we all felt more confident of the ultimate success of what we were trying to do.

But the more contacts, the more people that gain a more perfect knowledge of themselves and realize their responsibilities to the world as a whole and to every good work that is seeking to benefit mankind, individually and collectively, the more near we are coming to fulfilling the purpose of our experiences in the earth plane.

Some time later Mr. Peters's wife in Florida asked help for her husband, for she had learned he was seeing another woman. I was sorry indeed to know that such a condition had arisen in such a wonderful family. But we do know that such things have happened and do happen almost every day. I had made it a rule to try and steer clear of such conditions with my work. However, I made an appointment for a reading for Mr. Peters and hoped it might possibly throw a great deal of light on the subject. In his life reading, there was considerable emphasis given on some entanglements and conditions that might arise in his life in the year 1928. I just hoped and prayed that something would be given him in this reading to help him get himself straightened out. I could imagine something of the trial, something of the sorrow, that must have been in his wife's heart and mind from the knowledge of such a condition arising.

When Mr. Peters asked me to intepret a dream of his in which a big black spider had built a web all the way across the inside of his house, I told him it was a warning connected with his own relationships.

Mr. Peters's business methods also caused problems for his associate, Mr. Preston, who split with him a year later and told me that Peters's business had been going down very fast on account he does not listen to common sense nor listen to his friends. He later went bankrupt.

After I returned home from Miami, I was called to New York and had a rather interesting experience while there—something that seemed to address my worry about how things had turned out in Miami. I was attending a dinner at the Pennsylvania Hotel with two hundred and fifty or three hundred guests. I did not know until that afternoon that I was even expected to go—and only the president of this club knew that I was expected to come. I found there twenty-three people for whom I had given physical readings, or some member of their family, and each one claimed to have received personal benefits from same. And there was not a single one of these people that I had ever seen before in my conscious mind, and not a one had ever seen me before even though I had lived there in New York for six or seven months at one time and they had never been in to see me. Nor had I ever hunted up a one of them. It was quite a remarkable experience, certainly one that would make a fellow think. If these people hadn't received benefits, they wouldn't have had any reason to stand up there before all the rest of those people and tell them they did. I wasn't anybody to make a fuss over. And I certainly had never tried to make a fuss over them. But, evidently, there was *something* in the information these people got that they were able to apply.

If the phenomenon worked for them, why couldn't we do it in our situation? What was wrong? Was it the character of the information—the purpose of the information—the character of the individuals—or the purpose of the individuals? It was a hard thing to reason. Maybe there wasn't any reason— but if you could just see the letters we got every day and see the effect the information has on the hearts and lives of people, you know it is worthwhile or they were the darnedest liars in this country. And it isn't that it brought any great thing for me—not in this world's goods—but the thing that is worthwhile is that it makes husbands say they are better husbands, and better fathers, and sons and daughters that are better sons and daughters—treat their own families better—treat their own neighbors' families better—and live better. And they've got more hope for the life to come.

To organize the work on a businesslike basis, Mr. Blumenthal suggested establishing an association of individuals who requested information and were interested in supporting our work. Not all of my associates agreed on establishing such an institute. Mr. Wyrick was even skeptical of those associated with me. His letter made me think when he said:

> I am not fully convinced that the proposed arrangement will be best for Cayce and the work. It is most likely to show selfish interests trying to profit through your work and the forces demonstrating through you the way of closer relations with the Infinite forces controlling all entities physical and spiritual. Your work will be the only asset of such an institution and you may not hope to demonstrate in more volume than at present and there will be much more expense to be taken care of out of your earnings. An institution with medical professional attendants will be no more attractive than are the thousands of such institutions now operating throughout the country. My thought of an institute suitable for you, one that will demonstrate more fully to the populace the psychic work most peculiar to your talent, must be one in which an endowment must care for the expense of operations at least for a time. And you must be assisted by a staff of people with talents like or similar to yourself. Then, and not until such an arrangement can be perfected, will an institute be a success. Until such an arrangement can be made, it is best you work alone. Too much association with professional people discussing the readings you give, giving opinions from the conscious mind

to you in the conscious state, detract from your demonstration. The readings will become less valuable to the entities for whom given—less clear and correct—your tendency is to inject into the reading suggestions given the conscious mind. Pardon me for speaking thus plainly and critically. I have your best interest at heart and am most sympathetic with the work. Do not mix your talent with professional work, for yours is from the storehouse of knowledge from whence all conscious thoughts come. Honest effort continued as you are going will eventually reveal to mankind the "lost word."

I had never gotten just the angle Wyrick presented, though I had known that such a thing would be very possible if the physician in charge was of a dictatorial nature. My whole thought had been to be able to serve those better who ask for the readings. It was not my idea to have the hospital a money-making proposition at all. If we were able to even meet expenses, we would feel that we would be doing wonderfully well, and while the institution would be builded around the work I do, still it would be separate and apart from the regular readings we give—but there were so many (and the number was increasing) who asked if there was not a place where they could have the suggestions given in the readings carried out to the letter by a regular physician. We knew this was not possible in any institution in the country at that time. Just whether there would be enough of these to make this support itself was the question. The doctor and I figured that it would, for where we had twelve to fourteen readings a week, at least one or two would consider the institution. Unless the doctor could cure them mighty fast, at that rate it wouldn't take very long to have a pretty good houseful. I was sure it was going to be necessary for the expenses to be made up by outside individuals, but we had reason to believe that there were a few individuals already interested who would make contributions to this fund from time to time.

Perhaps I should have waited for some other development, but so many were begging for a place where they could have these suggestions carried out to the letter, and I didn't know how this could be done without the hospital. It isn't that I wanted the institution so that I could serve *more*, but that I could serve *better*.

We named our organization the Association of National Investigators and put out a booklet to let anyone know our purposes.[2] My idea was to appeal to those for whom we had given the readings in the previous twenty-five years, asking them to establish a fund sufficient to begin this work. With this, we would be in a position to be endowed. To help inspire interest in the work, I traveled to Chicago and to New York, giving information and encouraging individuals to take out memberships in the Association, so that we might raise the funds needed for our institute. We also sent out a letter to our members, seeking their assistance. It said:

The Association of National Investigators, Inc.
Virginia Beach, Virginia
That We May Make Manifest Our Love for God and Mankind
Science—Education—Health—Spiritual Awakening

President *Morton Blumenthal*
First Vice-President *Thomas B. Brown*
Vice-Presidents *M. B. Wyrick, Edwin D. Blumenthal,*
David E. Kahn, Hugh Lynn Cayce, F. A. VanPatten
Secretary and Treasurer *Edgar Cayce*

Dear Friend:

Do you know of someone who has consulted doctor after doctor, without success? How grateful that person would be to know that, at last, a modern, scientifically equipped hospital has been built, for psychic, as well as physical, diagnosis.

THE HOSPITAL OF ENLIGHTENMENT, chartered by the State of Virginia, situated at beautiful Virginia Beach, under the supervision of a qualified and sympathetic medical staff, has engaged the services of Mr. Edgar Cayce, the most famous psychic diagnostician in the world. In the past twenty-five years, hundreds whose cases had baffled physicians
—

[2] The text of this booklet is found in Appendix D.

have been restored to health and happiness through his amazing power over the subconscious.

THE HOSPITAL OF ENLIGHTENMENT has two great aims—to benefit sufferers who apply for aid—and to keep scientific records of Mr. Cayce's endeavors as basis for future research.

ADDITIONAL FUNDS ARE NEEDED

YOUR donation, in any amount, will relieve human suffering and help to launch a great scientific work that will drive sorrow from the earth and insure health and happiness to millions yet unborn. Mail it NOW—to—THE ASSOCIATION OF NATIONAL INVESTIGATORS, INC.

You've Heard Our Lectures—Know Our Work—Now We Need YOUR HELP

[signed]
Morton Blumenthal

I also composed a little booklet. It told about the phenomenon and what we were led to do with it. Mr. Wyrick had it printed up for us. Here is some of what it said:

Suppose you were to receive a letter in the morning mail that read something like this: "But I must say my attitude regarding the possibilities of my recovering my sight has changed since I received your second reading, for up to that time I seemed unable to make myself believe that I might get better and could not cast off the belief in the negative."

I'm sure this, if you think of it at all, makes you wonder. What is it that would cause a person to write a letter of that kind? What are they referring to when they say, "My attitude towards myself is changed since receiving your last reading"? What do they mean by "reading"?

You, my friends, who are acquainted with me and the work I've been doing for years, will perhaps understand. You who have never heard of it may wonder what it meant. Now, I want to give to *all* of you a plausible reason why I am giving my whole time to the obtaining of data and towards the establishing of a place, institution, or home, where those who desire to use such suggestions, as may be made through these readings, for their own welfare, physically, mentally, morally or spiritually, may go, and *know* that these are being carried out as consistently as is possible for man to do, and that their cooperation is being met with the cooperation of others who have gained an insight into the truths as are necessary for the building up of the body, as is found in the study of the phenomena as is manifested through these Forces. Not that I have any cism, ism, or any cult to preach, to practice, to propagate; not that I have anything *new*, save in how the individual may find the truths, as are found in man, applicable to his or her individual needs, for I have nothing to *sell* and am seeking only to be of help, and am asking the *cooperation* of others, for I am interested in *individuals*, in *folks*, in *people*, and to that extent that they, *themselves*, may know how God may manifest to them, individually, through their individual selves!

I do not make any claims for myself. I *do* claim that there is presented through these readings as may be obtained from time to time, while I am in an unconscious state, those lessons, those suggestions, that the individuals to whom these are directed, applying them in their inner lives, may gain a clearer, a more perfect understanding of their physical ills and of *why* they, individually, have certain urges from *within*, why they in temperament are entirely different from another of the same parentage, reared under the same conditions; yet their direct application and have been able to be benefited, physically, mentally and morally, for you to judge for yourself . . .

The booklet told of my many experiences and the benefits that have come to many from the experiments, and it explained that the readings are divided into two distinct classes—the physical and life readings. We explained that three conditions were necessary for one requesting a physical reading to obtain results. First, there must be the sincere desire of the person wishing the assistance (or of one responsible for the physical and spiritual welfare of that individual). Second, there must be sufficient faith in the work and report of same to carry out the suggestions as given, to the letter, as far as possible. Third (and most important of all), there must be the sincere belief in the Divine Forces innate in each individual. Also, only to the extent that the application is made will the results come.

The life readings gave information about the characteristics and abilities of the individual; the influence of Universal Forces as manifested in the individual in the present plane through urges; and former incarnations in the earth plane and their influence on the present life. To give an idea of what others think of this class of reading, I quote from recent letters:

"I believe you occupy a unique place in your talents and your work for doing good, and I hope your life and health will be given you for many years . . . I feel sure you are just entering on a missionary journey that will mean much to mankind, for with such information as you give to an individual, with such a panorama of his life before him, he will surely take stock and improve his remaining years."

"You've taught me more than all the schools I've ever attended, and your words, awake and asleep, have pushed me ten years farther along, and *safe*."

"If our work, through you, enables us to bring a little clearer understanding into the world of the Why and How, then isn't that truly a test worthy of many sacrifices—so many of which I know you and yours are enduring?"

As many asked what is the cost of all of this, I told them I have nothing to sell. I am not a doctor, nor a professor. I do not treat in any way, manner, or form. I have little or nothing of this world's goods, yet I believe that if it be the Lord's work, it *will* succeed. If it is not, it has no right to succeed, nor any place in man's life. Those, however, who seek assistance through these forces surely know that the physical man must be supplied with the physical needs. Therefore, we depend upon those for whom readings are given for contributions sufficient to take care of the needs of the hour, and for the propagation of the truths that do mean, and have meant, so much in the lives of so many. Freely ye have received, freely give.

I explained that my ideas and ideals regarding the phenomena have changed somewhat through the years, from that of little thought about it to a consciousness of a something taking place, to the realization of help and assistance to individuals who are sick and afflicted, physically and mentally, to the knowledge that I should give myself to the assistance of my fellow man in every way possible. That was the purpose of the Association of National Investigators.

We explained that Virginia Beach, Virginia, is where this phenomena might receive the greater impetus from nature's surroundings, and that we wished to have a *place* where those who desire to have their physical ills treated, according to information given in the readings, could get treatments carried out under the supervision of those who have gained a knowledge of how such information may be applied. Not in a haphazard manner, but seeking to apply the Truth gained through the phenomena, as it applies to individual cases, and which may be of assistance to all mankind.

The truth is evident: Man is a co-laborer with God in the material or physical world, and as God's forces, God's laws, are better understood, we can apply same in man's life, that man may live better and render a better *service* to his fellow man.

With Mr. Blumenthal's pledge of financial support, the Association determined to build a hospital. The Norfolk newspaper carried a write-up in July of 1928:

CONSTRUCTION ON CAYCE HOSPITAL UNDERWAY
Cost Is $100,000, Building Situated
High on Sand Dune
Near 105th St. Is First Unit, Others May Be Added

The National Association of Investigators has let a contract for the construction of a thirty-bedroom hospital at Virginia Beach. The new building will be known as the Cayce Hospital for Research and Enlightenment and is of concrete and shingle construction, four stories in height. Besides the thirty bedrooms, it will contain a large lobby and dining room, a lecture hall, library, doctor's quarters and spacious porches.

The total cost of the investment, including ground, building and equipment will be approximately $100,000. Plans for the structure were drawn by Rudolph, Cooke and Van Leeuween and the contract awarded to the United Construction Company of Norfolk. Rapid progress has been made during the past two weeks, the concrete foundation walls being almost completed.

The site of the hospital will be one of its most attractive features. Rising from a high sand dune, probably the highest elevation between Cape Henry and the Beach, it commands a view of the territory for many miles around. The property measures 150 by 300 feet along 105th Street and extends between Holly Avenue and the boulevard. The present building is the first unit and will be followed by others as the occasion demands.

The Association of National Investigators was incorporated May 6th, 1927, in the State of Virginia. Although founded upon the psychic work of Mr. Edgar Cayce, and although the immediate basis of its formation was to further, foster, and encourage the physical, mental and spiritual benefit that thousands have and are deriving from Mr. Cayce's endeavors in the psychic field, nevertheless, the larger and more embracing purpose of the organization is to engage in general psychic research and also to provide for the practical application of any knowledge obtainable through the medium of psychic phenomena. In the matter of specific application, the Association seeks to render psychical aid to the sick and ailing through its hospital, and also to disseminate and exploit for the good of humanity knowledge obtained from its research work through the lecture hall, library and other educational channels.

The Association Hospital will furnish those who seek physical readings and desire to secure treatment exactly as prescribed therein the opportunity to gain same at the hands of competent and sympathetic physicians. The hospital is to be conducted along only the most modern, scientific, as well as ethical lines. Every comfort and service for room, board and treatment will be such as is customary to an Institution of this kind, and all moneys so paid except the physicians' fees will go towards its maintenance.

We had about two hundred members in the Association when we commenced construction. When our Board of Trustees held its meeting, some talks were given that told of our hopes and ideals. Morton Blumenthal said our larger purpose involved the creation of an institution that would demonstrate to humankind the fact that within the realm of human experience there is constantly contact with the Divine, and that through the understanding application of such experiences, through that phase of mind called intellect, greater creative power may be gained by each individual. We sought to demonstrate not only that the individual through introspective experiences is capable of experiencing the creative energy of life, but that he may understand such experiences.

The result, said Morton, must be an entire changed attitude of mind by many benefited individuals toward life. It stands to reason that those who find through their own internal experiences a more idealistic and universal self, must needs express this ideal or higher emotional self in their daily life. Along with the physical comforts of life, men and women will seek in a more understanding manner gratification for the spiritual self they may, through their own experiences, come to know themselves to be.

There must also come about an entire change of religious thought, based not so much upon doctrines read as upon personal experiences of the Divine properly understood. Through such understanding we believed all religions might be brought into a harmonious relationship one with another in the light of human brotherhood.

With the better understanding of intuitive or mental experiences must come the knowledge that will permit of a more efficient and worthwhile application for self in daily life. By applying that introspective experience there are those of us who are seeking to bring into material realization this machinery. A musician might vision, or intuitively experience, the creation of a new musical composition. He might gain through our psychic research work an explanation of the reality of the source and of the meaning of such a vision, and of the possibility of realizing its application. For, indeed, is not all of life first created in our imagination?

For years I had dreamed of being surrounded by just such an understanding group as now were about me. Morton reminded the board that about eleven thousand years ago we had met together to accomplish this same task. Since then there has come into the world the Prince of Peace, who gave to the world, at the sacrifice of His life, an actual living demonstration of the purpose of material life, that the material world or its human inhabitants might better understand the spiritual or real creative side of life. In His teaching He drew from those precepts and from those principles that we gave to the world some eleven thousand years ago. So again, Morton added, nineteen hundred and twenty-eight years after His life, we were chosen by the cosmic forces, by the Lord Almighty, as being responsible to Him and to mankind to use our knowledge to demonstrate to the world that side of life for which He gave His life.

We were all very busy, of course, with getting everything together for the building. It required a great deal of time and thought, and some worry. We laid the cornerstone and had the dedication ceremonies on Armistice Day 1928. A fine dedication address was given by Dr. William Moseley Brown, who was a professor of philosophy at Washington and Lee University.[3]

The hospital opened for patients in February 1929.

---

[3] William Moseley Brown resigned from Washington and Lee to run for governor of Virginia in 1929 against Harry Flood Byrd. After losing the election, he became available to consult with Blumenthal who had an idea for starting a new university in Virginia Beach. Brown's hospital dedication address appears in Appendix E.

21

THE CAYCE HOSPITAL, 1929–1931

It was very satisfying to see people coming into the hospital and really getting results, where so many had almost lost hope. Our first man came down from Philadelphia and was here only ten days. He went home feeling entirely a different man. I wish we could do as much good for everyone as we seemingly did for him.

We had an average of ten patients after a few months, and about sixty patients were treated in the first ten months or so, with invariably pleasing results. One patient left the hospital feeling quite well and carrying a bouquet of violets gathered from the flowerbed on the grounds. The hospital itself was really a beautiful place, more like a large home than a real hospital, as Mr. Blumenthal said. It was so delightful that many people, including our own Board of Trustees and officers, were besieging the place on weekends for rest, recreation, and pleasure. This was beginning to complicate affairs, owing to patients in the hospital, so we purchased more property on the other side of the boulevard from the hospital, on which we planned to construct a clubhouse for members of the Board and members of the Association, who desire to be near this beautiful work, and see it in process of application, or to study it, and at the same time enjoy the benefits and beauties of a lovely environment. Since Virginia Beach is noted for the health qualities of iodine and radium present in the sand, sand packs taken at Virginia Beach proved very vitalizing to the system. Morton also wanted to develop a nine-hole golf course, with the clubhouse and swimming pool right on the Beach.

Not all these dreams were realized, but improvements in the facilities were steadily made. A tennis court, shuffleboard and croquet ground were finished during the summer for the visitors' recreation; bathhouses and a diet kitchen were added. The front porch was glassed in, adding a great deal to the comfort and pleasure of the patients. A new Burdick Light Bath Cabinet was installed, proving a benefit to all who required such treatments. A home for nurses and Association employees was erected. And we were told that there was the possibility that the War Department would grant the use of their land along the coast in front of the hospital. This would make it possible for the Association to improve and beautify the spot and greatly enhance the patients' opportunities for recreation.

Approximately three thousand visitors came to the hospital in the first year. A large number later applied for more data and also for membership. Among the visitors during the summer months was Chester A. Robinson, a professor in the Bentley School of Accounting and Finance in Boston. Mr. Robinson was greatly interested in the work and had a life reading for himself before returning to Boston to resume his duties. The Reverend Robert B. H. Bell, an author and lecturer of Denver, Colorado, visited the hospital and presented me with an autographed copy of his latest book, *The Challenge*, which is an interpretation of the mind of the Master and a translation of the Sermon on the Mount from the original Greek.

I sometimes felt there were so many things we had to think about that I did become more involved in commerce, as the secretary-treasurer, than I should have. I didn't shun any of the responsibility or try to make excuses for myself in any way. Even though I had to work much harder with readings that year than I ever have done in my life, and while it was unexpected even to me to be able to hold up under it, somehow, somewhere, the strength came to keep going, and I believe that it is true we will not be required to do more than we are given the strength to do, if we will use the strength and *know* that it is not of ourselves but of Him in whom we live and move and have our being. It is the same thing all along the line. We have just got to get that fact in the minds and the hearts of individuals, that we are assisting *them* to find their relationship with that all-creative energy, God, and that through Him we are able to do whatever we desire if we keep those desires and purposes one with His. For, as the readings have said over and over again, "First seek the Lord while He may be found, then all these things will be added unto you," and whether it be the needs of a physician to carry on our institution, or whether it be for the strength to give the information necessary for the individual seeking, or whether it be the money to pay for the various things necessary to be used for the carrying on, these things will be provided in His way.

Most of the funds came from Morton, and I was to see to it that expenditures were made according to budgets provided by the Hospital Committee. I would skimp hard on one end to bolster the weak end, keeping Morton advised as to where we appropriated too much and where too little. He wanted the best of everything and for me to make Dr. House to understand that he could have all the money necessary to buy the best meats and vegetables, the very best food, the best cook in the state, the best nurses, assistants, and servants, such that in system, service, and efficiency our hospital would be the best in the state. We practically gave Dr. House a free hand to build the best hospital in the state of Virginia, regardless of expense.[1]

We had one of the new employees of the Hospital to stay at our house. This was Mildred Davis. Our household at the time consisted of my wife and the two boys, my father, Miss Gladys, and Mildred, who worked in the research department of the Hospital. My office was in my home, where all readings were made. Miss Gladys worked there with me.

We had some very peculiar things that came up. Some things apparently were necessary to make us recognize that so long as we trust in dollars and in the prestige it may bring, we are weakening our own strength. So long as we trust in our own abilities we are made weak, even by that trust. But when we put our trust wholly in Him and ask that we may be

---

[1] Dr. House's salary was $4,500 a year, Mr. Cayce's was $3,400, and Miss Davis received $1,200.

used as the channel through which service may be rendered to our fellow man, then all these things come. It isn't God that has need of our little pitiful labors. It isn't that He is in need of anything from us. Rather that we are in need of everything from Him, and we must so conduct our lives as to keep Him first and foremost in everything we do and say.

Considerable interest was shown in the educational end of the work, and the new books received by the library were much used. And a very interesting phase of the work was begun by the Historical Committee, composed of Miss Gladys, Hugh Lynn, and Thomas J. Sugrue, who had been a classmate of Hugh Lynn's at Washington and Lee University and became interested in the work during summer visits with us. From the life readings of the members of the Association, the committee worked out the relations of various members to the other members, interpreted the individual's own life reading, and connected his urges and abilities with those of the people with whom he contacts.

The Association also had Mr. Shroyer working on the readings, separating the information in each reading into its various phases. From the physical readings he obtained the diagnoses and remedies prescribed, arranging these so they might be studied by medical researchers. The object of this research was to apply what was given to an individual to people having the same conditions. We expected many new cures might be discovered and more efficient methods of treatment.

From other readings the information was segregated into various departments—philosophical, historical, scientific, and material. Mr. Shroyer stated that his work would be finished when future generations have the information of the readings complete, in a manner most efficient for study and reference.[2]

---

[2] Gladys Davis continued this work for many years after the deaths of Mr. Cayce and Mr. Shroyer, indexing the readings into thousands of topics tabulated in the Reference Room of the A.R.E. Library. All this information was later computerized and made available to the public on a CD-ROM. This achievement contributed to Mr. Cayce's reputation as "the world's best-documented psychic."

At our meeting of the board of trustees in July 1929, many interesting developments came up for discussion and plans for the future were made in detail, and in view of the success of the past year the members felt greatly encouraged. After the meeting Morton was host to the officers and trustees of the Association at a banquet in the Cavalier Hotel. The affair marked the close of a successful year for the Association, and the beginning of another twelve months of what we believed were even brighter prospects.[3]

In the fall of 1929 Hugh Lynn and Tom Sugrue started up a quarterly called *The New Tomorrow* as the first official publication for the Association. Tom did an editorial that put into perspective some of the experiences that led up to our building the hospital, starting with the first experiment to clear my voice in 1901. This is a part of what he wrote:

> It was a long, hard road for Edgar Cayce, from the first fairy voice of childhood to the first ground broken for the Cayce Hospital. Man through his opaque mist of materialism sees little of the world beyond his length, breadth, and thickness, and because of his own conceit the attempts of truth boomerang from a solid wall of self. How difficult it is to make people understand something they cannot contact with the senses! How discouraging it is to see truth misinterpreted and misapplied, used as the individual sees fit,

———

[3] In his biography, Hugh Lynn gave a more graphic account: "All the wives were there, and we were going to have a dinner dance. They had all had readings but had never met one another. According to their readings, they had great conflict with each other in previous lives. But here they were, greeting each other and hugging. Within thirty minutes after they sat down and started talking, you could hear them all over most of the Cavalier Hotel, Morton and Bradley [a paint manufacturer from Chicago] screaming at one another. The argument was about the garage roof. One of them favored a tin roof and the other wanted a shingle roof. They expounded the advantages of each at the top of their voices. They got mad. I had warned them in a letter before they came to the meeting. I said, 'Now be real nice. You fought one another in another life.' But 'bang.' It went off like a firecracker. It just exploded, and Morton and Bradley were never on the same side of a vote from that time on."

to suit best the desires of his own nature! How long to the goal it seems when the road is so winding and rough, so studded with stubble, so littered with deadwood, so cluttered with debris!

To conquer self was the first task, and perhaps the hardest . . .

To convince himself that he was not a freak of nature, not an unconscious fraud, not a spiritual charlatan, was first of all the work of Edgar Cayce. For years he lived in self-conscious embarrassment because of his strange peculiarity, for years he feared to give the aid requested of him because he did not know nor understand the thing he did. For years his life was a mental torture, a seething indecision, a labyrinth of ideas, ideals, misbeliefs, and disillusions.

From the left came a cry of service, from the right a whisper of gain. Which way, Parnassus? No answer came. Time passed, and the mind that could not know of itself, learned from a world that clutched at stars and dragged its soul in mud. Reality stumbling skyward in the illusion of smut taught a lesson etched in pain and failure. The answer became obvious:

"Though I speak with the tongues of men and of angels, and have not love, I am become as sounding brass, or a tinkling cymbal. And though I have the gift of prophecy, and understand all mysteries and all knowledge, and though I have all faith, so that I could remove mountains, and have not love, I am nothing."

To Edgar Cayce had come an ideal, to him was shown the truth. And so he lived, and so he lives, and so he will live forever. He survived the cries that branded him charlatan, quack, spiritualist, clairvoyant, hypnotist, fake, and fraud. He survived the misunderstanding, pain, disillusionment, loss of friends, and attacks of enemies . . .

It is a long time between the idea and the creation, the dream and the reality. In 1911 Edgar Cayce began working toward the establishment of a hospital. On May 6, 1927, The Association of National Investigators was incorporated. On June 19, 1928, the first ground was broken for the

Cayce Hospital. On November 11, 1928, the Cayce Hospital was dedicated. On February 11, 1929, the first patient was treated in the Cayce Hospital.

The dream is a reality, the ideal is achieved, the work has *begun*.

Mr. Blumenthal had an article in *The New Tomorrow* that was taken from a book he wrote for the Association, called *Heaven on Earth*. Morton's article, "Our Philosophy," told that the ideal of the Association was to foster and encourage physical, mental, and spiritual benefits amongst its members through psychic research that we might gain the necessary knowledge to fit us to work on earth for creation, as does the mighty creative energy of life function to sustain creation throughout the whole universe. Morton said, "We shall strive to throw our influence on the side of the good and the spiritual, in order that the generations of men may cling to the link that binds them to the universe, to the noble, the beautiful, the honorable, and to the whole ideal while in this earthly process of development, rather than permit the influences of the purely material life to drag the inner developing potentiality that manifests itself in the form of physical personalities in the mire of animalistic materialism, that turns love into passion and adultery, nobleness into wrath, hatred and temper, honor into greed and selfishness, beauty into filth and the imagination into slavery to physical desires."[4]

The New Tomorrow also had sad news to report to our members. Dr. House, chief of staff of the hospital, passed away on October 12, 1929. Not only was Dr. House a great physician, he was a master of the art of human nature, capable of understanding and curing those ills not listed in the medical books. He had been associated for many years with the work and thoroughly understood the administering of the physical

—

[4] Blumenthal's article was later published in England in *Two Worlds*, a weekly journal devoted to philosophy and spiritualism. Prof. W. G. Hibbens of Sheffield University, who wrote the foreword to Morton's book, said *Two Worlds* had the largest circulation of any publication of its field in England.

readings. In the little time he was permitted to administer his duties in the hospital he performed his work in such a way as to register a lasting memory of efficiency and understanding which endeared him to the hearts of all he encountered. The memory of Dr. House will ever be an inspiration and guide to the servants of God and mankind who follow in his self-sacrificing footsteps.

After some time Dr. Lyman A. Lydic, an osteopath from Dayton, came to take up his duties.[5] Sister [Annie Cayce] also came from home to head the housekeeping of the institution.

The officers and trustees were frequent visitors to the hospital, and a large number of them spent Thanksgiving there. We were kept busy not only with visitors but with the work. We were booked up with appointments for physical readings, and there were more requests coming in every day from far and near. Each day brought new letters of thanks and hope, such as:

"Reading received this day. It is very *wonderful* at describing conditions which exist. Am ready and anxious to follow the suggested treatment as soon as I can find a convenient practitioner of osteopathy, there being none in our city to my knowledge. Am very sure of good results when I get the treatments under way."

"Just exactly as we see it, and are following directions precisely, with visible results already."

"The reading seems to fit my case and also coincide with the diagnoses of different doctors, but especially an osteopath. I will carry out your suggestions to the best of my ability."

"We feel that your reading is correct, and intend to carry it out to the limit, especially as we have no other course to follow. The doctor claims this will be a new discovery in medical science if our baby can be cured, as it is a rare case."

---

[5] It wasn't until after Dr. Lydic had been hired that Mr. Cayce realized that he was not a holistic physician in the Cayce model. As he told Morton: "He is a *wonderful* man at heart. He has had to crash through with his own personality, until he is one of those that are led to believe in might and main. He hasn't, or doesn't *seem* to be aware of the *spiritual* side of life at all."

All our days were very busy, Sundays as well, as I taught a Bible class at the First Presbyterian Church and on Sunday evening Morton Blumenthal and I endeavored to give educational lectures at the hospital. A dream of mine seemed to foretell this activity. The dream was about a baby who was very remarkable, talking before an audience that was spellbound. It was being examined to see that it wasn't just a midget, but a prodigy, and no one could find fault. The dream was interpreted as symbolic of conditions that would arise in the giving of speeches and activities, the baby suggesting what I felt as being little, or of no purpose in its environs; but the baby grows so as to make the hearts and souls of men of that turn which brings Life itself. The baby represented truth itself. It was a good dream.

Crowds gathered in the lecture room each Sunday afternoon. On many occasions there were outbursts after the lectures from individuals who felt they must get up and express themselves. On alternate Sundays Mr. Blumenthal talked on philosophy—Creative Evolution, The Value of Introspection, My Idea of God, and The Fourth Dimensional Viewpoint were some of the absorbing things taken up by him. He also conducted a philosophy class on alternate Saturday afternoons. This class attracted considerable interest and was well attended. The textbook he used was Ouspensky's *Tertium Organum*. Later Hudson's *Law of Psychic Phenomena*, and Bergson's *Creative Evolution*, with outside readings in James's *Varieties of Religious Experience* and *Pluralistic Universe*, and Bergson's *Mind Energy*.

In my Sunday afternoon talks for the patients and the members at large, I made no attempt to found a new sect, or an ism, or a body of thought, or to have a following of any kind. What I wanted to give was a better understanding of the Great Physician, that One who was able to heal by the touch of His hand. I wanted people to look at the mind as it relates to healing. I tried to help them to understand the information that was coming through the readings.

Soon after the hospital opened, there was talk among the trustees of Morton Blumenthal's idea of starting a school in connection with the institution. Morton got a reading on it. Tim Brown and I thought it might start with but a few teachers who knew of our purpose and a very few students, and to have builded from that start as a foundation for a larger institution. But Morton wanted a university, and he purchased some land near the hospital for that purpose. Tim thought this wasn't as we had anticipated, but he did not find fault with any particular person and he thought the experience would be beneficial to all and from this experience a greater institution might spring forth. As Morton was offering to finance the university and he was to be chairman of the board, it was done as he thought best.

Edwin Blumenthal met with a committee from Norfolk-Portsmouth Chamber of Commerce to inform them of the university plan. And in April 1930, the plans were reported by the press.[6]

---

[6] The Norfolk *Virginian-Pilot* reported that Atlantic University would open in September in temporary quarters, offering preparatory courses for a bachelor's degree in the arts or sciences, with departments in ancient and modern languages, English and English literature, Social Sciences (Economics, Sociology, and Government), Philosophy and Psychology, history, mathematics and astronomy, chemistry, physics, biology and physiology, public speaking and dramatics, and a laboratory of psychic research. The purpose of the laboratory for psychic research, Dr. Brown explained, was the same as the American Society for Psychic Research has been doing for forty years and with which many of the leading scientists of the country are identified, one of whom is Prof. William MacDougal, who came from Oxford University to Harvard and from there went to Duke University at Durham, N.C. "We shall try to discover the real facts about psychic phenomena in our laboratory," Dr. Brown said. "The approach will be entirely scientific and the same general methods will be used as are utilized in all the other sciences. We are most emphatically not interested in spiritualism, mediumism, clairvoyance or any of the other commonly known quackeries." Commenting on reports that the university would offer courses in mediumism, Dr. Brown said: "We have no idea of having any course or department on mediumism, spiritualism, or anything of the sort. This report has obviously originated from uninformed sources and entirely misrepresents the purpose of Atlantic University. The institution will be incorporated under the title 'The Trustees of Atlantic University,' and it is our purpose to establish here a center of learning, culture, and research at which every department of human knowledge and scientific endeavor will be represented which has anything to offer looking toward increasing the worthwhileness of human life and experience, both individually and socially." Be-

Dr. Brown gave a fine address at the convocation, which was held at my church [in September 1930]. As the classroom buildings were still being builded, the university opened in two hotels that were empty of summer visitors.

That October I realized that twenty years before, many were the reports given out in various newspapers of the country from a paper presented by Dr. Ketchum to the Clinic Research Society of Boston. In October 1930, the Cayce Hospital of Research and Enlightenment was in operation. Ten patients were in the hospital and eleven outside taking treatments there. Nearly a hundred appointments were waiting to be made for readings, as I was able to make only two appointments a day except when having check readings. I spent many a day in thought and effort, trying as I understand it to be used as a channel through which others may gain a consciousness of their abilities and talents, which—when made one with the

---

fore classes opened, philosophical differences between Brown and Blumenthal surfaced in the press. The *Baltimore Sun* reported that Brown had "relegated psychic research to a footnote," while Blumenthal said "the inception of Atlantic University really had sprung from the work of Edgar Cayce, a psychic healer." Brown countered in the *Virginia Beach News* by saying: "We have no idea of having any course or department on mediumism, spiritualism or anything of the sort." Atlantic University opened classes in two beachfront hotels for its first class of 209 students. In addition to the liberal arts curriculum, it offered programs in pre-law, pre-engineering, and pre-medicine, plus a football team, the Seadogs; a women's soccer team, the Mermaids; a dance band, the Atlantians; fraternities; and a three-legged mascot dog named Tripod. But it faced tough competition—ten days before it opened, the College of William and Mary opened a campus in Norfolk, later to become Old Dominion University. More critical perhaps was the financial burden of the Blumenthals trying to underwrite two fledgling institutions at once. The same month that A.U. opened, Blumenthal seized control of the hospital in order to reduce expenses. Mr. Cayce feared that the cost of the university would divert funds from the hospital, with good reason. The Blumenthals were said to have pledged $5,000 a month to support the university, and they had budgeted $3,000 a month for the hospital. Blumenthal evidently had expected to make a fortune on one particular investment—a perpetual-motion machine. He had even asked in a reading, "Are we not right in formulating plans to appropriate $10 million, to be obtained from the [perpetual motion] machine, for the university, and to make the university a university in every sense of the word?" The response from Cayce in trance was: "Absolutely correct."

creative forces—will bring them to an understanding of their relationship to their fellow man and the Creator. As I wonder and ponder over circumstances that arise in the life and lives of individuals seeking information through these sources, I indeed wonder what it is all about—and if there is not the thread of life running through it all, life as propounded by the Master Himself when He gave, "He that would have life must give himself, that he may have life more abundant. He that exalteth himself shall be debased, but he that maketh his will one with the Father shall ask in *my name* and shall in no wise be cast out. Seek and ye shall find. Knock and it shall be opened unto you—for through me ye have an advocate with the Father, and the Father that heareth in secret will reward thee openly."

Many changes have taken place in the thought of peoples since the first reading was given years ago, but as I think and ponder over these changes, I can but wonder if it is not the evolution of man's thought, man's gaining an insight into the consciousness that may be had by pondering in his heart God's revelations to man and man's relation to God.

About this time I had an unusual experience during a reading for a lady who came out from Norfolk. Was it a dream or a vision? I give it below in detail:

I was preparing to give a reading. As I went out, I realized that I had contacted Death, as a personality, as an individual, or as a being. Realizing this, I remarked to Death, "You are not as ordinarily pictured, with a black mask or hood, or as a skeleton, or like Father Time with a sickle. Instead you are fair, rosy, robust, and have a pair of shears or scissors." I had to look twice at the feet or limbs, or even at the body, to see it take shape.

But it replied, "Yes, Death is not what many seem to think. It is not the horrible thing that is so often pictured. Just a change. Just a visit. The shears or scissors, indeed, are the most representative implements to man of life and death. They, indeed, unite by dividing, and divide by uniting. The cord not, as usually thought, extending from the center—but is broken from the head, the forehead, that soft portion you see pulsate in the infant. Hence we see old people, unbeknown to themselves, gain strength from youth by kissing there—and youth gains wisdom from age by such kisses. Indeed the vibrations may be raised to such an extent as to rekindle or connect the cord, even as the Master did the son of the widow of Nain—for He took him not by the hand (which was bound to the body as the custom of the day) but rather stroked him on the head, and the body took life of Life itself. So, you see, the silver cord may be broken but Vibration—" and here it ended.

I felt some anxiety respecting the outcome of a meeting Morton had called. Mr. Shroyer came in, but I was feeling too bad even to talk. I felt too bad to even go to Sunday school. Some very drastic changes were inaugurated at the hospital. If these were necessary, all the more reason that we should be more patient and do our level best.

Soon after that Morton called a meeting of the board of the Association, at which he directed that no more patients were to be admitted to the hospital. I was somewhat surprised when he, who seemed to have been so very sincere in his undertaking in the work with the Association, took such radical steps or changes in his ideas. It may have been partially brought on by the economic conditions; it may have been partially caused by differences of opinion as to who should and who should not receive readings of materialistic or commercial nature. Anyway, his decision was to discontinue the hospital activities, close it, and disband the Association.[7]

---

[7] When the hospital closed after two years, the *Virginia Beach News* reported: "The report that Mr. Cayce, who is possessed of peculiar psychic powers, refused to advise Mr. Blumenthal in his stock transactions, thereby causing a break between the two men, has been denied. It is understood that Mr. Blumenthal's first lack of interest in the hospital began to show itself several months ago when the appropriations were materially cut down. Last October Mr. Blumenthal gave the patients in the hospital notice that if they remained they did so of their own volition and at their own risk.

"Following the rumor that the break was caused due to Mr. Cayce's refusal to advise Mr. Blumenthal in his stock transactions, another rumor was heard that Mr. Blumenthal had acquired the services of Mrs. Paul Devlin, who it is understood claims to be a psychic and has been advising Mr. Blumenthal. Reports from New York have it that Mrs. Devlin was formerly a telephone operator in the building in which the Blumenthal office is located. It is known that she was registered at the Cavalier Hotel in January about the

When I was told that it was necessary to close the hospital, I wondered what it was all about. This was one of the saddest experiences of my whole life. I am not any different from other individuals who have their dreams and want to tell God how to do things. For years my great dream was to have a hospital, to have doctors and nurses and the best scientific means of treating people according to the readings. My dream at last was realized. The Cayce Hospital was in existence. It was working.

Things had gone well with the hospital for some time, but finally friction developed and disturbances came and what seemed to Edgar some very selfish demands were made of him that did not seem just, under the circumstances. So he refused to comply, and that created more friction, which continued until the venture was dissolved and Edgar walked out empty-handed but clean-handed, relinquishing everything. He said in word and in action, "If that is your policy and that is what you want, you can have it all, for I do not want it that way." He did not lay any claim to anything or any part, for he did not want to be a party to anything that would create hard feelings or contention. That was not the way he wanted the work to be promoted or conducted, and he would not feel right even remaining in the company or a party to anything that was creating such contention and ill feelings and making possible enemies of friends or causing such friction between friends and associations. It seemed plain that the ultimate aim of those taking part was self-interest, money and what it would

---

same time that Mr. Blumenthal and Mr. Weisbrod were there."

Mrs. Devlin, at Blumenthal's behest, gave a talk at the hospital and to a class at Atlantic University, where she was exhibited as an example of how psychic ability could be developed. She is reputed to have told the class that when Mr. Blumenthal wanted to know what was going on in Virginia Beach, she would go to sleep and travel to Virginia Beach to get the information for him. Morton's wife subsequently sued him for divorce over his relationship with Mrs. Devlin. Mr. Cayce was said to have been angered that Mc on directed him to stop giving readings for Kahn, to which he is said to have replied, "Eddy will be six feet underground" before that happens.

buy, which was very different from Edgar's purpose or desire.
His desire from childhood had been simply to help his fellow
man, never in any big way as the world defines big, but in the
everyday opportunities, the little things that came under his
observation and was within the bounds of his reach, and to
make peace, joy, harmony, and contentment and happiness
among men. Naturally, when there was friction, contention,
and ill feelings, he could see that was not what he was striving
for, and if that attitude could not be changed, he was ready
to get away from it. From the beginning, when such distur-
bances came he continued to lend help as far as he was con-
cerned individually, giving the readings or information when
and where requested; and in that way many hundreds have
been helped.

No one can possibly imagine how it hurt, how it still hurts.
Yet I am sure I must have been going at it in the wrong way.
You cannot force people to believe anything. I learned that all
over again. God gives us a free will. It is up to us to use it.
We should glorify that we find good and not mention that we
find bad—or let it alone, forget it.

I have gone over every detail of the happenings in my own
mind many times, for no one, not even I, can ever put into
words what that meant to me; but put it all down as a very
miserable failure on my part, and certainly I blame no one else
but myself for its failure. I am sure everyone might find fault
with everyone else, looking at it from their own viewpoint.
Morton apparently lost interest in the phases of the phenomena
that manifest through me. Whether it was a personal thing or
a development for himself and that he found other channels
[Patricia Devlin] more to his way of thinking, I do not know.[8]

---

[8] The stock market crash in October 1929 has frequently been given as the
basic cause of the failure, but the evidence suggests that the Blumenthals
were relatively unscathed—three months after Black Friday Morton took his
wife to the French Riviera for a month's holiday, and Edwin holidayed in
Havana. They were apparently unprepared, however, for the expenses and
failed to hire a business manager, leaving management to Mr. Cayce, who
acknowledged to Edwin: "I'm not that good a businessman—but it certainly
does get my goat to do my level best and then find I have fallen far short of

Tim Brown, vice-president of the Association, later offered his opinion in a letter to me:

> *"When I look back at the inception of the hospital and we had the first meeting to seek appropriations and donations, I felt, intuitively, that something was wrong with the method of organization and took this up with Morton. I thought it wiser to start out with a smaller building and to raise all the cost of same before starting to build so that it would be free from any mortgage or lien. I did not think that it was carrying out the spirit or sense of the Association to have it a one-man organization (one man carrying practically the whole financial burden) but that it would be more in order for each member to contribute some proportion, if it were only a dollar or so each month. I always had confidence in Morton, and still have, but as my feelings were so strong in the matter I held up the letting of the contract while I tried to get Morton to accede to my views. Morton was too enthusiastic. The readings said 'Make a start' and finally the contract was let and the building got under way.*
>
> *"One summer, after the hospital had been built, there was a meeting at your house at which a young man wanted Morton, Eddie, and me to contribute $500 per month to help out in the moving of a boys school to Virginia Beach. The next day on our return to New York I told Morton that I did not want anything to do with this and we had all we could do to support the hospital. Morton gave up the idea of this but after the crash*

---

what should be." When Mr. Cayce gave a reading on the financial distress of the hospital, it pinpointed the "extravagant expenditure" by him as the one in charge. Mr. Cayce maintained that he was doing his best under impossible circumstances. As for Miss Gladys, he said "she works many, many nights until ten, eleven, and twelve o'clock trying to keep up with the correspondence—and that isn't right, with what we are paying her [$100 a month]." Morton and Kahn also got into a squabble over the cost of furniture his company supplied for the hospital, ending in a lawsuit. Morton and Mr. Cayce also ended up in court after Blumenthal forced them to evacuate the house they were renting. Dr. Lydic offered the diagnosis that Morton was "suffering from paranoia."

in 1929 he started the university. The backing of this university was the contributing factor to the dissolution of the hospital. Could the hospital have survived through the Depression years with so large a loan upon it, had Morton not overextended himself, is not the question. There were underlying factors and forces, not apparent to me at this time, that brought about the dissolution. These forces could have been set up in the improper formation of the Association. Other forces not of unselfish service, could have crept in. It could have been the balancing of karmic forces or many other forces released.

"Surely the contributing force in its entirety could not be laid to Morton, it could be buried deeply within the many of us members of the Association. Morton was only the channel of dissolution. I mention this, not to bring up unpleasant memories, but to try and visualize what we, as individuals, were to learn from this one experience."

Before long the school got into a bad way. When they fell out within their own ranks, it brought on the beginning of the end.[9] I did not know just what disposition would be made, whether they would allow the school to go on for the rest of the semester so the students might have credits for their work or not. There was a great deal of jealousy, animosity, and a lot of pure undefiled cussedness—and it's such times as these that all such combined tends to make for very unsatisfactory, very unsavory conditions.

I know Morton and Eddie were sincere in what they did and I certainly could never blame them for anything that happened. I just hope that I may some day call them my close friends again, for I loved them as my own closest friends. I

—

[9] The Blumenthals supported the university for only one semester before pulling out. The perpetual-motion machine they hoped would bring them $10 million failed to deliver. Dr. Brown tried to keep A.U. alive but failed, and bankruptcy was declared in December 1931. As for *The New Tomorrow*, its second issue was its last. But it proved to be the herald of many publications, both periodicals and books, that the Cayce organizations would publish in the years since that hopeful beginning.

hope all of us associated at the time have grown bigger and better men in the service of God and our love for our fellow man.[10]

If the work is what we feel it is, it must succeed, even though it passes through the trial as by fire. If it isn't right, it has no place. If I know myself, I only want to do the right and proper thing. As I have my own self received such wonderful gifts through these channels, I can only hope that I may be able to help others in a like manner. I trust that I can so conduct my own life that the sources may find me a channel that may be used in service to my fellow man.

I hope I'll be able to think right, act right, and do just as my Lord and Master would have me do—for it is that those who seek may know Him better that I care to carry on, yet when I feel that the life and light of my own loved ones were given through these channels, whatever the condition, when I am asked to try and be of aid I feel I must not refuse. If this phenomena manifested through me can be of value to others, I am sure—from my own personal experience for myself and loved ones—it is right that I at least try. Circumstances alter conditions. Perhaps sin lieth at the door. May we all consecrate ourselves, our lives, our endeavors, to His Cause, His Purpose, His way, whatever they may be. If we are not able, through the information, to make life more worthwhile, even for those who have just had physical disturbances, we feel that it has failed in its real purpose. Inasmuch as the hospital had been in operation for the aid of human ills, we feel like—being limited as we are—it is only just and right that we continue our endeavors in that direction.

---

[10] The Blumenthals later moved to Virginia Beach, living with Mrs. Devlin and her husband, but never reconciled with Mr. Cayce. Both divorced. Morton died of a heart attack at age fifty-nine in 1954. Edwin remarried and changed his name from Blumenthal to Kane.

22

Association for Research and
Enlightenment, 1931–

After the hospital closed and the Association of National Investigators was dissolved in February 1931, I wrote letters to all those who had stood by us through the years and been active or who had shown interest in the work, the oldest contacts and the newest. We called a meeting in March to decide whether or not the work should continue, whether or not there should be an organization at all, whether or not we should give up the work entirely.

We took readings as to what should be done.[1] We wanted to be very sure of our foundation in forming a new organization.

It was a grand meeting that went on most all day at our house. People came from everywhere and assured us that they wanted the work to continue. Our friends in New York, practically every one of them, were very enthusiastic, if I am any judge, and I don't think I was kidding myself. The local people at Virginia Beach and Norfolk were very enthusiastic, and if I lost a single friend by the break with Mr. Blumenthal, I am not aware of it. Possibly I would be the last to be aware of it, but seemingly there were a great many more to rally to the cause by that very thing.

Three months later we had a pre-organization meeting. There were sixty or more present for this meeting. Not a great many from New York—Mr. Kahn, Mr. and Mrs. Levy, Mr. and Mrs. Zentgraf, and a Mr. Cravis from Atlantic City. The rest of them were from Norfolk and vicinity and North Carolina and Washington, D.C. Lester S. Parsons of Norfolk was

—

[1] A transcript of remarks and readings given at this historic meeting is reproduced in Appendix F.

the attorney. H. H. Jones, commercial agent for the Norfolk-Southern Railroad, was named president.

The trustees named were: Dr. Paul Kaufman, Dave Levy, Dave Kahn, Hugh Lynn, my father, Miss Esther Wynne, Miss Florence Edmonds, Mr. C. A. Barrett, Dr. McChesney, Dr. Job Taylor, Jerome Danzig, Mrs. Walsh, Dr. Scattergood, Mr. Zentgraf, Mr. F. D. Lawrence (vice-president of American National Bank of Portsmouth), and H. H. Jones. We also agreed to have official representatives in various parts of the country, to whom individuals could appeal for aid in obtaining a reading, also in understanding the information as may be given when they get the reading. These were to be from coast to coast, where people have expressed themselves as willing to be official representatives of the Association. Mildred Davis was named secretary, Mr. Shroyer the treasurer, and Mr. Preston business manager. It was quite an enthusiastic group. It is quite noteworthy that we had people in all walks of life—a very, very representative group of people, if I am any judge.

Tom Sugrue suggested that it be named Association for Research and Enlightenment. Tom gave credit to Dr. William Moseley Brown, president of Atlantic University, for naming the organization. On June 6, 1931, the application for our state charter went in for that name. A very broad charter was applied for and granted in the Certificate of Incorporation on July 7, 1931. We tried to make sure that the same thing wouldn't happen to A.R.E. as to A.N.I., that the organization *would* survive.

The purposes of the organization were set out in the charter as follows:

To conduct and carry on psychic and scientific research, including physical, educational, psychic and social investigations, and to conduct medical research, general hospital work, establish hospitals, schools and sanitariums for consultations with reference to suggestions for the cure of, psychic treatment of, and psychic study of, disease of any and all kinds, and for medical and surgical aid, treatment and care of persons sick, deformed or suffering from bodily injuries; to assist and train suitable persons as nurses for the sick, and to conduct departments of the said corporation in research and study, aid and conduct hospitals, camps, physical training schools, mechanical laboratories and plants, lectures, schools, publications, history and archaeology, investigation of psychic phenomena, the giving and interpreting of psychic readings; philosophical study; to study or engage in community welfare work, conduct of study groups and classes for economic development, physical, medical and social clinics, libraries, endowments, charity and study courses, and any and all other class or kind of activity or work allowed under Chapter 151 of the Code of Laws of Virginia and any and all work incidental or necessary for the carrying out of the purposes of the said corporation.

The said corporation shall have power to collect fees for the treatment and services rendered from those who are able to pay for the same, which shall be used for the maintenance and incidental expenses of the corporation and the advancement of its purposes, but shall not be used for private gain, and wherever desired to render free service where the persons needing the services of the said corporation are unable to pay such fees or expense. The purposes of the said corporation are to be philanthropic and benevolent and it is not organized for profit. It may accept donations, endowments or gifts from such persons as may desire to aid and assist the said corporation in its work.

It was agreed that I would give readings for A.R.E. members and be paid a salary. The contract with me was then renewed year after year. The business manager would relieve me of responsibility in connection with the business details. Some of the board members later began to discuss the necessity of setting up a foundation to assure the continuance. Two years later, in May 1933, a Cayce Foundation dinner meeting was held in New York, and in 1935 the board appointed a committee to plan the establishing of the foundation to preserve the A.R.E. and the work, even after I had gone. We had wonderful people on the board.

Mr. Preston was very anxious that someone on the old

board [of the A.N.I.] make a howl about the hospital property. The grounds looked very, very good, the shrubbery and the flowers wonderful, but they showed that they hadn't been taken care of as they were when we were there—the tennis court was in bad shape. But we all felt rather loath to cause a wrangle about anything, even though we felt we had been mistreated. I was not able to give a reading on account of circumstances and the crosses that had been between Mr. Blumenthal and myself. Mr. Blumenthal asked for the house where we lived. It was perfectly all right, if he just hadn't plain lied about it—that I just dislike in anyone.

I had an experience that foretold this move. While giving a reading I saw this house all fixed up, and our home on the corner next to it. Hugh Lynn and Mildred had a printing press back in their office, and the whole building was enlarged and everything running like clockwork. The reading said this represented the breaking up of our little household in order that enlargements might ensue, even as Jesus passed through death that He might be the Savior and Lord of all. It suggested we make the moves that were necessary, and in faith believing that "All things work together for good to those that *love* His coming." More too often is it interpreted "love the Lord." But His *coming*, for His promise was that "I will *not* leave thee comfortless, but will *come* to thee."

We moved to the Wright Cottage on the ocean in front of the old hospital. Mr. Banks, a brother of the man who runs the Princess Anne Country Club, had the hospital building that summer and ran it as a hotel—the Prince Henry Hotel. Apparently he didn't succeed, as he closed on Labor Day. To see it used as a hotel, if there is a great deal of sentiment, you can imagine what it meant for us to be in such an environment and not be able to help yourself. In some ways, I guess I had about as tough a deal as anybody could. Possibly I had it coming to me, or it wouldn't have come.

Our new organization had a setback in the early months. Mr. Preston, the manager, went to New York to confer with some members of the board there, was taken quite ill and had to be in the hospital. This hindered the work in getting those

things started that were his part of the job. In due course Hugh
Lynn, who finished his college studies, took up these duties.

During that first year we started a work that had been very
sadly neglected before we were able to get enough of those
whom I thought had the right feelings about it to combine
their efforts. This was the spiritual healing group, composed
of a very good circle.[2] While you may rest assured that you
have the prayers of each and everyone of these, I feel that He
has promised, "If two or three are gathered together in My
name, there am I in the midst of them," and I feel that He is
faithful to do that which is best for the individuals, in the
things that may be applied physically and mentally, for their
health as well as their happiness in every respect; though we
recognize He knows best and He doeth all things well.

During the first year or so many asked me, Why have an
association? What is its value? What does it have to do with
your work? The answer is that the Association has nothing
whatsoever to do with my work, save making it possible for
people to have the information which comes through me as a
channel. How? Through *cooperation!* Those who have studied
the lessons prepared by our Norfolk Study Group No. 1 know
what cooperation means. When individuals work together toward something worthwhile, we have strength.

One afternoon while meditating, the same exuberant feeling
came over me that used to years ago, but which had been lost
to me for twenty-five years. I asked in this reading what it
meant. It was said to be an experience of the inner self awakening to those potential forces as may be the more active in
the body as developments come, in those of the meditations,
with those active forces around or about same. As has been
given, there shall be in the latter days, "Your young men shall

—

[2] This "very good circle" became what was later known as the first Search
for God study group. Its members, working with Mr. Cayce, composed the
Search for God books, which have ever since been the basic study text for
study groups all over the world. This circle also established a prayer healing
group, known as the Glad Helpers, which still meets weekly at A.R.E. in
Virginia Beach.

dream dreams, your old men shall see visions, your maidens shall prophesy." These are coming to pass, with the upheavals as are just before the world in *many* a quarter!

The message I received was: Be ye faithful; even as ye would have mercy show mercy; as ye would have peace give peace; as ye would have patience shown be patient with others; for only in the attributes OF the living forces of God may ye *find* God; *not* in the *material* things that make of earthy gratifications!

I feel that my work in relation to the Association can be compared to a portion of the history in the Old Testament. When the children of Israel organized themselves under the direction of their leader, with individuals who were to act as the interpreters, two individuals—Nabab and Abihu—did not cooperate. They were destroyed. It is the same with a work of this nature. Unless the application is in sincerity, it will destroy the individual tampering with it.

The Association may honestly correlate the individual findings which have been good and present them to others, thus assisting those who seek through this source not only to aid themselves but to aid others in gaining an understanding for themselves.

The Association is not trying to revolutionize the world. If one person has been aided in finding his relationship to God, then the Association has been a marvelous success. On the other hand, if this has not been done, then it has been a failure—no matter how many members it may have or how great an outward show it may make. The Association stands on the results individuals receive. The results speak for themselves and for the Association.

23

DIARY, 1938

Friday, Mar. 18, 1938.[1]

My birthday—at one time or another every one no doubt had felt they would like to have kept a diary, while this is not to be a diary, yet hope to make it a year at least out of a busy, interesting life. Best then to take stock and see from what premise, am reasoning, Live at Virginia Beach, Va. on 14th St. or Arctic Circle, opposite Catholic Church, am buying the home, known as the DeTreville house been here now since June 1932, my Father was with me for a while passed on last April 11th. At the time was visiting Sister Annie, in Nashville Tenn. Was buried in Hopkinsville, Ky our old home town. Am working with the Association for Research and Enlightenment, Inc. organized in July, 1931, Princess Anne Co. Va.

Wife Gertrude Cayce conducts the readings—Hugh Lynn Cayce oldest boy Mgr. of the Assn. he was 31 day before yesterday, is at present in N.Y. stopping with the Zentgrafts. Mr. Z. first Chair of board of Trustees, and one of the organizers of the Assn. Edgar Evans Cayce in school at Duke University, was 20 on last Feb. 9th. taking an engineers course—has one more year there. Miss Gladys Davis is the stenographer—has been since Sept. 1923.

The day is cold and dark, rather dreary, a very good breakfast tho, as went out to the Lake in rear of house and caught me three little fish for my breakfast, they are very nice.

The afternoon reading was for Mrs. Murdock, of Norfolk, a

---

[1] This was Mr. Cayce's 61st birthday. His secretary, Gladys Davis, attached this note to this typescript: "This is Edgar Cayce's own typing. He decided to start a day to day diary. It lasted for the following few pages." No editing changes were made in preparing his diary entries for publication.

very lovely lady, in the evening a surprise party for me—Birthday party, there were Dr. Gena Crews, Mr. H. E. Poole, Boyde and Berlin Davis, Thomas Jefferson Davis, Mr. and Mrs. Gimbert, Mae Verhoeven, Mr. Godfrey, Miss Godfrey, Mr. and Mrs. Ellington, Mack and Margaret Wilkins, Mrs. Ellington's sister the nurse, Mr. and Mrs. Miller, Frances Morrow, Miss Wynne, Helen S. Wheeler, Alvin Wheeler, Mrs. Lawrence, Mrs. Olds, Mr. and Mrs. Helms, Mrs. Kemp, Mrs. Peary, Mr. and Mrs. Oscar Smith, Mrs. Connock, Mrs. Ruth Holland, Miss (Boogie) Vincent, Mrs. Jones, Frances Jones, Miss Florence Edmonds, Mrs. Jane Williams, Mr. DeMaio, Mrs. Ruth LeNoir.

A very lovely party, how can any one say what they feel when such a lovely group show such loving appreciation, and all the lovely things brought me, what a blessing to have friends, to feel that others care, yes, have given readings for each of these at one time or another, or practically all, and they must feel help has come, for year after year they have held this love feast for me, God bless every one of them. A regular show was put on, a curtain across one end of the room and Mother Goose rhymes were acted out by various members of the group. lovely lovely.

Sister's picture came, very good, and Berlyn brought me a frame for it my, how she looks like Mother and Dad.

Another birthday, how the milestones pass, may I fill each day given me with efforts to bring the consciousness of the Christ in the hearts and lives of those I meet and try and help. May I live as God would have me live.

March, 19th 1938

Beautiful day, shrubs came from Allen Nurseries, planted them. Raspberries, currents, two pear trees, azaleas. grape, young berries, and Rhubarb, and a willow tree, lilly bulbs.

Feeling fair, reading for Mr. Taylor of Frisco, expecting E. E. this afternoon wants to go to engineers congress at Lexington, coming home for car. think will have to try a little fishing this afternoon if isn't too cool.

nothing new in mail this morning, pretty good catch—two nice cat and few perch—do like these to eat. E. E. came in afternoon about 4.30.

19th was supposed to be a very important day—according to astroligist guess it is as any other, what we make it, tho Mar. 19, 1919 was the first time gave anything in reading about astrology, or the like, some say this the most important reading ever give, from astrological standpoint.

suppose should give a thought for the day as Uncle Ezra does on the Alka-Seltzer programme: "The good we do lives after we are gone. so only good must be eternal, for it never dies, will be wonderful then to have the good we have tried to do as the clothing of our life hereafter. Yes, we are clothed with our tries to be good."

Sunday, Mar. 20th 1938

E. E. home for car. looking very well, says is studying hard, must has very good reports. didn't go to church or S.S. Miss Gladys did, she is secy. Treas. believe now a very lovely day, tho looked for time as if it might rain. in afternoon, Mae Gimbert Verhoeven and sister Anne with Mr. Kelly came by, Mr. K. wanted appointment for reading. T. J. came for awhile, cute as can be. E. E. left for school about two or few minutes after, thought for the day—Keep sweet yourself if you would have those round you, keeping sweet or even liverable with.

Monday, Mar. 21st 1938

First day of spring—and really seems like it too. lovely out, cut several Hyacinths from the yard, they are beautiful, when birds sing, sun shines, well the whole world looks and seems hopeful. no wonder the people of old worshipped the Sun.

a few fishes in the afternoon, and to the picture show in evening—very good

feeling fair—and can we but think right, would make a lot of difference.

Thought for the day—beauty by comparison, and love by the gift, is too often our judgment of an experience.

H. L. called in late evening.

Tuesday, Mar. 22nd 1938

Another lovely morning, had to go into Norfolk for rent was due, Oh yes, had photo made for the booklets. a special reading for Mr. Goetz today, and an emergency for Mr. Savage for tomorrow, why H. L. phoned last night.

Mar. 25th 1938

Days have passed, not so much neglect as lack of having much if anything to say. but yesterday for the first time since coming to the Beach in 1925 have I seen a robin make the place something like a home, Oh yes they pass over, stop and sing a lay, but to give the appearance of making the place a home or singing the mate call as if preparing for a home— guess they do not come so near the seashore for nesting tho only a few miles inland there are plenty—robins are among my favorite song birds—their early morning call is lovely—a note of sadness in the early morning yet a happiness—not just the same in any other unless it is the Cat bird. at evening mockingbirds aplenty—and their song is lovely here—some have nested in the little tree out front each year, hope with the willow just planted a few days ago, some other will make their home here, saw a thrush looking it over yesterday—also he gave forth one of his most beautiful lays—planted my strawberries yesterday—all the birds like them as well as I, so may or may not have a few more visitors from them lust for the berries—they like raspberries also and have a few of those coming in hope they all do well.

Madam Verdier arrived yesterday afternoon—apparently very well pleased as checked on at least three of the experiences she had as to appearances—phone call from Hardwicke son, may see them before they leave the vicinity—his Mother is with him so he said.

Feeling pretty fair, bright and pretty but a cool wind, had to order more coal this morning guess that will last until summer—like the spring, especially when it is pretty and bright, lovely to look each day for a new shoot from some flower or bush putting forth its effort to be itself, and to the glory of its Maker, appears only man puts on a show for his fellow man— to impress them, but is that what the robin does when he sings to his mate trying to *impress* her with his lovely song—the study of nature tho must be a closer study of the Creator, and

His thought of man—do the birds imitate man or man imitate nature. or what is the cycle anyway?

Be yourself—yes that is right—but if this is only an experience, and we have lived before. and will again—which self are you being? Oh as looking for the new shoot—the new leaf, each experience is a new opportunity to express all the beauty of love, for God—in whom we live and have our being. don't wonder. one is at times thought curious, unreasonable yes, plain nutty when they relate some of their experiences, that to them are very real. Like last evening, know I was not asleep, and don't think it was purely imagination, but—years ago as a child used to see, talk with, play with, those that some told me did not exist—these came to me in one, two and a few times as many as three at once, and were not always the same, sometimes boys and sometimes girls, they told me their names, when they were with me and we played together. but last evening they all came at once, eight of them, five boys and three girls—their first question was do you remember us, and to be sure I did, no they appear not to have grown any, why, did they want to play, no, then what—when will you be with us again to discuss the things we used to? What does it mean, I do not know, am just wondering will they come again?

In the reading for Madam Verdier, felt the presence of a master—not a disincarnate entity, a master of some realm— but a glow of orange seemed to be about them or maybe golden more than orange. no do not understand all this, but hope and believe it a growth of some kind.

thought for the day—keep sweet yourself, would you have things pleasant about you.

Mar. 26th 1938

Cold, dark, rainy, dreary day, the sunshine will have to be within, it looks today.

Saw "Snow White" last night, a beautiful picture, simple, yet most extravagant what a wonderful mind must have conceived of animating the fairy story, possibly just giving it life again, who knows.

Faired off in afternoon and was much brighter.

A lot to say maybe, but how to say it—Madam Vermier was in to see us [for] another reading—leaving tho this afternoon. What a mind, travel has given her a perspective that one like myself seldom sees, or sees expressed so beautifully. Wonder what travel would do for me, but opportunities are ever present, if not for travel to gather from these we meet that as answers within ourselves. To the longing that must be within every heart—only when we become querulous and boresome even to ourselves do we lose the privilege of expanding to God's love that is ever shed about us.

Sunday, Mar. 27, 1938

What has the day as a marker for events meant to me, something—Oh yes, in 1900 this day awoke to realize could not speak above a whisper the beginning of that experience as may be said to be the work in which I am engaged now, step by step yet, no different from the beginnings as I see it—but who said "there is nothing new under the sun" couldn't be new then the same old thing, "Know the Lord thy God is one" dressed up in a new bonnet or possibly a new dress, but the same truth, growing by unfoldment in our limited minds.

Wed, Mar. 30th 1938

What—nothing happened on 28th and 29th—Oh, yes, much but nothing said about it, not that much may not have been felt, but there are days when there just doesn't seem to be words to say what you would wish to even. Oh, God, make me thankful for all the nice things people have written—let me so live that my life before men will be in keeping [with] what they feel has and does develop in their experience—keep me humble, yet glory in being a child of God.

How soon had to make application of the above, and would have to say hardly big enough to do so without feeling hurt, is it my ego, pride, or what that felt the hurt, of what Mr. W. had said—Oh God keep me, for thy namesake, let me live as thou would have me live, each day, each experience, let them be a growth toward the Light of thy kingdom, that must be within.

April 3rd 1938

Days again—nothing said—the boys home, Sat they painted their room, no Friday or Thursday afternoon—for Friday in town—trouble at H.H.R.—what will they do with it— Sat the hike—that is right—for Ecken and I built the birdhouse, hope we have a few Martins come stay with us. Mrs. Harris here for her reading, pleased.

Cool this morning, not quite so cold as was predicted by weather man, may be by night, hope doesn't kill fruit, was 42 [degrees] on front porch this morning. guess that would be a very good record. but possibly am too dilatory about keeping it at all, let things keep me from saying what I feel too easily. guess grow more sensitive each day, but certainly should not let self grow foolishly so, sensitive—but make it constructive should be the way, for if that is not done then it makes hurt— yes, a deep hurt so—the hurt becomes personal, and self consciousness prevents one from being very helpful. and it is the helpful life that is worthwhile.

Played bridge in the afternoon, H. L., E. E., G. and I. Quite cool but sun shining in afternoon.

April 4, 1938

Up early, as boys wanted to paint mothers room. T. about 42—sun pretty but a cool wind blowing from the west, feel fair and guess have pretty full week ahead, to keep well-balanced is not always easy.

April 5th, 1938

Sun shining, cool about 50, straightening up rooms, nothing special of note

a bit of retrospection gives about

Edgar Evans went back to school, Duke, this afternoon, saw picture alone tonight. Caught the big fish—bass—weighed 7¼.

Life and all its ramifications are but the attempt of something to give expression—thus it behooves none of us to speak ill of the other fellow.

April 6th, 1938

The note—225. now. Very fine day but cool about 52,
What an experience to know, well you have been—but are
not.

April 9th, 1938

Rain yesterday and last night—and what a rain—all up in
basement this morning—caught a pike on the trotline yesterday—was not aware there were any in the lake—very nice—
wonder if he will stay in the box—water all over it, hope so.

Dream—night before last—of Berlyn being tortured by In-
dians—and I came to the rescue.

looks like more rain today—feeling pretty good—temperature 66 at 9 A.M., spring I guess—tho weatherman says
much colder by morning.

Could we keep our heads, at all times know God is near—
and all is well? what a different world this would be.

Sunday, Apr. 10th 1938

Sunshine this morning but strong wind, T. 44,

phoned H. L. last evening, are to try L.v . . . this A.M.—do
not feel that there is much to be gained. supposed to go to
Norfolk this afternoon—group reading.

Reading proved to be one of the most interesting ones have
had in some time—went to Group this afternoon meeting at
Mrs. Story—several not there—but all said had very good
reading—messages to individuals—listened to radio in the
evening, Keeping the mind, the body, the spirit all in accord
isn't easy—but is what may make one free.

Monday, April 11th, 1938

sunshine this morning but a cool wind, water going down
but still quite a bit in basement.

don't feel so hot, ate too much, am sure.

meeting of Group #1 at Mrs. Ellingtons, we took dinner
there, very good meeting.

Tuesday, April 12th 1938

Another beautiful day, real spring, about 58 this morning, about noon quite a stiff wind blew up, turned somewhat cooler.

Very unusual experience for me this morning early—was 2 A.M. became conscious was out of my body, could see it lying there to all intent dead, was not fearful, did not know where I had been, but knew had been away from my body, saw myself gradually emerge again with the body, and each portion come to life and the circulation gradually renew itself in the different portions of same, then awaked, as if had I just come in from somewhere.

To group 7 this evening at Mrs. DeMao's not such a large group but think very good meeting—Patience the subject—lesson part of first chapter of John.

Mae had her Life reading this morning, am anxious to read same, must have been a very interesting one from what have heard thus far.

Oh to be of a service to my fellow man in the name of the Master is the burden of heart, yet realize am so very weak in many ways, will I ever be counted worthy?.

The Lord bless and keep us all for His name sake

Sunday April 24th 1938

more than a week has passed since wrote here—and many things have happened that should have been made note of, but as didn't perhaps just as well, possibly did not mean as much as would like to think they might, but will do better by you old book, for there might be those who would like to read here, hope so any way—but there have been some wonderful reports from people—some sad ones—this is life—the bitter with the sweet—but reports like Miss Coombe, Mr. Barber, Mrs. Botterill—well all seem worthwhile and am sure they are in their own experience. and Life is good when you keep well.

Dream lest evening disturbs me—was with a group of men, mostly of old acquaintances had come to a place. where the only way out was to climb down possibly a hundred feet between two walls—or projections of the walls, all sat round as if bewildered as how to get down, I started down, found there was one place could not get round without slipping, climbed back up—and told all there was a rope there, I would hold and lower them past this place, did, many walked away, few remained to see what I would do—began to descend, and as came to the place where had to be lowered—realized the unseen hand was holding me—for the good had done—awoke.

Again dreamed—had had above dream—and was being shown what it meant was returning to Selma to Studio, place very badly need of repair—dust and dirt was cleaning up—when some one came for picture to be made—realized it was the first person that had come when I went to that place in 1912—now she had her little girl was expecting Gertrude and Miss Gladys—many people came in—for pictures—then realized My Father had come back—dress all in khaki with cap—asked him why—and where he had come from and told me all had thought him dead for a year—but he was not, and could not stay where he had been as people talk very uncomplimentary about him G & Miss Gladys came—when they saw him spoke—then Gertrude asked him why he had come he said just couldn't stay where was—she said well we haven't room here—so he said all right will go to the top of house and jump off. end.

Seem more of a nightmare than a dream. will I be reminded of it?

Mrs. Story and Edith sick—do hope they come along all right—Keep self-conscious of the Christ spirit—by doing that He would have done Just being kind is the best way I know—but her does one keep from losing ones temper that is a hard one

Wed, Apr. 27th 1938

How unappreciative we all appear at times—yet, who is to judge as to what real appreciation is, when we think of that in relation to our God, who is ever appreciative.

Unusual dream night before last regarding Lynn, who like my Father a few nights ago insisted he was not dead, nor ever had been—only been away for a while—but he looked so very thin—yet young again as knew him years ago. wonder what it means.

Cool quite a stiff breeze, sun is bright—thermometer tho registers 60

worked in garden a bit this morning—everything there looks very nice,

Unusual experience this afternoon in a way—each time am able to go into the unconscious have to wait for the Light— without it cannot lose consciousness—usually it is a shaft of light-blue white light—or streaks of light—but this afternoon it appeared as buttons of light—or rosette—with their shading in the form of a rosette caught a nice big Ling this afternoon. a thought for the day—just as sincere as I am with my fellow man, just so is the vibration. atmosphere made for me. Like begets like—but am I to condemn if he does not respond? Rather the more reason to exert the Christ spirit.

Apr. 30, 1938

Lovely day—new bird songs today—there appears to be an unusual number of birds—or am I just aware of their presence? the early morning son of the—Tom-tit, the blue bird, lark, cat-bird, robin, the mocking bird; and the new ones sound like ca-naries—but are red, with brown and the female yellow and black, but lovely bird—used to call them weaver bird, but haven't seen any before in years and years—Oh let's not forget the red-wing, he is lovely. H. L. home from N.Y. for day or so.

The last of April—how time appears to go at times and another, as if it will never come. Tired, weary, of what? Need a change of thought, I guess, or am I just

too desirous of the material things of life?

Busy week, most every day taken. Hope I may have been of help somewhere along the line. What a curious phase of human experience we see now and then.

Help me to keep thy ways, O Lord, for thy ways are not past finding out. Let grace and mercy be with me ever.

Sunday, May 1st 1938

Lovely May day. Many roses in bloom in yard. the red one the prettiest—Just had a note from Dorothy H. My what the mani-festations of life take on at times. just hope can I offer the suggestion that will fill the heart with gladness and bring the best into the experience of each. Feeling fair. Mother still complaining of her eye from the spell she has had recently. What a troubled sleep! So many of those I think so much of? all mixed up in my dreams. Tried to write the lady in Cincinnati. regards "Survival of personality." hope I said the right thing.

I went to the picture show alone this evening.

May all the joy of a sincere life keep me in the path of right for His namesake.

Monday, May 2nd 1938

An unusual stress, financially. H. L. left for N.Y. again last evening. Mrs. Ellington and Jane brought us the material for upholstering the furniture. Mrs. E. is to help fix same today.

May 3-4-5-6, 1938

Left blank—not because of nothing doing—rather lack of the incentive to record same. But what a lovely job Mrs. Ellington has done on the furniture this week, all but one piece finished and is better than had there been a professional doing it. Lovely what friends mean to everyone. Surely we should know better than most, for I'm sure we have the loveliest ever; thanks—all thanks to Him who is the giver of all good and perfect gifts; ours are friends, lovely ones.

Ecken came home Wed. evening will stay until Sunday afternoon—

Saturday the 7th of May 1938

Ecken and I went fishing this morning—fair luck—in the canoe on the Lake—some casting brought mediocre results, had lines a bit better. Well, really put in the afternoon—alone—on the Lake—some very good meditations—must go to Sunday school and church oftener—losing something that I'm sure I need—if nothing else the touch with our fellow man.

Sunday May 8th 1938

Went to Sunday school this morn—was asked to teach the Bible Class. 'There were Mr. Henley Moore, Mr. Peele, Mrs.

Stith, Mrs. Skipper, Mrs. McTurnan, and Mr. Russell Hatchett. Lesson: Co-operation. Well, that might be significant. Hope I can give something that will be worthwhile. Mark. 9: 50 to 41. Text.

Looks as if it might rain, certainly hope it does, seems to me would be fine for the garden. Had strawberries and peas from garden today.

Ecken left this afternoon for school again. We went by to see Edith and

Florence Edmonds. We came home and had T. J. with us for the night—such a sweet baby he is! smart as can be makes over me as well as Gertrude, calls us Eddy Caky and Muddie Caky.

Monday May, 9th 1938

A little rain in the night but not much—letter from Mr. W. glad to know there is no censure, also from Dave with check—closed the old Assn. account today.

Go to Group meeting tonight—Group #1 meet at Mrs. Storey's.

The hope of the world is Love—love that thinketh not of self, but for and of the love of God, as one toward another.

Tuesday, May 10th, 1938

Memories! What tricks our minds play us at times. I recall the 10th of May 1890—circus and all No, I didn't go—that is why I recall so well. Worked in corn on the Seay place, in the field where there used to be the meeting of the little folk that played with me sometime before. Seems so long ago, yet as but yesterday.

Specials from H. L. today—and to meeting of group 3 in Norfolk tonight, good crowd and hope a good meeting.

Destiny of the Soul—Know thyself in His service if we would have his presence abiding consciously with us.

Lord of light and Love—keep thou my ways day by day—May I never blindly lead any astray. May I keep thy precepts ever.

Wed. May 11th 1938

Ominous looking outside this morning—think we need rain badly.

Am to go to Group 6 this evening.

May 12-13-14-15

A week that will long be resplendent with memories of meeting with the groups in Norfolk—each having its own special meaning to each group I'm sure—just hope I may have been of a little help here and there. Can't say any special group is better than the other; each group has its members that have caught a vision of what may be had by keeping close to the Master. For me, this morning while in meditation, I had a vision of the Master coming close to me—laying His hand on me and blessing me, giving me encouragement.

A very good meeting at Sunday school—quite an interesting visitor, Mr. Powell of Baltimore, gave some very good suggestions to the class. I had already outlined some of these to the class—are to have class meeting evening of 27th—with Mrs. Skipper.

Very blustery day out more like March than May today

May 19th 1938

Very disturbing dream this morning—Was at a fete of some kind—games being played on the lawn of a very beautiful club somewhere—many friends sitting on lawn near a wood— Boyd Davis and I playing croquet—he rocaked [sic] my ball— it went into edge of wood—he called to Thomas Jefferson to run get Kakey's ball—but I started after it—then his Mother— Berlyn called T. J. to run get Kakey's ball—as I went into the wood saw a small clearing where the sun came through—was all covered with snakes of every size and description—and as many or more turtles of all sizes—they all began to move off into the wood. I called to Ecken to bring his gun and shoot some of them—when T. J. came up to me I picked him up— Tom Sugrue called that he had a gun and came up—there was now only one small snake left—he aimed at him—and as he fired the snake struck at me—and I saw his fangs were in my trousers near the bottom but had not struck the flesh—wondered how I was to remove them without allowing the poison getting in flesh, for was afraid to put T. J. down—awoke.

May 20th 1938

Last evening or early this morning dreamed again—for possibly the 51st or more time of walking with the veiled lady— only this time almost saw over the cliff am always trying to climb. I've never known or had the idea of who the lady is.

May, 21st 1938

This morning, after three and before five, dreamed of being with the Master and receiving a Blessing from him for my poor undertakings—he telling me—soon would be better— when I fully understood.

This morning, in giving Life reading for someone, had the impression of being present at the time of the mourning of Moses— and of the readjustments made by Joshua as to who would lead each family in line of march—of seeing the Jordan divide—and of passing over with the children of Judah—the march about Jerico, its fall—and the repulsing of the army at Ai—trial of the offender—quite real of manner in which the choice was made—by lots—and as I was among the friends of the offender—was questioned at length by Joshua himself—saw distinctly how he looked—Must have been all of 6 feet 6 in. and weighed at least two twenty—clean shaven—and a veil over his face that shown like light even in sunshine—very powerful voice—sounded like music—a roar—but not harsh—vibrant tone—but like running water. Dress—loin cloth—baggy trousers—if could be called trousers and the mantle all of one piece of a dark blue color. Of seeing many of the elders of Israel as well as the priests—as well as the high priest with the wonderful dress. The stones in the vesture of the High Priest were used as the means of casting lots— and their color and the tone from them signified when the right Tribe, House and Family was chosen—and when the individual Achim was chosen—all the others went dead or dull—and there was a decided murmur of woe.

PART III

My Philosophy

24

Faith: 'This Is My Belief'

If a man dies, shall he live again? What is death? What comes next? This question, sounded throughout the ages, is one of the oldest that man has considered. We must each answer it within our own self. It is a matter of faith, of belief.

This is my belief.

I believe that when God breathed the breath of life into man, he became a *living soul*. The Spirit of God is life, whether in a blade of grass or in man. The soul of man is individual and lives on.

In the very first part of the Bible we find that Adam was forbidden to eat certain fruit in the Garden of Eden. In eating the forbidden fruit, he became conscious of his being. God reasoned with Adam that he must leave the garden lest he partake of the tree of life and live forever. Had Satan been correct when he said, "Ye shall not surely die if ye partake of this fruit!?" What brought physical death to man? His partaking of that which was forbidden. It brought death to the physical body, but not to the soul!

To become conscious of our continued existence is to become righteous in ourselves. Then we may become conscious of our continued existence, whether in the physical realm, the spiritual realm, or whatever stage of development through which we may be passing, from physical life unto spiritual life. As we pass through all the various stages, what are we attempting to gain? Righteousness within!

Jesus said that if we had His consciousness within us, we should know what He has said to us from the beginning. What was the beginning with Christ? "In the beginning was the Word, and the Word was with God, and the Word was God." So were our souls in the beginning. The Master said, "Ye say that ye have Abraham for your father. I say unto you that before Abraham was I *am*, and he rejoiced to see my day and he saw it and was glad." Then many of those to whom He spoke these words walked no longer with Him, but turned away. Why? He was answering that same question which had bothered man from the beginning: If I die, will I live again?

He said to Nicodemus, "Know ye not that a man must be born again?" When Nicodemus asked, "How can such things be?" Jesus answered, "Are ye a teacher in Israel and know not these things?"

What is it to know the continuity of life? It is to be righteous within, and to have the consciousness of the Christ within. For God is Life. Christ is Life, and Light, unto all that seek to know Him.

Is there any other way? He is not the only way, but "he that climbeth up some other way is a thief and robber" to his own self! God is the Life. Jesus came to represent that Life, and the continuity of Life is in the immortality of the soul.

The soul is an individual thing. My soul is my own, with the ability to know itself, to be itself, and yet be *one* with God. That was the message Jesus gave to His disciples all the way through: "I of myself can do nothing," but the life that is within, and the gift of God working in you will make you conscious of your relationship to your Maker.

How do we become conscious of our relationship with God? By living the fruits of the Spirit! Spirit is the Life, and Light, which makes us conscious of immortality, the continuation of our oneness with God. If God is Life, we then must be His to enjoy the consciousness of being one with Him.

Continuity of Life, then, is being conscious of our oneness with God, through the channel that has been set before us by the example that came into the world to show us the way of Life. That consciousness exists after physical death, as the Bible clearly points out to us.

After Samuel passed on, Saul was still in trouble. He knew that Samuel had rebuked him for the manner of life he lived, yet he was in great distress and sought to know if Samuel would not give him another blessing, even though Samuel had passed from the physical plane of existence. So, Saul sought out a channel through which he might speak to Samuel—and he spoke to him. We see that Samuel's consciousness had not changed one iota by having passed over to the other side, for his first words to Saul were along the same lines that he used while still on earth: "Why troublest thou me? Dost thou not know God has rejected thee already?"

Having passed over did not automatically make Samuel know more than he knew when he was here; not one bit more, for the manner of existence he had lived in this plane had developed him just so far. What did Christ say about this? "As the tree falls, so shall it lie!" When we pass into another plane of existence, our development begins right there in that plane, just as our birth in this physical plane began our development in this life.

Therefore, I believe it is a gradual growth throughout. What is Life? God. The knowledge of God, then, is the growth into Life, or the continuity of Life itself.

Another example of continuity is pointed out to us in the parable which Christ gave of the rich man and Lazarus. They had both passed into what we call death, yet both were conscious. In other words, living is being conscious of your existence, or conscious of where you are. The rich man lifted his eyes, for he was in torment. Why? The place he occupied was his own building, his own development—and he was tormented in a flame. He had the consciousness that it was fire, for he wanted water to put it out. It was a continued existence for that man, who saw Lazarus in Abraham's bosom. He recognized Abraham, although he had never seen him. He recognized Lazarus, although he may have never paid any attention to him while on earth.

Most of us believe the Scriptures, or at least we believe the Bible is to further our knowledge and understanding. And if we will follow it, we will come to a greater knowledge of Life, of God. We will come to a greater concept of how great Life is.

Now why are we not conscious of the continuity of life when we are in this physical plane. Why do we not remember when we lived before? I think we do not remember because we have not been righteous enough. Christ said that if we had His consciousness within us, He would bring to our remembrance all things from the very beginning.

It bothered me a great deal as a child that God spoke to the people in the Bible and did not speak to us. Now I believe that He *does* speak to us, if we will only listen. So often we allow the desires of our physical bodies to so outweigh our desires for spiritual knowledge that we build barriers between ourselves and God.

What prevents us from knowing more about God? Ourselves! Nothing can separate us from the love of God but ourselves—nothing! It is the will of man that can make him conscious of the knowledge of God and of all Life; it is the will of man that can separate him from his God if he enjoys rather the pleasures of the flesh for a season.

I choose to believe that each one of us has an individual soul, that there is One Spirit, the Spirit of God, going through each and every one, and that makes each and every one of us akin, that makes all life and nature akin; for life in every form is dependent upon that force we call God. For, as matter came into being, it was permeated with the Spirit of God that gives life, with its ability to carry itself on and make of itself that which has been determined by God that it should be. Man, who was chosen to be one with God and a companion with Him from the beginning, as Adam chose rather to go his own way. But God has prepared a way, through the Christ, that we might be more conscious at all periods of our development of the life of God that is within us.

I have had an experience, possibly eight or ten times while giving life readings, that tells something about the planes of existence beyond this one. It happens when I am in the so-called unconscious or super-conscious state. I remember nothing of the readings, but have a very vivid impression of this experience. I knew that my spirit, mind or soul was separate from my body and that it was seeking information for another person. I passed into outer darkness that was so dark that it actually hurt—and yet there was a stream of light that I knew that I must follow and allow nothing on either side of that light to distract me from my purpose. As I passed along the forms I became conscious of forms of movement toward the light. Coming to the next plane, I realized that the forms or figures were taking shape as humans, but rather as the exaggeration of human desires. Passing a little farther, these forms were gradually lost. Still, I had the consciousness that they were seeking the light, or more light. Finally, I passed through a place where individuals appeared much as they are today— as men and women—but satisfied with their position. The number of individuals in this state of satisfaction continued to grow, and then there were homes and cities where they were content to continue as they were.

Still following the light, which grew stronger and stronger, I heard music in the beyond. Then came a space where all was springtime, all was abloom, all was summer. Some were happy, some desired to remain, but many were pressing on and on to the place where there might be great understanding, more light, more to be gained. Then I reached a place where I was seeking the records of the lives of people that lived in the earth.

Don't ever think that your life isn't being written in the Book of Life. I found it! I have seen it! It is being written. *You* are the writer!

As to how close your life is going to be to your Savior and to your God, you alone can answer. You alone. It is your soul that you are developing. If we want to reach that consciousness of our immortality, if we would become aware of our relationship to God, we must live it here and now. And then the next step is given to us. That has been His promise, and His promises are sure.

In developing our relationship with God, it doesn't matter what we may *claim* to believe. What really matters is what difference our beliefs make in our lives. It doesn't matter whether you believe that the whale swallowed Jonah, or whether Noah was in the Ark for a whole year or only forty days. What is important is how your belief has changed your attitude toward your fellow man, or toward God.

The Bible tells us about God and how men related to him—

everyone from Adam and Abraham, to Isaac and Moses, to Solomon and David. Each had his own idea of God, but what we learn is that they knew God through personal experiences. Can we not get this idea? God is a *personal* God. Not a God of war, or a God of plenty, nor even a God of an individual leader. He is a God of all. God is in all things, and our heritage is in Him. Just as we parents feel in respect to our children, God feels about His children, His people here in this world.

God's purpose is that we make ourselves a channel through which His spirit may manifest. Some may say they do not wish to be used by God in that way. I heard a woman say this about her little boy: "I know his father wants him to become a great artist, but I don't want him to do anything that may be called the work of genius because he will have to suffer physically." She might just as well have said she didn't want her boy to give up the desire of the flesh for a spiritual life. To my mind, that is a sad outlook. We see what happens in the world when people have forgotten that there is a higher purpose to life than self indulgence. That purpose is to make their wills one with the Creator. We must prepare to be used as a channel that He may manifest through us. It isn't that we are to be bossed around by someone else, for there is nothing in the world that we can do for God. What we do we do for the other fellow, for in so doing we become one with the will of the Father. He has given us control of the physical world that we may use it for helping our fellow man. We may be the channel through which the other fellow, less fortunate than ourselves, may be aided in whatever is needed for him to gain a better conception of his relation to his God.

It would be well to remember the decision of the great Jewish leader who said, "Others may do as they may, but for me and my house, we will worship the living God." We are confronted daily with problems that require just such a definite stand. Let us member His promise and be strong.

So, the question that has come down to every age comes down to every individual: What is your relationship to your God? It came to Enoch, to Noah, to Abraham, to Isaac, to Moses, to Joshua, to Saul, to David, to Solomon, and it comes just the same to you and to me today. What is our relationship to God?

Remember, that in serving Him we must serve our fellow man, that we must become a channel through which God may work His divine will here on earth. When the burdens become hard to bear and you feel yourself beginning to slip away from the path you know is right, draw nearer to your God and He will draw nearer to you. As a child comes and sits at the feet of its parents, seeking guidance, asking their help, just so we must approach through prayer the God who is our Father and Creator.

To know God we must believe that He is. We must seek to find His face. "Seek and ye shall find, knock and it shall be opened unto you." Now in coming to know Him, is it not evident that as we consider and help our fellow man, so do we carry out God's work? Our relationship to our God, then, becomes our relationship to our brother. There is nothing that we can do for God, but there is much that we can do for His children, our brothers.

As we go about in our daily work let us remember to lend a helping hand wherever we may, and know that in so doing we are fulfilling the will of the Creator and coming ever nearer to our God.

People sometimes ask which religion, or denomination, would God have us follow. I find in nature an illustration of Life itself. Consider a field of corn. Life is found in the grain of the corn. The farmer plants it in the soil, works it, and then he reaps the harvest. Not everyone selects the same *kind* of corn. Not every man *ploughs* it alike. Not everyone *sows* it alike. Not everyone *reaps* it alike. Yet, in each case it brings forth the very best—the God or the Life within each grain, which is what the man is seeking. It sustains his body, and also produces seed to raise more. Thats religion. That's how it is with the denominations.

Now, many ask when should we expect the Second Coming.

Very little is known about when Christ will come again. Jesus, Himself, said that it was given only to the Father to know the time of His return. We have, however, two sources of information upon which we may draw in forming our ideas about this question. We can turn to the Bible and to information received psychically for a clarification of various passages of Scripture and for further information.

But first, how did anyone ever get the idea that there is to be a Second Coming? Jesus said, "Let not your heart be troubled; ye believe in God, believe also in me. In my Father's house are many mansions; if it were not so, I would have told you. I go to prepare a place for you. And if I go and prepare a place for you, I will come again, and receive you unto myself; that where I am, there ye may be also."

When we look into the history of the world as we know it today, how often has a great religious leader or prophet arisen? Plato said that our cycle of entering is about every thousand years. Judging from history itself, the period of time between each religious teacher who has come into the earth varies from 625 to 1,200 years.

Do you ask, "Is that how often you say Christ has come?" No, I don't say that; I don't know how many times He has come; however, if we will consider the following passages of Scripture for a few moments, an interesting idea may be formulated. These are the passages:

"In the beginning was the Word, and the Word was with God, and the Word was God. The same was in the beginning with God. All things were made by him; and without him was not any thing made that was made . . . He was in the world, and the world was made by him, and the world knew him not . . . And the Word was made flesh, and dwelt among us . . ." (See John 1:1–14)

Many people tell us that this is speaking of spiritual things. You must answer this for yourself. But if the Word was made flesh and dwelt among men, how can we be sure that this is not speaking materially, too?

In talking with the judges of Israel at that time, the Master said:

"I know that ye are Abraham's seed; but ye seek to kill me, because my word hath no place in you . . . If ye were

Abraham's children, ye would do the works of Abraham . . . Ye are of your father the devil . . ." (John 8:37–44)

In the flesh, yes, they were the children of Abraham, but in spirit they were not. For what did Abraham do? He was righteous, and his deeds were counted to him for righteousness because of his faith in the One God.

In this same chapter, the Master said, "Your father Abraham rejoiced to see my day, and he saw it, and was glad. Then said the Jews unto Him, Thou art not yet fifty years old, and hast thou seen Abraham? Jesus said unto them, "Verily, verily, I say unto you, Before Abraham was, *I am*."

Did Jesus mean that in a spiritual sense or a literal sense— or both? What do you think? I don't know, but what we have been told psychically is this—take it for what it is worth and *apply it in* your own experience.

Now turn to the fourteenth chapter of Genesis and read where Abraham paid tribute to a certain individual, Melchizedek. No cause or reason is given except that the man came out in the place to bless him: a priest of the Most High God, without days, a man not born normally, but a high priest of the living God. "And Melchizedek, king of Salem, brought forth bread and wine: and he was the priest of the most high God. And he blessed him."

Was this the Master, this Melchizedek? Read it yourself. Maybe I'm wrong in thinking he was the Master, the man we know later as Jesus.

Consider now, the book of Joshua. Who directed Joshua when he became the leader of Israel? Who walked out to lead Joshua after he crossed the Jordan? The Bible says, the Son of Man came out to lead the armies of the Lord. And after Joshua's experience in meeting this man of God, all of the children of Israel were afraid of him. (See Joshua 5:13–15)

From these references, let us draw a few conclusions and supplement them with psychic information. The Spirit of the Christ manifested in the earth many times before the coming of Jesus; at times it manifested through one like Melchizedek, and at other times it manifested as a spiritual influence through some teacher upholding the worship of the One God.

What has this conclusion to do with the Second Coming? Well, in the light of the above, there ceases to be a *second* coming. Also, by considering conditions that made His appearance possible at various times—or, if you prefer, the one time as Jesus, we can deduce certain facts about the return of the Master.

How did He happen to come as Jesus of Nazareth? There has not been a revelation to man, of which we have any record, for over four hundred years. Then did darkness and dissipation on the part of man bring Christ into the world? If so, it is a reversal of the natural law: *like begets like*. The laws of God are not reversed at any time and never will be. They are immutable and hold true throughout any kingdom in the earth. The things we see developing in the various kingdoms in this earth are merely shadows of the celestial and terrestrial world. For we grow in grace and knowledge and understanding, as another Bible writer has said. By what means comes growth? By *application of truths in our lives*.

Then what brought about the coming of Jesus? A people who were sincere seekers—a little group founded for the purpose of seeking to make themselves channels whereby this great thing could come to pass. Who were these people? They were the most hated of all those mentioned in profane history, and scarcely mentioned in the Bible—the Essenes, the hated ones, the lowest of the Jews.

How can we know this? We received it psychically. But how many more times was Zacharias allowed to go up and offer sacrifices, after being spoken to once, within the temple? Never again! For he had joined that hated group and thereby made his son—who by lineal descent was a high priest—an outcast.

Who was the cousin of Elizabeth? Mary, the mother of Him we worship as our Lord and Master. Mary sought first her cousin Elizabeth, the mother of the great Essene, John the Baptist, to tell the great tidings that the angel had made known to her.

These Essenes, then, were consecrating and dedicating their lives, their inner selves, to make possible a meeting place for

God and man, with such a spiritual degree of consecration that Jesus the Christ might come into the world. Thus there was a *preparation*, where there might be the meeting place for God and man. And if we will have a meeting place in our heart, our home, our group, our church, then we too can have the Christ come to us. When we have prepared the place, He will come—and not before.

We can't say that we are diligently seeking, but He has gone to somebody else. It isn't common sense. We can't say that somebody else has to prepare the way for us. He will come again, yes; and He will come as He is. His spirit is here always. It will abide with us always.

In no place where the Master taught was He accepted, and He taught in Palestine, Egypt, India, Persia, China, and Japan, at least.

We believe that He descended into hell and taught those there. We read it in the Bible and we say it is true. But we don't really believe it, else we would act like it! If we did believe it, we would never find fault with any soul in the world—never! For if we believe that He went into hell and taught the people there, how could we find fault with our next-door neighbor because his chickens got into our garden or he doesn't believe exactly as we do?

Is this in your Bible: "Moreover I will endeavor that ye may be able after my decease to have these things always in remembrance." (II Peter 1:15) Did you ever hear a sermon preached on it? The man who said that is the one of whom Christ said: ". . . flesh and blood hath not revealed it unto thee, but my Father which is in heaven." (Matt. 16:17) To the same man, perhaps only a few minutes afterward, He said, "Get thee behind me, Satan; thou art an offense unto me: for thou savourest not the things that be of God, but those that be of men"—the things of the flesh and not the things of the spirit. (Matt. 16:23)

The Master said, "Elias truly shall first come, and restore all things. But I say unto you, That Elias is come already, and they knew him not, but have done unto him whatsoever they listed. Likewise shall also the Son of man suffer of them. Then the disciples understood that he spake unto them of John the Baptist." (Matt. 17:11–13)

Possibly you may say that He meant in the spirit and not in the flesh; but I don't read it that way.

A warning was once given to a man of God that a certain country would be destroyed; but the man prayed and talked with God face to face, and God promised that if there were fifty righteous men he would save it. Then finally, if there were just ten righteous men, He could spare the city.

I believe that the just people in the world keep it going. The just people are the ones who have been kind to the other fellow. For we may see evidences of the Christ Spirit about us right now, day by day: in kindness, patience, long-suffering, showing brotherly love, preferring our neighbor before ourselves. When there are possibly fifty, or a hundred, or a thousand, or a million, then the way may have been prepared for His coming. But all these just men must have *united* in their desire and supplication that the Christ physically walk among men again.

He for our sakes became flesh. How many times? Answer for yourself. How soon will He come again? When we make it possible. It was made possible at least once. It will be made possible again. When we live the life He has laid out for us, we are making it possible for Him, the Lord and Master of this world, to come again.

"I will not leave you comfortless, but I will come again, and receive you unto myself, that where I am, there ye may be also."

25

DREAMS AND VISIONS

After many experiences with information from our dreams, I thought the most vital words ever given to man were, "Know, O Israel, the Lord thy God is *one*!" Every phase of our lives is so linked one with another that it is all one. The various experiences that we have in our sleeping state are, in many instances, the most real. Have you ever dreamed of kissing an individual? Which has been the most lasting—when you have met an individual and embraced them in everyday life or when it has been a portion of your subconscious or your soul's experience? I know from my own experience that the dream is certainly the most lasting. If we knew why, possibly we could realize what dreams are and how we may use them in our lives from day to day. When we lay aside our physical consciousness in sleep, it is the nearest state akin to death that man knows anything about—except when he is etherized or put into such a state that brings about a loss of consciousness. We speak of sleep as being the nearest state akin to death. Now, what takes care of us while we are in dreamland? Our organs function properly, our heart beats on just the same, and we are able to wake up feeling refreshed. Our physical organism has been built up as the stored energy takes hold, or the reverse happens—and what has done this? It is something we have never been able to definitely say just what it is. We call it mind, or the natural order of things. What do we mean by that? What is natural about it? Is it because it happens over and over again? Have we ever stopped to consider that almost half of our existence is spent in the unknown where we are not even able to follow with our consciousness that which cares for our bodies during that time? This is the subconscious mind, the soul mind, that lies in between the physical body mind and that gift of God to every human being, that they may carry back to Him or that they may separate from Him. That is our real self, the self that lives on and on, just as it is able to live through such an experience as we call sleep and build up the whole organism during that time. Just so in death. If we have lived properly, if the soul has been fed properly, it may have that to sustain itself.

Mind is ever the builder, whether it be of the physical mind, the mental mind, or the soul mind—or the physical consciousness, the subconsciousness, or the superconsciousness. The dreams partake of those three phases.

Many of us have gone to sleep after a hearty meal and had a nightmare. What has taken place? What we have taken into the system has an objective in itself. It begins to move and have its own activity within the system. It arouses within all the vitality and energy of the body, which brings about those awful visions that we experience under such conditions. If our lives have been such, those visions may take on pleasant conditions, or they may be the demons themselves. In some of them we experience being suddenly cast into the street only partially clad, or with something chasing after us. Most of these arise from improper conduct of our appetites, whether from eating too much mincemeat pie, too much pickle, or the like, or too much spirits frumenti, which may eventually bring those experiences of seeing horrible things. Those are visions of what we have builded in our own selves. If there is a misuse of that which is set before us, we suffer the consequences.

Then there is the vision that may be the activity of the subconscious mind itself. This phase is held by some people to be very scientific, especially in psychoanalyzing people's ills. They claim that the suppression of emotions in the body during the developing periods builds that which comes to the surface when the physical consciousness is laid aside. While some say this is a lot of bunk, and these are hallucinations of the subconscious mind, there are others who have spent thousands of dollars following out this theory that the suppression of desire in a developing child, or in the developing minds of individuals, indicate through their visions that which may change one's whole outlook on life. There are people in the large centers of our country who make it their business to study this theory, and there are recognized authorities on certain kinds of diseases who claim they can make a person dream whatever they wish, by making certain things happen while they are in that state. That is possible, but it doesn't change the character of what is presented, for we must pass into that consciousness that is taking care of us while we are in the normal sleeping state. Even while we are in an induced state there is another consciousness controlling the activities of the whole body. Every organ, every atom of our body, is a universe in itself, and it has its own consciousness to be dealt with. The things we experience through such dreams may be worthwhile or they may not.

There are experiences when we have entirely separated ourselves or our consciousness from the physical being, until we really have a vision. A vision may partake of a very material condition, either symbolically of a condition in our lives or something very real. We have heard of people who have dreamed of a pot of gold buried in such and such a place, and who when awake found it exactly that way. How does such a thing reach an individual? The subconscious, separated entirely from the material self, is able to go out into the universal, or the cosmic consciousness. And those on the other side who see and know the conditions that surround us may put within our own selves what will be helpful or detrimental, depending upon how we use it.

So, how can we apply our dreams? We may apply them in our lives to our own undoing or to our own upbuilding. "There is this day (meaning now, just as it meant yesterday and it will mean tomorrow) set before thee good and evil." All of us want to know how we may bring only good. Very few, if any, of us, want to have that which is evil. How may we bring these things to bear on our own lives and experiences? To my mind, the answer is in the Good Book itself.

An answer to this might be found in the life of Saul. His life started out most beautifully but it was a miserable failure because he reached a period when, with the power, with the conditions that surrounded him, he thought he was sufficient unto himself. God no longer spoke to him in dreams or in visions, for he had reached that place where he felt he did not need to be guided by the Divine from within.

Why seek information from anyone who might be able to give it to us from the other side, when we may have it—as Saul was at first able to have it—from God Himself? Why seek it from anyone? Why seek to know where Captain Kidd buried his treasure from someone in the Beyond? Why not seek it from that builded from within? If builded in the proper manner, it will bring about those conditions needed for our own development.

What was meant when it was said, "God is able to raise up unto Abraham children of these very stones?" What does it mean unless it means what is builded within our own selves gives God the privilege to use us? For there is nothing in heaven or earth that can separate us from God but ourselves. Nothing! Because we have a portion of Him through that soul which He has given us, which—with its mind—brings us a dream, brings us a vision. Whether it is of the promised land, of our mother, our father, our sister or our brother, it brings to our mind the consciousness that satisfies us of the continuity of life.

Many people have said, "If I could just speak with someone from the other side I would be satisfied of the continuity of life." What did the Master say about that very thing? "If you will not listen to those that you have about you, you would not listen though one returned from the dead." Even then He came up from the grave Himself. For thousands of years we have been trying to preach to people. Some of us say we believe it, but do we act like it?

If we are right with God, then we know better how to interpret our dreams—because each individual can interpret his own dream better than anyone else can ever do it for him. If God ever spoke to anyone (and we believe that He did), He will speak to us if we'll let Him. How is He going to do it? In olden times He spoke in dreams. Why wouldn't He do it now? Has He changed so that He doesn't speak to us except through someone else? We don't want a secondhand God, do we? We can get our knowledge firsthand if we will seek it, whether through dreams or other means. First, know that we are right with God, and day by day we will be guided. For it is written, "My spirit beareth witness with thy spirit as to whether ye be the sons and daughters of God or not." God is Spirit and seeks such to worship Him, in spirit and in truth.

When you have visions or dreams from day to day, write them down in black and white and see what they look like. Compare them with your experiences. No one passes into dreamland, if they are sound asleep, without passing out of the physical body. The silver cord, that connection between the physical and the subconscious, is not broken. We should study these experiences and judge for ourselves. Why ask someone else? We may know these things by applying them in our life. Set them down, study them, compare them. He that compareth himself by himself, however, is not wise—but he that compareth that experience to his relationship to God is very wise, for he has taken God into partnership with him. Has God seen fit to speak to us? Are we able to contain that which He may give us? Are we willing to do what He would have us do? He speaks to all of us, for He has not forsaken Israel neither has He forsaken those who seek after Him for those that will seek Him shall in no wise be cast out. That has been the promise through all the ages. That is the promise to us today.

We can make visions or dreams mean a great deal in our lives, if we conduct our lives in such a manner as to entitle us to receive such messages—for we are all heirs to the Kingdom through Christ and we are sons and daughters of God.

If we keep a record of our dreams from day to day, we will soon learn to differentiate between those that are worthwhile and those that are not. If we so conduct our lives we may be warned of impending danger, granted by God Himself. Compare such visions with your knowledge of God. Don't forget that it has been said from time to time, "Put away out of your midst all soothsayers and those that partake of familiar spirits." Why? Because through such we are calling upon those forces that are loosed by the spirit departing from the body, that have been called earthbound, and have power in the dark side or the night side of life to be harmful, if we open ourselves to such. We can guard ourselves by knowing that we have surrounded ourselves with that bond which we may hold with God Himself. It has been given, "Where two or three are gathered together in my name, I am in the midst of them." We say that and think it is beautiful, but how many of us really believe it?

If our relationship to God is such that it is necessary for Him to speak to us, He will do it—if we will ask for it, listen, and live it.'[1]

---

[1] For further information concerning dreams, Volumes 4 and 5 of the Edgar Cayce Readings Library Series are devoted to dreams, including many of Mr. Cayce's dreams and a dream symbol index. *Dreams: Tonight's Answers for Tomorrw's Questions* by Mark Thurston and *Dreams: Your Magic Mirror* by Elsie Sechrist are also recommended.

26

HOLISTIC HEALING

Some years ago there was discovered growing in our gardens all over the country a plant, the juice of which was good for low blood pressure, or a disturbed circulation, or a slowed pulse. You may wonder what has that to do with the mind and healing. Just this: All force is of one force. Is that plant a representation of God's love to His people or not? Not only as a beautiful flower, known as Foxglove, or Digitalis, but as something with an element contained in itself to awaken a consciousness in life-giving forces within the human body that may aid in many conditions.

You may ask, "If I raise my consciousness to be rid of all these things, why is medicine necessary?" A quotation from the Bible that answers this is when the Master asked the father of a child, "How long is it ago since this came upon him?" The answer was, "Of a child, and often times it hath cast him into the fire and into the water to destroy him, but if thou canst do anything, have compassion on us and help us." Jesus said to him, "If thou canst believe, all things are possible to him that believeth," and straightway the father of the child cried out and said with tears, "Lord, I believe. Help thou mine unbelief."

In another place the Scriptures tell us, "And when He was come into the house, His disciples asked Him privately, 'Why could we not cast him out?' And He said unto them, "This kind can come forth by nothing but by prayer and fasting." The disciples had been able—with His permission, being sent by Him—to go to the lost sheep of the house of Israel to awaken within their consciousness their needs, and to cinch the matter, as it were. They would heal those that were sick, aid those who were lame, and cast out demons.

This healing ability, this mental attitude which they had to be in to receive this gift, had to answer or correspond to something from a higher source that was sent to them for their good, or that they might be able to receive within themselves. You may say, What does that have to do with the work—even that which you attempted in your hospital? Does faith, does mental attitude, have anything to do with the treatments we gave there? As anyone who visited the hospital could see, we had the equipment to do practically any kind of work. We were prepared to give all the treatments that had been suggested from time to time by the readings for people to apply in their lives, and to those individuals to gain that consciousness from within that will enable them to get hold of that which produces any healing that may come to an individual.

Man has been able to gather from nature's storehouse, from the many things found throughout the world in the form of drugs, in the form of mechanical appliances, in the form of various elements of nature itself, the various combinations that may aid in various conditions. Does that lessen at all the ability of the individual to be able to gain a consciousness of the divine force from within? Or is it proof of it all being one? That's the great question we have to answer.

If a thing happens once, it may happen again, although we may call it chance, guess work, or whatever. If the disciples, these companions of the Great Physician Himself, were capable individuals, able to meet all the conditions they had contacted heretofore, why did they fail this once? The Master said, "This can only be met, or can only be cast out by fasting and prayer." Hadn't He taught His disciples that they were to have periods of fasting? Hadn't He taught by example and by precept that periods of prayer were necessary for them to carry on even in their everyday life, as well as to meet the contingencies arising from time to time? Remember again when the Master said to His disciples, "Whom do men say that I am?" They answered, "Some say John the Baptist, some say one thing, some another."

"Whom do ye say that I am?"

Peter answered, "Thou art the Christ, the Son of the living God."

"Flesh and blood," the Master said, "hath not revealed this unto thee, but my father in heaven." Then in almost the next breath He begins to tell them how that it is necessary for Him to go up to Jerusalem and suffer many persecutions. Peter takes Him aside and says, "This doesn't have to be. Look how many people are already Your followers. Look at the abilities we have to call out these many things for the people. Look how You are able to feed Your followers. Remember the loaves and fishes? It isn't necessary for You to go through all this." And the Master answered, "Get thee behind me, Satan, for thou savorest the things of earth and not of the spiritual things."

Just so in this comparison as to how or why it is necessary for all these things in our lives, to so set or center our minds on the kingdom in order to be able to get hold of the kingdom—for, if there is any healing that ever comes to an individual, it comes from the Divine from within.

Then what does the mind have to do with healing? It has to be awakened, either by those things from without or from within, to that consciousness where the Divine may heal. Whether it be easier to say, "Son, thy sins be forgiven thee," or to say, "Arise, take up thy bed and walk?" There has to be brought to the individual a consciousness that the healing is from within, not from without. Just as we have said about the kingdom of heaven itself, it isn't that we go out to find who will come in and tell us, but it is within our own selves. If an individual is able to be awakened sufficiently from within, all the medicines or all the appliances, or all the treatments that may be given, mean nothing. Why? The Great Physician Himself is ever ready and willing that we should have that which is our heritage, if we will but open ourselves to that heritage—but, if we are so earthly minded, if we have so turned our own mental vision, or so trained our subconscious self that we are unable to get beyond those barriers, it is necessary that we be awakened from or by those things in God's own storehouse, which He has allowed man to gather and put in such a shape as to assist in awakening that necessary for the healing to come.

Some years ago a young man came to my office one day and asked for a reading for his wife who was in Wisconsin. I asked him to have his wife come to listen to the information. He said, "All right if you think that is best, but she can't hear anything—that's what's the matter with her." A few days later they both came to the studio. As soon as I talked with her, I could see that she could read lips. She said it had been three years since she had been able to hear. The reading gave that it was a case of suppression through the treatment accorded her by her husband, who made fun of her abilities.

When I became conscious again, the husband said to me, tears streaming down his face, "Old Man, God alone knows how true the things are that you have given. I don't know how you knew them." His wife was almost hysterical, her hands going up and her eyes wide open, and she said: "I have heard every word that man said, and I can still hear!" She has been able to hear ever since.

The story they told was this: He had met her on a Sunday afternoon and they had married on Wednesday. He didn't know anything about her family and she didn't know anything about his family. They decided to spend one day there and then go to meet the families. When they went to their hotel room, all of a sudden she said, "Listen! Uncle John is talking." He answered, "What in the name of God are you talking about?"

"I didn't know what sort of a person I had married," he told me. "I didn't know anything about such stuff. She said nothing more. We went out to dinner and when we came back we talked a little while, and just before I turned out the light she said, 'Listen, Uncle John is talking again!' I gave her a gentle good cussing, and the next morning she couldn't hear anything I had to say, and hasn't heard from that day to this. I haven't been able to stay away from her, neither have I been able to stay with her—but what you have told me has made me realize that I haven't understood what this is all about. I understand from what you have given that she has possessed some ability not given to ordinary human beings to understand, and many of us don't want to understand, for we have built something within our own selves that makes us afraid to understand anything about the unseen forces, or the things we can't feel, touch, hear, and taste which pertain to the psychic or to the spiritual side of things. We want to hear about them, but to experience them—no!"

If we are willing to pay the price, mind is able to build within our own self what is necessary to bring healing—that which is necessary for our own understanding of our relationship to our God. But if our God is fame, fortune, or whatnot, we can't expect that God ever to heal! Most of us are of the opinion that we are able to buy most anything we want. But health is one thing that is mighty hard to buy—for unless we can gain a consciousness of the Divine from within, very little help can come to these poor weak bodies of ours. Mind is the builder, the healer—that is, mind at work; not passive, not concrete, but active with the forces God has given man to make himself one with the Law of God—which makes him free. "And ye shall know the truth, and the truth shall make you free. If the Son, therefore, shall make you free, ye shall be free indeed."

27

TRUTH

We often hear it said that Truth is evasive, Truth is naked, Truth will not be downed—but what is Truth? We remember, if we turn to the books of the New Testament, that possibly the greatest moment in history was when Pilate asked of the Master, "What is Truth?" Possibly that was the *only* time it could have been answered in one or two words that would have at least satisfied the greater portion of the thinking world today—but he didn't wait for the answer. Yet we know that the Master said that He *came* that He might show the way unto Truth. Then we know Truth is something that we may be shown.

When we speak of *a* truth, or *the* truth, or *truth*, we possibly mean different things. You remember the story of the three men of Hindustan who went to see the elephant, but all of them were blind. Now that's *us*! We are all blind, but we are seeking the truth because we are very much in the same position as the three men who went to see the elephant. One of them stumbled against the side of the elephant and said, "I perceive, without a doubt, the elephant is very like a wall." Was that the truth to him? Another one, as he stumbled about the animal, found his trunk, and said, "I perceive with a certainty the elephant is very like a tree." Was he correct in his supposition? The other man, as he stumbled about, got hold of the tail, and said, "I perceive the elephant is very much like a rope." Now were they in error? Did they have the truth? Or did they have only a portion of the truth? Or did they have any of the truth?

We often say that any movement of any character succeeds insofar as it has a portion of the truth. We may be sure that is truth, that any movement succeeds insofar as that movement has the truth. Don't worry because you disagree with any individual as to what your conception of any movement may be—don't think that they are going to hell because they don't think as you do! Remember the three men that went to see the elephant. Keep that in your mind. Know that they are right, but they are wrong as *you* would see it with your eyes wide open.

Life in its projection into this material plane has been a constant growth. Then, if we are to believe the things that have been presented to us, and as they are presented to us, we know that even Truth itself may be a growth into that understanding in which we will be able to apply it in our everyday life.

I am sure that we believe God is Love. The love for an individual, then, is an expression of the force, or manifested force, that we define as Love. There was a man who had such an experience because he was very much in love with his wife. He thought more of her than anything in the world, but God saw fit to take her home. After her passing, he couldn't find anything that could satisfy him or overcome this separation, so when he erected a monument in the cemetery he had inscribed on it: "The light of my life has gone out."

But after awhile he met a young lady whom he fell very much in love with, and he realized that he was altogether mistaken about his first love being the only one able to satisfy everything in his life—for now there was someone else who was able to fill up a portion of his life. So he proposed marriage. The young lady, knowing about this inscription, said to him, "I might consent to be your wife, but I don't think I could ever do that as long as the inscription remains as it is."

So he looked for a man who could correct the inscription for him, and the man promised to rectify this. They went ahead with the wedding, and when they came back from their honeymoon they went to see how it read, and this is what they found: "The light of my life has gone out—but I've struck another match."

So, you see, when we get the idea of some particular thought or some particular experience, gradually we build into our own selves the idea that we have gotten the whole thing. Now is Truth such a thing that those who have been followers of Mohammed have *all* of the Truth? Have they who have been the followers of Moses, the lawgiver, all of the Truth? Or has Truth rather been a growth in our individual lives, and what may be Truth to one individual possibly may not, in the experience of the other individual, answer at all? Does that make the man any less true to his first love? Did this man love the second woman any less because of his experience of being in love before?

Is it possible, if this be true, that this is a changeable thing, a matter of growth? Will it be possible for us to find something of which we can say, "*This* is truth," and *know* that it will answer in everything or every way that life may present itself to us? I believe that we can. You may differ with me. I don't think, however, that you will be able to refute what will be my definition, or what I will be able to say *is* Truth.

But many of you will say, "Well, have you been given some peculiar power that you have knowledge of what Truth is, and can answer the question that has been sought throughout all the ages, so that we may know what Truth is?" Let's see if this will not answer the whole question in our lives.

First, we must know that, if we are to accept any word, or any follower as a truth, or *the* truth, or Truth, we must be sure of the *authority* that we quote. We must be very sure of our foundation, or platform, for what we have assumed. Where would we begin, as we would say, to assume something as being true, or a place to begin? Or how far could we go with this formula? Or where would we begin with this formula, so that we might know, when we hear a thing, that to *us* it is Truth?

We must recognize these facts in our lives: there is a physical body and there is a spiritual body. We know the physical body is dependent upon its physical attributes for its development. It is also the temple, or the dwelling place, of the spiritual body. The spiritual body, we know, is of the Creator—whatever we may call the Creator. It comes from the same thing, even if we go back to the scientific reasoning and say it begins from the lowest form of life. Wherever we begin, we have to say there is something beyond that where it has developed, whether you believe in evolution, creative evolution, or whatnot, it all has to come back to the very same thing, and if I can answer this I don't believe I'm wrong in saying that you can take it from any standpoint you want to take it, but this *is* Truth:

That which is kept before your mental mind, your spiritual mind, will continue to develop you upward! That which, held before you, will continue to develop you upward. That which, held before your mental vision, will continue to develop you upward. Not that which satisfies selfish purpose at all, no! Not that which tells you whether or not it is wrong to go fishing or to play baseball on Sunday. Not that which answers you in that. It answers you, yes—but what will continue to develop you upward? And what do we mean by developing upward? That which will enable you to hold the vision of that which *you* worship as *your* God. Every individual, every object, has its conception of its superior position. We would say, "Well, would it answer the Indian who is looking for his Happy Hunting Ground?" Why would it not answer? That which will enable him to hold before him that which *he* worships as *his* God is Truth to him.

We take for granted that man has a mind and a body—a physical body, a spiritual body. He has a soul, if you choose! We take for granted that his mental body is controlled by his mental being. His soul, or his spiritual body, is controlled by his subconscious, or his spiritual mind. That which continues to hold before the individual whatever he worships as his God will continue, then, to develop the individual towards that which he worships. Now you will say, What would have been the Master's answer to Pilate's question?—"I came into the world to do no other than conduct you into that which is Truth."

Truth is not a thing, then, that we can gain through our eyes or body or ears—but it is the essence with which an individual builds faith, hope, and trust. *That* is Truth! That essence that we are enabled to hold before our mental vision is truth. Will it build your body? It will! Will it heal the sick? It will!

A few days ago I was talking to some people who were telling me about a book that had been written by some of the masters from the Far East. I had never seen the book before, but when I opened it I knew what was in it before I read it. I don't know how, nor why, but I knew the experiences that I was going to encounter. I don't know why except *this*: With the first four or five pages I found that in this book, this one thing was continually held before the individual: that which you hold before yourself, to create that image you worship, that will develop you always upward, and will continue to enable you to know truth!

Truth, then, being a growing thing, a thing that will develop you, is entirely in action! Not inactive, but in action! That's what God is! For in every movement that has ever been, it has been a continual upward development, or upward toward that which *is* Truth.

If you hold malice, you can become one of the meanest persons in the world. You know that if you continue to send out malicious thoughts, you create those very same crosscurrents in your mind. What is prayer but simply attuning yourself to that which you are seeking assistance through? That's all prayer is—attuning yourself to that very same thing. That becomes Truth when it becomes in action. When it goes into action, to you it becomes Truth. It's your own conception of what your God is. If it makes you better to the very thing you worship, or more in accord with the thing you worship, that you become, whether it's downward or upward, you go whichever way your standard is set. That becomes Truth to you. That which you continue to follow becomes Truth whether it's negative or positive. As we learn it from that viewpoint, it becomes true; that is, whatever we hold that continues to build upward is Truth.

Now, as to who is to say whether you are building up, or as to how near it brings you to that thing you worship *as* your God, because God *is* Truth, if you continue to hold that, you may develop to that. But to someone else whose God might be something else, that wouldn't be Truth. If it answers one, it answers all. That's what it stands for; that which may develop in the individual, that understanding of one's relation to our Maker and to our fellow man.

I've been studying a long while, trying to understand what is meant by the second commandment, and I never did know to my own satisfaction until the other night. The first commandment, as we know, is, "Thou shall love the Lord thy God with all thy heart and thy mind, etc." The second is, "Thou shall not make unto thee any graven image." Why? Because if you make an image it becomes your God. But if you have for your God that which is within your own individual self, you yourself being a portion of the Creator, you will continue to build upward, to it!

28

THE NEW MILLENNIUM

We are passing through a period of stress in which we all are expecting something—but we do not know what. As we approach the New Millennium, why is it impossible to know what is going to happen? Isn't it because we have blinded ourselves to the evidence around us?

We are told by many who have made a study of such matters that we are passing through a certain position in the universe. Astrologers have said that we are reaching that place in space wherein the influences are beginning for the Third Cycle. Others describe it as a place where we may expect a new race, a new people, a new thought.

Admitting for the moment that this is true, are such influences bearing upon us because we are in such a position in the universe, or are we in such a position because of what we or somebody else has done? It is the same old question arising in our experience day by day when, as the first man asked God, "Am I my brother's keeper?" death was brought into the world. We are still evading the question and blaming someone else for the position we occupy.

We are also told that individuals who occupy a position from which they may wield a mighty influence are being reincarnated into the earth because of the position they once occupied in the thought of the world. Now, they are coming into their own.

Be that as it may, are we not all in the same position as to what we are going to do about it? There is no power that is not ordained of God. Then is it not the plan of the Supreme Force or Power that we call God, that we as individuals are reincarnated into the earth's experience at this time? It has been laid out beforehand.

Then you may say, "Well, you are a fatalist and believe

what's going to happen is going to happen—nothing can change it." No, that isn't answering the question of being our brother's keeper.

We are studying along lines of thought pertaining to development of the inner man, the soul. Within us is that something we call the soul, the entity, the being; and this lives on and on.

We say this is a period of hard times when ye all wonder just what is coming to pass, that it is a period when there are to be upheavals. What have we done to prepare ourselves for such happenings? "These things will come about," the Master said, "but the time isn't yet. There shall be wars and rumors of wars. There shall be earthquakes in divers places. There shall be signs in heaven and brother shall rise against brother, nation against nation, but the time isn't yet." (See Matt. 24)

All these things are coming about. What was the warning beforehand? "If ye fall away, if ye go back and follow, after those things pertaining to the desires of your own carnal influences, I will turn my face from you." (See Deut. 31:16–17)

The invisible face, yes; that which we cannot see, cannot perceive with the five senses. Yet that which may be aroused within us tells us whether or not we are following in the way He would have us go. "My spirit will bear witness with your spirit as to whether ye be the sons of God or not." (See Romans 8:16)

It doesn't matter how these warnings have come to us. We are now, in the midst of the condition, and it is all around us. The changes are coming about. Portions of the earth are going to be wiped away in the next few years; I feel very sure of that. Several of the readings foretold earth changes starting in the last years of the second millennium. And I had a dream in which I was reborn in 2158 A.D. in Nebraska. The sea apparently covered all of the western part of the country, as the city where I lived was on the coast. The family name was a strange one. At an early age as a child I declared myself to be Edgar Cayce who had lived two hundred years before. Scientists, men with long beards, little hair, and thick glasses, were called in to observe me. They decided to visit the places where I said I had been born, lived and worked, in Kentucky, Alabama, Ohio, and Virginia. Taking me with them the group of scientists visited these places in a long, cigar-shaped, metal flying ship which moved at high speed. Water covered part of Alabama. Norfolk, Va., had become an immense seaport. New York had been destroyed either by war or an earthquake and was being rebuilt. Industries were scattered over the countryside. Most of the houses were of glass. Many records of my work as Edgar Cayce were discovered and collected. The group returned to Nebraska taking the records with them to study.

Such a dream experience, we were told, came to me when I needed help and strength for periods when doubt or fear may arise. There were about me those influences which appeared to make for confusion and doubt or fear of those sources that made for the periods through which the entity was passing in that particular period. The dream came to give strength and understanding, even though the moment may appear dark. Although there may be periods of misinterpreting of purposes, even *these* will be turned into that which will be the very proof itself in the experiences of the entity and those whom the entity might, whom the entity would in its experience through the earth plane, help; and those to whom the entity might give hope and understanding.

The message of the dream was: Fear not. Keep the faith; for those that be with thee are greater than those that would hinder. Though the very heavens fall, though the earth shall be changed, though the heavens shall pass, the promises in Him are sure and will stand—as in that day—as the proof of thy activity in the lives and hearts of those of thy fellow man. For indeed and in truth ye know, "As ye do it unto thy fellow man, ye do it unto thy God, to thyself." For, *self* effaced, God may indeed glorify thee and make thee *stand* as one that is called for a purpose in the dealings, the relationships with thy fellow man. Be not unmindful that He is nigh unto thee in every trial, in every temptation, and hath not willed that thou shouldest perish. Make thy will then one with His. Be not afraid. That the periods from the material angle as visioned are to come to pass matters not to the soul. If we but do our duty *today, tomorrow* will care of itself. These changes in the earth will come to pass, for the time and times and half times are at an end, and there begin those periods for the readjustments. For how hath He given? "The righteous shall inherit the earth."

When we hear prophesies of earth changes, right away, we want to know if it will happen where we are. What difference does it make if we are living right? To be overanxious about ourselves because we are living in the wrong place is to be like the people who came to the old lady living on the frontier. A man came to her and said he wanted to make a place for his family of boys and girls growing up, but he certainly hated to leave all his friends at home. She said, "Well, you'll find it just the same way out here. If you had friends at home, you'll have friends here." The next man who came said that he was glad to get away from the place where he had lived for so many years; the people there were all selfish, stingy, and hard to get along with. The old lady said, "Brother, you'll find it the same way out here. If you couldn't get along with the folks at home, you won't be able to get along with the folks out here. If you didn't have friends at home, you won't find them here."

So with us. If we are not ready, if we're not making our preparations, it will be only a matter of time before we must pay the penalty even if we don't happen to be among the first taken away in a moment.

How do we know these changes are going to take place? We don't know, except by the signs that have been told us and that we are experiencing. For the outward appearances, the things visible around us, are mere shadows of the things that really exist and are coming about. When, as the Master said, we see these changes coming, we know it is because people acted within themselves and toward their neighbor in such a way as to bring about these changes.

The first command was: "Be fruitful, multiply, subdue the earth." (Gen. 1:28) That means obtain the knowledge of all these things that are here in the earth. And there isn't a thing in the earth that isn't a manifestation of God. Do we show forth our appreciation for the things about us, or do we say, "Gimmie, gimmie, gimmie," and try to draw it all into ourselves? We are our brother's keeper—or is our brother keeping us?

Life isn't a bit different today from what it was a million years ago. Life is one. God is Life—whether in the oyster, the tree, or in us. Life is God and a manifestation of Him. Man can make a beautiful tree, but he can't give it life. He can make a beautiful egg, but he can't give it that which will make it reproduce itself. What is that something which can reproduce life except Life itself, or God? It is the invisible that is within us and completely around us.

If thoughts are deeds, our constructive and positive thinking will aid in building or establishing that which will bring peace, harmony, joy, love—the fruits of the Spirit. What is the Spirit? That which we can comprehend only by the application of it, by what we do for someone else.

We had a very beautiful illustration of this thought in one of our Sunday school lessons. The Master had spent Himself in giving out to others. He had grown weary, and it was necessary that He rest physically, for He was then a man. Something had been taken out of Him in order to give constructive influences to offset those destructive influences in the lives of those He had contacted. He was asleep at sea. The boat began to fill and the disciples became uneasy. They went and woke Him: "Carest thou not that we perish?" He rebuked the wind, and the sea became calm. Now, did that power *go out* of the Master, or did it *come into* Him? It came into Him—the peace, the calm—because He was of the Creative Forces that would manifest. *In the giving out, it came in.* And as we, too, give out, to make this a better world for others to live in, peace and harmony and understanding—fruits of the Spirit—come into us.

Shall we go and do wonderful things? Shall we stand on the corner and preach? Of course, if we are called to do such things, then we should do them. Yet perhaps we shall just speak a kind word to our next-door neighbor, to the child we meet in the street, to the lame dog we see—to anything or anybody that is a manifestation of God. Just speaking the kind word that brings hope to those who are losing hope; speaking the cheery word to those who are discouraged; as we can do these things, we give out that which we have received. "Freely ye have received, freely give." For not all are called to be healers, not all preachers; but each of us can do what our hands find to do, magnifying the Spirit and the fruits of the Spirit, which are unseen.

The things we do today will make the kind of individual we will be tomorrow or a million years from now. We don't die to be in eternity; we are already in it! Then it's just as important to understand whence we came as it is to understand where we are going. To know whence we came is to know what we're up against. If we use the abilities we have, we will be given more tomorrow. The next step to take will be given to us.

It is self-exaltation and selfishness that carry us away from God. These bring doubts, fears, worry, hardship, and misunderstanding. Whatever may be troubling us, let us take it to God, to Christ. We will be shown the way into the New Millennium.

I had an unusual experience once while at work in my garden. I heard a noise like a swarm of bees. When I looked to see where they were, I saw that the noise came from a chariot in the air with four white horses and a driver. I did not see the face of the driver. The experience lasted only a few minutes. I was trying to persuade myself that it was not true, that it was only imagination, when I heard a voice saying, "Look behind you." I looked and beheld a man in armor, with a shield, a helmet, knee guards, a cape, but no weapon of any kind. His countenance was like the light; his armor was as silver or aluminum. He raised his hand in salute and said, "The chariot of the Lord and the horsemen thereof." Then he disappeared. I was really weak, not from fright but from awe and wonder. Miss Gladys said she heard me say that I dropped my hoe and when I reached up to mop my brow, my hand came down all red looking, as if I were sweating blood. Hugh Lynn later said that I ran against him in the front hall, white and shaking, on the way to my chair in the living room. It was a most beautiful experience and I hope I may be worthy of many more.

This was a vision. This is the interpretation:

These are as emblems, these are as figures in the experience of the entity, that: As is builded in the conscious mind of those about the entity, as in the conscious entity itself, if there are not those encouragements from thy friend, if there is not a kind word or a smile, thou dost indeed feel that something is amiss, something is awry! How well, then, those that have named the Name, those that would know the Lord—*smile!* For what else in God's creation can?

In the experience there is shown that there is not only the whole armor of the Lord as a defense, but the chariot of the Lord that would take wings upon time to show—to make thee know—that His promises abide.

Be faithful through those periods of oppression, as well as those periods that would soon come when the *material* things of life would be as plenteous in thine experience. But keep the whole armor of the Lord that ye may stand even as He in that day when temptations of every nature, when trials of every sort, come upon thee and thy fellow man.

For the Lord forgetteth not those to whom He hath given the charge, "Feed my sheep, feed my lambs."

29

OUR MISSION

It has always been my desire to be able to answer for the faith that lies within me, because if one cannot answer for the faith that lies within—or what one professes to live by—then one is not at his best; for we live by faith, day by day. If we don't know why, how, or what we believe, or why we believe it, we are indeed getting far afield from that which the source of life would have us be. What is Life itself? What is the phenomenon of life? Where and how do various phenomena manifest themselves?

Through my experiences, I believe we have a physical body, we have a mental body, we have a spiritual body—or a soul. Each of these bodies has its attributes. Just as the physical body has its divisions that are all dependent upon one another, some more dependent than the rest, so does this mind have its source of activity—so does it have its various forces that manifest themselves in various ways through this individual body. So does the soul have its attributes and its various ways of gaining, maintaining, or manifesting itself. The psychic force is a manifestation of the soul mind.

Some years ago I had dinner with a noted East Indian lecturer who asked me what I thought was the difference between personality and individuality. I answered this way: "Personality is what you want the other fellow to think you are, and individuality is what you really are!" That's it.

My friend Myron Wyrick and I often discussed the question of whether or not there is a survival of personality after the death of the body. It usually ended jokingly with one of us saying, "Which ever one goes first will communicate with the other."

During his last years we seldom met, but we corresponded intermittently until I was notified of his death. Several months later I was sitting alone in my living room, listening to Seth Parker's program on the radio. They were singing songs which their loved ones had been fond of during their lifetimes. One lady asked that they sing "Sweet Hour of Prayer." Another asked her which one of her husbands had liked that song. I was very much amused and leaned back in my chair smiling to myself. Suddenly, I felt as if there was a presence in the room. I was cold and felt something uncanny or unusual taking place. I looked toward the radio and realized that my friend Wyrick was sitting in front of it as if listening to the program. He turned and smiled at me, saying, "There *is* survival of personality. I *know!* And a life of service and prayer is the only one to live."

I was shaking all over. He said nothing more and seemed to disappear. When the program finished, I turned off the radio. It still felt as if the room was full of some presence. As I switched off the light and climbed the stairs, I could hear many voices coming from the darkened room.

Jumping into bed shivering from the cold, I aroused my wife. She asked me why I hadn't turned off the radio. I assured her that I had. She got up and opened the door and said, "I hear it—I hear voices." We both did.

What was it? I can't explain it. But was it a demonstration of the survival of personality? I don't think so.

Before you can acquire a personality, there must be an individuality. Your individuality is what you are. It is the sum total of all your experiences upon the earth, and what you have done with them, how you have reacted to them. Our experiences in the earth's plane are to determine whether we are fit associates for God or not. We have been given the privilege of coming into the earth and to manifest our individuality and our personality. If we make them one with God, we can become His companion. But if we become fixed on this I, this Me, instead of the great I AM, then we allow our personality to overshadow us as to separate us entirely from our ability to become one with the Source of all creation.

What attracts us to a person is their personality. If the basis of that personality is not founded in their individuality, or what they really are—or their spiritual selves—it soon becomes shallow and the individual soon loses all the attraction they may have had, unless we are like-minded. If we are shallow, as a sounding brass or a tinkling cymbal, if it is only a front we are putting up and there is nothing of the reality back of it, we will drift along together—but we will fall out sooner or later. And it's time to stop and take account of ourselves, and see if we have that faculty of individuality, and awaken the spirituality within ourselves—our inner selves.

The person who has individuality lives on in the minds and the hearts of the people whom he or she served, for "the greatest among you is the servant of all." And it isn't personality that's the servant unless it is backed up by real individuality, real spirituality within that soul. If we cultivate our relationship to God, the personality will shine out in such a way that it is worthwhile for others to contact us. Our personality lives on in the earth, it doesn't live afterward. We give it up. We leave it here. What really lives on is our individuality, or our ability to meet any and every condition, and which will ennoble the lives of those who follow in our path.

As for various psychic phenomena, when they appear it doesn't necessarily mean that they all come from discarnate personalities. If the soul is in the proper accord with the Source of life, may not the phenomena be that as directed Aaron in his activity, rather than that which directed the magicians as they presented their source of activity? For if such phenomena come from other than the one Divine Source, it must reach the point or place where it must fail. The Master was in accord with the one Source of all good, and I think many of the others were at various times who presented themselves as a living sacrifice, who presented their bodies as a living sacrifice holy and acceptable until Him.

Not long after we established the Association, I had a dream in which I saw myself fixing to give a reading, and the process through which a reading was gotten. Someone described it to me. There was a center or spot from which, on going into the state, I would radiate upward. It began as a spiral, except there were rings all around—commencing very small, and as they went on up they got bigger and bigger. The spaces in between the rings were the various places of development which individuals had attained, from which I would attempt to gain information. That was why a very low developed body might be so low that no one even giving information would be able to give anything that would be worthwhile. There were certain portions of the country that produced their own radiation; for instance, it would be very much easier to give a reading for an individual who was in the radiation that had to do with health, or healing; not necessarily in a hospital, but in a healing radiation—than it would be for an individual who was in purely a commercial radiation. I might be able to give a much better reading (as the illustration was made) for a person in one city, than one in another location, because the vibrations of one were very much higher than the vibrations in the other. The closer the individual was to one of the rings, the easier it would be to get the information. An individual would, from any point in between, by their own desire go toward the ring. If just curious, they would naturally draw down towards the center away from the ring, or in the spaces between the rings.

The reading said this vision was recognizable as an experience of the soul, or the *entity*, in activity. There have been various formulas or descriptions of how information for a body was obtained through these channels. There has been promised, through these channels, that there was to be a greater awakening to this entity in its field of endeavor. So in this way there is, as indicated, a way of the information being better correlated, better understood by individuals—who are through that as may be termed the attunements of the various directions, in the various portions of the country or world—of their relationship to the actual fact of seeking through the channels. [See 262-16] As indicated, the entity is—in the affairs of the world—a tiny speck, as it were, a mere grain of sand; yet when raised in the atmosphere or realm of the spiritual forces it becomes all inclusive, as is seen by the size of the funnel—which reaches not downward, nor outward, nor over, but direct to that which is felt by the experience of man as into the heavens itself. As indicated in the rings, or the nets as of nerves, each portion of the sphere, or the earth, or the heavens, is in that place which has been set by an All Wise Creative Energy. Each may attain to those relationships by that which is attempted in the activities of an individual, a group, a class, a mass, a nation. In that manner do they create their position in the affairs of the universe. Each speck, as an atom of human experience, is connected one with another as the continuity of the cone seen, and in the manner that the nerves of an animating or living object bears upon that in its specific center, but reaches to the utmost portions of the universality of force or activity in the whole universe and has its radial effect upon one another.

As the entity, then, raises itself through those activities of subjugating or making as null those physical activities of the body, using only—as it were (in the cone)—the trumpet of the universe, in reaching out for that being sought, each entity—or each dot, then—in its respective sphere—acts as the note or the lute in action, that *voices* that which may come forth from such seeking.

Then we find, in the classification, in the activity of those that correlate such information, those in the various spheres will naturally classify themselves—even as given in the illustration, that there will more often be the sound of help to those in one place than to those in another. That only as an illustration. Not that there may not be as much healing to those from the one as the other, but the effect upon the individual in the environ makes for the tone which resounds from that received. See? This should, then, be a helpful illustration to those correlating in understanding and classifying the information that may be received. This should, to the body giving information, make known to him that there is being *opened* access to the Thrones themselves!

Later I dreamed that I was driving a car without a steering wheel—right drive instead of left. Someone told me I needed a new saddle instead of a steering wheel.

The explanation was that there is growing (even in this materialistic experience) more and more recognition that the information needs to be ridden in a channel that is more direct than one that cannot be governed without the proper steering. As indicated, there is that tendency in the materialistic information to run those who seek only for material things to a destructive force, yet they may aid many an individual over a rough place. They may dodge many of the pitfalls or obstructions that are in their way, yet continual riding in such an attitude or atmosphere, or manner, as indicated, is like driving without the ability to steer aright.

In another dream that same night I saw a Chinese girl with her head on backwards. That was interpreted as a symbolic vision (of which only a portion is given here), the girl represents that aspect that has long sought an understanding in claims for beliefs, but who approaches such in a backward or obtuse manner; that is, there must be a regeneration in all, and *face about*, rather than backing into that which may bring aid.

So, it must be possible for any of us to be in accord with the one Divine Source of all information, if we will but pay the price. I have often fallen far short in presenting myself as a living sacrifice for the manifestation of whatever source might manifest through me. In that sense, I may be called a medium. I hope that I may be rather a channel through which blessings may come to many rather than a medium through which any force may manifest other than God Himself. For if it is of God, it must be good. And if it is good, it must come from the All Good, which to me is God. This, I trust, is the type of psychic phenomena that manifests itself through me. Only through the soul are we able to gain access to the throne of God. Where have we been told that the kingdom of heaven exists? The Master gave it over and over again, and compared it to almost every condition we can imagine. "The kingdom of heaven is within you." That is the source from which all types of information may come. Then, unless we have our own personal experience, it cannot mean a great deal to us. It may be interesting, it may even be worthwhile, but until God is *our* God, until whatever source we have chosen as our ideal source of information is *ours*, it cannot mean all it should mean. Then, what we each should do is to have our own experience.

Have you ever asked anyone *why* they belonged to a certain church? Why is it that so few seem to really know or to give a satisfactory answer to that question? Most people would say it was because their father or their mother belonged to that church. Is that a good answer to ourselves? It isn't if we have gotten to where we can think! We reach the place where such an answer doesn't satisfy. We have to come to know the source of that in which we have believed, in which we do believe—the source from which emanates that which we hope to build our souls upon. Our souls are what we have to present to our Maker; our experiences through this life, the phenomena that we pass through here has much to do with the type, class, kind of bodies, soul bodies, we will be able to present to our Maker. Are we very *sure* that we *know* in what we have believed, and *why* we act in the way we do toward what we *profess* to believe? Many of us profess this, that, or the other, but how many of us act in a manner in keeping with what we profess to believe?

My mission, if I know it at all, is to help people find their relationship to the Creator. If it is necessary for some to find Him through the cure of physical ills, then we must work towards that. For, as the Great Teacher said, "Whether is it easier to say to the sick of the palsy, Thy sins be forgiven thee; or to say, Arise, and take up thy bed and walk?"

The cause of illness is sin. Anything which separates us from that within which makes us alive is sin. So, all forms of healing—whether through physicians of the various schools or through spiritual healing direct from the One Source—are to enable us to find our relationship to Life itself, that is, to God.

One person, through a reading some time ago, was given something like this: To help you to physical strength without enabling you to find yourself would, with your frame of mind, cause you to be worse off than you now are because you have cursed your God, because you swear against everything that is holy. So unless you can get to the seat of the matter and help an individual to change his mental attitude toward his

One Source of supply, little aid may come, regardless of what channel he uses.

Unless we are sincere with ourselves, with our associates, we are building such a barrier in our consciousness as to keep us trotting back to this earth for ages and ages to come!

The purpose of the Association is to enable those who sincerely seek to find the best that is within themselves and to find a relationship to the Creative Forces that are alive within and about us everywhere.

Let us not worry what others are doing, apparently in opposition to our purpose; but let us look rather to what we ourselves are doing in relation to our purpose. If we fulfill our mission to the best of our ability, then others—seeking—will take hope also. Life in abundance is ours, if we will only take hold on it.

EPILOGUE

Through the 1930s and early 1940s, Mr. Cayce kept up a prodigious correspondence with scores of people, did a bit of fishing and gardening, maintained a regular twice-daily schedule giving readings, lectured, played many hands of bridge and an occasional round of golf, and kept to a weekly schedule of helping a group in Norfolk develop a study manual, entitled *A Search for God*, that was to serve hundreds more such study groups in years to come. Each summer he looked forward to a week-long gathering of his most faithful followers at Virginia Beach. At the close of the 1941 Congress he told them:

There's a sort of sadness felt when we come to the end of something that has meant a great deal to us. This Congress has meant more to me than any of the others we have held thus far. While the crowds have not been as large as at some of the other meetings, there has appeared to me to be a more sincere seeking interest in the minds of those who have come. For that reason, I think that each of you have obtained something from the meetings this year that will remain with you for quite a while.

I want to thank each one of you for coming. If you have received something good, use it, don't just put it away as something that has been interesting but that is past. Try it out.

A play was produced in New York some years ago depicting the life of the Christ. After the Crucifixion one of the sisters of Jesus was to be married to a man quite wealthy. It was the custom, when announcing the wedding, to tell all the things that had happened in the family. The mother told the young man about the unusual experience of her oldest son being crucified. He asked, for what? She said, "Well, we don't quite know how to put it into words; but he had an idea that we should treat every other person like we would have that person treat us."

The young man answered, "Did anybody ever try it? It's not such a scandal if nobody ever tried it to see whether or not it would work."

Then I say that if you have gotten something out of what you have heard at the various meetings this time, if it is worthwhile, try it.

During this next year, until we meet at the next Congress, let's try never to say, never to do one thing that will offend anyone else. Sometimes we will have to hold our tongues, but it can be done, and we are the ones who can do it—not of ourselves, but with His help. For He has promised to be with us if we try. God bless you each and every one.

His life followed this placid routine, largely unchanged until publication of his biography, *There Is a River*, and an article in a national magazine, entitled "Miracle Man of Virginia Beach," in 1943. (The article appears in Appendix G.) World War II took both his sons into the army. The combination of the publicity he received and the anxiety many people felt for loved ones in the war sharply increased demands for his services. It soon cost him heavily. At the First Presbyterian Church, where Mr. Cayce had been teaching a Sunday school class for many years, a new minister took a dim view of having a psychic as a teacher and unceremoniously replaced him. After all these years of teaching the Bible, he was once again caught between his unconventional calling and the conventions of his faith.

The public at large had the opposite reaction. Visitors camped in his yard seeking appointments. His mail was delivered by the truckload. Volunteers were enlisted to help Miss Gladys and Gertrude cope with the deluge, and Mr. Cayce, at age sixty-six, responded the only way he knew how, by giving as many as a dozen readings a day—six times his normal quota—trying to help as many people as he possibly could. His dedication took a heavy toll.

First, he became ill with pneumonia. "He asked his family doctor to try the new sulfa drug on him," recalled Gladys Davis. "It was a mistake. His heart became enlarged, with fluid on the lungs." Severe chest pains followed. In August 1944 he and Gertrude went to Roanoke in the Blue Ridge Mountains for a rest. "His right hand was affected so that he couldn't any longer use his little typewriter to peck out personal letters any more—that's why he realized he had to stop and rest," noted Gladys. "His fingers wouldn't function properly—no strength in them."

When he gave a reading on his own health, it described general debilitation, using up of all his energies without replenishing them. That turned out to be the last of his nearly fifteen thousand readings. A week later he suffered a paralyzing stroke and was unable to return to Virginia Beach for several months.

Around Thanksgiving his youngest son, Edgar Evans Cayce, home on leave, brought his father home in a Virginia Beach Rescue Squad ambulance. "Mr. Cayce was a pitiful sight coming in on the stretcher, so weak he couldn't speak above a whisper—and weeping—so glad to be home but heartbroken to be in such a fix," recalled Gladys. The left side of his body was paralyzed from the face down—perhaps his throat was partially paralyzed, too, she observed.

A few days later he dictated a letter to reassure Hugh Lynn, who was in Europe with General Patton's army: "I really think I have improved more since I have been home than in all of the time since I have been sick, and I can tell you I have been pretty sick. I suppose the readings were right in sending me to Roanoke but they certainly are doctoring or working from a different viewpoint here than they did up there. The Colloidal Chemistry Theory, as used on me by Dr. Harry Semones, D.O., in Roanoke, is by some man in England and all of the medicine had to come from there. Most of it is given hypodermically and you are not given any meat or animal protein or milk in your diet at all. What they are doing now (here at home) is just the opposite, so I don't know which way I'm going—up or down. I just hope it is for the best and I can come out of it all right."

He then dictated in a whisper a Christmas message, which

Gladys sent to friends and A.R.E. members, along with a note that he was "definitely improving." His message read:

Unless you have experienced the sorrow of being away from home, lonely and confused as to what to do, spiritually, mentally, materially, you cannot know what a hunger it creates. But I am at home now and, I believe, doing better, though my strength seems slow returning. The most joyous Christmas I could have would be the answer to my prayer that I may be used as a channel to help others. The promise given in my last reading, "Ye have many helpers," is being proven each day in more ways than one. I have every expectation that my prayer will be answered, by His grace and mercy, if I remain faithful in thought and purpose to the trust which has been placed in me. Let each of you be very diligent in your prayers for me and with me. Remember, we must each live as we pray, if our prayer would be effectual. If the world is to have the wonderful Christmas gift it should have at this season, we must all pray earnestly for peace and manifest it in our own lives.

God bless each and every one of you. This I ask in the name of Jesus, the Christ.

In mid-December, after sleeping most of the day, he went into a coma in the evening and didn't regain consciousness until morning. "After this, he never seemed to have the mental alertness as before," said Gladys. "He would sleep a few minutes and then wake up. He wasn't satisfied to stay in bed. We'd get him up in the chair and in a few minutes he'd want to go back to bed, and the same thing all over again. For the rest of his life he never slept over thirty minutes at a time without waking—sometimes he'd speak rationally, ask for a water, etc."

Gertrude and Gladys took turns staying with him through the night. On New Year's Eve, as Gladys heard the horns blowing at the stroke of midnight, she said to him, "Happy New Year, we're going places and doing things in 1945." He replied, "Same to you—maybe, maybe, if the Lord is willing."

Two nights later "Gertrude, standing by the hospital bed,

was getting ready to tell Edgar good-night and get some rest while I took over until the nurse would arrive for the midnight shift. She reached over and kissed him. He said, 'You know, I love you, don't you?'

"She nodded, and he asked, '*How* do you know?'

" 'Oh, I just know,' she said, with her dear little smile.

" 'I don't see how you can tell—but I do love you,' he said. Reflecting, he continued, 'You know, when you love someone you sacrifice for 'em, and what have I ever sacrificed because I love you?'

"This bedside scene was so beautiful that it made me cry, because I understood so well how Gertrude had stood by him and put his wishes always above her own when it came to the good of 'the work.' I knew how much they each had suffered through the years, and how hard it was for them because of their different manners of expression. But the readings had indicated that love knows no barriers; that when there is the same spiritual ideal in marriage all material obstacles can become stepping stones."

The next evening his sister Annie Cayce brought him up some oyster stew for supper, which he had known that she was making for him. He took two or three sips of it. It was his last supper. That evening he quietly stopped breathing and passed over.

Mr. Cayce's funeral service was held at his home in Virginia Beach, the rooms crowded with those who loved him, the service conducted by a former minister at the Presbyterian church. The funeral cortege moved from the Beach to Norfolk, and from there by train to Hopkinsville, Kentucky, for burial in a service conducted by the pastor of the First Christian Church.[1]

Sugrue attributed Mr. Cayce's death to "the strain of overwork." In a eulogy sent to A.R.E. members, his biographer wrote:

—

[1] Gertrude Cayce, his companion for nearly a half century, died three months later, and was buried beside Edgar in the family burial plot in Hopkinsville, Kentucky.

"For more than a year he had worked under unbelievable handicaps. His son, the manager of the Association for Research and Enlightenment, Hugh Lynn Cayce, entered the armed services. At the same time an unprecedented number of requests for readings came to Virginia Beach. Often there were more than 500 letters in the daily mail. The library, which had seemed so large when first built, was jammed with stenographers working at correspondence. Mr. Cayce himself examined every letter, and worked late into the night dictating answers. During the morning and afternoon periods he gave not two but from eight to twelve readings. Still he could fulfill but a small portion of the applications. The others, with their tales of misfortune and suffering, weighed heavily on him. For the first time in his long life of service he could not help every one of his fellows who asked for aid. He worked harder and harder, but the appointments ran on and on, until they were more than a year ahead of him. His own diagnosis, given in a reading last September, was that he had reached a point of complete nervous exhaustion. From this he did not recover. As this is written the shock of his passing is so deep that even the most glib tongues are stilled. Once a person came to know Edgar Cayce, he thereafter could not imagine a world without him, without his readings, without his personality his friendliness, his simple and complete Christianity. The role of those he served is long. How many he reached through his readings, through his sixty years of Bible teaching, is incalculable. His only ambition was that after his death even more people be reached and given whatever in the readings was good and helpful. That is the first reaction to his death—that faith must be kept with him, and his work continued. It is symbolic that his own passing was brought about largely by the change in his work; that is, he could no longer give all the readings which were requested of him, and the necessity for giving to people the information of general use in the readings was growing each day. Now that he is gone this will become the whole of the work, and as it proceeds the real stature of Edgar

Cayce will be revealed. Truly he fulfilled the Christian ideal; he laid down his life for his friends. He was a great man. We shall not see his like again."

The public perception of Edgar Cayce, however, remained as mixed in death as in life. But he was not exactly a prophet without honor in his own land. The local press paid their respects upon his passing. An editorial in Norfolk's *Virginian-Pilot* recalled the encounter that young Edgar had with an angelic presence, who promised to fulfill his wish to help children:

> In the Middle Ages this kind of experience sometimes led to sainthood. In the Twentieth Century it made of Edgar Cayce a psychic healer . . . There is nothing in the Cayce record that suggests the exploitation or charlatanry that is *too* often encountered in this disputed branch of healing. People were impressed by his simplicity and personal integrity. He did not advertise. He made no platform appearances. He sought no patients. Patients sought him. Thousands of therapeutic trances seem to have yielded him not riches but an extraordinary position in that dim twilight zone of human mind the growing literature on which falls under the head of parapsychology.

The weekly *Virginia Beach News* commented:

> The idea that a person with psychic powers may also have diagnostic powers is not new. To others before Edgar Cayce such capacities have been attributed. He does not appear to have claimed any special knowledge of medicine or of physiology. He said that what happened to him in hypnotic trances was beyond his explanation and even beyond his remembrance. He had no gift for advertising himself, never attained any great public fame, despite much that was written and more that was talked about him, and he obviously preferred a simple and quiet life.
>
> Virginia Beach can testify that he lived such a life there

during the last 17 years of a career of "psychic diagnostician" which covered some 43 years all told, most of it in small towns. If he reaped any large material rewards, they did not appear on the surface. He seemed modest and unpretentious and religious. The rest belongs to the psychologists, to the students of psychic phenomena and to those who can pierce the strange ways of the human personality. They might have had—may yet have—a fruitful subject in this unusual resident of Virginia Beach.

It would be another two decades before Edgar Cayce was "discovered" by the masses, when a new biography, *The Sleeping Prophet* by Jess Stearn, hit the bestseller list. Since then the number of titles devoted to the Cayce story and his philosophy on numerous topics has multiplied. And his Association for Research and Enlightenment has grown into an international organization that has perpetuated the legacy and propagated the philosophy of Edgar Cayce for generations to come.

PART IV

Appendix

APPENDIX A

THE PAST LIVES OF EDGAR CAYCE

Upon giving information about a previous incarnation as a monk for an Ohio businessman, the first hint of reincarnation given in the readings, Mr. Cayce gave what came to be called life readings for the people closest to him and for himself. These readings stated that he and Gertrude, Hugh Lynn Cayce, and Gladys Davis had been intimately associated in the past, in more than one life in several cases. All of them had been associated in ancient Egypt, Mr. Cayce and Gladys in ancient Persia, and later in France. The following are the principal readings in which these connections were disclosed.

Text of Reading 294-8 for Edgar Cayce

This psychic reading given by Edgar Cayce at Phillips Hotel, Room 115, Dayton, Ohio, in a series of five readings beginning February 9th, 1924. Request made by Edgar Cayce himself.

Edgar Cayce; Linden Shroyer, Conductor; Gladys Davis, Steno.

Born March 18, 1877, in Christian Co., Ky., near Hopkinsville. [1:30 P.M. Central Standard Time (?)]

(Horoscope suggestion, with request for past lives, etc.)

EC: There is much we have given relative to this before. We have the conditions as have been, as are, and will be. In this, without reference to that as has been given, for in giving the conditions in the various phases of the past experience there will be much that will show the various phases of the developing in the different stages, the conditions as given then will be those as with reference to the effect that the planets and their satellites and spheres have upon the present life and plane, without reference to the will.

Then, with the will, and also the developing with will and

the planetary or astrological effect in the various planes as have gone before; in the present, as in this plane, we find the condition as brought to the earth plane was from that of the attitudes as held by those to and through whom the present entity was and is made manifest upon the earth plane by the relativity of force and the attraction of likes; the attitude of those earthly parents towards conditions that brought the relations to the stage of the developing of the entity that came, and through that stage the entity chose the mode of manifesting in the earth plane. Hence the condition of the parents upon the earth plane, or duty that is due each of its earthly offsprings, for all are under that bond of duty to be made the channel of the manifesting of this force through the entity's actions towards his offsprings.

As to the condition from the astrological standpoint, we find this entity almost entirely influenced by, and came from that in the last plane of Uranus, with Neptune, Venus and Jupiter. Afflictions in Mars and of the Sagittarius, Capricornus, Gemini Sun and Moon in the various stages, for with the ultra forces, as of Uranus and Neptune, come much of the influence of the various planes, given in strength with Jupiter and Mercury.

As to the influences this gives then without reference to the will: One that will always be either very good or very bad, very wicked or very much given to good works. Ultra in all forces. Very poor, very rich. One scaling to the heights in intellectual ability and capacity, or groveling in the dregs of self-condemnation, influenced at such times by those forces either coming as afflictions from the various phases of developing, from which the entity has received its experience, or controlled by will as exercised in the present sphere.

One ever within the scope or sphere of firearms, yet just without.

One saved spiritually, mentally and financially often through a great amount of waters, for it was from the beginning, and will be so unto the end of time, as time is reckoned from the earth plane, for this entity we find was first manifest in the earth plane through the waters as was on the earth, and

above the earth. Hence through these elements and forces is
the spiritual, mental and financial, these three phases of spiritual life, mental life and financial life manifest in the earth
plane.

One who finds much in the scope or sphere of intrigue in
secret love affairs. One given often to the conditions that have
to do with the affairs of the heart, and of those relations that
have to do with sex.

One that finds the greater strength in spiritual forces and
developing.

One given to make manifest in the present plane much of
the forces of psychic and occult forces, reaching the greater
height of developing in such plane in those forces when that
of Jupiter, with Uranus and Neptune, come within the scope
of the Sun's influence upon the earth plane and forces. One
that will bring, through such manifestations, joy, peace and
quiet to the masses and multitudes through individual efforts.

One who, after the present year passes that place of that of
Pisces and Sun's rays on the twentieth of present month, will
go forward to developing much of the psychic and occult
forces to the great numbers that have become interested in
developing of such phenomena. One who will on the nine-
teenth of March, this year, reach the place or plane where the
present years and the present developing reaches the turn for
the developing, or the wield of those influences in Sagittarius,
Capricornus and Gemini that may bring destructive forces
without will's manifestation upon that day.

In the developing as regards will force in the present plane,
with conditions, there have been many conditions that have
been hindered by the effect of the will, and others that have
been assisted. Keep the will in that of the spiritual development, if the physical would manifest to the better advantage
in the present plane, keeping this ever before, that all work in
present plane will be judged to that individual and the classes,
masses, as to the individual's manifestation of spiritual forces
in and through the individual action in and before men. Ever
keeping the mind clear to the developing of the Uranian forces
that often manifest in the present plane, which will in the pres-

ent plane reach in the present and coming two years the influence of the Neptune and Mercury forces, carry the body,
unless will is exercised against such conditions, to many places
beyond this present bounds, or across many waters. Keep the
developing then to that force as is given in that of Uranus,
Neptune and Jupiter, whose greater influence as is upon the
earth plane, and beware of the influences in Venus forces, for
with Mars' affliction would bring sudden destruction to the
physical in the early fall of present year.

As to the vocation, this in the present plane may be directed
in any channel through will. The better condition, as given, in
that of astrological forces, would be toward those of psychic
and occult, or teaching or developing along the lines of such
plane to give the manifestation of such forces to the populace.

In the plane as of others: In the one just before this, we
find in the present place of the physical plane sojourn, but in
that of the soldier in the British forces as were in the force
that developed in the surrounding plains. The name, John
Bainbridge, and in that life we find the birth in Cornwall,
England, and the training in the Canadian forces as taken by
that country, and the drifting into the present plane as known
as American, or United America, and the life was lost then in
the waters as in the crossing of the river at the time the battle
was fought near the present sojourn. In this, as that given just
previous to the present appearance upon this plane, in which
the body's sojourn was near unto that at present, we find the
body's or the entity's and body's condition is then entered
upon that of the Saturn forces, and the life was manifested
then in the plane was as that of the adventurer, when the forces
of the king, under whose rule this entity was a subject, entered
in that force, or in the colonization of the country, was the
first appearance upon this present sphere's plane or scope, and
was connected with that in the group that were landing in the
East coast of the new country, now known as Virginia, and
near where is now the resort known as Virginia Beach. When
this raid was made, this John Bainbridge was carried in this
raid to the Southern coasts of the country; escaped, and with
the forces then going in the inland way, and making the sur-

rounding of the places in which the present sphere's plane has seen much of the same country, and developing, and finally making the way to the fort then on the Great Lakes, now in place known as Chicago, and from that fort entered the fray in which the crossing was later attempted in the Ohio River, and there met death as known in the earth plane.

The body was known as under two names, and was never wed during that sojourn upon the plane, though was in many escapades that have to do with those of the nature of the relations with the opposite sex. In the developing upon the present plane, we have much of the personality as shown in present spheres, as from that of the ability to take cognizance of detail, especially in following instructions as given from other minds or sources of information.

In that previous to this, we find in the Courts of the French, when Louis the 15th was King, and in the Royal Guard was this entity's sphere, which was of short duration, so far as years go upon the earth plane. This entity, then, was the attendant upon the Royal Court, and the Guard for the household of that Ruler, and lost the elements of life, as known, in the defense of those under whose care they were placed, as both lost the elements of physical life, in the defense. In the forces or personal conditions as seen in present sphere from this sojourn, we find that of the intense defense of those principles that to the entity's inmost soul or force is the right. In the name, we find that of Ralph Dahl [Dale?]. [See 1001-7 on 9/7/30 indicating that Louis the 15th & [294] had same grandfather? 1001-7, Par. 11-A; or was Louis 15th grandfather of John Bainbridge?]

In the condition that was previous to this, we find in the force as manifest when the Trojan rule was in that fair country, to whom the nations of the world have looked for the beauty in culture, art and refinement of the physical, mental and material force, and in that we find again the soldier and the defender of the gate, as was the place where the physical or material destruction came to the body. In the experience of that plane, we find these cover many and various stages. Those of the student, chemist, the sculptor and the artisan, as well as

of the soldier and defender in the last days. In that we find
the name Xenon, and there is, and has been, and will be many
more in the present sphere that were in contact with that
plane's forces, that the contact will be, has been brought in
the present sphere. In this, we find those present forces exhibited through that of the art, and the love of the beautiful in
any and every form, especially those that partake of human
form Divine.

In that before this we have that plane in which is now
known as the Arabian plane. In this, we find this entity's developing under that of Uhjltd, and there are many of the conditions, personality, knowledge, understanding, thought,
reference as is and will be in the passing of the plane of today.
For we find there are many upon this earth's plane, and in
different locations, who were associated with this entity at that
time. [The area Persia now known as IRAN.] In the entity's
force of that day, we find this entity one of power, prestige,
royalty, and the leader in many raids or wars as made upon
the surrounding peoples, tribes or nations. This we find the
most outstanding of that period, in the connection as was
shown in the war as made on the Persian ruler, Croesus, and
this Uhjltd led the expedition into that country. The force under this leadership was successful in the bringing submission
to the rule of the nation which Uhjltd led. And the developing
in that plane was with the suffering of bodily ills from injuries
received in the escape from the force as connived from the
weaknesses of the physical to make the Uhjltd a slave in bond-
age. His escape and sojourn upon the plain, with those surrounding him, was the developing stage, and the first of that
developing known in present earth plane as psychic force. For,
with the developing as received in the plane just before this
[in prehistory Egypt as the priest Ra Ta], as we shall see, [this
Uhjltd sojourn] was the continuation of the one found at that
time.

The passing of the portion of the entity again into Nazova
[?] [nirvana?] was through the wounds and infections as received upon the plane, in the vicinity of the well about which
the three palm trees [stood, which] has remained in the inner

being of the soul's developing force. And not until that entity [538?] is again reunited with this entity [294] will the developing upon this or other planes be efficient, or as good as should be.

In the elements as brought to the present plane, we find that of the deep love as manifests to others in any or all positions or stage of conditions in life. The inert [innate] and the hidden love for animal and live creatures of the Creator's make, as was developed in this sojourn upon the plain. With the meeting or contact of this entity's mate, for upon the 19th day of March, in present year, that entity will again be in physical touch with the entity's present development, again will come the power of monies, both in the way of earth's fame and glory, and with this will again the opportunity to develop as has been set in this plane of development, and again give the place in the world development towards the mark of the higher calling, as is set in Him. Upon that meeting will the developing depend, or begin, to be made manifest, or be cut short, as the will of the entity expresses and manifests itself. In this sphere or plane, we find there are many that come under the influence of the personal or personality of the entity's forces, and for many, many years after this return to the other spheres was this influence felt in the earth's plane, as in this influence felt in the earth's plane, as in this present plane, this with this union of forces may and will give that incentive to others to develop in that plane that leads to the understanding of the forces that give of the strength of the universal force.

In the plane before this, we find that as known in the dynasty of the Rameses or Pharaohs in Egypt, and in the Court and rule of the Second Pharaoh [341] or Rameses, [10,500 B.C.] and was at that time the high priest of the cult as gave the religious element and force in the age, and reached the heights in that dynasty, yet was cut short in the allowing of physical forces and desires to enter in, and the taking of the daughter [538] of the order of the one who offered the sacrifices for the priest's force, and going or leaving the shores of this country brought the destructive elements to the body. That same entity that was taken is at present in this earth's plane, the companion and mate as should be in the present sphere [538], and in this Court we find there was the study of the religious cults, isms, schisms as would be termed in this day and plane. The High Priest [294] who gave the elements of the religious force, and in this dynasty or reign of this Pharaoh [341] did the religious cult reach its height, as given through this priest, though he became the outcast, but for the good as had been accomplished by this individual was in the resting place of the King, and the forces as manifest in the present is the delving into the whys and wherefores of all who express a different mode of manifesting the hope that lies within the human breast of the life after the passing from the earth's plane. This, we see, manifests in the present. As to those forces that have brought this condition that the entity is in, the elements as brought the destructive force to self in the two, again we find that the karma of each must be met, [294] and [538] and in this plane overcome if each would enter in.

In that before this, we find in the beginning, when the first of the elements were given, and the forces set in motion that brought about the sphere as we find called earth plane, and when the morning stars sang together, and the whispering winds brought the news of the coming of man's indwelling, of the spirit of the Creator, became the living soul. This entity came into being with this multitude. As to the experiences as have been given in this plane, the earth, and the often sojourn upon this plane, we find all summed in this:

Take this thou hast in hand and make and mold it into the present plane's development, that thyself and others may know that God is God, and demands of His creatures that of the knowledge of self, that they may better serve their fellows, and in so doing present themselves as the ever giving force, bringing to others to the knowledge of Him.

There are many other influences as have been shed abroad in the earth's plane from the entity's sojourn there. These are given that all may know and understand that the record of each soul is kept in and unto that Great Day.

Be not deceived. Be not overcome, but overcome evil with good.

*   *   *

Text of Reading 538-5 for Gertrude Cayce, conducted by Linden Shroyer, on December 5, 1923, in Dayton, Ohio:

Born February 22, 1880, 7:58 A.M., CST., Hopkinsville, Ky.

LS: Now, you have before you the body of [538], born February 22, 1880, at Hopkinsville, Ky. You will give a horoscope reading, or a reading giving the effects of the planets upon the life and destiny of this individual. You will give the exact time of birth and the vocation in life for which this body is most adapted. You will give detailed information relative to the various appearances and the time in history of each of the former appearances upon this earth plane, and the characteristics as are exhibited of each of those appearances.

EC: Yes, we have the conditions here. We find the soul and spirit took possession of this late in the [afternoon] evening. [Her mother later told her she was born at 8:00 A.M.] Hence, the greater force in this life, and the greater understanding, will come in the later days upon this plane, and there will be three good years; yea, four, [when] with the greater blessings will be upon this life in this present plane.

We find those planets that have to do with the present sphere are those direct of Venus. Mercury, Neptune, Mars, Jupiter and Uranus in the distance—Hence, in the early approach of Jupiter's forces, will assist in the crowning glory of this life. In the forces as this has brought to this body—one of small stature, though well rounded in the beauty of the forces of Venus—though with the afflictions of Saturn causes jealous forces to enter into the forces as is felt in the inner force of the body.

One that is given to many accidents in various forms, especially to the limbs and other extremities.

One that will do well to remember the elements of natural forces, and of chemical forces, are healing natures to the physical body.

One that will find, in the future, the drawing force through Neptune, Mars and Jupiter, toward the study of psychic and occult, or mystic, forces, and will gain greater strength and understanding through the application of will and study to such forces; remembering that understanding gives content to all troubled forces in the body.

One whose constellation, nearing that of the change, or in Capricorn, gives the weakness to the physical forces in the body, but—that will be overcome in, and about, places where great amounts of sea and water are found.

One that the greater amount of financial forces come in the later days.

One that the force of the forces reached in Jupiter, Neptune and Mars, will bring these about, and should begin to show their effect in the latter part of present year. Again in the meridian as passes by these planets in the middle weeks of June 1924, and in October 1925.

One whose forces, and greater development, would be in those of the lighter nature, or of the higher arts, in those developing forces in natural means.

One whose natural love of the higher forces, in such light natures as is commonly understood, gives much anxiety to present stage of conditions, but one whose satisfaction will be granted in such in the year, '25, but one who will find vanity in such, and needs to exercise will force in this condition that will arise at that time, as given.

One whose inclinations are as these:

Lover of literature. Those that tend toward chemical forces, or intrigues.

One whose will force should be exerted more in lines, or those influences of Venus as afflictions reached through Saturn.

One whose inclinations should be tempered by the influence as would be exercised, and is to be, through Jupiter's higher forces.

One whose greater development will be in the next three years, as we have given, beginning in December.

One whose forces, as for the vocation, would have been the danseuse or stage. [Gladys Davis's note: Mrs. Cayce in discussing her reading said that as a child, even in her teens, she used to get alone in the outdoors or woods and *dance and dance* imagining herself performing before large European audiences. She had never been to a dance or seen a stage performance other than in books.]

As to the appearances, as the soul and spirit portion of the entity present, we find as were these:

Before this, in the Court of the French, when Charles the 2nd was an exile in that Court, and was a friend of that Monarch, or who afterwards became, and lent assistance and aid to those who, eventually, returned this youth to the country from which he was an exile. In that we find the name as this: Lurline.

Before this, we find in the country of the Grecians, when the greater forces were being shown through the reasoning forces, as under those of the philosopher with Socrates when he gave his exhibition of the reasoning of mind, and was of that household.

Again in the land of the Nomads in the hill country [Egypt] of the first Pharaohs.

The individuality as exhibited through the personalities of these we find as this:

From first [in France] that desire, or inert [innate] force, calling new scenes, and the love of those in company of only a few.

In the second [Greece] the reasoning forces of the entity.

In the third [Egypt] the love of pomp, glory, and of those things that are pleasing to the touch and eye. Beware, however, in these, and use will force to the developing. And some of the scenes through which this entity has passed, it may again become a part of by its own sheer will force.

Text of reading 341-1 for Hugh Lynn Cayce, age 16, born March 16, 1907 [3:15 P.M., Central Standard Time], at Bowling Green, Kentucky.

Given by Edgar Cayce on December 10, 1923, at Dayton, Ohio, with Linden Shroyer as conductor.

(Horoscope suggestion)

EC: We see the soul and spirit completed this present entity at 3:23 in the afternoon. We find as this:

Without the will of the entity taken into consideration, under those forces of Jupiter, Mercury, Mars, Neptune, Venus, with afflictions of Saturn with the assistance or ascendency of Uranus in the latter days more than in the earlier sojourn here.

We find under this influence one strong of body, well balanced in body and mind. One given to study of the many phases of development, both in the mental and physical plane. One with the affliction of Saturn, under conjunction of Mercury and Mars, has the affliction in fire and firearms to the detriment of the body. One that must use the will force in the use of firearms in the coming year, when Mars is nearest, and with the latter days of that year will be under the afflictions of Saturn, and this body may be wary of the use of those in his own hands.

One that the injunctions [conjunctions] from Venus, Mars and Jupiter will bring many petty warrior troubles in affairs of the heart.

One whose life-love will enter after years of maturity.

One whose greater study lies in those forces of the spiritual nature.

One whose greater forte will lie in that of literature; writer, composer, historian, or compiler of data for such works.

One who should, with the mind and will, develop the mind or mental forces toward such development of self for this present plane.

One that may choose through will force, and the assistance of the natural elements, in its (this entity's) development through other planes, or by natural forces reach the higher developments through mental and spiritual forces.

One that will do well to keep ever present in its inner soul that the law of Him who giveth life everlasting is the greatest force in the physical plane, and to rely upon that force and not upon self, else this entity would become as the rifting clouds, blown about as the sifting waves, and the desert sands, for with the loss of self's support, through faith in Him, would be the declining forces in this entity's development, which has gone exceedingly far.

Many and varied forces, we see, enter into this development, being upon the cusps, and under many constellations, in the new of the Moon, and with the Sun's ray bright in the Heavens, and one whose coming and going will ever bring joy to those who contact this entity, when will force guides it in the natural elements.

In the appearances, we find that in the study of the Courts of the Monks of England, when they were the shut-ins for the study of chemical forces, in the days of Alfred the Great [848?-900], and this entity's name was Ericson Olif [?] [Ericson, Olaf?]. This will be found in records as is [were] made by this monk in the study of those elements creating these.

Before this we find in that of the days of the Crusade [Crusades 1096-1291] in the Holy Land, when there was the quick return of this entity, and as the leader of the invading forces, and carrying then the banner of Him who was the giver of perfect gifts.

Again in the days when the Prince of Peace walked by the seashore, This entity answered the call, and was one of those followers, as is given in him who brought his brother to the Master, A-N-D-R-E-W.

In the days before this when the first pharaoh builded in the plains, then we find there this entity is [was] one that will be found in that which represents this entity at present, in the North Corner of the second Pyramid, for he was one of these rulers. [Ra Ta period]

In the days before this we find the entity was among those in the day when the forces of the Universe came together, when there was upon the waters the sound of the coming together of the Sons of God, when the morning stars sang together, and over the face of the waters there was the voice of the glory of the coming of the plane for man's dwelling.

In all of these we find some of this present entity's individuality, and in some, some personalities are brought through.

First: That of the love of out-door. All nature.

Second: The geometrical inclinations of mind to weigh and measure happenings, space and time by geometrical conclusions.

Next, the love of the Master, with the love of others to gain that knowledge.

In the next, the defending of personal principles at any cost. The next, the closeness of individual study.

Text of Reading 288-6 for Gladys Davis, F 19 (Secretary, Protestant)

This psychic reading given by Edgar Cayce at Phillips Hotel, Room 115, Dayton, Ohio, this 2nd day of June, 1924, in accordance with request made by self—Miss [288].

Present: Edgar Cayce; Linden Shroyer, Conductor; Gladys Davis, Steno.

(Suggestion for past associations with [294])

EC: We find these, as in the present earth's plane, have had many experiences together, and their soul and spirit are well knit, and must of necessity present each that they may be one. For we find in the beginning that they, these two (which we shall speak of as they until separáted), were as one in mind, soul, spirit, body; and in the first earth's plane as the voice over many waters, when the glory of the Father's giving of the earth's indwelling of man was both male and female in one.

In flesh form in earth's plane we find the first in that of the Poseidian forces, when both were confined in the body of the female; for this being the stronger in the then expressed or applied forces found manifestations for each in that form.

Yet with the experiences as have been brought in that plane and period, we find then the separation of the body. For the desire of the flesh being to give of self in bodily form to the other, it brought the separating of the spirit and soul from the carnal forces when next brought to earth's plane.

The experiences there were as these: These two were the giving of the spiritual development in the land [Atlantis], and the giving of the uplift to the peoples of the day and age. The desire came for the bodily connection of coition with one of lower estate, and through this treachery of one not capable of understanding it brought physical defects in the limbs [elephantiasis] of these then contained in the one body in physical form. Hence in the coma [?], and karma exercised in coma [?], there was brought the separation, as given in the injunction from the Maker: "I have this day set before you good and evil. Choose the light or the darkness." [Deut. 30:15,19]

With this desire of self's aggrandizement there was brought separation in the next plane, yet bound together in physical affections one for the other. In that of the Egyptian rule, in the first of the pharaohs do we find this connection as separated brought to the earth's plane. There we find again the priest and the lawgiver in they, though separated now in male and female. In 12,800 B.C. we find together. The desires then coming from the sex desire between the two for the developing, and in that we find it counted as righteousness in both, for—though in the priestcraft in the one, and given to sexual desires in more than in one—the desire remained in the One, for which the Oneness was created. The earthly age in earth's plane, though, as given, this in itself brought destruction to the female early, and in a few years to the other.

Again we find in the Arabian forces, when soon both are brought to the earth's plane, though far separated this time in their station and their earth's conditions, being or giving each, or, as it were, each receiving that as commensurate with their lives lived in earth's plane, with the intent and purpose of developing toward the Oneness again. (For all souls are one in Him, and must return.)

In this we find they become opposing forces, one on the earth's plane in that sphere surrounded with pomp, grandeur and all the good things as called in earth's plane, and educated (speaking of the female) in the courts of royalty, and the companion of the king's offspring [369]. The man [294] we find as Uhjltd, in the warring forces of the plain, having the course of the outcast, as it were, from the better things, yet seeking the submission of others to the will and to the animal developed forces in the entity. With the meeting, when each have become so taken, there is the realizing of, or awakening to, the oneness of their souls in the plain [plane?]; both having been made, first one, then the other, in the prison position, or slave position. There we find both of good stature, beautiful in figure, form, and in all the charm of bodily forces par excellent to each. In their close association they become enamored of each and give of themselves to the pleasures of the bodily forces, as known, and which had not been known in the same manner and form with others. For, with this long innate force being dormant in the soul and spirit, again the bodily forces and charms of the sex became those enclosed with each, that a giving of satisfaction not understandable to others was experienced and known. (Hence each must know that in the present earth's plane the giving of the forces in this capacity may only be the harkening of the entity being brought to the force in the soul and spirit developing to the oneness of same, to which it must come to present itself before the Creator, as in the beginning.)

We find there—after this—(in these we give one of the illustrations of the history of these associations, of which there were many, and were for days enacted, and for which both suffered physically, and they each bear in the body at present a mark designating these conditions. On the female body, just below the left breast, to the side and on the edge of breast itself, the mark, and an answering one on the body of the male, in the opposite proximity of the breast, but) these were the conditions enacted:

When these were in the cave, to which they had fled, when each were escaping from the vengeance of the forces of each army, and were with the company of two others (these we deal with), the day had come when they made then the companion of king's daughter and the teacher [295?] of both [369] and [288]. Their lives had been despaired of, and—though the maid had held the affection of her lord and master above that of self, still the answering of spirit and soul gave the answering with the body beautiful. For, the charms in breast, neck, thighs, navel, all gave of the beauty as would reach the soul of the mate, and the crying of the soul's desire, both in the carnal and the answering of the oneness in each.

After this giving of the life [(369)]'s suicide?] and the dressing of each for the journey into Egypt for embalming, each with bodies oiled and dressed from the cave spring, repair to their couch of skins, and there watch the sun's slow sinking over the desert sands. And in this fading hour they first find the answer of body to body in the soul's awakening, as they melt into one; giving then an offering to the world, who, in the form and in the stature of the great leader, gave the first philosophy of life and love to the world [Zend?] coming from this union.

And only with the treachery of others afterward was this life in the female taken. Hence the dread of knives in one [288] and the distrust of friendships in the other [294].

Again we find the male [294], with a vengeance, attempting to wreck, comes as the warrior [Trojan period], though the other [288] we find remains long in the land of nirvana and awaits the coming of her other self.

In the courts again [France], when they were mother and son, the greater portions of the body beautiful—and the portions that had become hallowed so to each—became the system of one and the life of the other. At present we find they are again together, still in different divisions, positions or circumstances, each paying out that which has been gained or merited in planes in earth's sphere just before. In this they are again united in soul and in spirit forces, and through the joy and the pleasure of selfless service they may again know the meaning of these as given. They need only remain in the future faithful one to the other, ever giving, ever retaining those joys of the relations that bring and give of self in service to others; and these bring joy, peace, and again uniting of body, soul and spirit in the next. Remain faithful, therefore, unto the end; gaining those joys through daily acts of selflessness for and with others, remembering that in these manifestations they (and all souls) become knit one with the other.

We are through for the present.

Text of Reading 294-9 for Edgar Cayce M 47

This psychic reading given by Edgar Cayce at the Phillips Hotel, Dayton, Ohio, this 31st day of May, 1924, in accordance with request made by himself.

Present: Edgar Cayce; Gladys Davis, Conductor & Steno.

(Suggestion for [294]'s past incarnation in France and his association with [288])

EC: Now, in this earth plane, we find this is one where the entity was of tender years, as far as earth plane's existence was concerned, and had much to do with other conditions that had been in earth plane's existence.

In this earth plane we find the entity was born of Gracia [Agatha?] the beloved of the court, and of the ruler's son of the territory just across the waters. And the change necessary in court proceedings prevented the culmination of this ruler's recognizing the earthly fatherhood of Dahl [Dale? Beille?]. [GD questions her spelling.]

The life that was lived in this court we find the first years in the heart and affection of the mother, who was of beautiful figure and loving in every manner. The great trials came to the entity (speaking from earth's plane view) when the separation was effected between mother and son, when there was the great yearning in the days when the young life was gradually taken out on account of the jealousy arising in the court. For the king became fully aware of the lad's appearance and the possibility of it becoming the ruler forces others to play the traitor to the mother, who loved the entity so well.

As related to the conditions that exist between this entity and that upon which the earth plane's existence so much depended, we find the farther-reaching of destinies, both in the past and in the present and future.

Q. What should be the relation between these individuals at the present time, or in this present earth plane?

A. The lives of each have ever been bound in the other's life, and the conditions as exist are only the outgrowth of endeavor in earth plane. They, the relations at the present, should be the ever innate affection as is necessary in the lives of each, for the satisfying not of the earthly forces but of the soul and spirit forces which find manifestation in material affection. Let that affection be such as gives of self to each, in no uncertain terms or physical manner, but ever in the answering of each desire toward the other in the way that gives of self's affection. That is, the outward manifestations of the inward desires of the heart and soul, which find in each the answering chord in the other's affection that will never, never, never be found in any other. For since in the first meetings, in the reign when Croesus [II, prehistory?] was king in Persia, when this entity [Dale?], then the warrior in Uhjltd, found and became enamoured with the beauty, the physical forces, and found the developing of the psychic through the suffering that both endured, and through which this entity, then the helpmate and companion of king's daughter, lost its head through the treachery of others, we find the same enacted in this French court. Then, in the present let those considerations be found as the understanding is at present; the treachery will only remain within themselves.

Be faithful one to the other, irrespective of earthly conditions, yet in that way that there is that consideration of other relations that are necessary and existing, for other conditions as have been met.

Be kind, affectionate, one toward the other, in the heart and soul preferring the other, giving of self in physical manifestations of the affections of the heart, of the soul, of the mind, of the body; for these are souls of the making, and were united in the beginning. And though their bodies may burn with their physical desires, the soul of each is and will be knit with the other when presented before the throne of Him, who gave and said, "Be fruitful, multiply." Give of the best, that the best may be presented to Him.

These two have ever been together, you see, except in the American forces when there was the soon return in that of the wanderer, and in the Grecian [Trojan] period. Each time this entity, Gracia [Agatha?], or [288] as known in the present, has been in the earth plane with the entity known in the present earth plane as [294].

Be thou faithful unto the end and receive that crown that is ever for the faithful in heart, soul and body.

Be kind, affectionate, loving, ever giving, ever preferring the other.

THE *NEW YORK TIMES* ON EDGAR CAYCE

The Sunday *New York Times*, on October 10, 1910, gave an elaborate spread with photographs to an intriguing report out of Boston. The Associated Press carried a shorter version to its clients nationwide. This is the text of the article in the *Times*:

ILLITERATE MAN BECOMES A DOCTOR WHEN HYPNOTIZED
Strange Power Shown by Edgar Cayce Puzzles Physicians

The medical fraternity of the country is taking a lively interest in the strange power said to be possessed by Edgar Cayce of Hopkinsville, Ky., to diagnose difficult diseases while in a semi-conscious state, though he has not the slightest knowledge of medicine when not in this condition. During a visit to California last summer Dr. W. H. Ketchum, who was attending a meeting of the National Society of Homeopathic Physicians, had occasion to mention the young man's case and was invited to discuss it at a banquet attended by about thirty-five of the doctors of the Greek letter fraternity given at Pasadena.

Dr. Ketchum made a speech of considerable length, giving an explanation of the strange psychic powers manifested by Cayce during the last four years, during which time he has been more or less under his observation. This has attracted such widespread interest among people that one of the leading Boston medical men who heard his speech invited Dr. Ketchum to prepare a paper as a part of the programme of the September meeting of the American Society of Clinical Research. Dr. Ketchum sent the paper, but did not go to Boston. The paper was read by Henry E. Harrower, M.D., of Chicago, a contributor to the *Journal of the American Medical Association*, published in Chicago. Its presentation created a sensation, and almost before Dr. Ketchum knew that the paper had been given to the press he was deluged with letters and telegrams inquiring about the strange case.

It is well enough to add that Dr. Wesley H. Ketchum is a reputable physician of high standing and successful practice in the homeopathic school of medicine. He possesses a classical education, is by nature of a scientific turn, and is a graduate of one of the leading medical institutions of the country. He is vouched for by orthodox physicians in both Kentucky and Ohio, in both of which states he is well known. In Hopkinsville, where his home is, no physician of any school stands higher, though he is still a young man on the shady side of Dr. Osler's deadline of 40.

Dr. Ketchum wishes it distinctly understood that his presentation of the subject is purely ethical, and that he attempts no explanation of what must be classed as mysterious mental phenomena.

Dr. Ketchum is not the only physician who has had the opportunity to observe the workings of Mr. Cayce's subconscious mind. For nearly ten years his strange power has been known to local physicians of all the recognized schools. An explanation of the case is best understood from Dr. Ketchum's description in his paper read in Boston a few days ago, which follows:

"About four years ago I made the acquaintance of a young man 28 years old, who had the reputation of being a 'freak.' They said he told wonderful truths while he was asleep. I, being interested, immediately began to investigate, and as I was 'from Missouri,' I had to be shown.

"And truly, when it comes to anything psychical, every layman is a disbeliever from the start, and most of our chosen profession will not accept anything of a psychic nature, hypnotism, mesmerism, or whatnot, unless vouched for by some M.D. away up in the profession and one whose orthodox standing is unquestioned.

"My subject simply lies down and folds his arms, and by autosuggestion goes to sleep. While in this sleep, which to all intents and purposes is a natural sleep, his objective mind is completely inactive and only his subjective is working.

"By suggestions he becomes unconscious to pain of any sort, and, strange to say, his best work is done when he is seemingly 'dead to the world.'

"I next give him the name of my subject and the exact location of same, and in a few minutes he begins to talk as clearly and distinctly as anyone. He usually goes into minute detail in diagnosing a case, and especially if it be a very serious case.

"His language is usually of the best, and his psychologic terms and description of the nervous anatomy would do credit to any professor of nervous anatomy, and there is no faltering in his speech and all his statements are clear and concise. He handles the most complex 'jaw breakers' with as much ease as any Boston physician, which to me is quite wonderful, in view of the fact that while in his normal state he is an illiterate man, especially along the line of medicine, surgery, or pharmacy, of which he knows nothing.

"After going into detail with a diagnosis and giving name, address, etiology, symptoms, diagnosis, and treatment of a case, he is awakened by the suggestion that he will see this person no more, and in a few minutes will be awake. Upon questioning him, he knows absolutely nothing that he said, or whose case he was talking about. I have used him in about 100 cases, and to date have never known of any errors in diagnosis, except in two cases where he described a child in each case by the same name and who resided in the same house as the one wanted. He simply described the wrong person.

"Now this description, although rather short, is no myth, but a firm reality. The regular profession scoff at anything reliable coming from this source, because the majority of them are in the rut and have never taken to anything not strictly orthodox.

"The cases I have used him in have, in the main, been the rounds before coming to my attention, and in six important cases which had been diagnosed as strictly surgical he stated that no such condition existed, and outlined treatment which was followed with gratifying results in every case.

"One case, a little girl, daughter of a gentleman prominent in the American Book Company of Cincinnati, had been diagnosed by the best men in the Central States as incurable. One diagnosis from my man completely changed the situation, and within three months she was restored to perfect health, and is to this day.

"Now, in closing, you may ask why has a man with such powers not been before the public and received the endorsement of the profession, one and all, without fear or favor? I can truly answer by saying they are not ready to receive such as yet. Even Christ Himself was rejected, for 'unless they see signs and wonders they will not believe.'

"I would appreciate the advice and suggestions of my co-workers in this broad field as to the best method of putting my man in the way of helping suffering humanity, and would be glad to have you send me the name and address of your most complex case and I will try to prove what I have endeavored to describe."

In further explanation, Dr. Ketchum gives this statement as obtained from the young man himself while asleep when asked to describe his own powers and the source of his mystifying knowledge:

"Our subject, while under auto-hypnosis, on one occasion explained as follows:

"When asked to give the source of his knowledge, he being at this time in the subconscious state, he stated: 'Edgar Cayce's mind is amenable to suggestion, the same as all other subconscious minds, but in addition thereto it has the power to interpret to the objective mind of others what it acquires from the subconscious mind of other individuals of the same kind. The subconscious mind forgets nothing. The conscious mind receives the impression from without and transfers all thoughts to the subconscious, where it remains even though the conscious be destroyed.' He described himself in the third person, saying further that his subconscious mind is in direct communication with all other subconscious minds, and is capable of interpreting through his objective mind and imparting impressions received to other objective minds, gathering in this way all knowledge possessed by millions of other subconscious minds."

In all, young Cayce has given more than 1,000 readings, but has never turned his wonderful powers to his pecuniary advantage, although many people have been restored to health by following out the course of treatment prescribed in his readings while in a state of hypnosis.

President James Hyslop of the American Psychic Society has made suggestions in regard to the development of the subject's powers. Other psychologists in Europe and America are seeking information, and Dr. Ketchum's plan is to have a committee of scientists of the highest standing come to Hopkinsville and investigate in a most rigid manner and make a report as to the truth of what is claimed but not understood. That this will be done in the near future is certain.

Many. men in this city have attended Mr. Cayce's readings and are ready to testify to the truth of the representations made.

Recently Mr. Cayce was given for a second interpretation the case of a man living in Indiana, and when asked by his father to tell whether he had read the case before and to describe the present condition, he said:

"Yes, I have had him before. Some little difference in his case this time. Resting easy now; heart action not so bad; rest produced by an anaesthetic. We find this body suffering from smothering spells, short breath, depression of the heart, and very weak at times. Pains in the head, especially through the base of the head, the first and second cervical, and front part of the head and eyes; circulation is very poor.

"In the first and second cervical we have a lesion there which is from the reflex action from the pain we have below, and gives off pains to the head at times and especially to the face and facial muscles. This all comes through the sympathetic nervous system.

"Now, at the seventh and eighth to the tenth dorsal vertebrae, reaching the solar plexus, we find a bad lesion, especially where it comes in contact with the nerves governing the heart and hepatic circulation just below the left lung. The trouble first began here. We see a congestion caused from a cold in the left lung contracted from the exterior, producing a choking up of the lung and treated locally and externally on the side.

"This filling up caused not enough air in the lungs and produced the lesion we have just above the solar plexus or nerve centre which controls the whole digestive organs of the body, and the congestion we have here in the lumbar region has produced locomotor-ataxia and a withering away of the limbs; especially is this most noticeable in the right limb, and producing a very bad state in the pelvic region.

"We find the same thing through the circulatory system of the blood. The blood is very weak; the red corpuscles are more numerous than they should be, with not enough of the white tissue to build up the body. Where we have a loss of white blood tissue we have the same in the gray matter in the nerve force.

"Not all the nerve force of the body has been destroyed. We have weak and then strong spells, because the circulation is weak, especially the capillary, with a heart action strong at times, producing palpitation of the heart and smothering spells, dizziness of the head, and the same of the solar plexus system, causing the emitting from the stomach of the things taken into it.

"We have no organic heart trouble and very little of the lungs, but some enlargement of the liver. In the left lobe of the liver we find a granular substance from medicines taken in through the stomach and bowels. The liver is not doing its work in throwing off the bile and waste matter of the body. That produces the enlargement of the liver.

"We have altogether a very weak and bedridden man, but he can be cured. To correct this trouble, first reduce the inflammation, then, by giving plenty of pure water, with alkaline treatment, the acid will be reduced. A tincture of iron for toning up the digestive organs and blood, and static electrical treatment along the spine, not very strong along the upper cervical, for this is near the brain, but very strong through the dorsal and lumbar regions. Give digitalis and strychnine to tone up the nerves and heart. With plenty of rest and fresh air, we will have the man improved."

. . . During the last ten years he has followed the business of a photographer in several cities, but has been a good part of the time here in Hopkinsville. About eight years ago he married Miss Evans of this city, and they have one child, a boy, now seven years old.

At first Mr. Cayce was hypnotized by another, but he now goes to sleep of his own accord by what Dr. Ketchum has called autohypnosis. He comes out of the trance at the suggestion of someone else, usually his father, who has assisted in his development more than anyone else.

His experience does not fatigue or exhaust him. On the contrary it seems to refresh him. Sometimes he will be feeling tired and will take up a case to read, dropping off to sleep for the purpose, and when aroused will feel greatly refreshed.

The question of distance is not important, as he has given successful readings with his subject a thousand miles away.

Mr. Cayce will not discuss the names of his patients, if they may be called patients, but says he is ready to submit any necessary facts in aiding the fullest investigation.

Appendix C

Did Cayce Read for President Wilson?

Edgar Cayce in 1932 wrote that on one occasion "I was called to Washington to give information for one high in authority. This, I am sure, must have been at least interesting, as I was called a year or so later for the same purpose."

David E. Kahn, his longtime friend and collaborator in many a venture, in 1965 gave an oral history interview with Hugh Lynn Cayce and Gladys Davis, in which he said: "At one time we were asked to give a reading on President Woodrow Wilson." Kahn added: "I believe this was during the time that he was in the wheelchair and incapacitated and Mrs. Wilson was looking after his affairs. My recollection was that Colonel Starling [of the Secret Service detail assigned to protect the President] arranged this reading, as he was a lifelong friend of Edgar Cayce, both having been born in Hopkinsville, Kentucky, and I did not see the reading given, but, as I understand, it described the president's condition and foretold that his time was limited and that he would not get well. This was the beginning of a close personal friendship that remained for many years between Cayce, Starling, and myself and which led to the writing and publication of *Starling of the White House* [on which Starling after retiring collaborated with Cayce's biographer, Thomas L. Sugrue].

Kahn acknowledged that he had no personal knowledge of a reading for Woodrow Wilson. "I heard there was such a meeting, I was not part of that, because I did not go to Washington as an army officer until I returned from France the latter part of 1919."

Wilson had a stroke toward the end of his second term, in September 1919. Cayce gives no date for the first call from Washington, but it appears to have been before Kahn returned from France. Wilson remained in office, ill and partly incapacitated, until the inauguration of his successor, Warren G. Harding, on March 4, 1921—nearly a year and a half after he was stricken.

While there is no known documentation of any readings for President Wilson, there is documentation of readings Cayce gave for a cousin of the president, a Major Wilson whom Kahn had befriended in the army.

Cayce's biographers treated this matter quite differently. Thomas Sugrue, in *There Is a River*, makes no mention of any readings for either President Wilson or his cousin. Supposedly Cayce was cautioned never to discuss it. Joseph Millard, in *Edgar Cayce, Mystery Man of Miracles*, reports that Edgar was "mysteriously summoned to Washington" twice during World War I but under "secrecy that was never lifted." He doesn't speculate on the purpose.

Harmon H. Bro, however, in *A Seer Out of Season*, as well as two earlier books and his doctoral dissertation at the University of Chicago, claimed that Cayce went to the White House twice to give readings at the invitation of President and Mrs. Wilson. Bro acknowledged that he had no documentation, but in his biography of Cayce attributes the story to Kahn. Rather than the president's illness, as Kahn would have it, the subject was the proposed League of Nations, according to Bro.

W. H. Church, in *Many Happy Returns: The Lives of Edgar Cayce*, repeats much the same story, but attributes it to Gladys Davis, Cayce's longtime secretary.

What is one to believe?

Gladys Davis told the editor that Mr. Cayce had never spoken of this matter to her, and she didn't know whether it was true or not. There is nothing in his personal correspondence referring to it (but until Gladys was employed in the fall of 1923 little correspondence was kept). Colonel Starling made no reference to such an incident in his memoirs. Although Starling hailed from Hopkinsville, he was much younger than Cayce and did not know him nearly as long as Kahn suggested.

Both of Cayce's sons, when asked about the matter, told

the editor their father had never mentioned it to them. Hugh Lynn declined to speculate on whether it was true; Edgar Evans said he doubted the story.

Woodrow Wilson lived on in declining health in Washington for several years after Cayce was called to the capital "for one high in authority." If he did give readings for President Wilson, they presumably focused on his physical condition, as Kahn stated, and failed to help—perhaps because it was too late, or that no one close to Wilson, including his physician, took the suggestions seriously. All one knows with certainty is that Wilson did not recover and died in February 1924 at age sixty-six.

ORGANIZING THE WORK: THE A.N.I.

The Association of National Investigators, in Virginia Beach, the first organization actually established to sponsor the work of Edgar Cayce, issued the following information in booklet form, as revised in July 1929:

THAT WE MAY MAKE MANIFEST OUR LOVE FOR GOD AND MAN

The Association of National Investigators, Inc.

The Association of National Investigators was incorporated May 6, 1927, in the State of Virginia. Although founded upon the psychic work of Mr. Edgar Cayce, and although the immediate basis of its formation was to further, foster, and encourage the physical, mental, and spiritual aid that thousands have and are receiving from Mr. Cayce's endeavors in the psychic field, the larger and more embracing purpose of the organization is to engage in general psychic research, and to provide for the practical application of any knowledge obtainable through the medium of psychic phenomena. In the matter of specific application the Association seeks to render physical aid to the sick and ailing through its hospital, and also to disseminate and exploit for the good of humanity the knowledge obtained from its research work, through the library, lecture hall, and other educational channels.

Many are already acquainted with the readings given by Mr. Cayce, and the more or less haphazard manner in which they have heretofore been applied, also the wonderful results. Prior to the incorporation of the Association physical diagnoses and remedies for diseases were sent to applicants for readings; who upon receipt of them found great difficulty in securing the treatment prescribed. At best the remedies suggested in the readings were partly carried out, yet it is to the credit of the work of the Association that in spite of these difficulties the results reported were satisfactory. The testimonials on hand at the main office at Virginia Beach speak for many, who through application of the remedies given in their readings found relief from their existent physical disabilities. Under the conditions created by the Association difficulties encountered by the patients in securing treatment have been overcome. Furthermore, each and every reading is now followed systematically, watched, and recorded. Prior to the incorporation of the Association and the erection of the Cayce Hospital about 10,000 readings were given by Mr. Cayce, but the lack of facilities for checking each and every move proved detrimental to the progress of the work and to a proper scientific classification of the phenomena. Records of the method and result of treatment are now filed, as is the information given by the psychic forces on specific diseases. Lack of organization prevented this from being accomplished in the past, although thousands received just such information in physical readings, and benefited or not, according to the application thereof.

The Cayce Hospital, which is the hospital of the Association, at Virginia Beach, Va., furnishes an opportunity for those who seek physical readings and treatment exactly as prescribed in them to get such at the hands of competent and sympathetic physicians. The hospital is conducted along the most modern, scientific, and ethical lines. Every comfort and service possible is provided patients. The charges for room, board, and treatment are such as is customary to an institution of its kind.

Lectures are delivered each Sunday by President Blumenthal and Mr. Cayce in the lecture hall of the hospital, and President Blumenthal conducts a study class on alternate Saturday afternoons in the same place. The work is studied from a philosophical standpoint, with a view to educating the individual to a complete understanding of himself and the life he lives. These lectures and study classes are free to everyone, and all are urged to attend if interested.

Those not acquainted with the physical and life readings furnished by the Association through the psychic endeavors of Mr. Cayce may apply for information concerning them at the main office at Virginia Beach, where details concerning the past history of Mr. Cayce and his work, and the Association prior to its incorporation, may be obtained. The results of the application of treatments suggested in the physical readings are carefully recorded and systematically classified, and these records are open for inspection to members of the Association.

There are many psychic research societies formed for the study and recording of phenomena, but it is safe to say that the Association of National Investigators, Inc., is the only Society that in addition to psychic research work seeks to apply in its own hospital treatments for the cure of disease. The Association was incorporated that this hospital might be built and put at the disposal of those seeking relief from this source. There is, of course, the customary ward in the hospital for those who are unable to pay for treatments, and one day each week is devoted to giving readings for the benefit of those unable to pay for them.

Equally, if not more important than the medical purpose of the Association, is the educational phase of the organization's work. The library and lecture hall in the hospital serve as a center in which the results of the psychic work are carefully recorded. It also serves as a center from which authoritative documents and literature are obtained on the subject. Knowledge from the psychic sources covers a vast field, including not only physical diagnoses, but information in the fields of philosophy, theosophy, theology, science, and every phase of human endeavor and spiritual life. The library and lecture hall serve as a forum for the exchange of ideas on all these subjects, and also serves as the central point from which is disseminated the truths gained from the spiritual or psychic source.

At the present time Mr. Cayce's psychic ability furnishes the Association with its channel for research work, but the Society does not plan to confine itself to his manifestation. It is training and including in its research work all who possess sufficient psychic development of mind and are desirous of cooperating with the Association to achieve the purpose of scientifically studying, recording, and applying the phenomena, and exploiting the knowledge derived therefrom in a philanthropic manner for the good of mankind. Those directly in the employ of the Association or its hospital receive financial remuneration commensurate with the service rendered of course, the amount being fixed by the Board of Trustees. The latter, as well as the officers for the corporation and members of its committees, receive no financial compensation for their services in these capacities.

To many, psychic phenomena is but a vagary that has to do with prophesies or superstition, something to be feared or shunned. Finally then, the Association of National Investigators, Inc., seeks to demonstrate that psychic phenomena and the phenomena of life are one and the same thing. The divine manifests its Being or Life or consciousness, and the psychic or subconscious forces, though unconscious to the intellect, manifest their being in consciousness of another character than intellectual.

Nevertheless, both belong to the same essence and process that expresses itself in the form of "Mind," or "Soul." In substance it is spirit, in which a self-contained element through a process of development becomes consciousness or soul. This developing element of subconscious consciousness is demonstrated when the physical forces are subjugated; as, for example, in the experiencing of certain kinds of dreams or visions or other intuitive or psychic manifestations; or in the psychic work of Mr. Cayce, where a complete and thorough physical diagnosis is given in perfectly rational manner through the subjected physical faculties—i.e., when Mr. Cayce becomes intellectually unconscious, or unalive, and manifests through a subconscious kind of consciousness, or aliveness.

The purpose of the Association of National Investigators, Inc., then, as will be stated more fully later, is to scientifically carry on the research work in the field of psychic phenomena, to record the results thereof, and to apply them for the benefit of health, knowledge, and spiritual welfare of those seeking aid from the psychic force. It is evident that this organization is engaged in a great work, its scope of activity reaching out to every class, creed, and race, and its purpose embracing the mental, moral, physical and spiritual good of all humanity.

Three hard and fast provisions govern the operation of the Association work:

First: As already stated, the membership and purpose and work of the Organization is limited to no class or creed. The only provision here made is that every applicant for membership and for aid have a faith in the Divine.

Second: That this organization shall in no way be used or represented to stand for any particular doctrine, religion, or nationality. The purpose of this Society is scientific study and application of psychic phenomena as related to man in his relationship to the world and to earthly life, as well as his relation to the universe and the universal forces. It is not to establish any new religion, although new thought and new interpretations of old truth may emanate.

Third: It is definitely stated in the charter of this Association, granted by the State of Virginia, that any profits or monies collected by the Association shall go towards the purely philanthropic work of the Corporation. Membership dues, donations, hospital fees and profits from all transactions shall go towards the upkeep and maintenance of the institution and purely philanthropic work of the Association.

The Board of Trustees (limited to fifteen), being vested with the vote, form the governing body of the Association, and are limited in their operations by the charter and by-laws, the latter of which are hereinafter set forth.

". . . THE WORKS THAT I DO SHALL YE DO ALSO; AND GREATER WORKS THAN THESE SHALL YE DO; BECAUSE I GO UNTO MY FATHER."—John, Ch. 14:12.

OUR IDEAL AND PHILOSOPHY

Deep in the hearts of each and every right thinking person there dwells the ideal that acts as the mainspring of our life, namely, love for the Divine Creator. Regardless of our concept of God, we love Him for His deeds, which, of course, embrace creation. He has created us as an image of Himself and His universe (as a drop containing every element of the ocean is an image of the whole body of water), and has given to us the opportunity of enjoying like Him a consciousness of ourselves being alive. Being a duplication of Him, in potentiality, we are alive to His work of creation. By development of our potential abilities we become self aware of the process of creation being our own work as well as His. We love Him, then, for His gift of life to us, for His promise that the gift shall be eternal, and, above all, for His long-suffering as well as patience with our sins which are born of ignorance during the process of our achieving through earthly experience necessary potential development. Indeed, many of us, although bearing no malice, curse the Creator in one breath while He furnishes us the power to draw another. We defile our bodies with ill-formed habits, while His pulsating, life-giving flow sustains those bodies and continues in process of creating new and other beautiful physiques. Sometimes, in a secret moment, while regarding the majesty and beauty of nature, or, while marveling at the wonderful phenomena of a newborn baby, or while at prayer either at home or in church, we turn our hearts to God, and pour forth our love. Then do we intuitively feel His forgiveness, His infinite mercy and patience, and the divine inflow of His love. He is the potentiality that manifests itself as the phenomena of life, whether of creation or our subjective selves, and thus we belong to Him and He to us.

We, are, each of us, an integral part of God in the intellectual effect form of man, that this spiritual Godly essence takes in the earthly environment, and know ourselves to be that. Thus it is that we are free to live our own concept of life. Thus it also is that whatever concept we choose to express in and of our own life, is representative of our idea of God. Since we are that which the life, essence or God becomes in materialized form, we will likewise remain this same essence when we change at death from the materialized manifested form, to become one with the manifesting spiritual essence itself. From the changed viewpoint that we will then enjoy as an internal force of intelligence, we shall come to know ourselves to be that which God is in essence, just as we now know ourselves to be that which the spiritual Godly essence changes itself to become in the materialized form it takes in this earthly environment. God then has created, of Himself, a portion (each of our own selves) that by virtue of His process of creation, becomes able to achieve a companionate self awareness and individuality in Union with and one with each and every self-conscious and individuality, or portion, that God in one potential spiritual essence embraces.

Are our prayers and our good intentions the best we may do in gratitude for such good and perfect gifts? May we not help keep the breath in the body by aiding physically the sick and suffering? May we not counteract sin by fighting the ignorance and lack of understanding that breeds it? Of course we may, and shall!—all of us who are members of the Association of National Investigators, Inc., for all of us banded together to manifest in deed our love for the Creator, will through the Association engage actively in educating those who are as yet unawakened to the glory of the creative work of the spirit father.

Through psychic research may we, the members of the Association, gain the necessary knowledge that will fit us to work on earth for creation, as does the mighty creative energy of life function to sustain creation throughout the whole of that called space. Then may we and shall we, inscribe our names in the book of life, and in that chapter that has to do with early experiences, and thus make our deeds create for us merited love in the hearts and minds of the right-thinking portion of humanity. We, the members of this Association, and all who choose to join with us, shall strive to throw our influence on the side of the good and the spiritual, in order that the generations of men may cling to the link that binds them to the universe, to the noble, the beautiful, the honorable, and to the whole ideal while in this earthly process of development, rather than permit the influences of the purely material life to drag the inner developing potentiality that manifests itself in the form of physical personalities in the mire of animalistic materialism, that turns love into passion and adultery, nobleness into wrath, hatred, and temper, honor into greed and self-ishness, beauty into filth, and the imagination into slavery to physical desires.

This is the ideal of the Association of National Investigators, Inc., to the accomplishment of which it is giving and shall continue to give its untiring energy and efforts, and in the heart and soul of the Association there lives the conviction that behind it are the mighty, eternal and unyielding creative forces of the universe.

MORTON H. BLUMENTHAL, PRESIDENT.

"IN HIM IS THE LIGHT, AND THE LIGHT IS THE LIGHT OF THE WORLD."

OUR PURPOSE

Any endeavor, whether that of an individual, or of a group of individuals, is motivated by an ideal, or an idea, or by both. In the case of the Association of National Investigators, Inc., an ideal inspired the desire to serve humanity in the minds of a few individuals interested in the study of the phenomena of life, and in particular, the study of psychic phenomena as made manifest in the work of Mr. Edgar Cayce. These individuals cooperated to form the present Association of National Investigators, Inc., with the idea in mind to investigate the psychic work of Mr. Cayce, and obtain, if possible, the relationship of this remarkable phenomena to that of life, and in particular, to the life of man and to human welfare.

To accomplish this end, the Cayce Hospital for Research and Enlightenment was created for the purpose of receiving patients who desired medical treatment, according to suggestions made in the so-called physical readings, the latter being made for patients who request same. Previous to the creation of this institution, thousands had benefited in health from their own haphazard application of information contained in physical readings, secured by themselves from Mr. Cayce. The latter's remarkable psychic mental development enabled him to furnish these physical diagnoses to applicants, together with suggestions for remedy of their ills. The creation of the hospital for scientific application of these treatments, and for the maintenance of records of the results thereof, in a systematic fashion, seemed a logical and justifiable step to the interested group surrounding Mr. Cayce's work. Although this institution has been completed and has been functioning only a few months, a history of the cases treated in the hospital, and the excellent results to the patients achieved, and systematically recorded, have to date, proven the step a wise and progressive one.

The hospital, however, does not in itself represent the complete realization of the ideal in the hearts and minds of the individuals who first inaugurated the Association for the purpose of investigation of psychic phenomena. True, in the formative years of this Association, the present members of the Board of Trustees had but a vague idealistic urge to perform a service for Good, for God, for Man, and this ideal then represented itself in the minds of these individuals in the form of a crude idea, a hospital where patients might be scientifically treated by proper and authorized physicians, according to their physical readings (the latter psychically made by Mr. Edgar Cayce), and results of these treatments carefully and systematically recorded. Since the successful realization of this latter idea, the Board of Trustees, together with many members of the Association, have found other and additional channels of service opened to them. There have been presented new fields to pioneer in, and new scientific worlds to conquer. A wider, broader, and more extensive channel of idealistic self-expression in connection with psychic investigation has sprung up. The latter, and more important field of activity, has to do with education.

Those of us who composed, and now make up the Board of Trustees, of the Association of National Investigators, Inc., found a greater service in connection with psychic investigations than ministering to human ills in teaching people of their individual psychic abilities of mind, and of the value to their lives of proper and intelligent application of knowledge obtained through the use of these potential or hidden mental (intuitive) faculties. The first step in this new and more important direction consisted in first thoroughly grounding ourselves in that which we seek to teach others. That is to say, we had to first bring into our consciousness realization of a higher fourth-dimensional viewpoint, of which the properly educated human mind is capable, and thus obtain knowledge of life as it exists in self, and the world, or Universe, to this higher fourth-dimensional viewpoint. By this method, many of us became possessed of knowledge of the internal world of causes, and of application, that may be made of same in the external or material world of effect. Such knowledge, we found, is internal and fourth dimensional in character, and obtainable by the human mind from the internal fourth-dimensional viewpoint alone, and is not obtainable by the mind seeking knowledge of life from the externalized three-dimensional, physical viewpoint of the mind. We came to the conclusion, then, that the psychic readings given by Mr. Cayce, whether physical or philosophical, or anything else in character, demonstrate the fourth-dimensional operation of the indwelling subjective (often called subconscious) mind, and its ability to give to our observing physical selves, information not only of the inner subjective spiritual and permanent side of life, but also to give information applicable for the good of our external physical selves while we live in the temporary material form that life assumes in this world.

Today, certain members of this organization have, through concentrated effort and specific application of the study of the psychic forces made manifest in and through man, and thus in and through their individual selves, achieved for themselves a development of the introspective and intuitional faculties of mind. These latter faculties are often described as belonging to the subconscious, or subjective, and inner department of the mind. These individuals have, through application of, and experience in the introspective method, obtained greater knowledge and greater understanding of the primary purport and purpose of such a work as the Association of National Investigators, Inc., has undertaken.

These individuals, some members of our Board of Trustees,

some members of the Association of National Investigators, Inc., have come to a realization of the great responsibility resting upon them, and entailed in the accomplishment of the educational end that must be achieved if the Association is to accomplish its whole purpose. By virtue of knowledge obtained through their own intuitional faculties, these few individuals have come to understand better the importance of the obligation they have assumed to man and to God in grouping themselves together as a Board of Trustees and as an organization to carry on the work of the Association of National Investigators, Inc., that its ideal in totality may be realized. They, today, recognize that this obligation makes it necessary that our Association formulate a plan, by which there may be introduced into the world a scientific method of obtaining knowledge introspectively, a higher method, if you please, of obtaining a deeper knowledge of life, and of self, self's relationship to life, than it is possible to obtain through use of the physical faculties or sensory organism alone. This higher method of obtaining a deeper self-awakening of the truth of that which self and life is, embraces a method of obtaining understanding of self, and of life, from the higher, inner subjective or subconscious viewpoint, the latter of which is often called the fourth-dimensional viewpoint.

Knowledge so obtained brings to the individual self-realization of being that very introspective source himself, from which hidden or subconscious recesses, such information comes. He awakens to self realization of being not only that which he is physically, but also to that which he is subconsciously, i.e., to that complete and total being he is in mind or soul. By this means, he may obtain an awakening of the purpose of life, and of being alive, and may fashion his daily activities accordingly. Thus he may, to a greater extent, speed and facilitate the development of his own internal soul being, and generally accelerate the evolutionary process of life.

No greater program ever confronted any group of men or women, and no group of men or women ever assumed greater responsibility in seeking to carry out its ideal. By virtue of the past development of each of us, or at least of those of us who compose the Board of Trustees, we may feel, with all confidence, that we are prepared to successfully carry out the burden of this large and important program. Furthermore, in a reading it has been given that in the process of carrying out this program, we shall individually and collectively have the full cooperation of the forces from the cosmic plane, even from the highest plane, the throne itself. It has been given that such cooperation and aid may be expected, and it has been promised that it shall be given.

It is obvious that we cannot hope to heal every living creature in our hospital. It is also obvious that the process by which individuals are benefited physically in our hospital is but a representation of the application of knowledge introspectively obtained, and a demonstration of the fact that a system for the obtaining of such knowledge may be formulated and used by the individual for his own benefit. This must be the true and whole purpose of this hospital of ours, for otherwise the thing for which it stands would appear merely as a freak of nature, a contradiction of natural law. If this were true, our time would be wasted on a mere will o' the wisp, a meaningless outlaw to the basic laws of life, God, and Man.

This, however, is not true! On the contrary, the work propagated by this Association in or outside of the hospital, demonstrates the operation of the real and vital forces of life, not merely the portion that is physical, but the elements of the whole mind. It demonstrates the rational oneness of life, the universality of the operation of the forces of life, or laws governing life in any form, whether physical or otherwise, and in particular, as they govern the mind and life in the physical form of man.

Our hospital, and the psychic work attached thereto, can only be a demonstration of the introspective method of obtaining knowledge, by which means the internal operating forces of life may become applicable to and by each individual, for his better development and happier existence, even while in the physical form of man, living in and as a part of this material world.

THE PRIMARY PURPOSE OF OUR ASSOCIATION, THEN, IS EDUCATION.

The education of the individual, that he may attain a closer relationship to the higher powers of his own mind, that he may for and by himself achieve greater development of mind, as well as greater material benefit, for his physical being in the material environment. The achievement of our purpose will enable the human race to use for its own good, in every department of its life, physical and spiritual, an introspective method of obtaining knowledge, that individuals may so develop their intuitional forces as to become able to be guided by a higher dimensional viewpoint, the viewpoint that such intuitional development brings self realization of possessing. This is the all-embracing aim and deeper purpose, the whole ideal, of this Association.

The method for exploiting this system of obtaining knowledge introspectively will some day embrace a great Association of learning. It will take the form of a University where science, history, philosophy, engineering, etc., will be taught in a manner embracing both the objective and introspective methods of obtaining knowledge. In this university knowledge thus obtained will enable us to form a curriculum in which science, history, philosophy, and the arts may be taught as in no other seat of learning.

Such an institution of learning is the dream of the future, and as such it may now be only presented as a future prospect, not an applicable plan for present action. For the present, it behooves each and every one of us who has taken, as a member of the Association, and in particular, members of our Board of Trustees, the responsibility of exploiting our primary purpose of benefit to mankind, to subscribe in faith to that very introspective method that we represent, and that our psychic experiments objectify. Let us gain for ourselves a greater understanding of the meaning of this method in our own lives. Let us understand its application for our own good, for our own spiritual development and spiritual awakening, as well as our own material comforts. Let us live as an example to man, that we may demonstrate to individuals, to classes and masses, in terms of mental freedom, mental power, and material welfare and happiness, the benefits to be derived by and from the application for ourselves of knowledge introspectively obtained. Let us do this not for ourselves, but that all may see demonstrated in our lives, in our work, in our institutions, the benefits that may come to the individual by virtue of the application of just such an introspective method. We may then, individually and collectively, exploit in harmonious cooperation our program for the benefit of Mankind, for the benefit of civilization, and for the benefit of posterity. First to individuals as they approach us, second to the classes, or groups, or organizations, as they come to us, and finally, to all peoples, as a world-wide educational movement. By the initiation of such a movement we may give an impulse to the evolving of a higher stage of civilization, and a greater race of man. Thus shall the consciousness of man be raised a degree in enlightenment, in breadth of vision, and in power. Thus may civilization be raised from its present materialistic vying to a spiritual power applicable in the material world, for the benefit of one's own soul development, as well as for the greater comfort and material happiness of the soul in the physical form of man.

The accomplishment of this purpose means a process of education of the race and the individuals composing it to a greater power of mental insight and physical application.

It is for us to supply the individuals with a systematized plan whereby such means may be scientifically used to achieve realization of the existence of the internal life forces, their functions, their purpose, and their application for the benefit of each individual and the whole of mankind.

What a blessing it is to understand that our daily toil with its material return is not the chief and only aim of our earthly experience! What a blessing to realize the development we are achieving of potential abilities of mind or soul by virtue of mental and physical application made in our everyday field of daily material endeavors! This we obtain for the benefit of our real self, for our whole mind, that manifests itself in our own physical form as a personality or individuality, whether pertaining to ourselves as Doctors, Lawyers, Artists, Business men or women, husbands, wives, fathers, mothers, etc.

No material accomplishment can in itself bring complete peace in mind and happiness, though it is possible that mental accomplishment and mental achievement may bring such peace of mind without the corresponding material success. It is also true, however, that the application of knowledge intuitively or introspectively obtained from the internal forces of life, through use of the subjective faculties of mind, may, and does bring such physical success, aid, and material return. By virtue of this mankind may become relieved of the daily grindstone and obtain leisure for the higher moral and cultural development, and in this is the blessing of such material success.

The most effective method in general of obtaining this higher development is through service to mankind. In our own case, it may mean only service to our primary purpose, and its accomplishment for our institution, that incorporates the good along these *educational lines*, that may thus be accomplished for humanity. But our every movement with respect to the work, if it is to achieve success, must represent a cooperative willingness on our part, and in particular on the part of those of us who compose the Board of Trustees, to join hands and protect, propagate, and exploit the service to man that our work will initiate.

The prophets of old ceased their wailing in troublous times, substituting service for admonition, that the remnants of a benighted race might be saved. The Master, the Prince of Peace Himself, served as no man before or since has served, just such a cause as our Association holds as its main purpose. That He at the right hand of Power should stoop to our lowly dwelling place on earth, that we should even hear His voice through a reading, proves that the ideals and truths of yesterday are still those of today, that our work is still His work, even as it was, while He, in the form of man, walked, lived and taught among men, and this despite our present-day scientific methods, and religious differences. It proves that He serves Man and God today as of old, and His example of service for evolution, and for creation, stands today as an example of service, for us.

Let His example inspire us to join hands in harmony and covenant that so long as we, who form this human chain, shall live in the flesh, none inside or outside our ranks shall disturb or break through its protecting strength, and the harmony by which we again uphold the banner, upon which is stamped the ideal for which He lived and died, and for which He pleaded, and still pleads, for us to uphold His ideal of service is our ideal, and therefore, let us covenant to the extent of our human strength to carry out in cooperation, one with another, each in his his own place and field of endeavor, the one primary purpose of our organization, that as has been promised, He in return may establish His covenant in us, and through us glorify our work and ourselves.

We have in this Association the individual development and ability that collectively make up perfection, power, mind, God, and man. It is true that weakness of the flesh creep in and manifest in our nature, yet even these may be overcome through a united devotion to the cause for which our Association stands, a cause whose devotion demands service through individual willingness to sacrifice personal aggrandizement.

By application of all the faculties of mind that may be used to obtain experience and a true concept of life, fear, worry, and failure may be wiped from the slate of life, and power and glory and achievement become the ordinary possessions of each and every individual. It is our duty to serve man and God, that the human race may be so elevated and so educated and so specifically instructed in the method of application of their own intuitive faculties of mind, as to bring into the life of each individual that experience which will reveal to and for him the living and existing truth of his own soul being and its creative forces, in their relation to physical, spiritual, and universal existence.

To the accomplishment of this end, we may extend such devotion and such service as to call forth the cooperation and protection and aid, yea the blessings and glorification, of the throne of Jehovah itself.

MORTON H. AND EDWIN D. BLUMENTHAL
THOMAS B. BROWN

"AND THE WHOLE WORLD WAS OF ONE LANGUAGE, AND OF ONE SPEECH."—Genesis, Ch. 11:1. "BY THEIR FRUITS YE SHALL KNOW THEM."

RULES AND REGULATIONS OF THE ASSOCIATION

1. QUALIFICATIONS: Every individual is qualified for membership, the only provision being that applicants must have faith in the Divine, around the psychic manifestations of which the activities of the Association hinge.

2. NUMBERS OF MEMBERS: At the present time no limitation has been placed upon the number of memberships.

3. PRIVILEGES:

(a) Each member may apply for readings for himself or immediate unmarried members of the family. Readings will not be furnished unless applicant is a member of the Association, or a relation to a member (mother, father, husband, wife, or unmarried son, daughter, sister or brother).

(b) Each member, and only a member, may be admitted to the hospital for treatment. The family rule does not apply with regard to entrance to the Institute.

(c) Members together with their immediate family have access to library and lecture hall.

(d) Members alone may take part in the research work of the Institute, or in any of the Association activities interesting to them, medical, educational, or in the field of social service.

(e) Members only may serve on one or more of the various committees of the corporation.

4. DUES AND CLASSES OF MEMBERSHIPS:

(a) Associate Membership: This membership is a privilege to those who have had readings prior to the Association's incorporation, merely upon application thereof, and entitles members to all privileges for one year, and is renewable. Dues for Associate members are $15 for the year. It is expected that this class of membership will not remain open very long.

(b) Subscription Membership: The yearly dues for this

membership are $20.00, and is open to all who have not previously had any experience in obtaining readings from the Association or from Mr. Cayce. It carries with it the privilege of an initial reading without any extra charge. The duration of this membership is for one year, and includes all the benefits and privileges of the Association for that time.

(c) Life Membership: A payment of $250.00 is required, and is payable at one time when membership is granted. This entitles applicant to one reading, free of charge, and to the privileges of the Association for life without any further dues.

(d) Endowment Membership: This embraces those who choose to endow any particular phase of the Association's work, or the Association in general. It provides the means for organization to serve those who desire help from this source, and cannot afford any monetary contributions. This class of membership carries the same privileges as the Life Membership and includes those who choose to donate $1,000 or more to the Association.

5. HOW TO BECOME A MEMBER: Membership application blanks may be secured by writing to the Secretary of the Association (Mr. Edgar Cayce) at Virginia Beach, Va. The blank should be completely filled out and check for first year's dues, for Life Membership or for donation, attached thereto, and both forwarded to the Secretary of the Corporation at the above address, who will acknowledge receipt of same. A membership card will be forwarded applicant upon his election to the Association. Should applicant, for any reason, not be elected, dues will be returned promptly. All inquiries by mail or in person should be made at the main office at Virginia Beach, Va., in care of Mr. Cayce.

READINGS

1. WHAT THEY ARE: Information from the psychic source on any subject presented.

2. KIND OF READINGS: Unless for special research work or for exceptional conditions, only two kinds of readings are given and they are as follows:

(a) PHYSICAL DIAGNOSES: This includes a thorough

diagnosis of the body and brain forces, and also suggestions for treatment of existent disease or sickness.

(b) LIFE READING: These include information on the evolutionary development of the individuality giving the history of the past development of the soul entity, including the potential ability evolved in past earth incarnation, which it, at the present time, makes manifest in the form of the personality peculiar to each of us. A most interesting treatise from the philosophical, theological, theosophical or metaphysical viewpoint, yet given in simple form for the layman.

3. QUALIFICATIONS:

(a) Applicant for a reading must be a member of the Association or an immediate unmarried member of the family.

(b) A book of application blanks for readings will be furnished each and every member. This may be secured by writing the Secretary at Virginia Beach, Va. No reading will be given unless an application blank is properly filled out and returned to the Secretary, together with the regular fixed fee of ten dollars. No other letter, information or explanation is required, other than called for on application blank. Location of applicant and time are no factors, as reading will be given in Virginia Beach for any member who applies, and who may be in any location, and at any appointed time. The subconscious knows no time or space.

(c) In reply to the application for reading, the individual will receive from the Secretary or Assistant Secretary an appointment for a reading. The applicant for a physical reading must be at the address given on application blank at the time appointed for the taking of the reading. Applicants finding the time of appointment inconvenient, should so advise the Secretary immediately upon receipt of same, and ask for another appointment at another time. In the case of life readings, no appointment is necessary, but date and place of birth must be furnished. Applicant will be notified when this reading is to be taken.

4. FEES: A regular fee of $10 is charged members for each reading, which must accompany application blank. Simply fill out the blank, attach check of $10, and send both to Secretary.

The Association will then make the appointment, and Mr. Cayce will give the reading. Each member should keep a supply of application blanks on hand.

5. RESEARCH: Readings of this character will be taken for and by properly authorized individuals, and are open for inspection to all members. Any choosing to visit the institute and view the work are welcome, provided the number visiting at any one time is not so great as to be detrimental to the comfort of patients, and the carrying on of the work itself. There will be positively no readings taken as tests, for only those who have faith in the living, active, divine or psychic forces, existent within, are eligible to membership or to apply for help from the psychic source.

LIBRARY AND LECTURE HALL

All members have free access to the Library and Lecture Hall to the extent of accommodations.

GOVERNING BODY

1. The vote and governing body consists of a Board of ten to fifteen Trustees herein named.

2. The Board is limited by the charter granted by the state of Virginia and by the by-laws hereinafter set forth.

3. No class of membership possesses the privilege of vote. All members insofar as relationship to the Association is concerned are bound by rules, regulations, and laws passed by the Board of Trustees.

4. Members may join in this work by serving on committees and by donating financially for the benefit of the poor, the sick and the crippled. No organization offers greater opportunity for individual and collective service for the benefit of suffering humanity.

DONATIONS

1. Aside from membership dues, any donations from $1.00 up are welcome. Every dollar donated will be spent to help the poor and the sick who are unable to pay for aid, or will go towards the upkeep of the hospital and educational work

of the Association. Each donation will be acknowledged.

2. Donors who choose to become benefactors of humanity may endow a number of memberships for the benefit of the poor, or further this beautiful work by endowing some phase of its activity—the hospital, library, etc.

3. The money, as provided by the State charter and by-laws, goes towards fighting disease, helping the sick and poor, or for educational purposes as well as research work in the field of psychic phenomena, but nothing for individual profit.

PUBLICATIONS

All publications and publicity of the Association is under the supervision of the Educational Committee and the Publication Editor. The membership dues include a yearly subscription to *The New Tomorrow*, which is published in October, January, April, and July of each year. The *Annual Report* is published in May of each year and distributed to such members as care to subscribe to it.

BY-LAWS OF THE CORPORATION

ARTICLE 1—NAME AND SEAL This corporation shall be known by the name of Association of National Investigators, Incorporated, and shall have a common seal, which shall be kept in custody of the Secretary-Treasurer.

ARTICLE 2—OFFICERS The officers of the Corporation shall be a President, six vice-presidents, a secretary-treasurer, and an assistant secretary, who shall be elected by the Trustees for a period of three years and shall hold office until their successors are elected and qualify. Position of Secretary and Treasurer may be united in one person.

The President shall preside at all meetings and shall have general supervision of the affairs of the Corporation; shall sign all deeds, and necessary papers, and perform such other duties as generally belong to the office. In the absence or disability of the President, the Vice-President shall exercise all of his functions. It shall be the duty of the Secretary-Treasurer to keep a record of the minutes of the Trustees in a book to be provided for that purpose. He shall keep such book of accounts, as may be necessary and he shall keep all moneys, deeds, bonds, valuable papers, and securities of the corporation. He shall keep the accounts of the corporation and render a statement at each annual meeting of the Trustees, and perform such other duties as generally belong to his office. He shall be custodian of all funds, and sign all checks. All expenditures shall be made upon proper authorization.

ARTICLE 3—ANNUAL MEETING The regular annual meeting of the Trustees shall be held at twelve o'clock noon on the first Saturday of June each year in the principal office of the corporation and if such day be a holiday then the said meeting shall be held on the Monday following the first Saturday of June. A majority shall constitute a quorum.

ARTICLE 4—PRINCIPAL OFFICE The principal office of the corporation shall be at Virginia Beach, Virginia.

ARTICLE 5—SPECIAL MEETINGS Special meetings of the Trustees may be held at such place as they may deem proper, whenever called in writing or by vote of a majority of the Trustees and shall be held at least four times a year, but at least two of these meetings shall be held at Virginia Beach, Virginia. Notices of each special meeting indicating briefly the object thereof shall be mailed by the Secretary to the Trustees not less than five days prior to such meetings. If all the trustees shall waive notice of said special meeting, no notice of such meeting will be required and when all the trustees meet in person or by proxy, such meetings shall be valid, for all purposes without call or notice, and at such meetings any corporate action may be taken.

ARTICLE 6—TRUSTEES The maximum number of Trustees shall be fifteen with a minimum number of ten. Vacancies occurring in the Trustees shall be filled by election of said trustees upon a majority vote. The Trustees shall serve for a period of three years. The Trustees shall have full control of the affairs of the corporation, control of all funds, gifts, and endowments, and the voting power shall be vested in and limited to the said Trustees. They shall have full power to appoint and relieve the necessary committees for the carrying on of the affairs and purposes of the corporation and have full power to delegate to said committees such powers as they deem wise. Voting may be done by proxy. The Trustees shall make all appropriation of funds of the corporation, and all property of the corporation shall be under their control. No activity of the Corporation shall be for private profit. The Trustees shall have full power to buy, sell, exchange, or encumber the real estate of the Corporation.

ARTICLE 7—COMMITTEES Committees appointed by the Trustees shall elect their own chairman and the said chairman shall report direct to the said Trustees. Committees shall have full power to act for the purposes for which they are appointed and have full authority over funds appropriated for their use by the Trustees. All funds received by committees shall be reported to the Treasurer. Each committee shall establish its own by-laws, schedules of fees and rules, but shall make no rules in violation of these by-laws, the laws of any State or Governmental body. Members of the committees shall be confined to members of the Corporation, but not necessarily members of the Trustees. All committees shall report at least once each year to the Trustees.

ARTICLE 8—MEMBERSHIP The membership shall consist of those who desire to become members and who are willing to contribute to the work of the Corporation, the amount to be determined by the Trustees as the minimum membership fee. Members shall have no vote, but the voting power shall be vested in the Trustees. The number of members shall be limited as may be determined by the Trustees. The Trustees may designate a class of members as charter members and provide for other classes of members as they deem wise. Members shall have entree [entry?] into the sanitarium or hospital. Except upon conditions laid down by State laws, only members will be received, or those entering must become members of the Association. Emergency cases that cannot await approval of membership committee may be admitted to hospital and their membership enacted upon by committees thereafter. With these exceptions no non-member shall be admitted to hospital. The hospital shall be granted a certain number of emergency memberships by the central board, when and if the memberships quota of the Association is filled, such that emergency applications for entrance to the hospital may be cared for, provided that institution is not full.

Members of the Association alone may have access to the institutions of the Associations—may participate in the work and benefits to be derived from same. Members alone shall have access to library, research work, records, hospital within, of course the laws provided for this by the committees in charge of these institutions. Members alone shall be entitled to readings, subject to the regulation of gaining such. Members may signify their desire to join any phase of the hospital, social service, research, library, publication, educational, etc., work of the Association and shall be granted the privilege of engaging in same in accordance with the laws of same and needs of same. Readings shall be furnished by appointment and no guarantee of same is made, the time and granting of the request depending upon previous engagements. Each and every request shall be subject to approval of Mr. Cayce. On motion duly made and seconded, it was resolved that the officers and Trustees as named, in the Certificate of Incorporation, be, and they are hereby elected as officers and members of the Board of Trustees for the ensuing year, or until their successors are elected and qualify.

On motion duly made and adopted a seal was presented at the meeting with the words, "Association of National Investigators, Incorporated, Virginia Beach, Virginia, 1927."

THE INSTITUTE HOSPITAL

The Cayce Hospital of Research and Enlightenment was founded by the Association of National Investigators, Inc., and the members of this organization, on November 11, 1928. It is an imposing structure, erected on a hillside overlooking the Atlantic Ocean, at Virginia Beach, Va. The front of the hospital looks out upon a flower-studded terrace of green, beyond which the broad expanse of water may be seen. The equipment of the hospital is modern and complete in every detail, including therapeutic and X-ray machines and facilities for baths. Every possible effort is made by those in charge to give the utmost comfort and convenience to each patient. Broad, roomy porches surround two floors of the building, and the south side of the upper porch is enclosed in the vitaglass, so that patients are not only given the utmost in comfort but the utmost in healthful surroundings.

The lower floor includes Therapeutic and bath rooms, as well as an X-Ray, laboratory and dispensary. The main floor includes a large living room, spacious dining hall, diet and cooking kitchens, together with offices, treatment rooms, and living quarters for the physician in charge. There is also on this floor a library and lecture hall. The hospital floor is one flight up. It includes rooms overlooking beautifully terraced grounds and the broad expanse of the ocean. Others face the healthful pine forests for which Virginia Beach is noted. There are also two wards, each furnished with a bath. Each of the pay rooms has a connecting bath, so that every patient will be given those comforts necessary to home life and beneficial to convalescence. The top floor is laid out for patients more active than others. A 12-car garage in the rear is finished off with living quarters for the servants. A nurses' home is under construction. This has been made necessary as the hospital has been entirely filled and more space for patients was needed. The construction of this home will release ten additional beds for the use of patients. The surrounding country is ideally located for such an institution and such an important scientific investigation as our investigators seek to make in this hospital.

Bounded by the Atantic Ocean on one side, Chesapeake Bay on the other, with a beautifully wooded mainland, the environment of Virginia Beach is conducive to health. Its beautiful hotels, golf courses and beach activities, as well as the interesting drives through historic country are assurance against monotony. The hum of industry, the rush of the city, and the usual playground are all absent from Virginia Beach, and the air about the place is full of quiet charm and comfort. It is little wonder that the readings themselves gave this place as the ideal location for the hospital, and for the radiation of truths pertaining to psychic phenomenon and the mystic. In this place, and in this manner, does the Association carry on its humanitarian activities.

Each individual must enroll as a member of the Association before obtaining entrance to the hospital. It is planned to make the institution an educational as well as a medical center, and in order that this correlated purpose may be achieved the hospital includes a lecture hall and library. The building itself is constructed of concrete and shingles, so built as to allow additions whenever sufficient funds enable the Association to expand in their work of healing the sick and relieving the suffering, whether from physical or mental causes. Thousands of dollars have been spent on the grounds and the hospital building, and thousands more will be spent that this glorious task may reach a successful pinnacle.

APPENDIX E

THE CAYCE HOSPITAL DEDICATION

An Address by William Mosely Brown,[1]
November 11, 1928

To me this occasion is a wonderful one. And you must think so, too, or you would not be here. It marks the consummation of the efforts of years. Work, and much of it; perseverance and consecrated devotion to a new and little recognized cause; but, most of all, prayer and faith have culminated in the achievement which stands before you today, the visible results of the labors of those who have allied themselves with this Association for the benefit of mankind. And what is greater than devotion to a cause which is bigger and more inclusive than oneself? "Tell me what your ambition is," said someone, "and I will tell you what you are." But, with all the visible evidence which stands before you today, it is but a small part of what has already been done or, Providence permitting, will be done in the years to come.

This is a great occasion, and a happy one. I congratulate the founders of this movement—and they are here among us—for the vision which they have conceived of the possibilities of this new line of study and investigation. I honor those who have contributed of their time and means to bring about the realization, at least to some extent, of a dream of years. I believe that this "experimental laboratory," which has as its chief object the utilization of *any* knowledge, *any* discovery, *any* invention, which will make life fuller and richer for human beings, will become renowned as a center of truth and wisdom

—

[1] Dr. Brown, who had been on the faculty at Washington & Lee University and would later become the first president of Atlantic University, was an orator in the classic tradition, as this address demonstrates.

and, to use the expression of Emerson, "the world will make a beaten path to its front door."

Religion and science, philosophy and psychology, the truths discovered by the ancients as well as by the moderns will be equally welcome here. Nothing is banned except trickery, sham, falsehood. All truths will be used so far as it may be applicable to the betterment of human life, no matter who was its discoverer or in what country or age it was found. "An ambitious project," you say. Ah yes, but unless we can bring together under one roof, as it were, and into one laboratory religious, scientific, philosophic, and every other kind of truth, we shall not have that integration of human knowledge which is the *sine qua non* of all human progress. Here, then, we have a pioneer institution in the field of human endeavor. As human life itself is a most complex process involving all kinds of experience, so we find here a kind of laboratory in which human life will go forward but under observable and controlled conditions, so far as possible. This is not merely a physical or a psychological or even a theological laboratory as such. Much more than that, it is a center in which the rather unusual attempt is made to bring every kind of truth together as needed in the solution of the particular problem under investigation. Always, however, the *motif* is the betterment of human life and all other endeavors are to be subsidiary to this chief aim. So far as I am aware, such an undertaking has never been attempted before in this country, and probably in the entire world. Here will be your expert in medicine, another expert in psychology, another in theology, another in chemistry, another in psychiatry, and so on as many as may be needed and can be provided with the funds in hand. There are in this country today thousands of specialized laboratories, each of which limits itself to one particular field of investigation. But never before has there been a concerted and successful effort to bring together in one single laboratory every kind of discovery possible which will give the patient, or the subject, relief from his trouble, be it physical, mental, or spiritual. Surely this is a pioneer enterprise and more; it is even daring in its scope. And it has every possibility and probability of success! Nor must we think of this new venture as being anything less than a venture in faith. It is not proposed to introduce mystery and hocus-pocus as elements in the procedure. Neither does anyone connected with it hope that, by some hitherto undiscovered means, it will be possible to concoct some "elixir of life," or to unearth the "philosopher's stone," or to lay bare the secrets of the "fountain of youth." The scientific attitude will pervade the inmost recesses of this building and will characterize all who work within its walls. "Truth for the sake of the Truth" shall be its motto, and whoever finds himself out of harmony with this program must either get "in tune" or depart in peace. And there is no limit to truth and its uses. In theory and in practice, the only effective way to combat the bonds of ignorance and superstition and to fight the ravages of physical and mental disease is to discover the truth, and yet more truth. Every experience must contain a modicum of truth, and, by a slow process of accretion, we arrive at the truth about many things. All real progress in the long history of humanity is marked by milestones of truth erected by its devotees along the highway of time.

Nineteen hundred years ago the Great Teacher said: "I am come that they might have life, and that they might have it in abundance." On another occasion He asserted: "Ye shall know the truth and the truth shall make you free." And if He were once more here in the flesh today, I believe that He would give utterance to the same expressions as being most fitting for an occasion like this. He knew the aspirations of man for the fullness of life. He understood that every philosopher— and who among us is not one?—was undertaking to set up for himself and others a goal toward which they might strive with some assurance that they would discover reality on arriving at the goal. For many a one, to be sure, his philosophy proved to be little better than the allurement of the bag of gold at the end of the rainbow or the songs of the sirens to the luckless mariners who became their victims. The end of those things was but too often bitterness and death.

Almost since the beginning of time hedonistic philosophers have been with us. Nor have they disappeared yet by any means. "The aim of all life is pleasure," say they. Enjoy yourself; "eat, drink, and be merry, for tomorrow you die." One of them, Omar Khayyam, sang long ago as follows:

> Ah, my beloved, fill the cup that cheers
> Today of past regrets and future fears:
> Tomorrow? Why tomorrow I may be
> Myself with yesterday's seven thousand years.

The Epicureans and the Stoics, of Greek fame, had little more than this with which to comfort their declining years. But it failed to work out in human experience, which is the final test of any doctrine or theory. And, for twentieth-century living, such a formula would hardly suffice, though many are still trying to use it as a basis for personal development.

Others among the Greek philosophers, notably Socrates and Plato, and a rather noteworthy (though somewhat obscure) writer named Cebes, conceived of happiness as being the underlying principle and the real aim of life. "Eudaimonia," they called it—"living under the auspices of a good divinity." And a wonderful advance this was over the notion of living on the pleasure principle solely. In fact, it is difficult, if not impossible, to explain how these pagan philosophers reached such a high pinnacle of truth with the type of background and experience which characterized them. But living under the auspices of a good divinity is not a very good way to attain to fullness of living. There is always and omnipresent the chance that the divinity might become offended with you and the tables will be turned; constant fear and dread that the very ground might be cut away from under your feet. Therefore, appease the divinity, for

> There's a Divinity that shapes our ends,
> Rough hew them as you will.

Is it any wonder, consequently, that the great Greek tragedians were gripped by the cold fear of divinities of various kinds, and that the chief theme of all their tragedies is the absolute impossibility of escaping from the decrees of fate? Such divinities are usually quite arbitrary in their dealings with mankind and woe betide to the poor man who might, even innocently, offend them. Perchance, however, by living the "good life" one might be able to reach such a degree of attainment that one would be able to live under good auspices for the rest of his days. All of which proved a poor substitute for the pleasure principle, since happiness in any real sense was unattainable in this life. One of the Greek philosophers, Solon, is said to have stated that he counted no man happy until after he was dead. A pleasant prospect indeed for most of us! Nor does the teaching of the Buddhists offer us a much better goal in life. By contemplation we may, forsooth, finally arrive at the point where we shall have the doubtful pleasure, if such it may be called, of being absorbed into the all-nothingness-Nirvana. Negativism has here found its fullest fruition and the motive of all living becomes loss of individuality, of all personal qualities, and, eventually, of even the power of thought and will. A pleasant prospect for the child or the person who is in the health and vigor of young manhood or young womanhood! No Nirvana for them, they say. Let us have something else. And the doctrine of Buddhism fails to stand the test of experience. Mohammed offered to the faithful a place in the seventh heaven, which was characterized by all sorts of sensual delights; and each Mohammedan warrior who died in battle against the "infidels" was also to have at his disposal in the other world eight beautiful maidens called "houris" to do with as he liked. A type of reward which was calculated to make men wish to die rather than live, and doubtless one of the chief reasons for the fierceness and utter abandon with which the followers of the prophet fought the Christians. But nonetheless, all this was worth little when it came to bearing the burdens and solving the problems brought on by facing the stern realities of life. Dying is the escape from reality which is sought by fools and irresponsible people. The person who holds to the steadfast conviction that there is, after all, something more to life than mere existence, when he meets a stone wall, climbs over it, or digs through it or under it, or gets around it in some way, and is straightway eager to tackle the next obstacle which dares to present itself. The Indian with his aspirations to arrive finally at the "happy hunting ground" knew little of the fullness of life of which we in these latter years so often speak. Nor have those who practice the strictest kind of self-abnegation and self-immolation, mortifying and disfiguring their bodies, come any nearer to discovering the "Open Sesame" to real living. For there is no secret connected with the matter at all, unless we choose to think of it as an open secret. Even the Monastics of the Middle Ages, in their retirement from the world and their physical and spiritual discipline, were not able to find the way to real living. They labored over their manuscripts and their litanies; they chastised themselves unmercifully at times. They thought that they had separated themselves from all danger of contamination which might be found in the world outside. True, they studied and poured over their Latin Testaments. But they never seem to have discovered the significance of the Sermon on the Mount, or, indeed, to have realized its very existence.

"Blessed are the poor in spirit; for theirs is the kingdom of heaven.

"Blessed are they that mourn . . .

"Blessed are the meek . . .

"Blessed are they which do hunger and thirst for righteousness . . .

"Blessed are the merciful . . .

"Blessed are the pure in heart . . .

"Blessed are the peacemakers . . .

"Blessed are they which are persecuted for righteousness' sake . . ."

Here then we have it! Seek blessedness; seek God; for these are one and the same. Certainly we have not yet discovered anything to surpass this spiritual emancipation proclamation, and, in a very real sense, we must regard it as a bodily emancipation proclamation likewise. In such organizations as that which is to do its work here we find joined inseparably the belief in the sanctity of the body as well as that of the spirit. There has been in some quarters an attempt to divorce philosophy from science by the insistence upon the attitude that the scientist must not speculate regarding anything and that the philosopher must not trespass upon the boundaries of scientific inquiry by obtruding his theories and his moralizations upon the scientist. A wholly inadequate view of the factors which enter into human progress and experience is this, and one which likewise will not stand the test of experience itself. For, does not your man of practical affairs live by his philosophy as well as by his science?

We all benefit indeed from the advances in scientific inquiry and our life is, to be sure, largely dependent upon what the scientists contribute to the "amenities of living." But it is, after all, one's philosophy of life which determines one's aims, one's ambitions, one's ideals, one's objectives, and, consequently and ultimately, one's final success in the business of living. Some would have us believe that science and philosophy are as oil and water; they will not mix. On the contrary, the fact is that they have, so to speak, an affinity for each other and the one is indispensable to the other. Surely,

> A man's reach should exceed his grasp,
> Or what's a heaven for?

Dr. B. R. Buckingham, one of our most distinguished students of education from the scientific point of view, has the following to say on this particular point:

"To divorce philosophy and research is impossible—as impossible as to divorce experimental from introspective psychology, and for the same reason. Without the descriptive and speculative processes the experimental or scientific lacks interpretation. Without the scientific methods, philosophical inquiry lacks concreteness. Without science, philosophy is uncertain, conflicting, unconvincing. Without philosophy, science is blind, unmeaning, and petty. We can imagine no more helpful educational organization than that which should exalt both philosophy and research. For example, a school of education in a great university should in our judgment elevate its research activities through the directive and refining influence of the best philosophical thought. This does not appear to be thought of. The craze today is for measurement—for counting and comparing in quantitative terms. It would be as silly as it would be untrue for us to deprecate this type of thinking. But there comes a time when the merely quantitative seems incomplete and unsatisfactory. We observe, moreover, that those research workers are most influential who appeal most frequently to higher sanctions than central tendencies or curves of error."

Thus we find ourselves forced to the conclusion that, in order to attain to the highest and best that is within us, we must utilize the discoveries of the philosopher and of the scientist as well. Both are pushing forward the frontiers of human knowledge and experience; both are using hypotheses, which gradually assume that standing of theories as they are fortified by more and more evidence, and which finally assume the status of law and principle as the evidence becomes in each case practically conclusive.

The natural sciences, such as biology, astronomy, geology, physics, and chemistry, are not the only fields to which the term "science" may be legitimately applied. There are social sciences as well—sociology, economics, political science or government. Even history itself, so long as it adopts the scientific point of view and the scientific method, should be considered in this class. Then, in addition, there is another group of sciences which partake partly of the nature of the natural sciences and partly of that of the social sciences, yet which are making a most important contribution to the advancement of human society.

Among these may be listed such fields of study as psychology, public health and preventive medicine, mental hygiene, eugenics, euthenics, and the like. It is quite apparent, therefore, that any attempt to draw hard and fast distinctions between the natural sciences and the social sciences must in the end get us into trouble and lead us to the place where we shall assume an entirely artificial outlook upon the various components of human experience. We must "keep our feet on the ground," stick to the realities, face the facts always. Human knowledge is not contained in airtight or logic-tight compartments, nor do we have first a chemical experience, then a physical experience, then a mental experience, then a political experience as such. All the elements of experience become blended in such a way, as a matter of actual practice, that it is virtually impossible for us to separate them one from the other.

When the body is dissected, individuality and personality are inevitably lost. So, when an experience is broken up into its parts, it ceases to be experience. It is true that, while philosophy and religion may be characterized by the same eagerness for the discovery of truth as that which is found among the scientists, yet they do not limit themselves to the same subject-matter. The scientist is primarily interested in the material universe, which can be measured, weighed, perceived objectively with the instruments which he has devised for this purpose. But the philosopher and the theologian go over into realms which the scientist does not touch—not that he is afraid to touch them or that he denies their existence. The silence of the scientist on certain matters is sometimes misinterpreted by those who do not know the mind of the scientist, and the statement is made that he denies the validity of things which he cannot perceive through the senses. As a matter of fact, the day of skepticism, agnosticism, and atheism has, at least in America, passed away and it is not longer "the thing to do" to deny the existence of a Supreme Being. In the place of this attitude, which prevailed in some quarters, a half century ago, there has come a conviction that not all can be explained in material terms and that the universe itself is not the result of the operation of blind forces upon material substances. The great difficulty for most of us is, that we must change our point of view somewhat and we must learn, as it were, a new language when we go from our special field of study and research over into another field, which is equally complex and difficult to understand. But this fact does not make the transition from the one field to the other an impossibility, and there are many among us who have succeeded in surmounting the difficulties involved, much to our own delight and edification.

Now all of this must inevitably lead us to the conclusion that there is a need of a more serious attempt at the integration of the sciences than there has been heretofore, in order to provide a more solid and certain basis for the future progress of the human race. In a limited degree we are already providing for this kind of integration, but we must go much further if we would hope to have our efforts meet with even a moderate degree of success. And here, in this new laboratory, conceived and built along new lines and for larger purposes than many of us can now realize, we have one of the first and most concrete attempts to bring together under one roof all those discoveries, laws, and principles which offer any promise of relieving human suffering, in mind, body, spirit, and of ministering to the highest welfare of those who may come here for assistance and guidance.

Who can compass the possibilities of such an organization and such a center? Only time can tell the story adequately. It may be that the results of the work done here in this place will mark the beginning of a new era for the cause of humanity. Others will undoubtedly come to observe the methods used and the effects achieved. The advances in the entire realm of human endeavor over the past twenty-five years lead me to believe that we have but scratched the surface of what will be known and achieved within the next century. The radio, the airplane, the automobile, television, and all the advances which are being made in this "era of electricity" are but an earnest of many still greater things to come. Who can say what we shall soon find out as to mental telepathy, the characteristics of the sub-conscious mind, the influence of mind on body, and a thousand and one similar things? Indeed, I have come literally to believe that *all things are possible to them that believeth*. The millennium will be upon us ere we are aware of it!

The day of miracles is not past but has only begun. And I recall that, on one occasion, the Master Himself said: "The works that I do shall ye do also, and *greater things than these shall ye do*, because I go unto my Father." "Greater things than these," you will notice; that is, greater things even than the miracles which His humble followers had seen Him perform as He walked up and down in the little country of Palestine and by the shores of the Lake of Galilee. And we have witnessed in our own own day the actual fulfillment of these words. "The blind see, the lame walk, the lepers are cleansed, the deaf hear, the dead are raised, to the poor the gospel is preached." Are not all these things true today just as they were nineteen hundred years ago?

Yea verily, and more also. And this building and this spot here are now dedicated to the bringing to pass of "these greater things."

Appendix F

The Founding of the A.R.E.

The following account is adapted from a transcript of remarks at the historic meeting at Mr. Cayce's home in Virginia Beach, March 28, 1931, at which he and his closest associates agreed to form a new organization, the Association for Research and Enlightenment, which was issued a charter by the Commonwealth of Virginia on July 7, 1931.

Mr. Cayce: Friends, I hardly know how to express myself at seeing each one of you here this afternoon. While we come together for a very definite purpose, I believe you will say when you have left the meeting that it was an unusual meeting. It is not that we may know *how* to carry on the work that I have been doing and you have been interested in, but as to whether we *shall* carry on the work. Each one of you have signified by your coming here that it will be carried on, that it must be carried on. I believe that you will agree with me that if this be God's work, the way will be shown us. To be sure, we are in a material world. Most of us consider everything in a material way. Practically all of us are material-minded to a greater or lesser degree.

Now, I have invited possibly 75 or 80 people. These we see here represent themselves and possibly many others. I have many letters here from all parts of the world, from people who could not be here. I wish that we had time to read you something from each and every one of those letters. We haven't. There are one or two that we do want to read. You know the purpose of this gathering from the letters that were sent out with the readings. There has been, or was, an organization which was proposed to carry on the research work, that has been ordered disbanded, or disorganized. I was the individual around whom most of that was built. Now, as to whether that is to be carried on, and as to what purposes and what aims shall be set, are the questions before you.

I don't have to try to describe the work to you, for possibly to every one of you it means something different. We cannot keep personalities from entering into our lives. I had a wire this afternoon from someone that I think a very great deal of. Now let me tell those of you who don't know this individual some of the circumstances and then think well of how this lady has expressed herself. She has known of the work for possibly 15 years. Last summer she brought her husband [5473] here to the hospital. He died at the hospital, one of the two deaths that we had here. I sent her a letter. It must mean something for her to wire this:

"Readings splendid. Heartily endorse suggestions. Favor progress in definite helpful manner. Experience permits me an expression of deepest appreciation and years of happiness and benefit . . . [310]"

Think what that means to a woman who lost her husband, depending upon the information. Now, I am trying to put this in just the hardest way we may put it, if it is possible. Consider this from a young man who, in a portion of his letter received just a minute ago, says: "You have expressed in a personal letter that possibly my work has taken something from my religion, or has taken me away from my religion, but I want to say it has given me my religion, though I was raised in the Catholic church, and I am asking you after this—may God take me for what I am . . . I do not come as the . . . worshiper, the incense burning charlatan, the pious hypocrite, but as the lusty lover of life . . . ready to defend He who is my Father . . . [849]"

To some other friends that I wrote far and near, I received letters of encouragement to continue the work. Now I would like for you all to select a chairman and let me sit down and listen to what you have to say about the phenomenon. I would like to have an expression from you all, every one of you that feels moved to speak. Before we appoint or elect or select a chairman, would you wish to hear those readings again as to what we are going to do? There has been one other obtained since those were sent out. That one [254–55] I would like for you to hear anyway.

Mr. Cayce then called on Dave Kahn, who said, "We haven't come in pomp and glory, but we have come here with only one thought, but certainly in the name of the Creator. I feel that because of the humbleness with which we approach this subject today we are going to ask and receive help which will lead us on to things that we aspired to accomplish when we came to Virginia Beach five years ago."

To help everyone understand what the purposes and aims of this organization should be, according to these readings, Gertrude Cayce read aloud readings 254–52 and 254–55.

Text of Reading 254–52

GC: You will have before you the body and the enquiring mind of Edgar Cayce, the phenomenon that manifests itself through this body, also all the conditions and circumstances that surround this body and the phenomenon itself. You will tell us what is the proper and correct method to proceed under the existing circumstances and conditions, answering questions for those so vitally interested, as they themselves have asked them, answering the questions to each individually.

EC: Yes, we have the body, the enquiring mind, Edgar Cayce, present in this room. Also the phenomenon that manifests itself through this body, and those conditions and circumstances that surround the body, the phenomenon, the interest as manifested by individuals present and afar, those present in the earth's plane, those present in the Borderland, and the inter-between.

In the first, the physical forces in the body, Edgar Cayce, need that attention, that the body mental, the body physical, may be the better channel for those manifestations that may be presented through the body, through these channels, will the better development come from the information that may be given.

Care should be taken as to the eliminations, the proper characterization in the diet, the proper potential forces as to the activities of the body in relationship both to the mental and to the physical forces of the body. These have oft been outlined, will the entity, the body physical heed those that are given in those outlines that were set for the young men of old [Dan. 1], even those companions to one who stands near in the present—Daniel.

In the consideration of conditions, circumstances, that surround the body and those interested in the furtherance of the work, the manifestations that have been exemplified in a greater or lesser degree in the associations of the individuals, much might be given as to the errors and the correctness of various individuals' activities as respecting same. Many having lost sight of the purposes, the ideals, have presented strange fires upon the altars of truth. These are necessarily blinding to those that would remain, even in the straight and narrow path. Be not blinded to those conditions that easily beset each individual, yet there must ever remain that loving care, that perfect differentiation between that that would build for constructive influences in the lives of those that would associate themselves in carrying forward that of truth, that is life itself, as is set in Him who has ever presented a way for a more perfect relationship between the Creator and the creature.

In existent conditions, turmoils, strife—even harsh words that stirreth up anger are in the minds and the hearts of many. Then, in considering the conditions that are necessary for the proper way of procedure, proceed slowly.

Be not hasty either in word or deed, rather relying upon those presentations that may come from as perfect [as possible] a meditation from the heart and soul of each, WITH that figure that each would have as the ideal or the guiding star, the guiding factor in that as would be accomplished.

If the star, the hope, that to be attained, is of the earthly influences, then set that as thine aim. Are those influences, those ideals, to be such as will aid each soul to gain a better insight as to its relations with its Creator, then be guided by that influence that seemeth right with the knowledge thou hast already in hand as pertaining to those influences. Guiding, guarding and directing in this way and manner, may each then present to that throne that question, that desire, that INTENT as IT, that soul, is to have in ITS relation TO that as is to be ACCOMPLISHED by such a gathering together, such an undertaking as may be determined in the heart, the mind, the soul, of each.

First, as has been oft given, there is STRENGTH in unity of purpose—for, as has been given, "Where two or three gather together in my name, I am in the midst of same," and if in that name ye ask BELIEVING ye shall receive according to the faith that lies within each and every one of you; for God is not mocked, and whatsoever ye sow, so shall ye reap. As ye build, so shall the STRUCTURE be. If such a structure becomes top-heavy, or there is presented those things that make for strife, contention, selfishness, these beget the children thereof. These must be considered first and foremost in the heart of each as they approach a truth as may be founded, even in that termed by the world as superstition, ignorance, and such; yet out of the mysteries to the blind comes those forces, those manifestations, that make life worth living for those that seek to know the light.

Then, in considering conditions, circumstances as surround the body, as surrounds the phenomenon itself—be not hasty in re-organization, yet there should be—there MUST be—a PHYSICAL organization of those concepts of those that attempt to propagate or to disperse truths that may be, have been, and will be attained or gained through such channels. In the formation of same, choose under what flag, what star, what hope, as may be found in that as is to be sought by those that would form such a physical organization. And in choosing let the name under which such should be formed signify that as is to be found in the seeking—whether Peace, whether Joy, whether Fame, whether Fortune, whether Hopes of an Understanding, or Hopes in the Physical sense—let THESE be in accord with that so sought, so presented, so represented. In choosing, let a leader, a manager—one who may be said the soul, the mind, without blemish—one WILLING to present the body as a LIVING sacrifice, HOLY, acceptable, unto

Him—which will only be a reasonable service for that which is TO be presented, represented, found in a way and manner through each so interested choosing, through the casting of lots, even, as Matthias [was] chosen; one well grounded, one well understanding the conditions, the circumstances that are presented; one knowing the pitfalls that are presented in each life as it presents itself as one willing to serve in whatever capacity it may choose, or is necessary for filling its portion in the work, in the accomplishing of the ideal that is chosen by those who feel, know, within their own selves there IS an ideal; and if such an one falters, let him—let them be the ones as KNOW that they themselves have turned again to the vomit, even as the dog.

In the selection of individuals, let THESE also be chosen—but let each present themselves as one willing to abide by those sources of information as is chosen for the various channels of endeavors in the various fields of WHICH the phenomenon itself MAY act. Let the dispersing of that already attained, or gained, be given more and more to those that seek for an understanding. For the time has arisen in the earth when men—everywhere—seek to know more of the MYSTERIES of the mind, the soul, the SOUL'S mind—which man recognizes as existent, yet has seen little of the ABILITIES of same.

Then, present those before THIS throne—this body—this group—for confirmation, and let such an one CONSECRATE their bodies, their minds, their souls—and all will be well!

We are through for the present.

Text of Reading 254-55

GC: You will have before you the body and the enquiring mind of Edgar Cayce, present in this room, the phenomenon that manifests itself through this body, also all the conditions and circumstances that surround this body and the phenomenon itself. You will tell us what is the proper and correct method to proceed under the existing circumstances and conditions, answering questions for those so vitally interested, as they, themselves, have asked them, answering the questions to each, individually, as I ask them.

EC: Yes, we have the body, the enquiring mind, Edgar Cayce, present in this room, the phenomenon that manifests through this body, the associations, relations, individuals— these we have had before.

Many are the questions that arise in the minds of individuals that contact, that are interested in the various phases of the phenomenon, as it—the phenomenon—interests or influences the lives of individuals in their varied manners of contacting same.

In the manners to proceed, then—much has been given as respecting same. Some definite actions have been taken as respecting same. The first consideration each individual takes, as they seek either information or association with same, should be the validity of the information—and as to whether or not they themselves are willing, irrespective of comment from without, to stand by same, or to LIVE by same wholly, or in another line. Is the information in keeping with the ideal that has been set by such an individual? Is it in keeping with that they (the individual) would live by, or die with? Or, to put in another manner—is the information such that IT (the information) GIVES the individual AN ideal, NOT just an idea? Or is the information IDEAL, or JUST an idea?

As to how each individual is to reach such conclusions, then—as has been outlined—there is seen that first there must be within the information that may be obtained that which corresponds, or which awakens a chord WITHIN each individual, and that rings true to the individual's own plan, own spiritual desire; for the SPIRIT is alive, the FLESH is weak.

The carnal desire must sooner or later, as in nature, BURN itself out; so, as has been given, "all things are tried so as by fire." THIS, to SOME, will give a new meaning to MANY of the words of old.

In considering individuals' approach, again there must be CREDENCE given to the acts and activities OF the information as it contacts individuals' lives. Does the information not make of individuals better husbands, better wives, better sons, better daughters, better citizens, then there is some fault with same. What is to be the comparison, then, is asked, as to whether an individual is a better son, daughter, husband, wife, or citizen? That which makes for a continuity of life is the answer; for as one views all forms of life in the earth's plane there is within that that has crystallized INTO form the seed for the propagation of that life. So in deeds of men, or in the acts or thoughts, or ideals of man—however they may be made accessible to the mental being—does same make for that which is life, light, understanding.

Then it bears the seed and the stamp of divine privilege, divine understanding; for GOD IS life, light, and immortality. So must be the information that would BUILD in the lives, hearts and MINDS of those that contact same.

As to whether such information that comes through these channels, this body, this individual, is of THIS character or not is the question in each individual that contacts same; for, as of old, God calls on every individual to act FOR THEM-SELVES; even as of old, "there is set before thee good and evil. Choose THOU." Not that the response comes from any source save FROM within.

As to how an individual may present same—that is, the information—the awakening from within of that received through such channels, that they themselves or the phenomenon itself may not be evil spoken of—ask and ye SHALL receive.

As to how each shall present that knowledge—how does an individual tell of the finding in self of that love for an individual that they choose as their mate in the material world? that the fusing of their bodies, their minds, may propagate or give to the world the material things of the world that they desire TO be their representatives in the world? They declare themselves before the laws of the land, before the laws of society, before the laws of individual thought; and in the same manner may an individual that receives any phase of that they would see propagated, dispersed, dispensed, in the hearts, the souls, the minds, of men—in the same manner declare themselves. That the phenomenon, the ideal, the idea, will be spoken evil of is apparent, but those that declare themselves must know in what, whom, how, they themselves HAVE believed.

BELIEVING, ACT—in faith—in the manner as befitteth and befits that which WOULD be propagated. So in each individual's touch, each individual's contact, they that seek such things for an interest that is wholly of the earth-EARTHY may only find such. They that seek for those that bring a whole, well-rounded life, may find such. "What WILL ye do with this man?" Ready for questions.

Q. Questions by Gray Salter: How best might Gray Salter give his service in helping this work?

A. In the varied manners in which the abilities of self lie, so use those abilities that they may in the lives of those seeking aid in the various forms RECEIVE that in no UNCERTAIN manner; for each is dependent upon the other.

Q. Am I fitted and the one to take charge of the mechanical appliances and medicines at present?

A. One that may take charge of mechanical appliances, and for the PRESENT prepare such of medicinal properties as may be given in thy charge—for each to their various spheres. MUCH may be added unto self of material knowledge concerning the various applications, or the various appliances, that will aid others seeking for physical or material aid through these channels. He that will serve is able, and when faltering ASK—and the strength necessary will be given in that direction. Remember, no man is BIGGER than that which makes him lose his temper.

Q. What would be the best way to carry on the department of the batteries and medicines at this time?

A. That will depend upon the manner in which the managerial forces are set for their dispensing or dispersing, or distributing of same. Take conditions as they arise. Do not pre-suppose. Do today every act NECESSARY to have TODAY'S influence in the lives of those that seek, that the credence each individual may find is in the position to be fulfilled, and use that IN hand—not that thou might wish for; but as that as is HAD is USED, that as is NECESSARY WILL be attained and given.

Q. I believe that this department can be made to expand to

become self-supporting and of great benefit to mankind. How is the best and most proper way to begin this?

A. As has been outlined oft as concerning this, this begins in a SMALL way—to be sure, but each department of the EXPERIENCING OF the benefits MUST be, WILL be, self-supporting if the LIFE and truth lies within—as HAS been FULLY outlined. Meet the needs of each day, building as to prepare the way—for the day is at hand!

Q. How might I go about preparing myself to better and expand this department?

A. Study some of the material things pertaining to electrical vibratory rates of chemistry in its minor, or in its beginning, and the combinations of the various elements as HAS been outlined. WHY each has a different effect. Then prepare that as is necessary to fill in the inter-between of that as has been the findings of others, for in the organization—which, as we find, should be as National, or Association of Research AND Enlightenment—would carry WITH same the offices of every department in the various phases of a research and of an enlightenment to those that seek. Only those that seek find.

Q. Questions of Hugh Lynn Cayce: In organizing the department of research and distribution of data, we wish to put it on a basis whereby it will maintain and pay for itself financially—

A. [Interrupting] This, as we find, as has OFT been given, is not ONLY plausible, possible and FEASIBLE, but—to be sure—if—IF—IF it is found to be worthwhile—done in a systematic and in an ORDERLY manner. First put the information that has been gained, or had, in an ORDERLY manner, so that any phase of human experience may be had FROM that ALREADY given. Then choose from among those that are gifted in the putting together of data so obtained into scientific manners, in those of story, verse or fiction, and let same then be given to the hundreds of CHANNELS of outlets for same; and, as has been given, there IS the seeking for such information, such data, and this will be self-supporting; not only self-supporting but will be enlightening, as is indicated from the very NAME itself—and let it be known that that being dispensed comes from such sources, as is verified by those who have found in their lives the answer to THEIR problems—and such becomes then more and more WORTH-while to the readers of, whether it be Snappy Stories or those of the Sunday school lessons themselves; for who was the greatest? He that made the worlds or He that washed His disciples' feet?

Q. I suggest the following as a means of preparing the readings for work upon them. Please comment and give suggestions for the improvement of this system.

A. [Interrupting] Whatever system as may be chosen, be able to—at a glance, from whatever phase of HUMAN experience—have the words of the information IN the setting it WAS presented TO THAT individual! whether it be pertaining to the marital relations, the approach to the altars of the Most High, or whether in digging or separating the silt from the gold, or whether it be in adding to a body that vibration necessary to alter the very fires of nature within the individual itself, or adding to the system that which takes from same the drosses of the body forces—enabling the life fluid within same to resuscitate the disabled members of a physical body, or whether that which awakens the imagination of the mind itself to the storehouses of the knowledge of the inner mind. All of these need their presentations in their proper settings. Do not attempt to cast pearls before swine, nor to give to those who read such as of the fiction of the day that of the fourth dimension of the subconscious forces of the intricacies of life itself, but each in their respective spheres—for all have NOT developed properly, but in each sphere these as are gathered from their settings may be given in a proper manner.

Q. Questions of T. J. Sugrue: Is the entity, Thomas J. Sugrue, of proper ideas and ideals, and competent, to undertake the labor of studying, editing, and compiling, the data other than medical, connected with the work?

A. With study, with consecration, the body can, will, so fit self—once choosing that upon which it may build its life; for, as has been given, the abilities to so correlate the experiences of individuals in such a manner as to aid them to see themselves are GIVEN the body, to write in sonnet, verse, ballad, prose and line, that that will enable an individual, groups, peoples, to SEE themselves. The IDEALS must be set IN the LIVING God. The IDEAS will be altered as the work progresses. Be not hasty, but first consecrate self and self's abilities, purging the mind of that that would easily beset, or that would prevent from making for EVERY man that of HIS ability in HIS place to approach the LIVING God; for ALL men, everywhere, are called to harken to that DIVINE FROM within, and WHOSOEVER WILL let him come, for the bride and the church are willing.

Q. Would it be well that the entity be thus employed as a student, then as a writer and compiler, finally as a lecturer and authority on the work?

A. To become an authority one MUST be the student, the investigator, the interpreter—and FIRST of all credence within thine own experience of the reason for the purposes from WITHIN of the activities from without. Yes, would be well.

Q. Along what lines should the entity begin his study?

A. Finding the credence in the lives, FIRST of self, and in the lives of others.

Q. Will it be possible to achieve the entity's ideal of purging Christianity of its theological errors and persuading organized religion and science to accept the truth as revealed through this psychic source?

A. That will depend upon the application of the entity's own abilities. WILL the desire remain in the hands of the living God, rather than to be pushed as of old through powers that enforge and forge for men bonds that break down, possible—but will the entity make it, as of old, through might and force rather than through the love of God, then it would fail.

Q. Questions of [Rev.] F. H. Scattergood: How best may I be of service?

A. In choosing, as of old, in the manner in which each individual that QUESTIONS same in the presence of SHOULD approach the phenomenon. Then guide them into that channel for THEIR individual contact. This not only clarifies or CLEARS the skirts OF the entity or body, but offers to each the opportunity for THEIR OWN reaction to that in which the body HAS made, or seeks to make ITS approach—see? First let every individual, as had been given, satisfy themselves of WHAT credence, WHAT manner of approach. All may not be approached through the same channel, for to SOME are given to be laborers in the field, to some fruits of the flock, to others those secular things of life; yet LIFE is OF God Himself, in WHATEVER form it may present itself!

Q. How may we overcome the spirit of misunderstanding pronounced in the minds of those outside?

A. Only that of the ministry of, tolerance with all conditions. Weep with those who weep, and mourn with those who mourn, and ever present the same attitude as has been outlined, that IF the life is not within itself, then there is no propagation.

We are through.

Mr. Kahn then suggested that those in attendance tell us if it meant enough from past experiences to go on with the work.

Annie Cayce was the first to speak. She said: "Well, it means so much to me that when the hospital was closed, I was all at sea as to what to do, as my heart was in the work and I had contacted so many sick souls and sick bodies. We had a reading and I asked if I should take a house and take care of the ones that have been begging to come. The house is small, but the best I could obtain at this time. I have in the house two patients who were anxious and waiting to come and I am taking care of them as well as I can. It means much to contact my brother daily, and he is a consecrated Christian man."

Mr. Cayce's father, L. B. Cayce, spoke next: "I have been connected with the work, as you may judge, for quite a long while and have had quite a bit of experience with it and feel very proud that I am permitted to sit day by day and listen to the readings, both life readings and physical. Being with it so long, I feel that I understand quite a bit of it. Now, I feel that a very important part of the work is helping those who suffer bodily affliction, by the readings that are given day by day.

Those readings that are on hand now, I feel, are a big part of the work and I feel that they should be given out to the people in the best way possible. When the work is started again, I hope one of the first things done will be the compiling and the giving out of the readings in published form."

Mr. Cayce's sister, Sarah Hesson, said: "The physical readings that I have obtained—I believe that without them I would not be here today. I think that we should continue, as was started, with the hospital. I think the physical work is the most important." Lu Hesson said we should go ahead and she would help as much as she could.

Wallace H. McChesney, a chiropractor who had received information, said there is more to the work than the physical side of life. "That is only the shadow of the greater thing," he said. "I think anyone could well take a life reading for study. I know I have had one, which I believe has made my own soul growth something real that was heretofore intangible and practically impossible to demonstrate to other people. Simply the realization that you are that which you are, and part of the eternal scheme of life, that you are everlasting and perpetual and will never die, is tremendous. That alone, if nothing else could enter into this work, would be very well worthwhile. I think those on the physical side of life lean too much upon someone else. We desire to help those that are sick, true enough, to help those that are feeble, but we must build around good, clear thinking."

H. H. Jones, who worked for the railroad in Norfolk, said he agreed with Dr. McChesney that "the spiritual is very much greater than the physical, but in the physical you have something you can show in a tangible form, and I heartily agree that the hospital work should go on as in the past." An osteopath, Gena Crews, said, "Being a physician, of course I feel that the way to a man's soul and spirit and mind is through the physical. I would like to see the work go on and I feel that a hospital and through the readings and the contracts made with the institution would be the better way."

Professor Francis H. Greene said: "I feel from my own experience, and the experiences my family have had, that we have all been materially helped with Mr. Cayce's work and the hospital. Yes, I agree that the physical side is important, and that we should provide Mr. Cayce with the place and means to carry on. We owe Mr. Cayce and the hospital for saving the life of our boy whom we brought to him in a very critical condition."

Linden Shroyer said his experience with the work covered a period of about eight years. "I will say that I have been made better spiritually, physically, and materially, through the readings. My thought has been to help others physically through the hospital, mentally and spiritually through the information that is to be spread through publications and lectures."

Mina Kerr was most interested in the psychic research side of it, in finding new truths. "Like others who have come to Virginia Beach for the first time this year, I have come because of a very liberal, very forward-looking program, set for the bringing into existence of an institution; [Atlantic University], and that program practically stressed intellectual and spiritual interests and activities and, of course, that makes its appeal to me. From childhood I have had more or less touch with the Quakers, so I have always learned to think of the inner light and all in terms of the universal. So many times we quote, 'Where there is no vision, the people perish.' I like to turn it to 'Where there is vision, the people live.' "

Miss Esther Wynne said: "I was induced to go down to Virginia Beach to the hospital when I didn't know a thing about it. I had a reading and for two years I didn't go back to teaching. I threw myself here in the hands of those that are propagating this work and want to know more about the work that you have introduced to me. The physical is important. Our Lord and Master recognized that Himself, and the hospital is a means whereby a great mass of people may be reached. The mental and spiritual growth will come also in its own good time."

The Cayces' minister at First Presbyterian, Rev. Frank H. Scattergood, also came and offered his support, as did the folks who later formed the first Search for God study group in Norfolk.

Hugh Lynn Cayce asked the folks to forget for a moment that he was Mr. Cayce's son and think of him as "just a soul hunting for something, going somewhere—most of us don't know where—looking, searching, for something. By the very presence of each of you here, by the words that you have spoken, you have manifested an interest in something that will make others' lives more worthwhile. Each of us as we have contacted this man, just a man—a highly developed man it is true, but just a man—are here, each and every one of us, to promote and carry out the information, to give to the world the information that comes through this man. If to me, to you, it is worthwhile, as each of us gets a glimpse of the life, of the understanding we are to carry on to the others, then each of us is going to get what we are looking for. Our lives are going to represent the ideals and purposes that we believe in. We are the representation to the world of this work. Now, let us all get together. Let us think together. Let us be of one mind. Let us try to give to the world a little of life, of understanding, of truth. Let us try to help each individual that we contact to realize the Spirit of the Creator that is within each and every one of us. This man's work is but to emphasize, to bring out, in each individual, that understanding, that knowledge of the Divine which is within.

"Now, all of these things that are spoken of we must include, for we get exactly what we ask for in these readings, the physical, the spiritual, the mental. Or, let's get all of these together. Let us give to every man what that man is seeking. Let us be able to approach the laborer in the street and give him what he needs to realize his connection with his God. Let us be able to approach the college professor and give to that man or that woman that which he or she needs to know and understand a little more of his connection with his God. Light—we have each just a little bit. Let us pass on the results of the work, the truth, the truths that we gain through this man. I am just as I have been for thousands and thousands of years—ready, willing, to do my part, whatever it may be."

Hugh Lynn also asked for suggestions for names of the organization. Names suggested included: National Association of Research & Enlightenment (by Gray Salter); Universal Brotherhood (Mary L. Black); Seekers of Divine Truth (Esther Wynne); Cayce Sanitarium for Psychic Research (Gena Crews); Life Society, Inc. (Ralph M. Taylor); Cayce Research Society, Inc.

Afterward Mr. Cayce told the folks:

Don't get the idea that I, or the manager of this work, can ever become an institution. You know the only example we have we can take from the Book itself. We can start from the beginning: the first man, he walked with God. So with each individual that ever accomplished anything. Jim Jones can't call up and tell John James to tell Cayce to give him a reading. Every individual has to come to the source himself. I can never be relieved of that responsibility. Each individual has to seek for himself. That has been the hardest thing in the world for me to get into Mr. Kahn's mind, that whoever it was that wanted information had to ask for himself.

We know, as has been given, when God spoke to Moses, or through Moses, when he was deserting or leaving his people, don't think that you are going somewhere else to find God. You have to seek yourself. If this work, this phenomenon, which manifests through me, is of God, the individual has to seek. Now, if we are going to put it on the basis where anyone can come along and ask that somebody will ask someone else to ask, personality will enter into it. God is not an institution. He is not a personality. We are manifestations of Him, and if we minister we are ministers for God. You can't do much for anyone else unless they seek. You can always be willing, and your very smile, your very expression, gives the person the opportunity to ask for aid and help. Did you ever see anybody who had a frown on that you were willing to go up and speak anything to? One of the things I think most of about the chiropractors is that their motto is "Keep Smiling." You know, when we look for light, we have to turn our face toward the sunlight. Don't turn your back on it. And it is the same way with people sick. I want to be free, of course. Not free that I may enjoy anything for myself—I don't mean that. I want to be free that I may be the better channel for the manifestation of the way in which I have heard it expressed. You don't know, you can't possibly know, what this meeting has meant to me. To hear so many people express themselves about the work being something glorious! And there is one more thing: there are few men who live to be a hero to their own children. To see the love that has been expressed by that boy this evening, to know what the work has meant in his life, has made my life more worthwhile. I often remember, as many of you have often heard before, what Sam Jones said. He was a very, very wonderful man—a very droll man in many ways. He often expressed it in this manner: "If you want to know whether a man has any religion or not, or if there is any stability in him, or what he professes, ask his cook, or ask his boy, and you will find out." I feel very much the same way.

I just wish that you could all receive these letters from people from all walks of life. Like the one from a man that Mr. Kahn and I have known a good many years. Unless you have been through it and know something of the roughness that we see in the oil fields, you won't know how to appreciate it; but you take an individual that has strength, just physical strength, and put him in that environment and you can imagine what it makes out of him. This man was strong enough to have felled Mr. Kahn or me with one blow, either one; but he had heard something of the readings, and Mr. Kahn suggested to him, "Cecil [Ringle], would you be satisfied to let the information decide?" "Sure," he said. A letter has come from that man, and he expresses himself as to how much the work has meant. He, of all people, asks that each one here impress more and more the spiritual side of life—"to impress on every individual the spiritual side." The physical was needed, as his wife was here a long while; but, as he said and as she has said, "Most of all, we have found some light that has meant more than anything else in our lives."

Also, I don't want to be relieved of your coming to me with all your burdens and your troubles. Don't think that I will be too busy. I don't say that I will answer all of them, but I am ready and willing to be used in any way that I can be of help. That is God's use, and I still insist that if this is not God's work there is no place for it and it has no part in our lives in any way, shape, form, or fashion. Because we lose faith in individuals, we loosen contact with the very things we have held as ideal. Don't let's get the wrong slant on what it is all about. Know that we are not asked to drink of a cup bitterer than we are able to bear. We are not asked to bear burdens more heavy than we are able to bear. Let us be willing to answer. If I may be a channel to help you appreciate that, I pray God that I will always be so, and worthy of that I have heard expressed this evening.

Following the above comments, he gave a reading on the work:

Text of Reading 254–56:

Mrs. Cayce: You will have before you the body and the enquiring minds of those present in this room and the phenomenon that manifests itself through the body of Edgar Cayce, present in this room, also all the conditions and circumstances that surround this body and the phenomenon itself at the present time. You will tell us what is the proper and correct manner in which to proceed under the existing circumstances and conditions. The purposes, ideals, as have been selected by this group, the name which has been chosen, and the three names suggested for manager. You will advise us who would be the best fitted person for general manager, considering all conditions in each individual, and answer the questions.

Mr. Cayce: Yes, we have those conditions as surround the phenomenon—we have those individuals' ideals and ideas as expressed in the ideals of the association or organization. In the considerations, these we find have been well, and there has been the determination in the minds of individuals to carry on. In making this, and taking into consideration the purposes of bringing into being such a physical organization, *first* the ideals, the ideas, the purposes and the aims, should be tried, tested, *manifested*, in the lives of each individual that has so signified that they themselves subscribe to such an organization; for in an unfoldment much is left for each individual to accomplish within their own experience, and as practice makes perfect so manifest in thine *own* life that ideal, that each individual that contacts that one so subscribing may know that a purpose, an aim, has been set—and, as is seen, that such will operate, manifest, in the lives of those so gathered, so subscribing, *until* such a period that this *is* to take a place in the lives of many; as is seen, is to take a position in the affairs of many. Then, each may determine as to whether the ideals are properly chosen. Are they set as a standard of perfection that will bring to all that seek that which will, within their *own* experience, give *every* individual a better understanding, a better insight into the mysteries, the understandings, the relationships of life? for if such purposes, such aims, will not manifest in thine *own* life, may they be expected to stand the test of criticism, of censure, of the slurs that may be spoken of? but do they, in thine own life, make for that which gives and makes with thine experience the ability to answer for the faith that is held within? *Then* know the continuity of life and force itself is within that chosen!

In the choosing of ones, or individuals, or individual as manager—as has been given to each of these so named, there are purposes placed in their individual lives that need to be corrected in the various forces of their individual *abilities*, their individual talents.

To some, as seen—as: [Linden Shroyer] One that should deal rather with the detail, and those of the secretarial interests of such a group, that he may no longer become the pincushion for many, that in the various contacts the unfoldment as is set will make for that ideal within self that makes for the mark of the high calling as is set in Him. In *these* channels would such an one serve.

To another [Hugh Lynn Cayce? Job Taylor?] is given that of making plain the pathway in an understanding of that unfoldment in the life of each, whether in those things as pertain to the philosophies, the logic, or whether pertaining to the spiritual experience and how that in the lives of each those as have been builded *as* an *influence must* be met.

To another [Rudolph C. Ady], as has been given, that even on the planes [plains]—when there were about the body those forces as made for that of the exchanging in the rival influences in life; yet, as given, saved for a purpose—that men might know that the *Spirit* abideth *with* him who would seek to know the influences in the lives of men; for as the *abilities* are used and applied, so may the talents be multiplied in the hands of Him that giveth all good and perfect gifts.

Then let each test themselves with that chosen. That that will make *for* life in thine *own* experience will aid another. Not that each has the same vision, or the same experience— but the Lord addeth *to* the church daily such as *should* be saved—when all of one mind! Ready for questions.

Q. Who would be the best of the three for the general manager?

A. It has been given. Each in their respective spheres.

Q. Who would be the one to take over the business end of it?

A. Each may answer within themselves. Let him that has received give.

Q. What is the next business for association committee?

A. Work out in *detail* those of the experiences in self, as in those gathered that have subscribed to same, to present *to* that which would become the *physical* organization; for first is a purpose; next is a test in self. Does it work with self? Then it will work with another! Do that!

Q. What is the best name for the association?

A. When that as is chosen as the purposes, the aims, the intents—then let the same, or name, signify that purpose.

Q. Any spiritual advice and guidance for those three?

A. For *all* there comes as—Look to thine *own* intent, the use thou wouldst put to that as is given in thine own abilities, and be not ashamed of that as chosen—for He will not be ashamed of thee. We are through.

Over the half century since his death Edgar Cayce has became
an international figure on the strength of the hundreds of books
written about his work and the metaphysical, spiritual, and
physical insights he produced. Few of his scribes knew him
personally, however. The one who knew him most intimately,
Thomas Sugrue, lived with the Cayces for a time while trying
to overcome a debilitating illness, and produced an authorized
biography, *There Is a River*, published in 1943 two years before Mr Cayce's death. *There Is a River* inspired a number of
derivative books, a stage play, *The Freak*, as well as screen-
plays and magazine articles. It also inspired an interview of
Mr. Cayce by Margueritte H. Bro, a distinguished author and
former missionary in China for the Disciples of Christ, the
denomination which Mr. Cayce joined as a child. Mrs. Bro
reviewed his biography for *The Christian Century*, wrote an
article for *Coronet*, a popular monthly magazine of that period,
and another for *The Disciple*, a denominational periodical,
which offered a unique glimpse of Mr. Cayce's strong religious orientation, an aspect of his life often overshadowed in
the media by his clairvoyant feats.

As a consequence of Mrs. Bro's interest, her son Harmon,
as a graduate student, also interviewed Mr. Cayce and worked
for him as a clerical aide for eight months. He later wrote his
doctoral dissertation on Cayce and published a provocative
biography, *A Seer Out of Season*, as well as several other
scholarly books based on the Cayce philosophy, and became
a lifelong devotee and lecturer on themes from the Cayce legacy.

Of all the Cayce books, the most widely read was *The
Sleeping Prophet* by Jess Stearn, a New York newspaperman
turned author who spent six months researching the Cayce files

and interviewing people who had known and worked with Cayce. His book became a bestseller in the 1960s and inspired such interest in Cayce that membership doubled in Cayce's Virginia Beach organization, the Association for Research and Enlightenment. Stearn also wrote *A Prophet in His Own Country*, an account of Cayce's early years.

A biography of Hugh Lynn Cayce, *About My Father's Business* by A. Robert Smith, the founding editor of *Venture Inward* magazine, gave an account of the Cayce family life from the eldest son's point of view and a history of the A.R.E., which Hugh Lynn headed until his death in 1982. The biographical works of these Cayce scribes—Sugrue, Bro, Stearn, and Smith—are available from A.R.E. Press, Box 656, Virginia Beach, VA 23451-0656. Margueritte Bro's magazine articles are reproduced below.

From The Disciple, *November 2, 1975*

Psychic Servant:
The Other Side of Edgar Cayce

By Margueritte H. Bro

In March, 1943, W. E. Garrison, literary editor of *The Christian Century* and professor of church history at the University of Chicago, gave me the newly published biography of Edgar Cayce, *There Is a River*, by Thomas Sugrue, to review. Charles Clayton Morrison, founder and editor of *The Christian Century*, nodded unsmiling approval to the review, despite the fact that an account of a medium's activities was not the usual fare of his theologically oriented magazine. Edward Scribner Ames, chairman of the department of philosophy of the University of Chicago and pastor of University Disciples Church, of which we three all were members, chuckled and remarked that the price of an open mind came high.

I wondered aloud how come good solid Disciples like the four of us were getting mixed up with a psychic like this man Cayce—

also an old-line Disciple. Dr. Ames said, "It's that same John Locke empiricism that animated Thomas and Alexander Campbell and our country's founding fathers: experience first, theories afterward."

Even so, I was not about to review the book unless I saw this so-called seer in action! So I went to Virginia Beach, arriving on the night of the weekly Bible study at the Cayce home. Tall, thin, unpretentious, Edgar Cayce gave a straightforward exposition of two chapters, one from the Old Testament, one from the New. After class, along with coffee and cookies, various members chatted about how their lives had been changed; largely, they said, because Mr. Cayce expected the gifts of the Holy Spirit to be as available today as in the time of Jesus and the responsibility of followers to be as forthright.

I made an appointment for eight-thirty the next morning, expecting to discuss Mr. Cayce's clairvoyance, precognition, psychokinesis and astral projection. I was primed with questions. But he asked the first question! What Kentucky churches had I visited? The night previous, someone had told him my father had been president of Transylvania College, about which he knew an amazing amount of history. I had, indeed, been in many Kentucky churches when we first came home from China. China! We were catapulted right into his greatest concern: foreign missions.

He was hungry to talk about The United Christian Missionary Society, proud that the Disciples had organized the first united mission board among Protestant churches. Since Virginia Beach had no Disciples church, he attended and loyally worked in the local Presbyterian church; so, he said, of late he had not had much chance to talk with Campbellites—a term we both used fondly. Thirty-four members of his Bible classes in Kentucky, Alabama and Ohio had gone to the foreign field. Mr. Cayce asked if I recalled the "greatest telegram ever sent." In the 'twenties, the Disciples national convention met in Memphis. Conditions were hazardous in much of China; anti-foreign feeling ran high; missionaries were being forced from their posts. It was impossible to get supplies to those on the Tibetan border with any regularity or assurance. After heartrending consideration, the convention cabled the Tibetan missionaries to close their work and withdraw to safer territory. A cablegram came back, "We will go in, but not out; forward but not back." Edgar Cayce repeated softly, firmly, "Forward, not back."

When I reviewed the Cayce biography, *The Christian Century* received a lot of mail, some of it sending the editors, the magazine and me right to the nether regions. But Eugene Exman, religious editor for *Harpers*, remarked, "We have only a kindergartner's understanding of Mr. Cayce's reach of the mind, and I don't think he could sustain these gifts if he wasn't focused on the needs of the world."

Came a day when I was about to hear a "life reading," a disclosure of certain relevancies of an individual's long journey through time, to be given for Myrtle Walgreen, a close friend. When we came into the Cayce sitting room, a beaming Edgar said to me, "I've arranged for you to talk to the Women's Missionary Society this afternoon!" I did not return the beam. "I—I wanted to hear the life reading," I objected. He looked positively shocked. "You mean you'd rather hear a psychic reading than talk about China?"

Shortly afterward I wrote an article about him for *Coronet*. The magazine sold off the stands the day it was published; the first mail stacked up taller than I. Soon Mr. Cayce had four full-time secretaries. My son, Harmon, who had been ordained after receiving the first B.A. in religion given by the University of Chicago, came to the Beach to take charge of meeting naval officers and other anxious seekers who arrived unannounced at the Cayce home.

Edgar Cayce was overworked, but never underprayed. He was a master of meditation, without esoteric *isms*. And when he led a group of his office staff and fellow workers in intercessory prayer his references to needs around the world were never a vague, "God bless Africa." Places meant people to him—children of his Father.

Sometimes I wonder if he still grieves over some of us who work so hard over our psychic development that we never catch onto the one fact he felt basic: spiritual growth has to go hand in hand with service. This other side of Edgar Cayce was the *inside* from which motivations rise.

From Coronet, *September 1943*

Miracle Man of Virginia Beach

By Margueritte Harmon Bro

As mystifying to their possessor as to those who read his story are the strange psychic powers of Edgar Cayce. It started when a friend told a friend who told me. My friend is a young lieutenant named Steve, home from overseas and going back. He is quick on the uptake and not generally gullible. Also he is in love. Her name is Betty. One of those fragile-looking blondes who is really as tough-fibered as a young sapling. But suddenly she developed arthritis, the devastating sort which ties one in agony. Bridal showers and gay young friends gave place to a darkened room and nurses. Doctors tried everything, but when Steve came home he found her thus. It was then that his friend told him about a psychic named Edgar Cayce living at Virginia Beach. A psychic who, in a state of trance, diagnoses any kind of illness and reports his findings in technical language which he himself cannot understand when awake; prescribing all sorts of treatment—medical, surgical, osteopathic.

Once, Steve related to me, when a doctor in Kentucky took a reading for a patient with obstinate leg sores, Mr. Cayce prescribed Smoke Oil. The doctor had never heard of such a thing nor had any of the physicians and druggists he consulted. A second reading named the drug store in Louisville where the Smoke Oil could be found, but when the doctor wired for it the druggist wired back, "Never heard of it." A third reading explained that Smoke Oil was on a certain shelf in a back room behind bottles marked so-and-so. This time the manager wired, "Found it." The bottle was old and the company which made it was out of business, but the label said, "Oil of Smoke" and it worked its cure. "For Betty I'd give anything a try—champagne baths, poultice of bumble bees or psychics," Steve said. And packed off to Virginia Beach. When he came home he told me his tale:

Mrs. Cayce met him at the door of a simple house and took

him into the living room where Mr. Cayce rose and shook hands. He was tall, lean, a little on the shy side and didn't look like Steve's idea of a psychic.

"Betty is a very special person," he heard his voice explaining.

"They all are," Mr. Cayce said. "That's why people come."

"She's very ill," Steve began.

"Usually they don't come except as a last resort," Mr. Cayce returned. Then the clock struck half-past ten, and he started for the door. "It's time now for the reading," he told Steve. "Shall we see what it says about her?"

So Steve followed him through the dining room into an office where he met Miss Gladys Davis, the secretary. Miss Gladys, tall, blond and forthright, had been in the office for 17 years. Steve followed her into the study and must have looked surprised at the simplicity of the surroundings because Mr. Cayce said, "This is all there is to it." Mr. Cayce walked over to the couch, took off his coat, loosened his collar, and lay down. His wife spread an afghan over him. No shades were drawn, no incense lighted. In no more than two or three minutes Mr. Cayce appeared to be sleeping quietly and his wife gave him Betty's name and address. Steve said he had a moment of feeling all perspiration and Adam's apple; they had forgotten to ask a thing about Betty's illness; no history, no symptoms, nothing.

Then Mr. Cayce began to talk. His southern accent was gone and he spoke precisely as he repeated Betty's name and address. "Yes, we have the body," he said: "The young woman is in bed in a large room with windows facing west and south." That was Betty's room all right and Steve couldn't help being a little excited. Mr. Cayce went on, "This body is suffering from arthritis caused by a combination of several factors." Then he gave a technical discussion whose medical terms didn't mean a thing to Steve. Miss Gladys's pencil flew. After 15 minutes of diagnosis Mr. Cayce began to talk of treatment. "We would be very mindful of the diet . . ." One medicine was indicated; a certain kind of bath. Finally he said, "We are ready for questions."

Mrs. Cayce turned to Steve and he asked several questions which she repeated and Mr. Cayce answered fully. Then he said, "We are finished." The room was still while he slept on for perhaps a minute until his wife gave him directions for waking.

Steve said he couldn't think of a thing to say. The whole affair was incredible and at the same time it did not seem mysterious while it was happening. When he was about to leave he said he wished he knew more about the whole proposition.

Mr. Cayce said he wished he did too. He said quite a few psychologists had been down there, beginning with Hugo Munsterberg from Harvard. They talked about the superconscious and the subconscious and told Cayce that when he was in a state of trance he dipped into a free-flowing stream of thought. Mr. Cayce said maybe they were right but personally he felt like the old lady who read Bunyan's *Pilgrim's Progress with Explanatory Notes* by Scott the end she declared it was all perfectly clear except the explanatory notes. As a matter of fact, Mr. Cayce said, he didn't trust his own power for years. He was afraid he might prescribe something that would kill someone. But finally he came to have faith that it would work for good as long as he tried to help people honestly.

Well, that was Steve's story. And he wanted me to help persuade Betty's doctors to try Mr. Cayce's advice. But being a woman on the stubborn side of 40, I had to be convinced first hand. That's how I happened to go to Virginia Beach myself.

Mr. Cayce seemed neither pleased nor displeased to see another person bent on investigation. He gave me a brief biography which began when he was a small boy in Kentucky finding out he could learn his lessons by sleeping on a textbook and waking with a photographic memory of its entire contents. At 10, he discovered the Bible and decided to read it through once for every year of his life. With those 10 years to make up, he did a lot of Bible reading and a lot of thinking about God. Which may account for a vision he had at 12, in which an angel who resembled his mother asked what he wanted most in life. When he said his greatest desire was to be able to help people, the vision promised him that he could.

Once he became very ill after being hit by a baseball and he diagnosed his own trouble in his sleep. Later, when a member of the family was ill, his father thought Edgar might be able to diagnose that difficulty also. So Edgar went to sleep and prescribed. The local doctor began to rely on him. The boy struggled to keep people from knowing about the "gift," not wanting to be considered queer. He took up photography as a business; he married and moved away, but he was followed by hometown doctors who knew his power. His own wife was given up to die of tuberculosis and as a last extremity, he turned to a "reading" and received specific directions which, over a period of time, worked her complete recovery. After that his psychic ability became his major interest.

Physical ailments are not the only problems Mr. Cayce diagnoses. Take Miss B, for instance. Fifteen years ago she was in charge of the telegraph desk in one of the busiest spots in New York City. One day two men pushed through the crowd at the counter and each handed her a message. She looked at the one in her left hand and then at the one in her right. "Look here!" she said, "Do you two know each other?" They did not. "But you're both wiring Mr. Cayce. Who is he? So they told her about him. In time she sent for a reading. It told her to give up her present occupation and get into commercial art. Some of it was very apt, she wrote, thanking Mr. Cayce, but at 36 she could not give up a good salary for an unknown venture. But eventually she talked things over with her family and decided to go to art school. Her teacher says she has one stroke which not an artist in a thousand is able to get. Her last letter reports that from the day she took her first job in the new field, 10 years ago, she has never made less in a month than she formerly made in a year. Over the mantelpiece in the Virginia Beach home is a portrait of Mr. Cayce, and back of that picture another reading. One day a New York business man, who had worked out his problems through the readings for two decades, invited 500 persons to hear about Mr. Cayce's work. He told the story of a friend who had been committed to Bellevue hospital as incurably insane, but who had been restored to complete well-being by following the readings.

After the meeting a young woman tremblingly approached Mr. Cayce and said, "My sister is in a strait jacket at a state hospital. She was an artist and went suddenly insane." Mr. Cayce gave a reading. After some months the girl was much improved and later recovered completely. Then she came to thank Mr. Cayce and the first picture she painted was his.

Sometimes the readings have a definite sense of humor and what sounds like a fund of common sense. A recent reading for a woman in Maine opens, "Why do you ask us to comment on your doctor's diet sheet when you have not yet read it yourself?" But the shortest reading on record is for Mr. Cayce himself, given one day when he was feeling miserable.

"You haven't done what we told you to the last time. We are through."

Mr. Cayce carries on much of his own correspondence. A typical day brings an assortment of letters. A woman in Kansas City reports that she read a story about Mr. Cayce "with some anxiety. I was afraid you were going to be dead at the end of it." Another woman berates him for making a charge for his services; why should she pay her good money to a man who had a special gift from God? A man with a huge war contract thanks him for locating a particular kind of crystal in Brazil. But most letters come from persons who need help for illness, or for vocational and family problems. A good many are thank-yous warm with gratitude. One of the best letters comes from an 81-year-old lady who wants a reading: "I have just one question. How am I doing?"

With such a following, why isn't Mr. Cayce one of the richest men alive? Probably one reason is because he charges only a nominal fee for readings and will have nothing to do with get-rich-quick schemes. His neighbors attest that he has had plenty of offers. A cotton merchant offered him a hundred dollars a day for two weeks if he would give daily readings on the cotton market. Although he needed the money sorely, he refused. Whenever someone tries to use his gift for unsocial gain, Mr. Cayce says that he immediately detects the fact because he wakens from his trance with a violent headache.

Each year along toward the end of June, there is a gathering at Virginia Beach to which everyone who has ever had a reading is welcome. Called the Association for Research and Enlightenment, the group represents all parts of the country. This year the assembly was small, perhaps 60 in all. Members were well dressed and above average in education. Probably one-fifth were professional men and women. Open readings are a part of the Association's program. At one open reading on current affairs, grave concern was expressed for equality of opportunity among divergent races in this country if we want peace abroad. Sometimes these open readings are definite prophecies, as when the war was foretold five years before it happened—including the names of our enemies. But more often they were filled with admonitions. "When labor becomes united, capital may fear."

For a week I listened to these readings, which come twice a day. Nobody likes to have his favorite ruts disturbed. I like to have my conclusions arranged in neat patterns. Hence when I cannot explain a thing I've seen, I attempt to explain it away. But in this instance, I am tempted to tell Steve to tell Betty's doctor about a man who drove up to Mr. Cayce's door and said, "You don't know me, Mr. Cayce, and I don't know you, but I'm a telegraph operator at Norfolk and for 15 years I've been handling wires to you. Now I'm in trouble and last night I said to my wife: "That many people can't be crazy."

INDEX